Fabricating the Keynesian Revolution

Studies of the Inter-war Literature on Money, the Cycle, and Unemployment

This book is about the emergence, during the inter-war years, of what came to be called "Keynesian macroeconomics." It accepts the novelty of that formulation, as represented by the IS-LM model, which in various forms came to dominate the subdiscipline for three decades. It argues, however, that the IS-LM model did not represent a radical change in economic thinking, but rather was an extremely selective synthesis of themes which had permeated the preceding literature, including Keynes's own contributions to it, not least the *General Theory*. Hence the book questions the appropriateness of thinking of that development as the outcome of a "Keynesian revolution" in economic thought, partly because the most radical aspects of Keynes's own intended contribution were excluded from it, but mainly because IS-LM is better viewed as the end result of twenty years or more of intellectual development to which many others besides Keynes contributed.

David Laidler has served as Professor of Economics at the University of Western Ontario since 1975. He has also taught at the University of California, Berkeley, the University of Essex, and the University of Manchester. Professor Laidler was the 1972 Lister Lecturer for the British Association for the Advancement of Science and was elected to the Royal Society of Canada in 1982. He is a former president of the Canadian Economics Association (1987–88), and in 1994 he was joint recipient of the association's Douglas Purvis Memorial Prize for a significant work on Canadian economic policy. Professor Laidler is a specialist in monetary economics and its history and is the author of a number of books, including *The Demand for Money: Theories and Evidence* (4th ed., 1993), *Monetarist Perspectives* (1983), *Taking Money Seriously* (1990), and *The Golden Age of the Quantity Theory: Development of Neoclassical Monetary Economics, 1870–1914* (1991). He has also contributed to such journals as the *American Economic Review,* the *Economic Journal,* and the *Journal of Political Economy.*

Historical Perspectives on Modern Economics

General Editor: Craufurd D. Goodwin, Duke University

This series contains original works that challenge and enlighten historians of economics. For the profession as a whole it promotes better understanding of the origin and content of modern economics.

Other books in the series:

William J. Barber, *From New Era to New Deal: Herbert Hoover, the Economists, and American Economic Policy, 1921–1933*

William J. Barber, *Designs within Disorder: Franklin D. Roosevelt, the Economists, and the Shaping of American Economic Policy, 1933–1945*

M. June Flanders, *International Monetary Economics, 1870–1960: Between the Classical and the New Classical*

J. Daniel Hammond, *Theory and Measurement: Causality Issues in Milton Friedman's Monetary Economics*

Lars Jonung (ed.), *The Stockholm School of Economics Revisited*

Kyun Kim, *Equilibrium Business Cycle Theory in Historical Perspective*

Gerald M. Koot, *English Historical Economics, 1870–1926: The Rise of Economic History and Mercantilism*

Odd Langholm, *The Legacy of Scholasticism in Economic Thought: Antecedents of Choice and Power*

Philip Mirowski, *More Heat Than Light: Economics as Social Physics, Physics as Nature's Economics*

Philip Mirowski (ed.), *Natural Images in Economic Thought: "Markets Read in Tooth and Claw"*

Mary S. Morgan, *The History of Econometric Ideas*

Takashi Negishi, *Economic Theories in a Non-Walrasian Tradition*

Heath Pearson, *Origins of Law and Economics: The Economists' New Science of Law, 1830–1930*

Malcolm Rutherford, *Institutions in Economics: The Old and the New Institutionalism*

Esther-Mirjam Sent, *The Evolving Rationality of Rational Expectations: An Assessment of Thomas Sargent's Achievements*

Yuichi Shionoya, *Schumpeter and the Idea of Social Science*

Juan Gabriel Valdés, *Pinochet's Economists: The Chicago School of Economics in Chile*

Karen I. Vaughn, *Austrian Economics in America: The Migration of a Tradition*

E. Roy Weintraub, *Stabilizing Dynamics: Constructing Economic Knowledge*

Fabricating the Keynesian Revolution

Studies of the Inter-war Literature on Money, the Cycle, and Unemployment

David Laidler

CAMBRIDGE
UNIVERSITY PRESS

PUBLISHED BY THE PRESS SYNDICATE OF THE UNIVERSITY OF CAMBRIDGE
The Pitt Building, Trumpington Street, Cambridge, United Kingdom

CAMBRIDGE UNIVERSITY PRESS
The Edinburgh Building, Cambridge CB2 1RP, UK   http://www.cup.cam.ac.uk
40 West 20th Street, New York, NY 10011-4211,USA   http://www.cup.org
10 Stamford Road, Oakleigh, Melbourne 3166, Australia

© David Laidler 1999

First published 1999

Printed in the United States of America

Typeface Times Roman 10/12 pt.   *System* DeskTopPro$_{/UX}$®[BV]

A catalog record for this book is available from
the British Library.

Library of Congress Cataloging in Publication Data

Laidler, David E. W.

Fabricating the Keynesian revolution : studies of the inter-war
literature on money, the cycle, and unemployment / David Laidler.

p.   cm. – (Historical perpectives on modern economics)

Includes bibliographical references and index.

ISBN 0-521-64173-X (hc.). – ISBN 0-521-64596-4 (pbk.)

1. Keynes, John Maynard, 1883–1946.   2. Keynesian economics.
3. Economics – Methodology.   4. Money.   5. Business cycles.
6. Equilibrium (Economics)   I. Title.   II. Series.
HB99.7.L28   1999
330.15'6 – dc21   98-38614
                                                                CIP

0 521 64173 X hardback
0 521 64596 4 paperback

Contents

Contents

ix

Preface

This book takes up the story of the evolution of what was to become macro-economics, beginning at the time of World War I, where my book *The Golden Age of the Quantity Theory* ended, and concluding just before World War II, in the early years of what soon came to be called the "Keynesian revolution." I hope that it will attract readers not just among specialist historians of economic thought but also among honours undergraduates and graduate students with a particular interest in macroeconomics.

Certain assumptions are so routinely made in modern macroeconomics that it must be difficult for students to grasp just how controversial they ought to be. Markets are assumed to clear, so that agents' plans are always fully co-ordinated; and the plans themselves are assumed to have been formulated in the light of a "true" model of the economic system to which all agents had access. Fully articulated model economies, built on these foundations, certainly have their attractions. Their structures are such that their exponents always know exactly where they are in their arguments and exactly where, among their assumptions, the origins of specific conclusions lie; and even the most sceptical critic of modern macroeconomics must sometimes feel that this is how economics always ought to be done.

It must be pointed out, nevertheless, that assumptions made to render economic models analytically tractable (which surely is our main reason for assuming clearing markets and universally held rational expectations) do not, as a matter of logical necessity, provide a good basis for understanding the world we actually inhabit. I do not raise this issue as a prelude to one of those attacks on modern economic theory to which ageing economists are unfortunately prone, nor shall I embarrass the distinguished authors of a long list of presidential addresses, special lectures, and so on, devoted to just this theme, by citing particular examples of what I have in mind here. I am still prepared to judge models on the basis of their predictions rather than their assumptions, and, more to the point, I also appreciate that there can be considerable scientific value in learning how to analyse previously intractable problems, even if that does require loosening up the contacts between theory and empirical evidence for a while. I also believe, however, that it is unnecessary, and probably unwise, for the discipline to forget what it previously thought it knew, pending the outcome of its latest theoretical explorations.

xi

Modern macroeconomics, that is to say, is fine as far as it goes, but perhaps it doesn't go everywhere we might want our students to be taken; and it is demonstrable that a tendency for interesting ideas to get lost, often for no better reason than a change in intellectual fashion, is particularly great in this area. For most of the twentieth century, the failure of markets to co-ordinate choices was taken as much for granted as their success is nowadays; and, quite frequently, a chronic state of misinformation among agents was held to have a crucial bearing on what then happened, just as, to the contrary, we nowadays usually stress the rationality of agents' expectations as a critical factor conditioning market outcomes.

To be sure, and as the reader of the following pages will discover, older analysis was crude stuff by the analytic standards set by modern macroeconomics, and to be sure also, most of its exponents had no idea of how really difficult it would have been to do things in a manner that nowadays would be regarded as adequate. But defenders of modern macroeconomics sometimes counter their heterodox critics with the assertion that its most objectionable (to those critics) assumptions will be removed just as soon as it achieves the level of technical sophistication needed to remove them in an acceptably rigorous (to those defenders) fashion. If this defence is seriously meant, then it must also be granted that modern macroeconomics, as it now stands, is not the only available source of economic understanding. Other approaches, less logically tight in their current states of development, and starting from other bases, may still have something to teach us.

This observation, moreover, yields a discomfiting implication about modern macroeconomics, and to bring it to the attention of serious students is another contribution which can be made by a historical study such as this. No methodological injunction has been more influential over the past twenty-five years than that we should model agents as forming their expectations on the basis of a "true" model of the economy they inhabit. The trouble is that economists' capacity to recognize a true model extends only to imaginary economies of their own creation; economics is an empirical science, and so its practitioners do not now, nor ever can, know what would constitute a "true" model of the real world economy, which is the ultimate object of their study. All they can do, at best, is to analyse agents' expectations as the predictions deriving from the model which, in light of the current, and always finite, stock of empirical evidence, seems to be doing "best" for the moment; and, more often than not, economists, let alone the agents they are studying, will not even be able to agree on which model that is.

Economists are the agents who, in an economic system characterized by a division of labour, create the models which others can then use to process information and make decisions; and "the history of economic thought" is the label we attach to the body of empirical evidence on how they have, up to now, carried out their task. As the following pages will show, that evidence reveals economists to have been habitually heterogeneous in their views of how the economy functions, and routinely wrong into the bargain. The macroeconomic ideas of earlier periods were (at best) the latest word, but not the last word; and there is no reason to suppose that more ambitious claims on behalf of modern macroeconomics, or of any future macroeconomics for that matter, can ever be justified. The methodological injunctions about how to model expectations that underlie modern macroeconomics do seem unduly restrictive in the light of empirical evidence of the type presented in the following pages.

This book is strongly out of sympathy with the romantic notion, so often found in undergraduate textbooks, of the subdiscipline's development as a series of revolutions and counter-revolutions, each engineered by some heroic figure (or villain, depending on one's perspective) in the teeth of some atrophied but stubborn orthodoxy (or vital but all-too-fragile truth, again depending on one's perspective). I would be delighted if my scepticism about this way of looking at things influenced even a few student readers. Economics has indeed changed more rapidly at some times than at others, not least in the 1930s; and some economists have indeed been a great deal more creative than others, not least Keynes. But for any new idea, or set of ideas, to catch on, it must be created, its relationships to existing notions must be explored, its novelty, not to mention its importance, must be recognized, and all of this must be conveyed to other practitioners of the discipline, who in turn must accept it in sufficient numbers to make a difference to what is then transmitted both to students and to the public at large as contemporary economics.

The negotiation of the many steps between the formulation of some initial insight and its attainment of a place in the mainstream of the discipline thus requires not just the efforts of an individual or a small group of individuals working in isolation, but ongoing interactions among those who at any time make up the economics profession, as well as interchanges among the ideas, well established and less so, which make up the subject. Complex issues arise along the way, such as the content to be attributed to words like ''originality'' and ''importance,'' whose resolution in any instance is once more a social, not an individual, matter. Small wonder, then, that ideas have a tendency to change as they make this journey, even those which successfully complete it, let alone the many others that get bogged down along the way, and that they sometimes take on forms that their progenitors did not foresee, and would not have encouraged.

All of this is well enough known to historians of economic thought, but I am already aware that one or two of my specific applications of this point of view in the following pages will run counter to some strongly held positions. To give one example: About a quarter of what follows is devoted to the work of Keynes, evidence enough, I hope, of the importance which I attach to his work, and of the respect which I think it deserves; but I do not believe that Keynes's work was anything approaching the be-all and end-all of what the 1920s and 1930s added to economics, for either good or ill. To give another example: I am aware of, and shall discuss, the important non-Keynesian tradition in monetary economics that existed at the University of Chicago in the 1930s; but I do not think that the tradition in question was either as original or as singular as it has sometimes been portrayed.

I make no apologies for holding these views, nor any others that I shall express herein. Even so, I have not written this book as a polemic. I have simply attempted to tell the story of the development of certain economic ideas as that story appears to me. In doing so, I have relied first and foremost on my reading of primary sources, and in what follows I have resorted rather frequently to direct quotation in support of my narrative. In this way, I hope that readers who disagree with me about any particular point will be able to go directly to the sources of my views and test for themselves those views, as well as their own, against the evidence. After all, the decisive element in any debate in the history of economic thought must always be what the primary literature actually says.

At the same time, I have made extensive use of earlier contributions to the secondary literature, though obviously not exhaustively so, for I doubt that it would be possible in a professional lifetime to read all that has already been written on the Keynesian revolution itself, let alone on the broader spectrum of inter-war macroeconomics. My debts to previous work will nevertheless be evident and will, I hope, have been adequately acknowledged; but in order to keep my narrative to a manageable length, and accessible to those student readers whose attention I would particularly like to attract and retain, I have tried to avoid long and distracting debates with particular contributors to the secondary literature. Where there are what I believe to be important points of agreement or disagreement, I have noted them and outlined the factors upon which they seem to me to hinge. As far as possible, however, I have tried to confine such matters to footnotes and to deal with them briefly.

I make no claims to comprehensiveness for this book. It is not by accident that its title refers to ''studies of'' rather than to ''a history of'' inter-war macroeconomics. Nevertheless, it covers a rather wider range of topics than one usually encounters in works dealing with the inter-war years. Indeed, I suspect that part of the disquiet, referred to earlier, that my views on some issues may provoke will stem from no more than their being discussed in a somewhat broader context than usual. But that is for the reader to judge; and in any event, only when historians of economic thought cease to argue with one another will their field be well and truly dead. If some of the positions I take up here generate a little constructive controversy, then perhaps that will be no bad thing.

Acknowledgements

I began work on this book during the academic year 1991–92, when on sabbatical leave from the University of Western Ontario. My first and most important debt is to the Lynde and Harry Bradley Foundation of Milwaukee, Wisconsin, which not only provided financial support for research and clerical assistance during that and the subsequent two years but also supported me with research-time stipends that enabled me to devote full time to this study in 1991–92 and to enjoy reduced teaching loads during the two subsequent years. The concentrated effort during the early stages of my work which that support permitted was quite indispensable. My second debt is to the Social Sciences and Humanities Research Council of Canada, which since 1994 has given me the financial support that has enabled me to see the project through to completion.

In the course of writing this book, I have picked many brains, both in correspondence and in conversation. None of the following should be held responsible for anything that is said in what follows, but all have been extremely helpful at one time or another. Let me thank the following: Bill Barber, Jack Birner, Mark Blaug, Charles Blitch, Mike Bordo, Filippo Ceserano, Victoria Chick, Bob Clower, Avi Cohen, Marina Colonna, Bernard Corry, Allin Cottrell, the late Lauchlin Currie, Bob Dimand, Patrick Deutscher, Joel Fried, Milton Friedman, Harald Hagemann, Dan Hammond, Rolf Hendricksson, Peter Howitt, Sue Howson, Lars Jonung, Mike Lawlor, Fred Lee, Robert Leeson, Axel Leijonhufvud, Assar Lindbeck, Perry Mehrling, Allan Meltzer, Paul Mizen, Don Moggridge, the late Johan Myhrman, Denis O'Brien, Michael Parkin, the late Don Patinkin, John Presley, Christof Rühl, Malcolm Rutherford, Tom Rymes, Paul Samuelson, Roger Sandilands, Anna Schwartz, Mario Seccareccia, George Selgin, Neil Skaggs, John Smithin, Franco Spinelli, George Stadler, Ian Steedman, Otto Steiger, Frank Steindl, Erich Streissler, George Tavlas, James Tobin, Hans-Michael Trautwein, Giancarlo de Vivo, and Geoffrey Wood.

I have had invaluable research assistance from Peter Ash, Toni Gravelle, Loretta Nott, and the late Sharad Sharma and bibliographic help from Jane McAndrew. Yvonne Adams, Jane Dewar, Darlene Goodine, and, in particular, Leslie Farrant provided much needed help with word processing.

At one time or another I have enjoyed the hospitality of the Stockholm

School of Economics, the University of Hohenheim, and the Centre for Economic Studies at the University of Munich. Last but not least, let me thank the C. D. Howe Institute of Toronto for allowing me the use of office and word-processing facilities away from my academic home at the University of Western Ontario, thereby doing much to speed the progress of this project.

Though everything that follows appears in its current form for the first time in this book, I have published a number of individual articles on particular topics since 1991, and relevant material drawn from them has been incorporated herein, with permission of the relevant copyright holders. I make the following acknowledgements: to Marina Colonna and Harald Hagemann for permission to incorporate, in Chapter 2, passages from my "Hayek on Neutral Money and the Cycle," which appeared under their editorship in *Money and Business Cycles: The Economics of F. A. von Hayek*, vol. 1, Aldershot, Hampshire, Edward Elgar, 1994, © Marina Colonna and Harald Hagemann; to Cambridge University Press for permission to incorporate, in Chapters 2 and 3, passages from my "The Austrians and the Stockholm School: Two Failures in the History of Modern Macroeconomics?" which first appeared in *The Stockholm School of Economics Revisited*, edited by Lars Jonung, Cambridge University Press, 1991, © Cambridge University Press; to the managing editors of the *European Journal of the History of Economic Thought* for permission to incorporate, in Chapter 4, material that first appeared in my "Robertson in the 1920s," *European Journal of the History of Economic Thought*, vol. 2, no. 1, Spring 1995; to the editors and publishers of the *Journal of Political Economy* for permission to incorporate, in Chapters 8 and 9, material that first appeared in my "Hawtrey, Harvard and the Origins of the Chicago Tradition," *Journal of Political Economy*, vol. 101, December 1993, © 1993 by the University of Chicago Press, all rights reserved; and to the editors of the *Journal of Economic Studies* for permission to incorporate, in Chapters 8 and 9, material that first appeared in my "More on Hawtrey, Harvard and Chicago" and "Hawtrey, Harvard and Chicago – A Final Comment," *Journal of Economic Studies*, vol. 25, no. 1, 1998, © MCB University Press. Last but not least, I am grateful to the Royal Economic Society for permission to quote extensively from their edition of *The Collected Writings of John Maynard Keynes*.

Introduction

CHAPTER 1

An Overview

The Nature of *The Keynesian Revolution*

Economics was subjected to a major re-arrangement of ideas in the late 1930s. So dramatic was the change that it was quickly classified as a revolution; more specifically, following Lawrence Klein (1949), it was labelled *The Keynesian Revolution*. It is, of course, far too late to do anything about this label, so thoroughly is it established in our vocabulary; hence its appearance in the title of a book whose main aim is to explore the relationship of the change in question to the earlier ideas out of which it was fashioned. And yet my choice of the word "fabricating" to characterize its creation is carefully considered. I do wish my title to suggest that an element of myth-making is involved whenever the phrase "Keynesian revolution" is deployed, that the re-arrangement of ideas to which it refers was neither revolutionary in the usual sense of the word nor by any means uniquely Keynesian in origin.

In the intellectual world, the word "revolution" conjures up an image of the overthrow of some dominant orthodoxy by a new idea or set of ideas that forces a systematic rethinking of a whole discipline. The Keynesian revolution is, to be sure, often portrayed as having accomplished such a feat in economics. John Maynard Keynes himself seems to have thought that that was what he was up to in writing *The General Theory of Employment, Interest and Money* (Keynes 1936). In 1935, he wrote to George Bernard Shaw as follows: "I believe myself to be writing a book on economic theory which will largely revolutionise – not, I suppose, at once but in the course of the next ten years – the way the world thinks about economic problems" (Keynes 1936, as reprinted 1967, back cover). And many people subsequently took him at his word. How else is one to explain that his publisher, Macmillan, thought that the posthumous appearance of the paragraph in which those words occur, printed on the back cover of the once-standard "Papermac" (*sic*) edition of that book, would elicit respect rather than provoke mirth?

It is the contention of this book that there was no overthrow of an old economic orthodoxy after 1936. What happened was altogether more mundane, though perhaps a good deal more useful: economics acquired a new formal model, around which there would, in due course, develop an orthodox body of analysis called macroeconomics. That model was remarkably simple and therefore easily grasped and eminently teachable, but it did not sound new themes. Rather, it synthesized and permitted orderly debate about questions which, far from being revolutionary in the sense of superseding what had gone before, had themselves permeated the complex discussions of money, the cycle, and employment that had taken place in the years after World War I. The formal model in question, known as IS-LM, was extracted from Keynes's *General Theory* by a number of that book's younger readers. A careful, not to say selective, reading will confirm that an informal version of the model was there to be found, and a reading of what went before it (or at least of what was available to the mainly English-speaking economists who expounded the model) will confirm that it was not to be found elsewhere. Keynes's status as the crucial contributor to what followed is not, therefore, in question. All the same, the ideas which IS-LM organized, as opposed to that model's way of organizing them, had been well established in the earlier literature, and the model itself omitted many important elements of the new message which Keynes was trying to convey in 1936.

The years between the wars had seen intense debate among competing schools of thought. No single orthodoxy, moribund or otherwise, dominated at that time. Keynes's attempted intellectual revolution of 1936 was an effort to set up ideas of his own as the basis for a new orthodoxy where none currently existed, not an attempt to overthrow an already established order; and, as we shall see, he was by no means the only one engaged in such a project. Many of his contemporaries (Austrian cycle theorists, American institutionalists, and many others) were attempting to do exactly the same thing. No one succeeded in that effort, not even Keynes, and if the state of economics before 1936 more closely resembled the state of European Christianity in the early sixteenth century than the state of the French monarchy before 1789, then the development of economics after 1936 also bears more resemblance to a successful counter-reformation than to a triumphant revolution. The new orthodoxy that IS-LM epitomized brought order to macroeconomics for thirty years or so, and, as I shall argue later, it did so while, indeed by, judiciously selecting among the competing doctrines of the inter-war years, accommodating some and excluding others.

Formal Models in Economics

Economists like formal models, sets of well-specified assumptions from which, by a mechanical process of logical inference, an array of predictions may be derived. They do so with good reason, because models, once constructed, become substitutes for creative thought and make their results widely accessible. They are usable by anyone who has mastered their mechanics, and teachable to anyone who has not. They are not, of course, foolproof when it comes to application. It takes a certain skill to distinguish those situations in which the inevitably approximate relationships between their assumptions and reality are relatively harmless and those situations in which such relationships can be misleading; and where the properties of the system itself depend upon the magnitudes of particular parameters, experience is needed for choosing the right ones to plug into given circumstances. All the same, when we use a formal model, we increase the amount of established knowledge that is brought to bear upon a problem, thus reducing our reliance on intuition and imagination, and we increase the chances that our analysis of it will be helpful.[1]

It may be, as older economists like to believe, that intuition and imagination become sharper with experience, but it is certainly the case that younger economists are just as capable as anyone else, indeed perhaps more so, of mastering the logical structure of formal models. Such constructs provide a short-cut whereby the less experienced are enabled to catch up with the state of knowledge in an area, and a model that is new is particularly useful and attractive in this respect. To the extent that a model formalizes what was already understood by experienced practitioners of the discipline, it makes that knowledge more readily and widely attainable; and to the extent that it incorporates novel insights, these are equally accessible to all who master the model's properties, regardless of the state of their initial understanding. Often the first reaction of experienced economists to a new model is that it contains little, or even nothing, that is new, whereas the less experienced may simultaneously treat it as pathbreaking. Sometimes each group is right from its own standpoint.

Seldom will any new model embody all that was previously, albeit informally, understood about a problem. If an area is interesting, it is also likely to be controversial, and a new model usually will systematize one viewpoint, or at least a subset of viewpoints, to the exclusion of others. Therein we see both a strength and a weakness of a discipline driven by a strong preference for formal reasoning. If a particular approach is fundamentally incoherent, it will not be amenable to framing in terms of a model, and it will inevitably and appropriately lose ground when an alternative is so formalized. But the actual construction of a coherent economic model, as opposed to its dissemi-

---

[1] The reader will note that it is Marshall's conception of theory as an "engine of analysis" that underlies this discussion. Theories, conceived of as a set of testable propositions, are best thought of as being specific special cases of these broader constructs, incorporating particular restrictions upon their parameter values, and perhaps specific hypotheses about the sources of disturbances impinging upon the system. Thus, though IS-LM in and of itself has no empirical content, it is well known that very different propositions about the behaviour of an economy may be derived from it, depending, for example, on the assumptions that are made about the interest sensitivity of the demand for money and the way in which the supply of money is determined in the economy to which the framework is applied.

nation, requires a good deal of creativity and technical capability. It is quite possible, at a particular time, that a perfectly reasonable idea will fail to find proponents capable of giving a formal account of it, whereas an alternative idea will be more fortunate. In that case, a promising approach can easily become lost to view, and an ultimately less useful set of insights can come to dominate an area, at least for a while.[2]

Formal Models in the 1950s

In the late 1950s, a would-be economist was thoroughly drilled in the properties of a well-defined set of models. In microeconomics, Marshall's partial-equilibrium supply-and-demand apparatus, various models of the perfectly competitive and monopolistic firm, and some version of a two-person, two-input, two-output, general-equilibrium structure formed the theoretical core of the typical honours undergraduate curriculum; and in macroeconomics that role was played by the IS-LM model, a formulation of what had come to be called "Keynesian economics." To be sure, advanced students of macroeconomics were also exposed to business-cycle theory, usually of the multiplier–accelerator sort, and perhaps some macroeconometrics in the Klein-Goldberger (1955) tradition, but as often as not those were presented as extensions of the IS-LM framework, the former dealing with factors causing the IS curve to shift systematically over time, and the latter as a quantification of a rather elaborate version of the same basic framework.[3] When, as late as 1973, that acute anthropological observer Axel Leijonhufvud visited the "Econ" tribe, he noted that among its Macro sect the cross labelled "IS-LM" appeared to be a totem of ritual significance equal to that of the cross labelled "S and D" among the socially superior Micro sect.

IS-LM

IS-LM lay at the very heart of orthodox "Keynesian" macroeconomics for three decades or more, and it was also an important component of the first

---

[2] Though good, and not so good, ideas seem to come and go with greater frequency in macroeconomics than in microeconomics, I do not think that the latter area is immune to the phenomenon. The comings and goings of oligopoly theory, and the closely associated appearing, disappearing, and reappearing taste for game theory in the area of industrial organization, are surely cases in point.

[3] Presentation of an approach is one thing; its actual ancestry is another, however. Both the development of business-cycle theory and the evolution of macroeconometrics from the late 1930s onwards are beyond the scope of this book, though the former topic is discussed briefly in its final chapter. An article by Patinkin (1976b) is still the standard treatment of the latter, though Morgan (1990, ch. 4) has provided important material. Suffice it here to say that in each case, Keynes's *General Theory* (1936) and the IS-LM model which grew out of it, though influential, were by no means decisively so.

serious challenge to that orthodoxy: *monetarism*, as it came to be called. It was not immediately apparent in the mid-1950s, when that challenge was first mounted, that Milton Friedman's capacity to get different results from his professional colleagues concerning, say, the relative influences of monetary policy and fiscal policy on output depended not so much on his using some different model of the economy, but on his attributing different orders of magnitude to certain key parameters of a commonly used system. Nor was it obvious that his monetary theory of inflation stemmed from concentrating on the economy's properties in regions where output was capacity-constrained, rather than being free to expand in response to changes in the aggregate demand for goods and services. However, in the early 1970s, Friedman did make those matters clear, and the IS-LM model played a prominent role in his exposition.[4] Thus it was only with the rise of ''new-classical'' economics in the 1970s and 1980s that IS-LM began to lose its dominant position in the macroeconomics curriculum.

The IS-LM model itself is easily expounded. In its simplest form, taking the price level P as given, it determines the levels of real output and employment in a closed economy as functions of autonomous private expenditure A, government expenditure G, and an exogenously given quantity of money M. Specifically, with C expenditure by households, I expenditure by firms, G expenditure by government, Y real income, and r the rate of interest, it postulates

$$Y = C + I + G \tag{1.1}$$

$$C = c(Y), \qquad 1 > c' > 0 \tag{1.2}$$

$$I = A - i(r), \qquad i' < 0 \tag{1.3}$$

$$M/P = m(Y, r), \qquad m'(Y) > 0, \quad m'(r) < 0 \tag{1.4}$$

Equations (1.1) – (1.3) can be solved and graphed as the downward-sloping curve IS in Figure 1, and equation (1.4) as the upward-sloping curve LM, and the equilibrium levels of Y and r are determined at their intersection. Obviously, the less sensitive is expenditure to the rate of interest [the smaller in absolute value is i'] and the more sensitive is the demand for money to the rate of interest [the larger in absolute value is $m'(r)$], then the more sensitive

---

[4] See Friedman (1974, pp. 29–40). Though Friedman's explicit deployment of IS-LM analysis there came as something of a surprise, the apparatus was already in fairly widespread use to illuminate certain aspects of what came to be called the ''monetarist controversy.'' See, for example, Laidler (1969, pt. I).

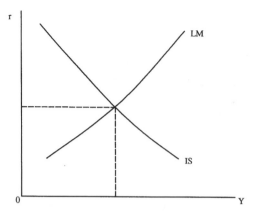

Figure 1. The IS-LM diagram.

is the level of income to variations in *A* and *G*, and the less sensitive to variations in *M* and *P*, and vice versa. Hence the model, even in this primitive form, enables one to construct a variety of stories about the factors, including price-level stickiness, determining income and employment and the relative effectiveness of fiscal and monetary policy in offsetting their undesired effects. In more elaborate versions, combined, say, with a so-called aggregate supply curve, relating output to the price level, or a Phillips curve, relating output to the rate of change in the price level, it can also be extended to the analysis of inflation; open-economy extensions are also available, and so on.

The Orthodoxy's Version of "Classical" Economics

Though a few economists of the post-war years objected vehemently to identification of the IS-LM model with John Maynard Keynes's *The General Theory of Employment, Interest and Money* (1936), including some who had been closely associated with Keynes in the 1930s – for example, Joan Robinson famously took to referring to that model as "bastard Keynesianism" – that orthodox view of things nevertheless came equipped with a version of history to support its legitimacy. According to that history, before 1936 there had existed a body of macroeconomic theory to which the label *classical* had been attached and which had proved incapable of dealing with inter-war macroeconomic experience in general, and the Great Depression in the United States in particular. That classical economics was said to have had at its heart a belief that the economic system could find equilibrium only at full employment, and hence had nothing to say about chronic unemployment. It based that belief on the postulate that money wages and prices were flexible and that the rate of interest would always harmonize saving and investment plans. Though it lacked a theory of employment and output, classical economics had attempted to explain the price level, using a device called *the quantity theory of money*, whose exponents had, however, failed to notice that it was not a theory at all, but a tautology, and hence vacuous.

According to that narrative, Keynes, reacting to the evidence presented by the real world around him, where, he had noticed, money wages and prices were sticky, particularly in a downward direction, produced an alternative and radically different macroeconomics in which such stickiness led to un-employment equilibrium as the general case. That macroeconomics also showed that, even if wage and price flexibility did exist, to rely on it to generate full employment was logically equivalent to relying on monetary policy for this purpose. Because Keynes had also demonstrated that mone-tary policy was an unreliable tool, with its effectiveness depending upon its capacity to influence the rate of interest, his analysis had revealed fiscal policy, particularly as it involved variations in the level of government de-mand for goods and services, to be a more appropriate remedy for depres-sion. In that story, the IS-LM model was a geometric exposition of such revolutionary insights, and to acquire mastery of it simultaneously made them part of one's own intellectual equipment and relieved one of any need to investigate just what economists might actually have been saying be-fore 1936. Modern macroeconomics had come into existence in that year, and anything that had been written beforehand was of purely antiquarian interest.

Exploded Myths

If all of this seems like something of a caricature, it was nevertheless a caricature whose features at one time appeared in many textbooks. But even in the 1950s there were things that a student might learn that did not quite fit into the story. The *General Theory* had been published in 1936. If it really had been written in reaction to the American Depression, and had been original in making the case for fiscal policy as a way out, how had it come about that most of President Roosevelt's allegedly Keynesian "New Deal" policies had been put in place a few years before its publication? If "classi-cal" economists had believed that market mechanisms automatically rendered wages flexible, why was it that some people seemed to have been advocating a *policy* of money-wage reductions in Britain in the 1920s? And why had John Hicks, in contrasting the economics of "Mr. Keynes and the Classics" in a 1937 article which was much read by undergraduates in the 1950s, attributed to the latter a version of the IS-LM model in which the price level was given?

Or, again, if the classical economists had believed that the rate of interest always equilibrated saving and investment at full employment, where did the Swedish economist Knut Wicksell, who apparently thought that the failure of what he called the *market (or money) rate of interest* to do just that was an important source of inflation, fit in? And didn't Wicksell, who wrote well before World War I (e.g., 1898), have a predecessor in the early nineteenth century in Henry Thornton (1802), who was an important exponent of the "bullionist" position and therefore a classical economist? What, too, was one to make of the "Chicago oral tradition" to which Milton Friedman (1956) drew attention, in which the quantity theory of money was said to have been a theory of the demand for money, not an accounting identity at all? And the list of discrepancies could go on.[5] We have come a long way in sorting out these and other puzzles, too, in the past forty years. Even though some of the old myths about Keynes and the classics recounted here still put in an appearance from time to time in the textbooks, they have, by and large, been exploded before the eyes of anyone who takes the history of economic thought even slightly seriously. From the early 1960s onwards, such scholars as Harry Johnson (1961), Robert Clower (1965), Axel Leijonhufvud (1968), and Don Patinkin (1976a) have set in motion a reappraisal of Keynes's work and its place in the development of economics.

 It is, by now, well understood that advocacy of fiscal policy as a device for combatting unemployment, particularly cyclical unemployment, was a commonplace of the inter-war (and indeed earlier) economics literature. Not least, as Barber (1985) has documented, was that true in the United States, so much so that it would have been extremely surprising if implementation of the New Deal had had to await the publication of what was a book about economic theory rather than policy, and written in another country too. It is also well known that the postulate of money-wage stickiness, particularly but not solely in a downward direction, was a central feature of efforts to explain why the business cycle was characterized by fluctuations in output and employment, rather than mainly in prices, from the 1870s onwards, and that this postulate had made occasional appearances in the so-called classical literature long before that.[6]

As to Wicksell, his originality in linking questions about the causes of inflation to a failure of the rate of interest to co-ordinate choices about saving and investment is now widely recognized, as is the fact that his insight was of far-reaching influence in the subsequent development of macroeconomics; and there is a closely related literature of considerable size debating the

---

[5] The two foregoing paragraphs derive from my memories of apparent conflicts in the various arguments to which I was exposed as an undergraduate in the late 1950s.

[6] Notably in Henry Thornton (1802), but also in William Stanley Jevons (1863). On this, see Laidler (1991, pp. 95–106, 116, fn. 9).

proper classification of Henry Thornton's economic thought.[7] The Chicago
tradition, too, has been much discussed, and though Friedman's suggestion
(1956) that the University of Chicago was the home of a unique version of
the quantity theory of money which treated this doctrine as a theory of the
demand for money has not withstood scrutiny, its reputation as a place where
at least some people resisted "Keynesian" ideas has been confirmed. Even
so, some commentators have suggested that Friedman's own theoretical notions have owed less to his Chicago predecessors than he was initially willing
to concede.[8]

Some Remaining Questions

If advocacy of fiscal policy, a belief in money-wage stickiness, and an
appreciation of inter-temporal allocative problems involving the capacity of
the rate of interest to co-ordinate saving and investment, which once seemed
to be defining features of the Keynesian revolution, were all prominent
features of the pre-1936 literature, another question naturally arises: Was
Keynes's own economics after all unique, or was it anticipated elsewhere in
the literature of the 1920s and 1930s? That question, too, has been much
discussed since the early 1960s, and not surprisingly the answer seems to
depend upon just what it is that one thinks Keynes's key contribution to
economics was, or, as it is sometimes put, what the *central message* of the
General Theory was.[9]

That the phrases "Keynesian economics" and "IS-LM analysis" were
widely treated as synonyms in the 1950s has already been noted, and appropriately so in the eyes of some commentators, but only some. For example,
Leijonhufvud (1968) argued that what he called "the economics of Keynes"
was something rather different, dealing with the disequilibrium behaviour of
a monetary economy and with its capacity to co-ordinate economic activity,
rather than with the equilibrium properties of a comparative static model.
Self-styled *post-Keynesians*, whom Alan Coddington (1976) characterized as
fundamentalists, moreover, have claimed to be custodians of, and to be
building upon, what they regard as the real message of the *General Theory*,

---

[7] For a brief account of those matters, along with references to relevant literature, see Laidler (1987).
[8] On the origins of Friedman's Chicago tradition, see Friedman (1956, 1974), Patinkin (1969, 1974), Humphrey (1971), Laidler (1993, 1998), and Tavlas (1997).
[9] For example, Don Patinkin (1976a, pt. 1, 1987) discussed that issue extensively, as did Allan Meltzer (1988), though they came to very different conclusions about what Keynes's central message actually was. I shall take this matter up in more detail in Chapter 10. Suffice it here to say that, in my view, Keynes thought he had more than one message to convey in 1936 and that the trouble with that particular debate hinged upon its participants paying more attention than was warranted to the word "central."

which the IS-LM model simply ignores. In that view, the analysis of decision making in conditions where the uncertainty of outcomes cannot be rendered analytically tractable by application of the calculus of probabilities, the light which that throws on the nature of a monetary economy, and its implications for the appropriate role for government in economic life are of the essence.[10] Thus, what Keynes ''really meant'' when he wrote the *General Theory* has been, and remains, controversial, as does its relationship to what went before. These, however, are not the only questions, nor even quite the central questions, to be addressed in the following pages, as I shall now explain.

An Outline of This Book

The IS-LM model made its first explicit appearances in the literature in 1936 and 1937, and it summarized most, though not all, of the macroeconomics of the inter-war years that eventually found its way into the post-war textbooks. Though its components were certainly to be found in the *General Theory*, many of them had been developed elsewhere long before 1936; and many intriguing ideas that also had been much discussed in the 1920s and 1930s, including some that originated in the *General Theory* itself, found no place in it. IS-LM was, in short, what new models always seem to be, a highly selective synthesis of several pre-existing strands of economic thought. Even so, the fact that IS-LM was less, and more, than a summary of the *General Theory* does not mean that economics took a wrong turn in focusing on it. Rather, it means only that the *General Theory* was one among several sources of what came to be post-war orthodox macroeconomics. Like all orthodoxies, that one took what fitted into it from earlier literature, while ignoring much else, regardless of the particular source involved.

This book, then, is about that earlier literature, including the *General Theory*, about what IS-LM took from it, and about what it left out. It does not purport to be a comprehensive history of inter-war macroeconomics. It has almost nothing to say about the development of macrodynamic econometrics during that period (Morgan 1990, ch. 3 and 4), about open-economy macroeconomics (Flanders 1989, ch. 4–10), or about the analysis of inflation which developed as a response to the hyperinflations following World War I, particularly in the German-language literature (Ellis 1934, pt. I–III). It is also

---

[10] Paul Davidson (1972), Hyman Minsky (1975), and Victoria Chick (1983) were important contributors to the ''post-Keynesian'' interpretation of the *General Theory* and its place in the history of economic thought. Post-Keynesian macroeconomics is, of course, far more than an approach to doctrinal history, but it is beyond the scope of this book to discuss its nature. The books by Chick (1992) and Colin Rogers (1989) are representative of this strand of modern economic thought.

highly selective in its treatment of the work of monetary heretics. Underconsumptionism is discussed, but social credit, stamped money, and a myriad of other schemes are not. Moreover, because it is concerned with analytic ideas and is conceived of as a series of related studies, rather than as a continuous narrative, its organization is at least as thematic as it is chronological, as we shall now see.

The Wicksellians   PART I

The first theme in inter-war macroeconomic thought that we shall take up here was directly inspired by Knut Wicksell's contributions, made long before World War I, a theme that Axel Leijonhufvud (1981) called "The Wicksell Connection," which involved refocusing the attention of monetary economics away from the interaction of money and prices and towards the influence of the rate of interest on saving and investment. Wicksell's analysis of *monetary equilibrium* and the capacity of a modern banking system to undermine it by setting the interest rate at the "wrong" value are briefly discussed, as a prelude to a more detailed account of the two divergent paths along which these ideas developed, those taken by the Austrians and the Stockholm School, to which Chapters 2 and 3, respectively, are devoted.[11]

The Austrians, Ludwig von Mises and Friedrich von Hayek in particular, brought Wicksell's notions of monetary equilibrium and disequilibrium into close contact with a deductivist approach to economic analysis that encompassed theories of the inter-temporal allocative mechanism in general, and capital theory in particular, that had been developed by an earlier generation of Austrian economists. In so doing, they created, by about 1930, a coherent (by the standards of the time) model of their own, very different from IS-LM, a model which dealt with the influence of monetary factors on the size and composition of the economy's capital stock, particularly by way of the *forced saving* that they believed took place when, in conditions of full employment, the banking system granted new credit to firms. Their model's policy implications, for conditions prevailing in the 1920s and 1930s, verged on the nihilistic. To the extent that there ever existed a body of economic thought that urged reliance on the self-equilibrating properties of a market economy as the best means of dealing with unemployment – a contention that exponents of IS-LM could contrast with its properties to the benefit of their own framework – it was that body of Austrian theory. Far from being some hang-over from the classical economics of the nineteenth century, however, Austrian cycle theory was itself one of the newest and demonstrably

---

[11] I have previously discussed Wicksell's contribution in some detail (Laidler 1991, ch. 5).

most original bodies of doctrine developed in the inter-war years, although one which was driven into obscurity by the subsequent success of IS-LM.[12]

The Stockholm School, as certain members of a younger generation of Swedish economists were eventually to be called by one of their number, Bertil Ohlin (1937), began its work at about the same time, and from exactly the same starting point as the Austrians. The Swedish economists, however, explicitly rejected Austrian capital theory and moved in a different direction. Noting that saving and investment decisions, which the rate of interest had to co-ordinate if the economy was to function smoothly, were inherently forward-looking, they made the influence of expectations on current spending decisions the centrepiece of their analysis. But these Swedish economists were never able to formulate a coherent theory of the evolution of expectations over time, and so, rather than producing a well-defined model, they created instead a method of dynamic analysis from which a seemingly endless array of what they called "model sequences" could be derived, which in turn formed the analytic basis for a pragmatic approach to macroeconomic policy in which both monetary and fiscal measures could, depending upon circumstances, be usefully deployed for stabilization purposes.

The Marshallian Tradition in Britain

Chapters 4–7 deal with the principal features of the British literature of the 1920s and early 1930s, to which Keynes, beginning in 1923, was an important contributor, and out of which his *General Theory* was ultimately to develop. The starting point here is the legacy of Alfred Marshall, for although Wicksell had drawn on Marshall, Wicksell's work, if not quite unknown, seems to have had little direct influence on British economics before 1930.[13] As is explained at the beginning of Chapter 4, Marshall bequeathed to his successors a stock-supply-and-demand version of the quantity theory of money as a theory of the price level, a vision of the business cycle as a cumulative-demand-driven phenomenon in which businessmen's expenditure plans were accommodated through a banking system at interest rates which failed, for a while at least, to keep pace with their profit expectations, and the

[12] Hayek's disappearance from the literature was discussed by Hicks (1967, ch. 12). It seems to have been that paper which first drew the attention of post-war readers to the important role played by Austrian theory in general, and Hayek's contribution to it in particular, in the development of inter-war macroeconomics.

[13] Wicksell's only account of his cumulative process analysis to appear in English during his lifetime was a succinct paper that was first presented to the British Association for the Advancement of Science and published in the *Economic Journal* (1907a); that paper seems to have made no impression at the time of publication. Wicksell did correspond with Marshall, but the letters reproduced by Gårdlund (1958) dealt with capital theory, rather than monetary economics.

idea that money-wage stickiness was responsible for the cycle being a thing of real rather than purely nominal fluctuations.[14]

In the 1920s, the English economists who followed Marshall's lead most closely were Frederick Lavington and Arthur Pigou, and their work, along with that of Dennis Robertson, is discussed in the remainder of Chapter 4. *Lavington* Like Marshall, they regarded the cycle as driven mainly by investment demand, and they were extremely sceptical of the capacity of businessmen to make well-calculated, let alone rational, investment decisions. Hence they *Pigou* emphasized the role of collective waves of what they called "error," successively optimistic and pessimistic. Though they thought that price stabilization would modify the severity of cyclical swings, they departed from Marshall in doubting that it would eliminate them. Lavington, moreover, extended Marshall's version of the quantity theory and discussed the demand for money as a liquid store of value, held, by analogy with banks' holdings of cash reserves, as a contingency against uncertainty. In his view, shifts in the demand for money, as business confidence waxed and waned over the cycle, would provide accommodation to its fluctuations in addition to that afforded by an endogenous response of the money supply emanating from the banking system.

Robertson also attached considerable significance to the role of "error" in creating cyclical fluctuations, but he believed that investment booms were *Robertson* sometimes the results of desirable technical innovations. For him, the central tasks of monetary policy were, first, to distinguish between the *appropriate* fluctuations in output that they brought about and the *inappropriate* fluctuations that would usually be overlaid upon them, and, second, to encourage the former and eliminate the latter. In elaborating that argument, Robertson developed an analysis of forced saving that in many respects ran parallel to that of Mises and Hayek, but, working in close collaboration with Keynes, he integrated that analysis with a Marshallian treatment of the stock demand for money. That, in conjunction with his scepticism about the efficiency of market mechanisms when left to themselves, led him to share with Pigou and Lavington a cautiously optimistic, rather than nihilistic, view of the powers of stabilization policy, both monetary and fiscal.

The work of Keynes and Ralph Hawtrey in the 1920s is taken up in *Keynes* Chapter 5. In the *Tract on Monetary Reform* (1923), Keynes touched only rather briefly on cyclical questions, but a typically Marshallian belief that price-level variations were the *sine qua non* of the cycle was quite apparent in what he wrote there. A much more comprehensive monetary theory of the

---

[14] The argument first appeared in the account of the cycle given by Marshall and Marshall (1879), and it became a regular feature of Cambridge writings on cyclical unemployment thereafter. On this matter, see Laidler (1991, ch. 4).

cycle is found in Hawtrey's writings. He located the proximate cause of output fluctuations in variations in what he called *effective demand*, the economy's rate of flow of nominal expenditure, arguing that money-wage and price stickiness prevented them from having consequences for the price level alone; and he attributed variations in effective demand to monetary sources.[15] In Hawtrey's analysis, an *inherently unstable* process of money creation and destruction was perpetually causing discrepancies between the supply of money and the demand for money, which in turn affected expenditure flows as agents attempted to restore equilibrium to their cash balances. Hawtrey was optimistic about the capacity of monetary policy to mitigate, though probably not eliminate, cyclical fluctuations in practice, but his insistence that no policy which failed to bring about variations in either the quantity of money or its velocity of circulation could affect output made him acutely sceptical about the powers of fiscal policy.[16]

Keynes's status as an exponent of a largely monetary theory of the cycle, closer to Hawtrey than to Robertson and Pigou, was confirmed by his two-volume *Treatise on Money* (1930a). That book is the central topic of Chapter 6. It is notable for, among other things, its belated introduction of Wicksell's ideas into the British literature, and one of its avowed aims was to integrate Wicksell's analysis with the Cambridge version of the quantity theory. Keynes's version of Wicksell emphasized the effects of interest-rate variations on the demand for output – particularly of long rates on investment. It was very much in the spirit of contemporary Swedish work and went strongly against the grain of Austrian cycle theory.[17] Concern with long, rather than short, rates of interest as the key link in a monetary explanation of the cycle and an accompanying pervasive emphasis on the problems of co-ordinating saving and investment decisions were only two of the notable innovations of

---

[15] It should be noted that the essential features of Hawtrey's analysis were first published in his 1913 monograph *Good and Bad Trade*, which appeared before World War I. See Laidler (1991, pp. 100–112). In the light of Hawtrey's extensive influence in the United States, particularly in the late 1920s, it is interesting to note that, according to Hawtrey, the empirical experience that prompted the analysis presented in that book was the American crisis of 1907.

[16] Hawtrey was, that is to say, the originator of what later came to be called the "Treasury view," whose locus classicus was Hawtrey (1925). Note that in the 1937 article in which Hicks first developed the geometry of IS-LM, he formulated that position in terms of a verbal account of a vertical-LM-curve version of this framework, as did Friedman as late as 1974 (pp. 137–143).

[17] That was why he drew criticism from Hayek, who by that time was based at the London School of Economics and was heavily engaged, in collaboration with Lionel Robbins, in introducing Austrian ideas to an English audience. The introduction of Austrian ideas about the cycle into British discourse was but one aspect of an altogether broader assault that Robbins was launching against the dominance of Marshallian economics in Britain. On the microeconomic front, the assault was more successful, for it was from the London School of Economics that Continental general-equilibrium theory began to permeate British thinking, notably, but by no means exclusively, in Hicks's *Value and Capital* (1939).

the *Treatise*. Among the others was the deployment of what amounted to Lavington's analysis of the demand for money as a liquid store of value in order to model endogenous fluctuations in velocity. Even so, the *Treatise* was ultimately unsuccessful, albeit in an extremely interesting way. It contained extensive discussions of wage stickiness and its consequences for output and employment over the course of the cycle, but it failed to integrate those real fluctuations into the formal analytic structure which it expounded. The *Treatise*'s theory of the cycle was thus, as many critics, both friendly and unfriendly, would quickly point out, a theory of fluctuations in the price level, not in income and employment.[18]

[margin handwriting: Treatise lacked formal analytical structure]

None of this is to say that English economics of the inter-war years neglected the problem of unemployment per se; far from it, but when that issue was the main concern, the analysis deployed was not cycle theory, but rather a comparative static Marshallian supply-and-demand apparatus, modified in one way or another to accommodate what seemed to be relevant institutional features of the labour market. Chapter 7 begins with a brief discussion of some key pre–World War I contributions to that essentially Marshallian literature on unemployment, those by Beveridge (1909) and Pigou (1913) in particular. It goes on to show how their emphasis on market frictions, seen as impeding both wage flexibility and inter-sectoral labour mobility, permeated much of the British discussion of those matters in the 1920s. Contributors to that discussion also understood that what we would now call general-equilibrium problems had to be addressed when discussing economy-wide unemployment. Pigou, whose book *The Theory of Unemployment* (1933) was much, and somewhat unfairly, criticized by Keynes in the *General Theory*, paid considerable attention to them, without, however, completely solving them.

Widespread unemployment and deficient output were not brand-new features of the British, or any other, economy of the 1920s. They had occurred often enough and lasted long enough in earlier periods and in other places to inspire a dissenting tradition in economic analysis which treated them as the norm, rather than as deviations from an equilibrium which, frictions aside, would occur only at full employment. Malthus, Lauderdale, and Sismondi are among the names associated with this "underconsumptionist" tradition in the early nineteenth century, and in the period dealt with by this book, its leading British exponent was John A. Hobson. That approach to the theory of unemployment is also discussed in Chapter 7, along with the work of Richard Kahn and Jens Warming, who between them developed an analysis of the so-

---

[18] For a friendly critic who made that point, see Robertson (1931a), and for a less friendly commentary, see Hayek (1931b, 1932a). These matters will be discussed further in Chapter 6.

called multiplier effects of public-works expenditures at the level of the economy as a whole.

American Analysis of Money and the Cycle

The literature to which Keynes's *General Theory* was most immediately related was predominantly British, but IS-LM analysis ended up at the heart of a macroeconomic orthodoxy which was to become at least as much American as European, if not more American. How the ideas of Keynes came to America, or at least to Harvard, very quickly indeed in the late 1930s is a well-known story, but Chapters 8 and 9 deal with highlights of the development of American macroeconomics in the 1920s and early 1930s, before that arrival.[19] In the 1920s, the United States was by and large prosperous and had only recently acquired a central bank. It is shown in Chapter 8 that questions about the use of monetary policy for stabilization purposes, which such neo-classical economists as Marshall and Irving Fisher had analysed before the war, continued to be much discussed there, not least because Fisher himself remained professionally active right through the period in which we are interested.

In the 1920s, Fisher was the main proponent of legally mandating the Federal Reserve System to pursue a price-stabilization rule.[20] Opposition to reducing monetary policy to such a rule, and indeed to using it for stabilization policy more generally, came from exponents of a version of the nineteenth-century Banking School needs-of-trade doctrine who were particularly influential at the Federal Reserve Board until the early 1930s. That doctrine had been kept alive in the United States, long after it had faded into relative obscurity in Britain, by James Laurence Laughlin and his followers, some of whom had been his students at the University of Chicago; and in its American version it developed a distinct, if somewhat superficial, resemblance to Austrian cycle theory.[21] A more middle-of-the-road position, influential at the Federal Reserve Bank of New York, saw a positive role for stabilizing monetary policy, but it was argued that in order to implement

---

[19] Colander and Landreth (1996) edited an interesting collection of the recollections (not always mutually consistent and accurate) of those who participated in bringing Keynes's ideas to America.

[20] On the pre–World War I discussions of the role of monetary policy in stabilizing economic activity, from which Fisher's post-war views developed, see Laidler (1991, ch. 6).

[21] Earlier (Laidler 1991, pp. 163–164) I briefly discussed Laughlin's views, but Neil Skaggs (1995) has provided an altogether fuller account of them. It is ironic that Laughlin, the arch-opponent of the quantity theory of money, should have been based at the University of Chicago, where Henry Parker Willis, a leading exponent of what Lloyd Mints (1945) would come to call the "real-bills" doctrine in the 1920s and 1930s, was among his students. See Chapters 8 and 9 for further discussion.

such policy, central bankers would need more room for manoeuvre than any rule would allow them. Allyn Young, who taught monetary economics at Harvard until 1927, was an important and influential academic exponent of one version of that point of view, strongly influenced by Hawtrey's ideas.[22]

Already in the 1920s the United States was home to an empirical tradition in business-cycle analysis whose closest parallel in Europe probably lay in the German historical tradition. In the 1920s and 1930s that tradition was associated in particular with Wesley Clair Mitchell of the National Bureau of Economic Research. Like many of his contemporaries, such as Alvin Hansen and Young, Mitchell was cautiously optimistic about the possibility of rendering cycles less violent in the future by way of a policy mix that would include the collection and dissemination of systematic data on the economy's current performance and likely future performance, not to mention the judicious use of counter-cyclical public-works expenditure programs, among other measures. And as Barber (1985) has shown, under the auspices of Herbert Hoover, secretary of commerce for much of the 1920s, that agenda had considerable political support.[23] Underconsumptionism, too, was a highly visible feature of American economic thought in the 1920s, promoted in particular by William T. Foster and Waddill Catchings, and notably supported among the academic community by Paul Douglas of the University of Chicago. The policy views of these underconsumptionists were, of course, vigorously activist.

The downturn which began in mid-1929 and rapidly grew into what Friedman and Schwartz (1963) would later call the "Great Contraction" changed the focus of American macroeconomics. Developments in its wake are discussed in Chapter 9. As we shall see, adherents of the needs-of-trade doctrine saw no need to change their minds about how the monetary system worked, even in the light of the new evidence, and they took a nihilistic position on policy questions which matched that of their Austrian contemporaries quite closely. Specifically Austrian ideas had been gaining a foothold in America at that time. For example, Gottfried von Haberler, who visited Harvard in 1931–32, was at that time an able exponent of the doctrines of Mises and Hayek. Among those who had been cautious advocates of monetary stabilization policy in the later 1920s there was also considerable pessimism in the wake of the contraction, and just as in the British economics of the period,

---

[22] Though Young was important as a policy adviser, having, for example, been Keynes's opposite number in the American delegation to the Versailles conference, his main influence on American economics was exerted as a teacher.

[23] Barber (1985) also noted that much of the impetus for the activist streak in American policy discussions in the 1920s came from the successful performance of the government in organizing war-time economic activity in 1917–18.

and in some cases under its influence, doubts about the expansionary powers of monetary policy were widely expressed. In the early 1930s, too, Joseph Schumpeter, appointed at Harvard in 1932, brought his own brand of cycle theory to America. Very much like Robertson, he stressed the role of technical change in driving the cycle, but he nevertheless took a pessimistic view, more in the spirit of Hayek, of what activist policy could achieve in the face of the depression.[24] For a while he exerted considerable influence, not least on Alvin Hansen, then at the University of Minnesota. Those two were intellectually coherent in their pessimism, but there were others who were far less so, notably some of Schumpeter's fellow contributors to *The Economics of the Recovery Program* (Brown et al. 1934), who were also based at Harvard.

Pessimism about the efficiency of monetary policy also marked the work of Paul Douglas, who re-emerged in the early 1930s (after a brief hiatus) as a vigorous supporter of underconsumptionist doctrine. He integrated its policy implications into a rather comprehensive democratic socialist program for reforming American social and economic life. Economic planning was to be a prominent feature of his program, as to a lesser extent it was in that envisaged by Mitchell in the 1930s. Though Irving Fisher retained confidence in monetary policy as the contraction gathered momentum, he developed what he called "The Debt-Deflation Theory of Great Depressions" (1933) to explain the severity of the slump.

Almost, but not quite, alone among his contemporaries, for Carl Snyder of the Federal Reserve Bank of New York held similar views, Allyn Young's sometime protégé Lauchlin Currie, at that time an instructor at Harvard, and Hawtrey's assistant during his visit to that department in 1928–29, offered a monetary explanation for the contraction. He argued that mistaken policies, based on the needs-of-trade doctrine, had initiated a downturn in the money supply in 1928–29 and then had failed to prevent it from getting out of hand in 1929–32. These are ideas which we nowadays associate with the Chicago tradition, as are Currie's 1934 proposals to put the monetary liabilities of commercial banks on a 100 per cent. reserve basis. As we shall see, elements of these ideas were indeed taken up at Chicago, or developed there independently, at about the same time, notably by Jacob Viner and Henry Simons, with the latter making them part of a radical liberal (in the old-fashioned sense) policy agenda. In addition to "100 per cent money," as Irving Fisher

---

[24] It is worth remarking that Schumpeter's views on the cycle had in good measure already been anticipated in the United States by Mrs. Minnie Throop England (1912, 1913) in papers in the *Quarterly Journal of Economics* and *Journal of Political Economy*, and such contributors as Irving Fisher and Alvin Hansen were familiar with her work before Schumpeter arrived on the American scene. On her contribution, see Robert Dimand (1995).

would come to call it, the monetary aspects of that agenda encompassed a legislated price-level stabilization rule similar to that which Fisher had first proposed in the 1920s.[25]

Keynes, the Classics, and IS-LM

Evidently the intellectual milieu into which Keynes introduced his *General Theory* in 1936 was diverse, to say the least. Chapter 10 deals with the book itself, and Chapter 11 deals with the reaction to it on the part of those who were already well-established contributors before its appearance – for example, Frank H. Knight, Pigou, Robertson, Viner, Hawtrey, Hansen, and Ohlin. Chapter 12 goes on to discuss the emergence of the IS-LM model in the writings of younger commentators – Roy Harrod, John Hicks, Oskar Lange, Abba Lerner, James Meade, Brian Reddaway, and Joan Robinson – as a way of expounding the issues raised by the book.

This is no place to offer more than the briefest sketch of Chapter 10's treatment of the *General Theory*. Suffice it to say, first of all, that the static nature of most of the book's analysis is stressed, as is its relationship to the literature on the problem of unemployment discussed in Chapter 7. The embryonic, albeit informal, IS-LM-style analysis that it develops in dealing with the parallels between the effects of money-wage cuts and of monetary expansion is recognized, but so is the amount of space devoted to the role of expectations in economic life and to an analysis of secular unemployment reminiscent in some respects, as Keynes himself recognized, of earlier under-consumptionist doctrines. The relationships between what Keynes had to say about certain issues in 1936 and what others had said about the same matters earlier are also discussed, such as those between his evident lack of faith in the inter-temporal allocative efficiency of market mechanisms and the prevailing scepticism among his Cambridge predecessors and colleagues about those same matters, between his theory of liquidity preference and Lavington's earlier treatment of the same issue, and between his notion of effective demand and Hawtrey's version of that concept.

In light of those relationships, which Keynes did not acknowledge, it is hardly surprising that some of his "classical" reviewers, Pigou and Knight in particular, were scornful of his claims to novelty. Chapter 11 begins with

[handwritten margin notes: Keynes effective demand vs. Hawtrey's effective demand]

---

[25] Even so, the Chicago department was far from united in its views. Indeed, there was considerable acrimony, particularly between Paul Douglas and Frank H. Knight. See Stigler (1988, ch. 12). Though the immediate occasion of their quarrel seems to have been the question of renewing Henry Simons's appointment, Knight also seems to have harboured a deep distaste for Douglas's public advocacy of activist policies. As Reder (1982) has recounted, relations between Knight and Viner were also cool, although correct.

a discussion of their reactions, where it is shown that those two nevertheless missed one valid and crucially important point that Keynes was making, namely, that there was a close analytic similarity between expansionary monetary policy, on the one hand, and a policy of money-wage cuts, on the other, and that the explanation of unemployment was to be found not in the labour market but in the determinants of aggregate demand in the economy. Hawtrey and Viner recognized that element in the *General Theory* and welcomed it, while criticizing other aspects of the book. They expressed doubts about Keynes's identification of liquidity preference with the demand for money per se in the context of a complex financial system, as well as his claim that the phenomenon was capable of permanently disrupting the capacity of interest rates to co-ordinate saving and investment and hence was capable of generating chronic unemployment. Along with Robertson and Ohlin, they also argued that the static nature of Keynes's analysis rendered it not only intellectually retrogressive but also a good deal less useful than much that had gone before it. Though the phrase is Alvin Hansen's, those critics all shared the opinion that the *General Theory* was "not the foundations of a new economics."[26] But anyone who believes that Keynes did not intend to found a "new economics" and did not take seriously the radical elements in the book's arguments must contend with what he said in his 1937 reply to those critics in the *Quarterly Journal of Economics*, which is discussed at the end of Chapter 11.

Chapter 12 brings the fourth part of this book to a close. It discusses the way in which a number of Keynes's younger readers extracted versions of the IS-LM model from the *General Theory*. It shows that some of them, for example, Brian Reddaway and James Meade, presented systems of simultaneous equations essentially similar to those set out earlier, though richer in detail in Meade's case, as reflecting the central message of the book, and how others, notably Roy Harrod, Oskar Lange, and John Hicks, were inclined to treat IS-LM as a more general system, not specifically Keynesian, and capable of encapsulating, as special cases, the main views of both Keynes and his predecessors, with the role of the interest rate in the demand-for-money function being a key factor differentiating those cases from one another. Hicks's extension of IS-LM to encompass an endogenously determined money stock is also discussed, as is his treatment of the relationship between a simple dynamization of the system and Wicksell's treatment of monetary equilibrium, thus bringing this book's narrative full circle.

---

[26] Note that this phrase, which occurred in the original version (1936) of Hansen's review of the *General Theory*, was deleted from later reprints of it.

Conclusions

The final chapter discusses how IS-LM was related not only to the *General Theory* but also to the literature discussed in earlier chapters. The static nature of the system is re-emphasized, but it is suggested that, despite this, the IS curve can be thought of as summarizing certain essential features of the analysis of inter-temporal co-ordination issues which followed from Wick- sell's contribution. It is further suggested that the LM curve performs a similar task on behalf of earlier work more closely related to the quantity theory of money, particularly in its Marshallian stock-supply-and-demand formulation. Thus, the model is presented as a subtle, though highly selective, synthesis of important and often apparently conflicting elements from the earlier literature. It is nevertheless noted that some elements of the earlier literature are missing from that synthesis, not least one that Keynes (1936) had particularly stressed, namely, the importance of uncertainty and associated problems concerning the role of expectations in conditioning forward-looking behaviour.

   Chapter 13 also briefly discusses the subsequent development of dynamic analysis, based on multiplier–accelerator interaction. It is argued that that class of models had little to do directly with Keynes's influence, but that with appropriate assumptions about passively endogenous velocity and/or money, they could be presented as dynamizations of an IS-LM system in which the LM curve was essentially horizontal, a configuration in which the quantity-theory element would disappear entirely from the system. The later revival of the quantity-theory tradition, in the guise of ''monetarism,'' and the subsequent re-emergence of a deductivist approach to macroeconomic issues, known as ''new-classical'' economics, related in some respects to Austrian ideas of the 1920s and 1930s, are noted, but not analysed in any detail.

The Lessons of the Studies

To the extent that the studies in the following chapters yield lessons, they are that the macroeconomics of the inter-war years was the product of many intellects and that, rather than being swept away by a Keynesian revolution, key features of that body of thought were in fact synthesized into a simple and easily grasped IS-LM model, around which debates could be, and were, organized for the next thirty years or so. To argue that an important branch of economics evolved in such an untidy and piecemeal fashion out of the interactions of many contributors, albeit with some, not least Keynes himself, playing larger roles in the process than others, does not make for as much drama as would the alternative of this branch of economics being destroyed and then reborn as a result of the superhuman efforts of a single creator. Perhaps, however, we should not be surprised that this way of telling the story of the 1920s and 1930s seems the more accurate one. I hope that the following studies will help make the case for doing so.

PART I

The Wicksellians

CHAPTER 2

The Austrian Theory of the Trade Cycle

Wicksellian Origins

Knut Wicksell's work provided a crucial link between neo-classical monetary theory, built around the quantity theory of money, and the analysis of the interaction between saving and investment during the inter-war years, out of which so-called Keynesian economics was, in due course, to develop.[1] But if Wicksell's ideas had an influence on those whom we nowadays regard as Keynes's predecessors, those ideas were just as seminal for their opponents. In particular, Wicksell provided the starting point for the Austrian trade-cycle theory which, before 1936, seemed at least as likely as any other body of analysis to be about to dominate the subdiscipline; and that doctrine offered an interpretation of macroeconomic behaviour, not to mention a set of policy recommendations, that no one could describe as proto-Keynesian. Indeed, the reader who looks in this chapter for points of contact between that theory and the IS-LM model will find virtually none.

Austrian cycle theory was largely the creation of Ludwig von Mises and Friedrich von Hayek, but it also had a number of non-Austrian adherents. Outstanding among the latter was Lionel Robbins, who was instrumental in bringing Hayek to a chair at the London School of Economics in 1931, thereby ensuring that over the next five years or so his work would have a major impact in Britain, and indeed in the English-speaking world more generally.

The Cumulative Process

The particular contribution of Wicksell upon which the Austrians built their cycle theory was his so-called *cumulative process* analysis. Wicksell treated the cycle as fundamentally a real phenomenon, reflecting waves of innovation

---

[1] Wicksell's influence on inter-war macroeconomics was pervasive, so much so that Leijonhufvud (1981) referred to one important theme that ran through it, namely, the role of inter-temporal allocative failures in generating cyclical fluctuations, as "The Wicksell Connection." For a detailed and penetrating account of the relationship between Hayek's cycle theory and Wicksell's work, see Trautwein (1996)

and the fluctuations in investment that accompanied them, and he regarded monetary matters as, at best, of secondary importance in this context.[2] He developed his cumulative process analysis not with a view to understanding the cycle, but mainly as an aid to understanding the problems raised by secular price-level movements, particularly as they occurred in a monetary system dominated by commercial banks but nevertheless anchored by adherence to the gold standard. His aim was thus to extend the quantity theory of money, as he had inherited it from classical theory, to deal with the old problem of such price-level movements in the context of a new and contemporarily relevant set of institutional arrangements.

At the heart of Wicksell's analysis was the postulate that when the rate of interest at which commercial banks stood ready to lend, the *market or money rate of interest*, lay below the *natural rate of interest*, to be defined in a moment, entrepreneurs would be induced to increase their borrowing from the banks and bid up the prices of the factors of production; the increase in nominal factor incomes, thus induced, would in turn ensure that the money price of output would also increase. Given Wicksell's usual assumption about price-level expectations, namely, that the current period's prices were expected to prevail in the following period, these mechanisms would raise prices period after period, so long as the discrepancy between the two interest rates persisted. Wicksell, however, looked to the workings of the gold standard to remove the discrepancy in question and hence to restore price-level stability to his economy: rising prices would cause an increasing demand for gold currency on the part of the non-bank public; the banks would thus lose reserves and in response would raise the money rate of interest. The system would therefore, in due course, settle down at a new higher and, according to Wicksell, metastable equilibrium price level.[3]

Though that analysis was conceived by Wicksell as extending rather than replacing the quantity theory of money, the quantity of money itself, which he usually thought of as consisting solely of what we would now call currency, played a passive role in the process of price formation. Credit granted by the banking system was the active element there, driving up input prices when it was granted, and output prices when the goods whose production the

---

[2] Patinkin (1965, note E) provided the best single account of Wicksell's monetary economics. See also Laidler (1991, ch. 5). Boianovsky (1995) has explored the relationship between that monetary economics and Wicksell's cycle theory.

[3] Note that this analysis by Wicksell would, with a given stock of gold, have the banking system's reserve ratio smaller in the new equilibrium than at its starting point. Other monetary economists, notably, for example, Hawtrey (e.g., 1913) and Fisher (1911), who also analysed cumulative processes similar to (though by no means identical with) that of Wicksell, were more concerned with banks having a desired reserve ratio. That is perhaps one reason why their analyses led to monetary models of cyclical fluctuations. On Hawtrey, see Chapter 5, and on Fisher, see Chapter 8, "The Quantity Theory and the Cycle."

credit had financed were sold. Moreover, because Wicksell thought of the proceeds of those sales as being used by entrepreneurs to pay off their bank loans at the end of each period, questions about whether or not the bank deposits created when loans were made might exert a subsequent influence on prices, over and above their first-round credit-market effects, did not arise. But it is only if such questions do arise that it becomes natural to extend the money concept relevant to the quantity theory to encompass bank deposits, and that Wicksell did not usually do. Thus, when in some of his expositions of the cumulative process he found it convenient to leave a gold-standard world altogether and analyse the operations of what he called a "pure credit economy" in which currency did not exist, his analysis seemed to supersede the quantity theory altogether, rather than supplement it.[4]

Monetary Equilibrium

In particular, Wicksell's analysis attributed inflation not so much to an increasing quantity of money – not at all in the case of the pure credit economy – as to the existence of a discrepancy between the money interest rate and natural interest rate. The significance of that shift in emphasis becomes clear when we consider Wicksell's conception of the natural rate of interest: he thought of it as being determined by real factors, that is, non-monetary factors, and in particular those having to do with saving and investment. Thus, for Wicksell, price-level movements, far from being purely nominal phenomena associated only with the monetary system, were, as Axel Leijonhufvud (1981) in particular has stressed, also associated with a failure of market mechanisms to co-ordinate choices about the inter-temporal allocation of real resources. Price stability, on the other hand, was symptomatic of *monetary equilibrium*, which Wicksell associated with successful inter-

---

[4] Elsewhere I have discussed this point at greater length (Laidler 1991, pp. 127–135). As Tom Humphrey has pointed out to me, there is at least one passage (Wicksell 1898, pp. 109–110) in which Wicksell, or his translator, used the word "money" to characterize bank deposits. However, that passage is devoted to arguing that they play a passive role in the system, accommodating but not causing changes induced by the interest rate, and indeed in one place (p. 109) they are referred to not as "money" but as "money loans." Humphrey (1997) has argued that because bank credit expansion is a necessary condition for a discrepancy between the money and natural rates of interest to persist in Wicksell's pure credit economy, his analysis should be regarded as lying in the same quantity-theory tradition as Irving Fisher's treatment (1911, ch. 4) of "transition periods." I have no differences with Humphrey about what those two authors said, nor about the fact that their work had a common root in the classical quantity-theory tradition that originated with Thornton (1802). The fact that Fisher attributed a causative, rather than purely permissive, role to bank credit creation in his analysis of transition periods seems to me, however, to be an all-important difference between his work and that of Wicksell, particularly in light of the subsequent development of monetary economics. For discussion of Fisher's work, see Chapter 8, "The Quantity Theory and the Cycle."

temporal co-ordination. Wicksell, however, was anything but systematically precise about the associations involved.

In some places he defined the natural rate of interest as that which would bring about equilibrium between saving and investment in a frictionless barter economy, and in one place in particular (Wicksell 1907a, p. 214) he defined it as the marginal product of capital; he also consistently argued that equality between market and natural rates of interest would lead to zero credit creation and price-level stability. But would saving and investment be equal to one another at a rate of interest equal to the marginal product of capital (we should add "per unit of capital" here) in a growing barter economy in which saving and investment were positive? Furthermore, in a growing economy, the price level could hardly remain stable if there was also zero credit creation: Which phenomenon would then characterize monetary equilibrium in this case? And in a world with heterogeneous output, precisely what sense does it make to try to reduce the marginal product of capital (per unit of capital) to a ratio determined purely in the production sector to which the market rate of interest may then be equated?

Wicksell probably was aware of each and every one of those problems. In *Value, Capital and Rent* (Wicksell 1893) he had shown himself aware of the interdependence of any scalar measure of the capital stock and the structure of relative prices in a multi-commodity world; so it is unlikely to have been an accident that in his most careful analysis of the cumulative process, in Chapter 9 of *Interest and Prices* (Wicksell 1898), he made just the right assumptions to ensure that problems associated with that interdependence would not be encountered.[5] There, the economy's stock of fixed capital was exogenously given and unchanging, while working capital and output consisted of the same wage goods, produced by a constant labour force (in co-operation with fixed capital) over a uniform period of production. In such a world, the following hold: the marginal product of working capital (per unit of capital) is indeed well defined as a pure rate of flow per unit of time; saving is zero and hence is equal to investment when the money rate of interest is equal to the natural rate of interest; and in the latter circumstances there is neither credit creation nor price-level movement. It takes very little in the way of changed assumptions to disturb all that theoretical coherence, and Wicksell's other expositions of his analysis tended to be less precise the closer they came to being applications to reality.

Some intellectual muddles lead to dead-ends, and others prove seminal.

---

[5] For further discussion of the role played by a natural rate of interest determined purely by the conditions of production in Wicksell's analysis, and the difficulties involved in such a concept in the context of a multi-product economy, see, e.g., Hansson (1990, pp. 263–268), Kompas (1989, ch. 4), and Rogers (1989, pp. 27–39).

That which Wicksell bequeathed to twentieth-century economists is firmly in
the latter category. Indeed, it would be difficult to think of any muddle in the
history of economic thought which produced so wide-ranging and creatively
constructive a set of responses as this one. We shall see in the next chapter
what Wicksell's younger compatriots, who came to be called *the Stockholm
School*, made of it, and later we shall see that there was a far-from-trivial
element of Wicksellian influence on English macroeconomics too. But here
we shall deal with the Austrian response to these puzzles.

Austrian Economics

Ludwig von Mises and Friedrich von Hayek, the two originators of Austrian
trade-cycle theory, were also the immediate intellectual ancestors of modern
Austrian economics, some of whose exponents still subscribe to the cycle
theory in question. It should be made clear, therefore, that Austrian economics, like economics of any other variety, has evolved over the years and that
some of its more striking late-twentieth-century characteristics were either
less important or completely absent from the work which concerns us here,
particularly the work of Hayek. In the 1920s and early 1930s, for example,
as judged by the standards of the time, Hayek showed no aversion to mathematics. More substantively important, he was an exponent of and contributor
to Walrasian general-equilibrium analysis, which he referred to as ''the modern theory of the general interdependence of all economic quantities, which
has been most perfectly expressed by the Lausanne School of theoretical
economics'' (1929, tr. 1933, footnote on p. 42). The idea of competitive
markets as being in a constant state of evolving disequilibrium as they process
and disseminate information and incentives among agents, which we nowadays associate so strongly with Hayek, did not become central to his thought
until after the appearance of his 1937 paper ''Economics and Knowledge.''[6]

Deductivist Methodology

Some characteristics of modern Austrian theory nevertheless marked the work
to be described here. There was, for example, a strong individualist tone to
the Austrian trade-cycle theory of the inter-war years, and, closely associated,
it was underpinned by a deductivist methodology. The Austrians thought of
economic theory as being mainly a matter of deriving results from premises

---

[6] That element in Austrian analysis developed not so much from its exponents' work on the
cycle as from their contributions to the ''market socialism'' debate of the 1930s, whose
discussion would be beyond the scope of this book. For useful discussions of Austrian ideas
about equilibrium and disequilibrium in market processes, see Boehm (1990) and Kirzner
(1990).

that, being self-evidently true, could yield only true conclusions. Hayek, in 1929, say, was not dogmatic in his adherence to deductivism and individualism; but when it came to understanding the trade cycle, the relative weights which he was willing to accord empirical evidence and deductive theorizing were clear enough:

> Even as a means of verification, the statistical examination of the cycles has only a very limited value for Trade Cycle theory. For the latter – as for any other economic theory – there are only two criteria of correctness. Firstly, it must be deduced with unexceptionable logic from the fundamental notions of the theoretical system; and secondly, it must explain by a purely deductive method those phenomena with all their peculiarities which we observe in the actual cycles. Such a theory could only be "false" either through an inadequacy in its logic or because the phenomena which it explains do not correspond with the observed facts. If, however, the theory is logically sound, and if it leads to an explanation of the given phenomena as a necessary consequence of these general conditions of economic activity, then the best that statistical investigation can do is to show that there still remains an unexplained residue of processes. It could never prove that the determining relationships are of a different character from those maintained by the theory. (1929, tr. 1933, pp. 32–33)

For Hayek, then, statistical investigation was helpful in describing the "given phenomena" in need of explanation, but only those explanations rigorously deduced from the "fundamental notions of the theoretical system" had scientific validity; further statistical investigation could not refute such explanations. Lionel Robbins was surely referring to Austrian cycle theory when he concluded his famous attack on "quantitative economics" with the following remark:[7]

> ... a few isolated thinkers, using the despised apparatus of deductive theory, have brought our knowledge of the theory of fluctuations to a point from which the fateful events of the last few years can be explained in general terms, and a complete solution of the riddle of depressions within the next few years does not seem outside the bounds of probability. (1935, p. 115)

How restrictive such deductivism will be in practice will depend very much upon how widely spread are the boundaries that define which "fundamental notions" are admissible; and even in the 1920s and 1930s the Austrian economists were, following the founder of their school, Carl Menger, strongly committed to the idea that maximizing individuals responded to the information and incentives conveyed by relative prices. They were also strongly committed to the analysis of inter-temporal allocation, developed by Men-

---

[7] Robbins's *Nature and Significance of Economic Science* (1935), from which the following quotation is taken, was and remains the classic statement of the case for deductivism as the appropriate methodological approach to economic analysis.

ger's successor as Professor of Economics at Vienna, Eugen von Böhm-Bawerk.[8]

Capital Theory

Austrian cycle theorists' commitment to Böhm-Bawerk's capital theory is of particular importance in the current context. As the Swedish economist Gunnar Myrdal would put it,

> it is not surprising that it was the Austrians who found the connexions with Wicksell: Wicksell himself was a pupil of Böhm-Bawerk and he put his thoughts into forms and constructions based directly on Austrian habits of thought. (Myrdal 1931, tr. 1939, p. 7)

The "Austrian habits of thought" which Wicksell had utilized characterized consumption goods as *goods of the first order* and pictured them as being produced with the aid of intermediate goods, known as *goods of higher orders*, by way of a *roundabout* process in which the passage of time was of the very essence. In the Austrian view, a decision on the part of consumers to save was simultaneously a decision to consume at some time in the future, while a decision to invest was a decision to devote currently available resources to the production of goods of higher orders. The latter would then be used to produce goods of the first order, consumption goods, which would become available only after some lapse of time.

Austrian capital theory claimed that the roundaboutness of production, even in a multi-product economy, could be characterized by an economy-wide average period of production, which purported to provide a scalar measure of the time that elapsed between the moment when the production of higher-order goods began and that at which the resulting first-order goods were consumed. It also postulated that more roundabout methods of production were more productive and that the marginal productivity of roundaboutness diminished as the period of production increased. To put matters in modern terms, the Austrians, and Böhm-Bawerk in particular, believed it possible to measure the economy's capital stock by a scalar – the average period of production – and to embed that measure in an aggregate production function characterized by diminishing marginal productivity.[9] As we have already seen, Wicksell knew that there were problems there, and skilfully avoided them, and as we shall see in the next chapter, his Swedish successors

---

[8] See Menger (1871) and Böhm-Bawerk (1884) for their most important contributions. Streissler (1990) has provided an excellent and succinct account of the evolution of the Austrian theory of capital.

[9] See Rogers (1989, pp. 35–39) for a succinct discussion of the relationship between these Austrian ideas and the issues debated in the so-called Cambridge controversy of the 1960s.

took the exposition of those problems by Gustav Cassel (1903) and Irving Fisher (1907, 1930a) as the starting point for their own development of his ideas. The Austrians, that is, Mises, Hayek, and their followers, did not understand the significance of those problems, however, and, as I have already noted, adopted Böhm-Bawerk's capital theory as one of the "fundamental notions" from which they deduced their theory of the cycle.[10]

It followed immediately that, for the Austrians, it was the interest rate's role in the economy to maintain harmony between consumers' plans for the time path of consumption and the economy's time structure of production. For example, a shift of preferences towards more saving would mean that consumers wished to defer more consumption into the future; the rate of interest would fall, and firms would be induced to undertake more roundabout production methods. When the latter came to fruition, the resulting output would satisfy the delayed demand for extra consumption goods which had been implicit in the initial act of saving. The value of the rate of interest which would thus equilibrate the inter-temporal allocation of resources was, of course, precisely Wicksell's natural rate, and he had explicitly grounded that concept in Böhm-Bawerk's capital theory in Chapter 9 of *Interest and Prices*. Elsewhere, as I have noted, he had been more vague in his exposition.

Credit, Inter-temporal Allocation, and the Cycle

Wicksell had argued that under a gold standard, those mechanisms, whereby drains of gold from (and into) the banks would influence their lending rate, would tend to keep the market rate of interest moving towards its natural value. He had, however, also analysed a pure credit economy, from which those mechanisms would be absent; but he had done so before World War I, in the heyday of the gold standard, when a pure credit economy had been more of an interesting theoretical abstraction than a practical possibility. The war changed all that, and monetary systems more closely approximating Wicksell's theoretical case became the norm in Europe, even if only, as it seemed at the time, temporarily. That lent real urgency to the problems raised for Austrian analysis of inter-temporal allocation in Wicksell's pure-credit-economy case, problems which Mises, who had broached those issues even before the war, albeit rather briefly (cf. Mises 1912), characterized in the following terms:

> ... it would be entirely within the power of banks to reduce the rate of interest ... provided that in so doing they did not set other forces in motion

---

[10] It was not until 1941, in his *Pure Theory of Capital*, that Hayek systematically took up those problems. By that time, Austrian cycle theory, if not quite defunct, was already well out of the mainstream of macroeconomics, as Hicks (1967) has recounted. For a constructively critical assessment of Hayek's *Pure Theory*, see Steedman (1994).

which would automatically re-establish the rate of interest at the level determined by the circumstances of the capital market, i.e. the market in which present goods and future goods are exchanged for one another. The problem that is before us is usually referred to by the catch-phrase *gratuitous nature of credit*. (Mises 1924, tr. 1934, p. 352, italics in original)

In the absence of gold convertibility, following Wicksell's reasoning, "it is impossible to see why rising prices and an increasing demand for loans should induce [banks] to raise the rate of interest they charge for loans" (Mises 1924, tr. 1934, p. 356).

Mises's Insights

Mises based his solution to that problem on a criticism which a number of other economists, such as David Davidson and Cassel (1923, p. 416), had levelled at Wicksell, namely, that he had not paid sufficient attention to the possibility that a divergence of the market from the natural rate of interest might have consequences beyond changing the price level.[11] Mises put the point as follows: ". . . if the rate of interest on loans is artificially reduced below the natural rate . . . then entrepreneurs are enabled and obliged to enter upon longer processes of production" (Mises 1924, tr. 1934, pp. 360–361). But that lengthening of the period of production, that increase in investment, would not be taking place in response to an increase in saving on the part of consumers. Hence it would involve a dislocation of the inter-temporal allocative mechanism, with the result that "a time must necessarily come when the means of subsistence available for consumption are all used up although the capital goods employed in production have not yet been transformed into consumption goods" (1924, tr. 1934, p. 362). Such a dislocation could not persist, however. Inherent in it was an excess demand for current consumption goods which would raise their prices relative to those of intermediate goods and hence future consumption goods. "That is, the rate of interest on loans . . . again approaches the natural rate" (Mises 1924, tr. 1934, p. 363).

That view of the operation of banking, thought Mises, "leads ultimately to a theory of business cycles" (1924, tr. 1934, p. 365). That theory would focus on banks engaging in credit creation and hence setting in motion a process of investment which in due course would be cut short before completion by a shortage of saving. Further injections of bank credit could prolong, and indeed accentuate, disequilibrium in the inter-temporal allocation of resources, but they could not, according to Mises, prevent its ending in a crisis

---

[11] Davidson's contributions to that debate remain untranslated from Swedish. See, however, Uhr (1987) for a readily accessible, albeit brief, account of his views. That the substance of those views was known to Hayek is apparent from *Monetary Theory* (Hayek 1929, tr. 1933, p. 115, fn.).

whose salient characteristic would be a stock of partly completed investment projects. The longer the continuation of credit creation delayed that outcome, the more severe would these symptoms be when they finally did materialize.

As early as 1924, then, Mises had produced a clear and complete outline of Austrian trade-cycle theory, and that outline made an appearance in the writings of his younger colleague Hayek in the following year (cf. Hayek 1925, tr. 1984, ch. 1, fn. 4, pp. 27–28). The subsequent filling-in of that outline, to the point at which it arguably became, in the early 1930s, the most coherent short-run macroeconomic system available, was largely Hayek's work. In the process, Hayek introduced a strong element of Walrasian general-equilibrium analysis into the system, with whose aid those theoretical ambiguities, noted earlier, in Wicksell's concept of monetary neutrality were resolved.

The Walrasian Element in Hayek's Analysis

Hayek's article ''Intertemporal Price Equilibrium and Movements in the Value of Money'' (1928, tr. 1984) was at least as much Walrasian in its approach as Austrian (though Walras was not explicitly cited therein). That article developed the idea that physically similar goods, separated in time, were appropriately treated as distinct entities whose relative prices were determined within a general-equilibrium system which extended over time. For that insight alone it had an important place in the development of general-equilibrium theory.[12] But it attempted to go further (not successfully, by modern standards, to be sure) by introducing both money and productivity growth into the system in order to propound the following message:

> . . . given a general expansion of production, the maintenance of equilibrium requires a corresponding reduction in prices, and in this case any failure of prices to fall must give rise to temporary disruptions of the equality between supply and demand. (Hayek 1928, tr. 1984, p. 74)

An appropriately falling price level could, however, be achieved ''only if the monetary system was one in which any change in the quantity of money was excluded'' (Hayek 1928, tr. 1984, p. 97). In fact, however, ''it is impractical to regulate the monetary system in this way'' (Hayek 1928, tr. 1984, p. 97), so a monetary economy was very likely to suffer temporary disruptions. Here we have two essential, and closely related, conclusions of Austrian business-cycle theory. First, in order to maintain equilibrium in the

---

[12] Interestingly, though hardly by coincidence, Hayek's contribution here runs closely parallel to that of Erik Lindahl (1929b), who noted the relationship of Hayek's work to his own. Martin Currie and Ian Steedman (1989) have provided a systematic comparison of the developments of Hayek's and Lindahl's analyses of these issues in the late 1920s and 1930s.

inter-temporal allocation of resources in a monetary economy when that economy was growing, a *constant quantity of money*, or, more generally, a constant rate of flow of money expenditure (and hence, by implication, a *falling* rather than a *constant* price level), was required; and second, malfunctions of the monetary system were the *sine qua non* of departures from equilibrium in the inter-temporal allocation of resources. But though those conclusions were stated in Hayek's 1928 paper, their derivation was not fully developed. That derivation hinged on the outcome of a conceptual experiment in which the nominal prices of the factors of production were held constant while their productivity increased and while the future prices of output varied, depending upon the behaviour of the quantity of money. The prediction that any variation in the quantity of money would move *relative prices* away from their equilibrium values was, however, asserted rather than derived.

> If, during such a general expansion of output, the expectation is held with certainty that the prices of products will not fall but will remain stable or even rise, hence that at the point more distant in time the same or even a higher price can be obtained for the product produced at lesser cost, the outcome must be that production for the later period, in which supply is already at a relatively adequate level, will be further expanded at the cost of that for the earlier period, in which supply is relatively less adequate. (Hayek 1928, tr. 1984, pp. 92–93, original in italics)

What was missing there was an explicit mechanism whereby money creation could distort relative prices, but it is clear enough that Hayek was well aware both that such a mechanism was required and what its general nature would be. His failure to deal with those issues reflected not ignorance of them, but simply the fact that his paper was not primarily meant to be a contribution to cycle theory: "It is not our task here to elaborate these reflections into a theory of economic crises, especially since our neglect of the phenomena of credit would mean that any such theory at which we arrived would be completely lacking in reality" (1928, tr. 1984, p. 102). The requisite elaboration would, in any event, soon follow, in *Monetary Theory and the Trade Cycle* (1929, tr. 1933) and particularly in *Prices and Production* (1931a).

Hayek on Forced Saving and the Crisis

Harald Hagemann (1994) has shown that among German-speaking economists in the 1920s, a common line of attack on general-equilibrium analysis of the type deployed by Hayek in 1928 involved drawing attention to its apparent inability to explain the facts of the trade cycle. Hayek's development, after 1928, of Mises's sketch of trade-cycle theory was, quite self-consciously, intended as an answer to such criticism. He conceded that "the logic of equilibrium theory . . . properly followed through, can do no more than demonstrate that . . . disturbances of equilibrium can only come from outside . . . and that the economic system always reacts to such changes . . . by the formation of a new equilibrium" (Hayek 1929, tr. 1933, pp. 42–43) and that this property would render any explanation of the cycle that relied solely upon such theory inadequate. But, at the same time, he was unwilling to abandon it.

> The obvious, and . . . the only possible way out of this dilemma, is to explain the difference between the course of events described by static theory (which only permits movements towards an equilibrium, and which is deduced by directly contrasting the supply of and the demand for goods) and the actual course of events, by the fact that, with the introduction of money (or strictly speaking with the introduction of indirect exchange), a new determining cause is introduced. (Hayek 1929, tr. 1933, p. 44)

The specific feature of a monetary economy which Hayek emphasized was the phenomenon known as *forced saving*, which had (as Hayek himself showed in 1932) intermittently attracted the attention of monetary economists since the beginning of the nineteenth century.[13] The particular institutional arrangement which gave rise to that phenomenon was in fact already beginning to change, at least in the United States, even as Hayek was developing its implications, a point to which we shall return later. Suffice it for the moment, however, to note that Hayek took for granted a banking system whose monetary liabilities entered circulation by way of loans made to traders and manufacturers. He built his explanation of the cycle on the potential implicit in that institutional fact for the creation of money to affect not the general price level (a concept for which he had little use) but the intertemporal relative price, the market rate of interest, which was crucial to the capital market's co-ordination of saving and investment decisions.

In that view of things, banks would play a dual role in the monetary system, acting not only as creators of money but also as intermediaries between savers and investors, and any expansion of credit on their part would involve placing in the hands of investors newly created purchasing power which had no counterpart in an increase in voluntary saving. That purchasing power would be taken up by borrowers only at a rate of interest below that which would equate investment to voluntary saving; and it would be used by them to acquire resources for investment. In a fully employed economy, these would have to be bid away from consumers, thus creating an involuntary cut in real consumption – forced saving. For Hayek, it was that

---

[13] Hayek identified Jeremy Bentham and Henry Thornton as the originators of the analysis of forced saving, and the idea was also said to be found in the writings of Malthus, Mill, and Walras, among others. For references to this literature, see Hayek (1932b) and Björn Hansson (1987).

first-round credit-market effect, as we would now term it, that was critical in undermining the co-ordination of inter-temporal allocation, rather than any subsequent consequence of money creation for the level of money prices. That latter effect would be present in the system, to be sure, but it would be incidental to what he regarded as the main story, which would involve the influence of the banking system's behaviour on *relative prices*, not on some artificial statistical aggregate such as the *general price level*, which, Hayek believed, was of no significance for individual behaviour.[14]

Thus the introduction of forced saving into the picture established the conclusion that Hayek had asserted in 1928; namely, that with velocity assumed constant, monetary neutrality required zero credit creation and, in a growing economy, falling prices.[15] Clearly, the assumption that the experiment began at full employment was crucial to Hayek's conclusion that credit creation would divert resources from consumption to investment, but his deductivist methodological principles required him to start his conceptual experiments from just such a state of affairs:

> ... we can gain a theoretically unexceptionable explanation of complex phenomena only by first assuming the full activity of the elementary economic interconnections as shown by the equilibrium theory, and then introducing, consciously and successively, just those elements which are capable of relaxing these rigid inter-relationships. (1929, tr. 1933, pp. 95–96, original in italics)

If, like Hayek, we begin with an economy in full-employment equilibrium whose rate of interest is at its "natural level," so that saving and investment are equal to one another, and then disturb that equilibrium with an injection of credit made possible by a fall in the rate of interest, and if we believe in the relevance of Böhm-Bawerk's capital theory, we necessarily induce a move towards a longer average period of production. However, we induce no accompanying tendency for consumers voluntarily to defer their consumption

---

[14] Here Hayek followed the lead of Mises in arguing that the notion of a general price level on which the quantity theory of money concentrated inevitably obscured the relative price changes that were required to bring about the fluctuations in quantities of goods supplied and demanded which had to lie at the heart of cyclical fluctuations. See, e.g., Hayek (1929, tr. 1933, pp. 106ff.). It is interesting to note, in this regard, that an incomplete "Fisher effect" of inflation expectations upon the nominal interest rate does indeed change a crucial inter-temporal relative price. Hayek was aware of that concept and indeed used it to great effect in criticizing Keynes's (1930a) discussion of the "Gibson paradox" (the tendency for high prices and a high nominal interest rate to coincide, and vice versa) in his review of the *Treatise* (Hayek 1931b). Nevertheless, in *Prices and Production* he explicitly denied its relevance to cycle theory. See Hayek (1931a, p. 14).

[15] Unlike their English contemporaries Dennis Robertson (1926) and Arthur C. Pigou (1929), the Austrians did not carefully distinguish between economic growth that involved an expanding population, with *per capita* income held constant, and growing *per capita* income, usually taking it for granted that it was the latter case that was interesting. On Robertson and Pigou on this issue, see Chapter 4.

plans until new, more roundabout production methods bear fruit. In due course, therefore, consumption demand will materialize before the goods available to satisfy it are available, just as Mises had suggested in 1924 (cf. Mises 1924, tr. 1934, pp. 362–363).

At this point, unless there is a further injection of bank credit which creates another round of forced saving, the price of current relative to future consumption goods rises, which, in the context of Hayek's model, is simply another way of saying that the market rate of interest rises. However, resources already committed to more roundabout production methods are now locked into partially completed projects and cannot be re-allocated to meet current consumption demand. According to Hayek, the resulting coexistence of an excess demand for consumption goods and an excess supply of non-consumable intermediate goods is the defining characteristic of the crisis phase, the upper turning-point, of the cycle. Such a crisis, moreover, is the inevitable consequence of any credit creation on the part of the banking system. Its occurrence can be delayed, at the price of increasing its severity, but it cannot be avoided.

Some Weaknesses

But why should such a disequilibrium resolve itself into a collapse of output and employment? Why could resources not be re-allocated to the production of consumption goods? Hayek's efforts to deal with these questions in the London School of Economics lectures on *Prices and Production* (1931a), in which he introduced Austrian cycle theory into British discourse, were perfunctory. They rested on a particular postulate about the production function ruling in consumption-goods industries, namely, that the degree of substitutability between labour and other variable inputs, on the one hand, and capital equipment, on the other, was sufficiently small that a shortage of finished, and hence usable, capital equipment would make it impossible to employ existing supplies of variable inputs.

> In the actual world ... the single workman will not be able to produce enough for a living without the help of capital and he may, therefore, temporarily become unemployable. And the same will apply to all goods and services whose use requires the co-operation of other goods and services which, after a change in the structure of production of this kind, [i.e., a truncated move towards lengthening the period of production] may not be available in the necessary quantity. (Hayek 1931a, p. 84)

Hayek himself must have been dissatisfied with that explanation of why unemployment followed the crisis phase of the cycle, for the section of *Prices and Production* in which it appeared was considerably extended in its second edition (1935). There, for example, he faced the fact that depressed economies seemed to possess a good deal of unutilized but *completed* capital equipment. That fact was, he argued,

> a symptom that we are unable to use the fixed plant to the full extent because the current demand for consumers' goods is too urgent to permit us to invest current productive services in the long processes for which (in consequence of "misdirections of capital") the necessary durable equipment is available. (Hayek 1931a, 2nd ed., 1935, p. 96)

Significantly, too, in that later edition of *Prices and Production* there is a brief reference to the role of downward stickiness in money wages as a factor contributing to the onset of unemployment, a phenomenon conspicuous by virtue of being ignored in the first edition, and indeed in *Monetary Theory and the Trade Cycle* (1929) as well. That belated introduction of wage stickiness into his framework in 1935 presumably reflected the influence of British discussions on Hayek's thinking, for wage stickiness had often been invoked there from the 1870s onwards and, as we shall see in due course, continued to be frequently invoked throughout the inter-war period.[16] Though those additions still left Hayek's 1935 explanation of unemployment severely deficient by modern standards, they did bring it closer to the standard prevailing in the contemporary literature than had those he had offered in 1931.

The foregoing criticism rests heavily on the wisdom of hindsight, but it is worth noting that Evan Durbin (1933), an Oxford economist, then recently appointed as Hayek's junior colleague at the London School of Economics, who had great sympathy with his basic theoretical vision, nevertheless produced a powerful contemporary critique of Hayek's proclivity to neglect the phenomenon of unemployment and to begin his theoretical experiments from a state of full-employment equilibrium. As Durbin pointed out, the "English view" (Durbin 1933, p. 134) of the relationship between consumption and investment over the course of the cycle was that they were complementary: The rate of investment expenditure would vary in the same direction as consumption expenditure for the simple reason that "the demand for capital is derived from the demand for consumption of goods and therefore increases with any increase in the profitableness of producing consumption goods" (Durbin 1933, p. 135). In Hayek's analysis, to the contrary, "the two groups of industries . . . are *competing* for the services of the ultimate factors of

---

[16] Robbins (1934) also invoked wage stickiness, but he was inclined to treat it as a new postwar phenomenon rather than as a chronic property of labour markets, which is how it appeared in Cambridge contributions to this discussion. Indeed, the idea of wage stickiness as lying at the root of cyclical unemployment was fully discussed by Marshall and Marshall (1879) and Pigou (1913), among other pre-war sources. Among those writing in the Austrian tradition in Britain, it was probably Evan Durbin who paid most attention to the manner in which stickiness of nominal contracts, and wages in particular, could affect the course of the cycle. See, e.g., Durbin (1935, pp. 54ff., 159ff.).

production, and it is . . . silly to imagine that the real output of the two types of production can move upwards at the same time'' (Durbin 1933, p. 137, italics in original). Which view was correct ''depends on the assumptions that are made about the condition of total unemployment, or the distribution of unemployment'' (Durbin 1933, p. 139).

In Durbin's view, Hayek's analysis was appropriate only if the assumption of full employment was maintained. But

> given unemployment in the capital good industries – the type of unemployment which clearly exists during any period of depression – it follows at once that the more normal view that profits in the production of consumption goods and the real output of capital move together can be justified by the most rigid logic. (Durbin 1933, p. 141)

Furthermore, those same considerations tended to undermine the quintessentially Austrian notion that an increase in voluntary saving would, by way of its effects on the rate of interest, induce an increase in investment. As Durbin noted, an increase in saving would, in the first instance, reduce the profitability of consumption-goods production and might ''involve a short period contraction in the demand for new capital.'' Thus, *''an increase in saving may cause a general depression''* (Durbin 1933, p. 92, italics in original), a result quite antithetical to Hayek's views on the causation of the cycle.[17]

Rising Inflation and the Boom

We have already noted Mises's belief that, at best, continued credit expansion on the part of the banking system could prolong the boom phase of the cycle, but could not prevent the ultimate crisis from materializing. Sustained credit expansion would, in his view, lead to ultimately unsustainable inflation, a reversal of policy, and collapse. In 1924, Mises was writing in the aftermath

---

[17] Durbin nevertheless hesitated to offer fluctuations in the saving rate as an important causative factor in the cycle. Such an explanation seemed to him to be contradicted by the fact that variations in investment expenditure led those in consumption at cyclical turning points, a fact which, incidentally, John M. Clark (1917) had already shown to be quite compatible with such an explanation, once the accelerator mechanism was understood: it was the desired services of capital equipment, and hence the capital stock, not the rate of flow of investment, that should respond to the level of output, according to that analysis. Durbin thus remained sympathetic to the main thrust of Hayek's analysis of the interaction of saving and investment in a long-run context and shared much of Hayek's policy pessimism.

Durbin, along with his fellow Oxonian Hugh Gaitskell, who largely shared his Austrian sympathies, though admirers of Hayek, were nevertheless already in the early 1930s leading figures among the younger Labour Party intellectuals associated with the Fabian Society. Durbin became a junior minister in the post–World War II Attlee government, but died by accidental drowning in 1948 at the age of 42. Gaitskell served as chancellor of the Exchequer in 1950–51 and was later to be leader of the Labour Party. He, too, died relatively young, in 1963, without achieving the prime-ministership.

of the great central European hyperinflations, and as a description of what were then recent events, it is difficult to quarrel with his analysis.[18] But the proposition that not just continuous inflation, but continuously increasing inflation, was the inevitable consequence of attempting to stave off crisis by monetary means became a central feature of Austrian cycle theory, allegedly logically implied by its basic postulates. When, in 1934, Lionel Robbins wrote the following passage, it was meant to characterize booms and crises in general, not merely one particular historical instance thereof:

> Once costs have begun to rise it would require a continuous increase in the rate of increase of credit to prevent the thing coming to disaster. But that itself, as we have seen in the great post-war inflations, would eventually generate panic. Sooner or later the initial errors are discovered. And then starts a reverse rush for liquidity. The Stock Exchange collapses. There is a stoppage of new issues. Production in the industries producing capital-goods slows down. The boom is at an end. (Robbins 1934, pp. 41–42)

Hayek's Accelerationism

Hayek's treatment of that matter was more extensive than the brief arguments by assertion that we find in the writings of Mises and Robbins, but nevertheless his logic was not entirely convincing. In *Monetary Theory and the Trade Cycle* he reasoned as follows:

> If the new processes of production are to be completed, and if those already in existence are to continue in employment, it is essential that additional credits should be continually injected at a rate which increases fast enough to keep ahead, by a constant proportion, of the expanding purchasing power of the consumer. (Hayek 1929, tr. 1933, p. 223)

The logic there was correct as far as it went; but it seemed to imply that a constant *proportional rate* of credit expansion would enable the new higher *relative* price of capital goods to be perpetuated. It did not imply that the proportional rate of credit expansion must *rise*, and the inflation rate *increase*, to stave off the crisis. And, indeed, in the particular passage from which we have quoted here, Hayek went on to argue that "a moment must inevitably arrive when the banks are unable any longer to keep up the *rate of inflation* [N.B.: not the *rate of increase in the rate of inflation*] required . . ." (Hayek 1929, tr. 1933, p. 223, italics added).

It is worth recalling at this point that Hayek's own analysis of forced

---

[18] Mises made important contributions to contemporary debates about the hyperinflations. Here he was an exponent of an explanation based on the quantity theory, supplemented by a subtle analysis of the effects of inflation expectations on price-setting behaviour and on the velocity of circulation. Some of that analysis found its way into the second (1924) edition of his *Theory of Money and Credit*. On this matter, see Laidler and Stadler (1998).

saving had led him to conclude that it would be a feature of any economy in which the rate of bank credit creation was positive. In a growing economy, he had argued, monetary neutrality therefore required not a stable price level, but a falling price level. That observation was not merely a theoretical curiosity: in the 1920s the United States experienced rapid real growth, rapid credit expansion, but essentially stable prices. Those facts had led Hayek and his colleagues, before the events of 1929–33, to warn of the likelihood of a severe crisis in that economy, a prediction to which both Gottfried von Haberler (1932) and Lionel Robbins (1931) would later draw attention when arguing in support of Austrian theory. But if the logic of Austrian theory implied that forced saving could be compatible with stable prices, or even prices that did not fall rapidly enough, it is difficult to see how it could also predict that such a state of affairs would inevitably degenerate into rising inflation if attempts were made to sustain the forced saving in question.[19] Even so, despite these logical problems with his case, it would be a travesty to suggest that Hayek did not, after all, believe that once a process of forced saving got under way, an inevitable crisis could be delayed only at the price of *rising* inflation. He clearly did, and he paid considerable attention to the issue in the first edition of *Prices and Production* (1931a).[20]

Contemporary Doubts

The weakness of Hayek's logic on this point, however, did not go unnoticed among his contemporaries. For example, in his review of that first edition, Piero Sraffa suggested that just as capital accumulation induced by voluntary saving was sustainable indefinitely, ''equally stable would be that position if brought about by inflation; and Dr. Hayek fails to prove the contrary'' (Sraffa 1932, p. 47). He also noted that credit creation would not necessarily distort relative prices if the banks made loans to consumers in the same proportion that consumption would bear to output were there no credit creation. In their

---

[19] This point was emphasized by Gottfried von Haberler in his discussion of Austrian theory in *Prosperity and Depression* (1937, pp. 51–53). Haberler had earlier been a rather uncritical exponent of Hayek's analysis (e.g., Haberler 1932).

[20] For that reason, Hayek acquired a reputation in the 1970s as someone who had anticipated the accelerationist doctrines of Milton Friedman (1968). As should be apparent from the following discussion in the text, however, the connection between Hayek's analysis and that of Friedman is extremely tenuous, for the simple reason that Hayek made no reference to the influence of inflation expectations on the formation of money wages and prices, a matter which is quite central to Friedman's analysis. It is interesting to note that Erik Lindahl (1930) did introduce endogenous inflation expectations into an analysis of a very Hayekian process of forced saving and did conclude that continuously rising inflation was a possible outcome. See Chapter 3, ''Substantive Analysis.''

"Annual Survey of Business Cycle Theory: Investment and Saving in Business Cycle Theory," published in the first (April 1933) issue of *Econometrica*, Alvin Hansen and Herbert Tout also argued that Hayek's own logic seemed to imply that forced saving could be prolonged indefinitely by maintaining a constant proportional rate of credit creation; and they went on to argue that "the persistent steady pressure of forced saving would be beneficial to society. What is disturbing is *fluctuations* in the quantity of bank credit, causing now a large volume of forced savings, and now a complete cessation thereof" (Hansen and Tout 1933, p. 140).

Hansen and Tout's criticism provoked Hayek's most sustained defence of his position on this matter. "Capital and Industrial Fluctuations – A Reply to Criticism" was first published in the April 1934 issue of *Econometrica*, and subsequently it was appended to the text of the second edition of *Prices and Production* (Hayek 1931a, 2nd ed. 1935). There Hayek was clearer than he had earlier been that he was concerned with *continuously increasing* inflation, as opposed to *constant but sustained* inflation:

> It is only a question of time when this general and progressive rise of prices becomes very rapid. My argument is not that such a development is *inevitable* once a policy of credit expansion is embarked upon, but that it *has to be* carried to that point if a certain result – a constant rate of forced saving, or maintenance without the help of voluntary saving of capital accumulated by forced saving – is to be achieved. (Hayek 1931a, 2nd ed. 1935, p. 151, italics in original)

But beliefs are one thing, and the ability to derive them by logical argument is another, and as the following passage shows, Hayek was no more able to do that in 1934 than he had been five years earlier:

> A constant rate of forced saving . . . requires a rate of credit expansion which will enable the producers of intermediate products, during each successive unit of time, to compete successfully with the producers of consumers' goods for constant additional quantities of the original factors of production. But as the competing demand from the producers of consumers' goods rises (in terms of money) in consequence of, and in proportion to, the preceding increase of expenditure on the factors of production (income), an increase of credit which is to enable the producers of intermediate products to attract additional original factors, will have to be, not only absolutely but even relatively, greater than the last increase which is now reflected in the increased demand for consumers' goods. Even in order to attract only as great a proportion of the original factors, i.e., in order merely to maintain the already existing capital, every new increase would have to be proportional to the last increase, i.e., credit would have to expand progressively at a constant *rate*. But in order to bring about constant additions to capital, it would have to do more: it would have to increase at a *constantly increasing rate*. (Hayek 1931a, 2nd ed. 1935, pp. 149–150, italics in original)

That argument is logically correct. If the period of production is to be progressively lengthened, then inflation must indeed increase, but the foregoing discussion also concedes, as had that in *Monetary Theory and the Trade Cycle*, that a constant proportional rate of credit expansion would suffice to sustain and render viable a once-and-for-all step change in the time structure of production. But that was, of course, precisely Hansen and Tout's point, and Sraffa's too. It is difficult to avoid the conclusion that when dealing with these matters, Hayek was not always clear about the distinctions, first, between a constant arithmetic rate of change of money and prices and a constant proportional rate of change, and second, between rates of change and rates of acceleration, both arithmetic and proportional, of the relevant variables. And it is equally difficult to avoid the suspicion that his confusion here led him to assert a result that the logic of his own model would not support.[21]

Policy Pessimism

That weakness in Austrian business-cycle theory was anything but a minor matter, for its exponents took a strong policy stance on the basis of what they believed to be their model's logic, and in the early 1930s in particular, when the Great Depression had become a world-wide problem, that stance mattered.[22]

---

[21] Austrian cycle theory was, of course, far from being the only approach to that topic in the German-language literature of the time which emphasized the scope for bank credit creation to influence the rate of capital accumulation. Thus Joseph Schumpeter (1912) and L. Albert Hahn (1924a) both propounded versions of a theory in which bank credit creation could support investment in fixed capital equipment which might embody new technology. Though both of them recognized that such a process could proceed at an unsustainable rapid pace, thus producing a cyclical downturn, they saw nothing inevitable about that, particularly Hahn, who in his earlier expositions of the matter had been extremely, perhaps even naively, optimistic about the capacity of the banking system to sustain expansion. See Ellis (1934, ch. 18) for an account of that approach, which bore a strong resemblance to that of Dennis Robertson (1926) described in Chapter 4. The point here is that it was precisely their predictions about the logical inevitability of either rising inflation or economic crisis that distinguished the Austrians' analysis from that of their contemporaries, so the claims by such as Sraffa and Hansen and Tout that they had exposed an analytic weakness in those predictions were extremely important.

[22] In particular, Robbins's adherence to Austrian theory made him an opponent of public-works expenditures, a position whose adoption he later characterized as "the greatest mistake of my professional career" (1971, p. 154). Howson and Winch (1977, pp. 57–63) and Moggridge (1992, pp. 496–506) have discussed, among other issues, Robbins's policy disagreements with Keynes while he was a member of the committee of economists associated with the Economic Advisory Council set up by the British government in 1930. It should be noted that Robbins's devotion to free trade, at a time when Keynes was advocating protectionist policies, was perhaps a greater source of friction between them than was Robbins's opposition to expansionary domestic policies (Robbins 1971, pp. 151ff.).

The Dangers of Expansionary Policy

Specifically, the Austrians claimed that their model implied that any attempt to counter depression by way of expansionary monetary policy, far from ameliorating the situation, would make matters worse. As Hayek put it in his review of Keynes's *Treatise on Money* (1930a), in which Keynes had strongly advocated "cheap money" (i.e., a deliberate policy of driving down market rates of interest) as a cure for depression, "any attempt to combat the crisis by credit expansion will . . . not only be merely the treatment of symptoms as causes, but may also prolong the depression by delaying the inevitable real adjustments" (Hayek 1932a, p. 44).

And it was not only monetary policy which was bound to fail in Austrian eyes. If the key feature of economic crisis was an excess of capital and a dearth of consumer goods, then public-works policies would only make those symptoms worse, as indeed would any measures designed to stimulate consumer expenditure: ". . . the granting of credit to consumers, which has recently been so strongly advocated as a cure for depression, would in fact have quite the contrary effect" (Hayek, 1931a, pp. 85–86).

Once a depression had started, that is to say, Austrian analysis led to a degree of policy pessimism verging on nihilism. The only cure

> is the most speedy and complete adaptation possible of the structure of production to the proportion between the demand for consumers' goods and the demand for producers' goods as determined by voluntary saving and spending. . . . The only way permanently to "mobilise" all available resources is, therefore, not to use artificial stimulants – whether during a crisis or thereafter – but to leave it to time to effect a permanent cure by the slow process of adapting the structure of production to the means available for capital purposes. (Hayek 1931a, pp. 86–87)

The Need for Neutral Money

Better by far, then, to prevent the crisis from arising in the first place, and Austrian theory was, as we have seen, clear about its fundamental cause. Only a discrepancy between the natural and market rates of interest, to use Wicksellian language, could lead to overinvestment; and though such a discrepancy could arise either from some technological or expectational shock hitting the natural rate or from a disturbance originating in the banking system, the appropriate preventive policy was the same in either case: maintain a state of neutral money by instituting a policy of zero money-income growth. In turn, but only if what we would now call the income velocity of circulation of money remained constant, that policy goal required constancy of the money supply. The Austrians knew full well that velocity did in fact fluctuate, and hence they understood that maintenance of perpetual monetary neutrality was hardly practicable.[23] Furthermore,

> it could be attempted only by a central monetary authority for the whole world: action on the part of a single country would be doomed to disaster. It is probably an illusion to suppose that we shall ever be able entirely to eliminate industrial fluctuations by means of monetary policy. The most we may hope for is that the growing information of the public may make it easier for central banks both to follow a cautious policy during the upward swing of the cycle, and so to mitigate the following depression, and to resist the well meaning but dangerous proposals to fight depression by "a little inflation." (Hayek 1931a, pp. 108–109)[24]

It has been noted earlier that, his dissent from certain aspects of Hayek's cycle theory notwithstanding, Durbin (1933, 1935) shared Hayek's policy pessimism. Though he understood that the existence of unemployed resources meant that "a little inflation" could hasten the recovery of an already depressed economy, he nevertheless believed that such a cure could only be temporary, and that another downturn was bound to occur in due course. Only a painful long-run readjustment of the capital intensity of production would produce a permanent cure: "We must choose between the relief of inflationary policies and temporary prosperity or settle down to a cure which is slow, which is devoid of spectacular success, and which in the first instance is as painful as the disease" (Durbin 1933, p. 177).

In the early 1930s, policy pessimism of that type was by no means confined to adherents of Austrian theory. Thus, in 1933, Sir Theodore Gregory, a colleague of Hayek and Robbins at the London School of Economics, argued that to deny "that the universal abandonment of the gold standard and the inauguration of a régime of competitive exchange reductions, accompanied by public works expenditure, are the best means of overcoming the difficul-

---

[23] Hayek discussed the behaviour of velocity in terms of a very clumsy and mechanical analysis of the transactions process, worrying, for example, about the effects that vertical integration in an industry would have on that parameter. See, e.g., Hayek (1931a, 2nd ed. 1935, pp. 118ff.). It should be noted that the main purpose of Durbin's *The Problem of Credit Policy* (1935) was to analyse the problems involved in stabilizing money income in the face of variable velocity, taking account of what later came to be called the liquidity-preference theory, as developed by Robertson (1926), Keynes (1930a), and Hicks (1935), among others. Hence Durbin's treatment of those issues was a good deal more sophisticated than Hayek's.

[24] It is worth noting that the word "inflation" in this quotation probably should be read as referring to expansion of the money supply, or of the rate of flow of nominal expenditure, rather than to an increase in the price level. That is certainly how Hayek's colleague Durbin used the word at that time: "By 'inflation' I shall mean . . . any increase in the quantity of effective money" (Durbin 1933, p. 73, fn. 1.). The passage just quoted from Hayek thus refers to the dangers of attempting to mitigate unemployment by expansionary monetary policy, rather than directly to those involved in attempting to exploit an inflation – unemployment trade-off, and therefore is not quite as modern as it looks.

ties of the moment'' (Gregory 1933, p. xii) was not ''tantamount to adhering to one type of monetary theory, viz. that propounded ... by the Viennese School.'' He noted his disagreement with some of their basic tenets, but nevertheless suggested that ''they are right in thinking that in the course of the upward movement of the trade cycle profound modifications in the structure of production take place and that monetary policy or theory cannot be negligent of this aspect in putting forward remedial measures'' (Gregory 1933, p. xiii). Furthermore, as we shall see in Chapter 9, such anti-activist views were quite widely held in the United States; and we shall see in Chapter 7 that some British economists of the period thought that the cause of unemployment lay in a chronic maladjustment of the real wage and that it was not susceptible to measures not directed at that variable.

Nevertheless, though there were many more policy pessimists than there were Austrian cycle theorists, the analysis of the latter was of particular importance in the early 1930s. It was that body of thought, above all, that seemed to provide a theoretical basis for the pessimism in question, and for a while that theoretical basis was the most coherent to be found in the academic literature. It was only with the arrival of the IS-LM model in 1936–37 that such ceased to be the case.

Austrian Analysis and IS-LM

A comparison of Austrian cycle theory with the IS-LM model which would in due course come to dominate macroeconomics yields a catalogue of opposites. Where the IS-LM model is static, the passage of time is a central feature of Austrian theory; where the IS-LM model focuses on an *inadequate level of aggregate demand* as the cause of depression, Austrian theory focuses on an *inappropriate composition of the supply of output*; where the IS-LM model suggests that both monetary policy, involving shifts of LM, and fiscal policy, involving shifts of IS, can be used to alleviate unemployment, Austrian theory suggests that the use of either will only make matters worse; and where IS-LM implies that with no policy changes the economy is likely to remain in depression, Austrian theory would have it that such inaction provides the best assurance of eventual recovery. It would be difficult, in the whole history of economic thought, to find coexisting two bodies of doctrine which so grossly contradict one another.

Though there was no overt debate immediately after 1936 between ''Mr. Keynes and the Austrians,'' in the sense of an explicit exchange on the relative merits of these two systems, there surely was a silent debate in the minds of many economists as they decided which body of doctrine to adopt. And here there is some anecdotal evidence that the policy pessimism that flowed from the Austrian framework was one factor leading to its demise.[25] It is nevertheless well known, and will be amply confirmed in the following chapters, that there was nothing new in the relatively optimistic policy prescriptions which were so easily expressed in IS-LM terms. Cheap money and/ or plentiful money, not to mention public-works expenditures, had been widely advocated as cures for depression long before 1936.

The Austrian theory to which this chapter has been devoted was in fact a novel and potentially revolutionary doctrine whose policy implications challenged what had, by the 1920s, become conventional wisdom, but because that challenge was based on what seemed to be a coherent body of theory, it attracted much attention and not a little support, its policy implications notwithstanding. It was also the Austrians who helped bring the analysis of Wicksell to the attention of British readers, and in that respect their efforts should be seen as part of a broader process whereby continental European economic ideas, centering on general-equilibrium analysis, challenged the dominant Marshallian orthodoxy in British economics. Even so, the Austrian path was not the only one that followed on from Wicksell. In Chapter 3 it will be shown that the Stockholm School, as they came to be called, had set out from essentially the same theoretical starting point as had the Austrians, but they moved in a very different direction, producing analysis that emphasized the level of aggregate demand, rather than the structure of aggregate supply, as the crucial factor in economic fluctuations, and whose policy implications were much more optimistic into the bargain. In those respects, their work represented a variation on the Wicksellian theme which was much more in harmony with the mind-set out of which IS-LM was eventually to grow.

----

[25] On this matter, see Friedman (1974, pp. 162–163), who suggested that his own relative imperviousness to Keynesian ideas, when compared with Abba Lerner's eager embrace of them, can perhaps be explained by the fact that the monetary economics to which he was exposed at the University of Chicago in the early 1930s was imbued with none of the policy pessimism which Lerner encountered at the Austrian-dominated London School of Economics. Friedman's characterization of Austrian analysis as a variant on the quantity theory of money in this context is, of course, inaccurate, but that does not affect the substance of his argument.

CHAPTER 3

The Macrodynamics of the Stockholm School

Methodological Preconceptions

Austrian cycle theory was based upon a model of the economy, well specified by contemporary standards, from which specific predictions and policy implications clearly flowed. Those Swedish economists, later known as the Stockholm School, whose basic contributions were systematically introduced to English-speaking readers by Brinley Thomas (1936), built upon Wicksell's insights, as had the Austrians, but they produced an altogether more diverse body of doctrine.[1] The individual contributions of the leading members of that group, namely, Erik Lindahl, Erik Lundberg, Gunnar Myrdal, and Bertil Ohlin, can be differentiated from one another rather clearly, and one cannot sum up their substantive content in a single, clear "central message" in whose development and articulation the various members of the Stockholm School were self-consciously attempting to collaborate.

If the Stockholm School did not produce a coherent and unique theoretical message, and I do not mean this remark to disparage their efforts in any way, it nevertheless added ideas of lasting importance to the analytic method of macroeconomics, and in particular dynamic macroeconomics, as Björn Hansson (1982) has demonstrated beyond any reasonable doubt. These economists did not treat macroeconomic theory as in and of itself a body of substantive hypotheses about how the economy functions, but rather as an "engine of analysis," to use Alfred Marshall's famous phrase, indispensable to the formulation of such hypotheses. As a result of their efforts, it became a much more powerful engine for their formulation. Gunnar Myrdal's dictum that "the first requirement for receiving sensible answers is to have raised sensible questions" (Myrdal 1931 tr. 1939, p. 209) sums up perfectly the attitude of the Stockholm School towards the role of deductive theory.

---

[1] The label Stockholm School was not attached to that group until 1937, when one of their number, Bertil Ohlin, drew attention to the close relationship between some of their contributions and some of the central ideas of Keynes's *General Theory* (Ohlin 1937). Brinley Thomas spent a year in Stockholm in 1934–35, and as Shehadi (1991) has recounted, the lectures he gave at the London School of Economics upon his return, which formed the basis of *Monetary Policy and Crises* (Thomas 1936), helped to undermine the dominance of Austrian ideas there and to prepare the way for the acceptance of Keynes's *General Theory* among the younger economists at the London School.

Dynamic Method

The Stockholm School's essentially Marshallian attitude to economics ensured that their analytic contributions would be open-ended. Rather than one core theoretical structure, as in the Austrian mould, we find in their work a series of what they sometimes called *model sequences*, dynamic models in modern parlance, often with important differences among their characteristics, and each one potentially of empirical relevance under the appropriate circumstances. In Erik Lundberg's words,

> . . . we may introduce time elements in order to carry . . . static theory further. In reality, of course, there are an infinite number of time-lags that could be considered. . . . If it does not seem satisfactory to qualify the results of static analysis by general statements about the time-consuming nature of the tendencies found, an infinite number of possibilities opens up for dynamizing the static relations. . . . Theories of the business cycle tend . . . to follow as many lines of explanation as there are possibilities of disrupting static relations. (Lundberg 1937, p. 51)

That theoretical eclecticism led naturally to policy eclecticism. One can find model sequences in Swedish work which seem to imply that Austrian-style inaction on all fronts might be the best option available in the circumstances, but there is never any suggestion that the circumstances in question could characterize anything other than a special case. In the vast majority of cases they analysed, policy activism, specific to the individual case in question, did seem to be called for. Thus the Stockholm School's contributions to the development of analytic methods also provided a logical foundation for the pragmatic eclecticism which marked the macroeconomic aspects of what Erik Lundberg (1985) was later to call *the Swedish model* of an essentially social-democratic policy regime.[2]

The contrast between the macroeconomics of the Austrians and that of the Stockholm School is stark. Only two features are common to the two, namely, the dynamic nature of the analysis (in strong contrast to the comparative statics of IS-LM) and an explicitly Wicksellian pedigree. It might seem, at first sight, utterly astonishing that two bodies of economic analysis, developed at the same time, and in response to the same theoretical puzzles bequeathed by a single person, could move apart so rapidly; but only at first sight, as we shall now see.

---

[2] Erik Lundberg's posthumously published 1981 Mattioli Lectures (Lundberg 1996) offer an insider's account of the development of Swedish economics both before and after World War II and, like his 1985 account of those matters, emphasize that there was a good deal more to the Swedish model than macroeconomics.

The Stockholm School on the Natural Rate of Interest

Wicksell's difficulty in providing a coherent and consistent definition of the natural rate of interest has been noted earlier, as has the fact that the Austrians' "solution" to that problem had involved them in a more thoroughgoing application of the capital theory of Böhm-Bawerk than Wicksell himself had usually been willing to pursue. Only once, in 1907, did Wicksell characterize the natural rate of interest as being the marginal productivity of capital:

> ... the interest on money is regulated in the long run by the profit on capital, which in its turn is determined by the productivity and relative abundance of real capital, or in the terms of modern political economy, by its *marginal productivity*. (Wicksell 1907a, p. 214, italics in original)

Elsewhere, as has also been noted, he had side-stepped the problems involved here, whereas the Austrians simply ignored them, at least until the end of the 1930s. In contrast, the Stockholm School had fully grasped those problems by the end of the 1920s and had tried thereafter to work out their implications for Wicksell's analysis. Specifically, they understood that the idea of an aggregate stock of capital with a well-defined marginal product that existed independently of the value of the market rate of interest was, except under very special circumstances, theoretically indefensible. Hence they rejected just that aspect of Wicksell's analysis that lay at the very foundation of Austrian cycle theory.

Cassel and Irving Fisher on Austrian Capital Theory

Wicksell's intellectual stature notwithstanding, he was something of an outsider to Swedish academic economics during his working life. The central figure among his Swedish contemporaries was Gustav Cassel, who subjected Böhm-Bawerk's capital theory to lengthy criticism in his monograph *The Nature and Necessity of Interest* (1903, esp. pp. 55–67). In the course of that criticism, Cassel made the point that " 'the period of production' might perhaps be made a fruitful conception if there was only *one* period of production in all different branches of industry. But we know that this is not the case, not even approximately" (Cassel 1903, p. 65, italics in original). Cassel took up questions of capital theory again in his textbook *The Theory of Social Economy* (1918, tr. 1923), where, though he recognized that "the equation between capital value, interest, and rent provides the required connection between the price of the object and the price of its use," he was also at pains to argue that, in general, "none of the three quantities – capital value, interest, and rent – is independent, and none determined by the others. They are all three equally unknown quantities of the pricing process, and are only determined by it, and all together" (Cassel 1918, tr. 1923, vol. I, p. 208). Thus, though Cassel accepted the essentially Wicksellian conclusion (without citing Wicksell) that "*the true rate of interest, for any form of loan, is that which is necessary in order to prevent variations in the general price level*" (Cassel 1903, p. 168, italics in original), he clearly rejected the idea that such a "true rate" could be derived solely from an analysis of the economy's time structure of production.[3]

Now, difficulties with the notion of an aggregate capital stock have most recently attracted attention during the so-called Cambridge controversies of the 1960s, but they were known (albeit carefully evaded in his monetary writings) to Wicksell and, as we have now seen, they were touched upon by Cassel as early as 1903. Their most thorough treatment in the literature of the time, however, was that by Irving Fisher in his *Rate of Interest* (1907), later much revised under the title *The Theory of Interest* (1930a), and that work, too, was known to the Stockholm School.[4] Thus Lindahl explicitly cited Fisher's *Rate of Interest* (e.g., Lindahl 1929b, tr. 1939) in a manner that suggested thorough familiarity with its contents, and Myrdal, though not at the point in question citing any particular work, referred to Fisher by name in a context which makes it quite clear that he had in mind either the 1907 or the 1930 book, or both (Myrdal 1931, tr. 1939, p. 49). Lundberg (1930, tr. 1995) also showed some familiarity with Fisher's work on capital theory. In any event, as we shall see in due course, the line of analysis which the Stockholm School followed in dealing with the difficulties addressed by Cassel's and Fisher's critiques of Böhm-Bawerk was also completely Fisherine.

Fisher's critique of Böhm-Bawerk, which was more sympathetic than Cassel's, was also a good deal clearer, analytically speaking. In his view, "a serious defect in Böhm-Bawerk's concept of an average production period is that it lacks sufficient definiteness to form a basis for the reasoning he attempts to base upon it" (Fisher 1907, p. 56). Even in the case of a single good produced over time with a single input there were problems in deciding which average would produce the "right" measure of the period of produc-

---

[3] I am indebted to Michael Trautwein for helpful discussions of Cassel's role in offsetting the influence of Böhm-Bawerk's capital theory on the younger Swedish economists.

[4] In his essay "The Wicksell Connection" (1981), Axel Leijonhufvud attributed no influence to Irving Fisher on the European economists who built up a macroeconomics on Wicksellian foundations in the inter-war years. If we consider Fisher only as an exponent of the quantity theory of money, as set out in *The Purchasing Power of Money* (Fisher 1911), which is what Leijonhufvud seems to have had in mind, then his judgement seems to me to have been correct, at least as far as the Stockholm School was concerned. But Fisher's influence in the area of capital theory (Fisher 1907, 1930a) is a different matter, as I here argue.

tion. Different averages, geometric, harmonic, arithmetic, would yield different results, and as Fisher noted, Böhm-Bawerk had offered no justification for assuming that a weighted arithmetic mean, with the weights being the quantities of input applied for each relevant length of time, would provide the appropriate measure. But, Fisher went on,

> suppose the question of the correct formulation of the average production period for an individual article to have been satisfactorily settled, in what manner is it proposed to combine the production periods of different articles? Here are involved, considerably magnified, all the well-known difficulties of constructing a serious index-number. Supposing the average production period of cloth is 2 years and iron 5 years, how are we to obtain the average production period for cloth and iron? . . . are we to weight these two commodities according to the value of the amounts annually consumed? If so, will not the rate of interest be involved in the value of the cloth and the iron? (Fisher 1907, p. 57)

Fisher had, moreover, already pointed out to his readers that the physical productivity of capital assets was measured in units whose diversity prevented them from yielding any measure of the marginal product of capital per unit of capital with the unit-free dimensionality of an interest rate.

> It is evident that if an orchard of ten acres yields 100 barrels of apples a year, the physical-productivity, ten barrels per acre, does not of itself give any clew [*sic*] to what rate of return on its *value* the orchard yields . . .
>
> It seems at first sight very easy to pass from quantities to values, – to translate the ten acres of orchard and the 100 barrels of apples into dollars. But this apparently simple step begs the whole question. The important fact, and the one lost sight of in the productivity theory [of interest], is that the value of the orchard depends upon the value of its crops; and in this dependence lurks implicitly the rate of interest itself. The statement that "capital produces income" is true only in the physical sense. . . . That is to say, *capital-value does not produce income-value.* On the contrary, income-value produces capital-value. (Fisher 1907, p. 13, italics in original)

Those arguments by Fisher were, of course, incontrovertible, and, more to the point here, they were utterly devastating to any notion of a Wicksellian "natural" rate of interest derived solely from the characteristics of the economy's production side.[5] They did not contradict Cassel's conclusions about this matter, but they added considerable sharpness to them.

---

[5] The problems revealed by Fisher's analysis were exactly those which would later surface in the co-called Cambridge controversies about capital theory, as discussed by Geoffrey Harcourt (1972) and Rogers (1989), among others. Fisher is usually given insufficient credit in this later literature for his contributions to capital theory, though see Velupillai (1975) for an important exception to this neglect.

An Alternative Conception of the Natural Rate

The Stockholm School, not least Lindahl, understood the relevant implications quite clearly, putting the matter as follows:

> Only under very special assumptions is it possible to conceive of a natural or real rate of interest determined purely by technical considerations, and thus independent of the price system. For this to be true it must be supposed that the productive process consists only in investing units of goods or services of the same type as the final product. (Lindahl 1930, tr. 1939, p. 247)

And only a year later, Myrdal remarked that

> The idea of physical productivity presupposes . . . that there is only a single factor of production, besides waiting, and only a single product and that, moreover, both are of the same physical quality. (Myrdal 1931, tr. 1939, p. 50)

The upshot of that, in Lindahl's words, was that

> under more realistic assumptions it is not possible to measure the investment and the product in the same real unit. To compare services invested and the resulting products, they must be expressed in a common unit which presupposes that the price relation is given. Then the real rate of interest does not depend only on technical conditions, but also on the price situation, and cannot be regarded as existing independently of the loan rate of interest. (Lindahl 1930, tr. 1939, p. 248)

Thus the concept of the natural rate of interest which underlay Wicksell's notion of monetary equilibrium had to be reformulated so as to avoid that difficulty, and for the Stockholm School, the way forward began with another of Fisher's insights, namely, that as far as existing real capital was concerned, "capital value . . . is . . . only a price reflection of the two magnitudes: Net return and 'market rate of interest' " (Myrdal 1931, tr. 1939, p. 62). It was a short step from there to noting that for a stationary economy, "the condition for monetary equilibrium could be formulated as the condition of *equality between the capital value and the cost of reproduction of existing real capital*" (Myrdal 1931, tr. 1939, p. 70, italics in original). Generalizing that conclusion to a growing economy in which there had to be net investment, Myrdal concluded that a margin over and above the natural rate of interest thus defined would be required:

> The profit margin which corresponds to monetary equilibrium is, therefore, the *complex of profit margins in different firms which stimulates just the amount of total investment which can be taken care of by the available capital disposal* [i.e., saving]. (Myrdal 1931, tr. 1939, pp. 82–83, italics in original)

In short, the Stockholm School addressed exactly the same Wicksellian muddle as did the Austrians, namely, that

> the "normal rate of interest" must now, according to Wicksell, (1) equal the marginal technical productivity of real capital (i.e. the 'real' or 'natural' rate of interest); (2) equate the supply of and the demand for savings; and, finally, (3) guarantee a stable price level, primarily of consumption goods.
>
> Wicksell assumes that these three criteria . . . are equivalent . . . but he cannot prove it. (Myrdal 1931, tr. 1939, pp. 37–38)

But they resolved that muddle in a very different way. Rather than making the foregoing condition (1) the basis for further analysis, they discarded altogether the idea of a well-defined marginal product of capital per unit of capital for the aggregate economy, settling instead on condition (2). At the same time, as we shall now see, they also discarded condition (3), that monetary equilibrium defined in that way implied anything at all for the behaviour of the price level. They did so, as I shall now show, because their essentially Fisherine approach to capital theory forced them to pay close attention to the role played by expectations in the inter-temporal allocative process.

The Role of Expectations

To argue that the nominal value of the capital stock is the result of discounting a future stream of nominal income by the nominal rate of interest, or rather by the term structure of nominal interest rates, makes it impossible to avoid questions about how the expectations of agents about future income are formed, and about how those expectations impinge upon the determination of current prices and of interest rates. There did, of course, exist a Fisherine solution to certain aspects of that Fisherian problem, in the shape of his well-known analysis of the influence of expected inflation on nominal interest rates: the "Fisher effect," so called, which Fisher (1896) had in fact developed from certain insights of Alfred Marshall (1887, 1890). It had been known to Wicksell, who had not, however, fully integrated it into his cumulative process analysis, and Hayek had rejected its relevance for trade-cycle theory entirely.[6] Not so the Stockholm School, however: Lindahl in particular paid close attention to its implications and developed it in conjunction with something rather akin to an early, albeit incomplete, version of the rational-expectations idea.

Like Wicksell, Lindahl thought that a satisfactory theory of the price level had to do more than explain that variable's behaviour under a gold standard. The case of a "pure credit economy" in which "the credit system is . . . so

---

[6] On this point, see footnote 14 in Chapter 2.

developed that there are *no cash* [i.e., currency] *holdings*'' (Lindahl 1930, tr. 1939, pp. 139–140, italics in original) therefore attracted much of his attention, and, as we have already seen in discussing the work of Mises (1924) in Chapter 2, such a system was, in the post–World War I years, a good deal more than a theoretical curiosity. In common with Wicksell (and with many others), Lindahl habitually identified money with currency and thought of the quantity theory of money as being relevant only to an economy in which currency circulated.[7] Thus he argued that

> the [quantity] theory fails entirely under the simplified assumptions . . . which imply *inter alia* that there are no cash holdings in the community. A theory of the value of money which has any claim to generality should be in a position to explain changes in price levels in a community of this kind also. The problem must therefore be attacked from some other starting-point. (Lindahl 1930, tr. 1939, p. 141)

Inter-temporal Allocation and Perfect Foresight

The starting point in question was the same as that for Hayek (1928) (whom Lindahl explicitly cited), namely, the "general theory of price . . . extended to include . . . the treatment not only of the relative prices in each period, but also of the price relations *between* the different periods included in the dynamic process" (Lindahl 1930, tr. 1939, pp. 141–142, italics in original). As did Hayek, so, too, did Lindahl understand that the interaction of saving and investment lay at the very heart of the determination of inter-temporal relative prices. Instead of a version of the quantity equation, he based his analysis on what amounted to a consumption function formulated in nominal terms. Specifically, with E being nominal income, s the fraction of income saved, P the price level of consumption goods, and Q their quantity, he wrote (1930, tr. 1939, p. 142)

$$E(1 - s) = PQ \qquad (3.1)$$

and went on to argue that

> starting from our basic equation we may lay down that . . . a change in the price level for consumed goods (and services) presupposes that the nominal income allotted to consumption has been altered relatively to the quantity of consumption goods. (1930, tr. 1939, p. 146)

But that allotment, being the outcome of a savings decision, was inherently forward-looking. Therefore, "individual anticipations of coming price developments are to a certain extent the causes of actual developments themselves.

---

[7] See Fregert (1993) for an interesting commentary on Erik Lindahl's work on monetary policy, stressing its reliance on Wicksell's model of a "pure credit economy."

The other factors in the equation adjust themselves to this anticipated development of the price level'' (Lindahl 1930, tr. 1939, p. 147).

Here Lindahl was taking up a central theme of Myrdal's doctoral dissertation (1927), where it had been argued, in the words of Lindahl's brief review of the work,[8]

> that changes have effects on the system of prices . . . before the changes have happened, and this result is produced through anticipation of what will happen. Thus, in every moment the pricing is a *functionally indeterminate* system, where among the primarily determining factors are also the anticipations of future changes and the valuations of the risk element in these anticipations. (Lindahl 1929a, p. 89, italics in original)

Indeed, as Lindahl (1930, tr. 1939, pp. 147ff.) was showing, in the limiting case of perfect foresight, which he had developed at greater length in his essay ''The Place of Capital in the Theory of Price'' (1929b, tr. 1939), any time path for the price level was compatible with the maintenance of equality between saving and investment. That was so because ''a shift in the price level that is foreseen by everybody early enough can be taken into account in all contracts for the future'' (Lindahl 1930, tr. 1939, p. 148), and ''the rate of interest must adjust itself to this anticipated price development, if the system is not to break down'' (Lindahl 1930, tr. 1939, p. 149).

On that point, Lindahl, and indeed, following him, the whole of the Stockholm School, differed radically from Hayek. Where Hayek had argued that ''monetary neutrality'' required a constant rate of flow of money expenditure and hence, depending upon the presence or absence of real growth, a falling or a constant price level, Lindahl's Fisherine emphasis on forward-looking expectations led him directly to the conclusion that monetary equilibrium was potentially compatible with any conceivable price-level behaviour.[9] In Myrdal's words, which echo Lindahl on this matter, ''the development of the price level would seem to have nothing to do with monetary equilibrium'' (Myrdal 1931, tr. 1939, p. 133). But that conclusion was, as Myrdal immediately noted (and as Lindahl also understood), too sweeping. It held only in conditions of perfect-foresight equilibrium. However, as Lundberg (1930, tr. 1995) in particular pointed out, ''the assumption that individuals' expectations are 'rational', in the sense that they are realized, . . . identical with

---

[8] Myrdal's thesis remains untranslated. In his review, Lindahl referred to a possible influence of Keynes's *Treatise on Probability* (1921) on Myrdal, but Assar Lindbeck has suggested to me in private conversation that perhaps that was a result of Lindahl's wishing to be polite to the editor of the *Economic Journal*. Frank Knight's *Risk, Uncertainty and Profit* (1921) was, Lindbeck has further suggested, a much more important influence on Myrdal at that stage in the development of his ideas.

[9] Thus, Hayek's rejection of the relevance of the Fisher effect for business-cycle theory, as noted in Chapter 2, footnote 14, had important consequences for his views on the appropriate stance for monetary policy.

Lindahl's hypothesis that the future is wholly foreseen . . . is also identical with the static premise'' (Lundberg 1930, tr. 1995, p. 34), by which he meant that it robbed the passage of time of any essential role in economic analysis. Only if ''individuals are mistaken in their anticipations [would] the time distances . . . influence price formation'' (Lundberg 1930, tr. 1995, p. 34).

Imperfect Foresight and Dynamic Analysis

''The case of imperfect foresight,'' discussed by Lindahl (1930, tr. 1939, pp. 150ff.), in which expectational errors were of the essence, was, moreover, the empirically relevant one. In such a case ''it is no longer possible . . . to regard the actual development of the price level as determined in the last resort by the expectations of individuals concerning this development'' (Lindahl 1930, tr. 1939, p. 151). The role of ''primary changes,'' particularly, but not solely, those emanating from monetary policy, and the manner in which those interacted with expectations about the price level and with its actual behaviour required analysis; and such analysis had to be explicitly multi-period in nature. Moreover, in that empirically relevant case, Lundberg in particular was extremely doubtful about the relevance of Myrdal's notion that future prices would affect current prices, with ''the connecting link . . . composed of anticipations'' (Lundberg 1930, tr. 1995, pp. 34–35).[10] Rather, he argued that once an economic model treated the passage of time as crucial, in the sense of permitting expectational errors to occur, then ''a theory would require the price level during a period to be determined by total economic change during earlier periods . . . expectations during a given earlier period have to be based entirely and exclusively on the price constellation during this and previous periods'' (Lundberg 1930, tr. 1995, pp. 34–35).

The development of methods to cope with such analytic problems was, as noted earlier, arguably the central distinguishing feature of the Stockholm School's contribution to the macroeconomics of the inter-war years. Both the *temporary-equilibrium approach*, later popularized by Hicks in *Value and Capital* (1939) and more recently used by Robert E. Lucas (e.g., 1972) and others as the basic tool of new-classical macroeconomics, and disequilibrium

---

[10] As noted earlier, and as now will be apparent to the reader, the Stockholm School came tantalizingly close to developing the idea of what is now called ''rational expectations.'' Even though, as we have now seen, Lundberg actually used that very phrase, he related it to perfect foresight, rather than to expectations formed with reference to a correct model of the economy with which they are concerned. In the absence of that all-important latter idea, the shift in emphasis from forward-looking to backward-looking expectations in the analysis of the Stockholm School during the 1930s appears to have been progressive rather than, as we would now think, regressive.

dynamics, based on the *ex ante–ex post* distinction, which from the late 1940s onwards was to become the standard tool for textbook expositions of the multiplier process and multiplier–accelerator interaction, are of Swedish origin. The former was contributed by Lindahl (1930, tr. 1939), and the latter was developed collectively. It had roots in the work of Lundberg (1930, tr. 1995), and Myrdal (1931, tr. 1939) did much to advance it, but it did not reach full flower until the appearance of *Studies in the Theory of Economic Expansion* (Lundberg 1937).

In Lindahl's formulation of the temporary-equilibrium approach,

> we imagine [time] to be subdivided into periods . . . so short that the factors *directly* affecting prices, and therefore also the prices themselves, can be regarded as *unchanged in each period*. All such changes are therefore assumed to take place at the transition points between periods. The development of prices can then be expressed as a series of successive price situations. . . .
>
> [These are] *equilibrium* states in the sense that there will be equality between supply and demand during the period. (Lindahl 1930, tr. 1939, pp. 158–159, italics in original)

But, as he was explicitly to concede in 1939, that method was somewhat limiting. The problem was that

> during each period there is present a latent disequilibrium, and that is the reason why the equilibrium achieved during the period is found to be only temporary. The driving force in the dynamic process thus lies entirely in the sphere of expectations, and this curtails the usefulness of this method as a basis for the construction of exact model sequences. (Lindahl 1939, p. 69)

The alternative *ex ante–ex post* approach was more flexible, because it permitted inconsistencies between the expectations and plans of different agents to exist *ex ante* and to lead to explicitly disequilibrium situations at the beginning of the period that would then be resolved during it. But as Myrdal put it in a passage added to the 1939 English translation of *Monetary Equilibrium*, "the element of greater realism which the period analysis gains by introducing the time-sequences as an object for study must be paid for by certain very unrealistic approximations" (Myrdal 1931, tr. 1939, p. 43). In particular, the period of analysis itself, "the unit period . . . must . . . be chosen of different length in dealing with different problems" (Myrdal 1931, tr. 1939, p. 44), thus introducing an arbitrary element into the very heart of the method. In raising those matters, Myrdal was echoing Lundberg's conclusion that "the question of the 'right' unit-period is a *real* problem" (Lundberg 1937, p. 47, italics in original).

Nevertheless, when applied to analysis of the establishment and maintenance of equilibrium in the inter-temporal allocation of resources, the method brought an extra degree of clarity to the discussion, one whose value it would be difficult to exaggerate, as Myrdal's statement of the matter illustrates: [11]

> "In such an *ex post* calculus there is ... by necessity an exact balance between the invested waiting and the value of gross investment. Looking forward there is no such balance except under certain conditions which remain to be ascertained. In the *ex ante* calculus it is a question not of realized results but of the anticipations, calculations and plans driving the dynamic process forward. ... The real problem to be solved in monetary theory is: How does this tendency to disparity in the savings–investment equation develop into an *ex post* balance? (Myrdal 1931, tr. 1939, p. 46)

But clarity there was indeed bought at the cost of generality, and that is one reason why, when it came to substantive theoretical results, the Stockholm School generated a series of special cases, rather than any overarching generalization such as dominated the conclusions of the Austrians.

Substantive Analysis

Lindahl's 1930 essay, first of all, worked out the properties of what its second chapter called "the cumulative process caused by lowering or raising the level of interest rates." Like Wicksell before him, and like his Austrian contemporaries, he concentrated on the former inflationary case. He explicitly examined the consequences of assuming that once inflation had started, "individuals, and especially entrepreneurs, expect the rising price movement to continue" (Lindahl 1930, tr. 1939, p. 182). Wicksell had only occasionally touched upon that matter, and Hayek had ignored it, surprisingly, because it was in fact precisely that factor that made the characteristic Austrian prediction of an ever-increasing inflation rate as the alternative to economic crisis logically tenable.[12] As Lindahl argued, if inflation itself engendered expectations of further inflation, that

> will make longer investments ... appear still more profitable ... than when only the change in interest rates was taken into account. This will accelerate the transfer of factors from the consumers' goods industries, with the result that the rise in prices of consumption goods will proceed at an ever increasing pace. Since this transfer of factors to longer processes will continue, the

---

[11] As Joan Robinson (1939) noted in a review of the English translation of Myrdal's book, as a means of dealing with the fact that saving and investment decisions were taken independently of one another, the *ex ante–ex post* distinction was "clearly superior to the device evolved by Mr. Keynes for the same purpose ... the peculiar definition of savings in the *Treatise*" (Robinson 1939, p. 494). For a discussion of Keynes's treatment of these issues in the *Treatise*, see Chapter 6.

[12] Thus, if anyone should be credited with anticipating Friedman's "accelerationist hypothesis" (1968) in the inter-war years, it should be Lindahl rather than Hayek. See Chapter 2, footnote 20, for further discussion of this point.

disproportion between incomes and the supply of consumption goods will not be removed and the rise in the price level of the latter will be cumulative, until the process is brought to an end by a crisis. (Lindahl 1930, tr. 1939, p. 182)

Endogenous Responses in the Distribution and Level of Income

However, that outcome was not, in Lindahl's view, inevitable. It was but one among several that were possible. He understood well enough that given an initial situation of full employment, tendencies towards forced saving and inflation were inherent in a reduction in interest rates, but he also noted that redistribution of income away from wage-earners was possible in the wake of such a cut if money wages were slow to adjust to inflation. With complete price and money-wage flexibility, so that "there [was] no time lag in the effects and counter effects of rising capital values and prices of consumption goods, prices would soar upwards to an indefinite extent" (Lindahl 1930, tr. 1939, p. 172); but Lindahl went on to qualify that conclusion in the following terms:[13]

> Under more realistic assumptions . . . the time lag hinders the increase in capital values from causing a corresponding rise in the prices of consumption goods. On account of the stickiness of wages, workers' demand for consumption goods will increase only slowly. And entrepreneurs who experience the largest increase in incomes, may be assumed to save a large part of it for investment in openings which have now become profitable. (Lindahl 1930, tr. 1939, pp. 172–173)

In that way, resources to support a process of capital deepening might come from an increase in voluntary saving induced by "the alteration in the distribution of income due to the shift in the price level" (Lindahl 1930, tr. 1939, p. 175), and in the presence of such an equilibrating mechanism there was no need to expect any crisis to ensue.

As we saw in Chapter 2, the Austrians usually started their analysis of the cycle from a state of full employment.[14] Brinley Thomas (1936) was critical

---

[13] In modern rational-expectations models, a cut in nominal interest rates will lead to lower inflation, because only such an outcome is compatible with an equilibrium in which expectations are satisfied. As Peter Howitt (1992) has argued, however, such an equilibrium is (absent perfect foresight, and on very general assumptions about how agents learn) unstable, so that if a cut in interest rates initially creates a disequilibrium, the rational-expectations equilibrium will not be attained. Lindahl's analysis here should therefore be interpreted as dealing with the system's out-of-equilibrium dynamics.

[14] Durbin (1933) had taken Hayek to task on this same issue, as was noted in Chapter 2, "Some Weaknesses." Later in the 1930s, Hayek did, somewhat grudgingly, display a willingness to relax that assumption. He remarked that earlier expositions of his ideas had been "frequently criticised for . . . failure to take account of the existence of unused resources. It still seems to me that to start first from a position of equilibrium was logically the right procedure. . . . But . . ." (Hayek 1939, pp. 5–6).

of that aspect of their work: "... it is legitimate and necessary in dynamic theory to assume unused resources; and if Dr. Hayek had done this, he would have had to alter some of his conclusions" (Thomas 1936, p. 103). And indeed, the Swedish economists, with whose work Thomas was mainly concerned, quite frequently discussed the properties of upward cumulative processes that began with some resources idle. Lindahl, for one, did so, showing that if the nominal interest rate were to be cut, "the resulting development [would] imply both an increase in incomes, accompanied by an increase in the demand for consumers' goods, and an increase in the production of these goods" (Lindahl 1930, tr. 1939, p. 178). More significantly, a recurring theme in the writings of the Stockholm School in the early 1930s was that falling output and rising unemployment might characterize the downward cumulative processes arising from the market rate of interest being set above its natural level in an economy characterized by money-wage stickiness.

Lindahl also treated that latter case, albeit in less detail than he treated the expansionary case. He noted that with wage flexibility, the process would be essentially the same as in the expansionary case, with all relevant signs reversed, but he went on to point out that "if ... wages are assumed not to be flexible, the price fall will cause unemployment" (Lindahl 1930, tr. 1939, p. 185), and that "while lower rates cause an increase in production when unemployed resources make this possible, higher rates have the opposite effect, and the movement may continue indefinitely" (Lindahl 1930, tr. 1939, p. 186).

Bertil Ohlin (1933, tr. 1978, p. 379), in whose work analysis of output (as opposed to price-level) fluctuations in general, and contractions in particular, received a good deal more emphasis than it did in Lindahl's analysis, significantly extended that argument with the suggestion that wage stickiness would cause "resilient consumption," which in turn would put a brake on the economy's contraction.[15]

The Swedish economists did not confine their analysis to the consequences of interest-rate movements induced by the banking system. Myrdal, in particular, paid careful attention to the sequence of events that would follow an autonomous increase in the economy's saving rate, developing an argument that may fairly be characterized as a version of the "paradox of thrift":

> It is then obvious that the increased saving immediately brings about a rupture of the monetary equilibrium in the capital market; for free capital disposal has increased, but not real investment. A downward Wicksellian process has thus been started.

---

[15] Indeed, endogenous output changes were sufficiently prominent in Ohlin's discussions of these matters that Hans Brems (1978) made a powerful case that he should be considered as having anticipated Keynes's treatment of them in the *General Theory*. Patinkin (1982, pp. 53–54) has discussed Brems's interpretation of Ohlin's work and has disagreed with that claim.

> Furthermore, it is obvious that real investments not only do not increase but must even decrease. For increased savings, defined to mean decreased demand for consumption goods, necessarily bring about some decrease in the prices of consumption goods. This fall in prices must itself tend to lower capital values by influencing anticipations; with the consequence that the profit margin will move in the negative direction, which naturally means that real investments will decline. . . . A downward Wicksellian process has thus been brought about by increased savings, where, paradoxically enough, the *increase* in savings continuously results in a *decrease* of real capital formation. (Myrdal 1931, tr. 1939, pp. 106–107, italics in original)

One characteristic of the foregoing argument is worth particular attention, namely, its postulate that an increase in saving will set in motion a process in which producers' expectations of the future demand for consumption goods, and hence their demand for investment goods, will also be depressed. That stands in sharp contrast to Austrian analysis, where an increase in saving implied an increase in the future demand for consumption goods and led to a fall in the rate of interest, which induced the increase in investment needed to provide them. As we saw in Chapter 2, Evan Durbin (1933) also stressed the capacity of an increase in saving to depress investment by way of its effect on profit expectations, arguing that it was characteristic of what he termed "the English view" of the relationship between consumption and investment over the course of the cycle, and that the failure of Austrian analysis to recognize that possibility represented a serious flaw.

Equilibrating Tendencies

As in Lindahl's analysis, so the downward process envisaged by Myrdal in the passage just quoted would be ongoing, without a well-defined floor to limit income's fall. But Myrdal did qualify his analysis somewhat. To begin with, he noted that its properties rested on the assumption of what he called "a free currency," that is to say, a system in which the banking system would passively adjust the quantity of money (currency) supplied to the economy's demand for it; "under more realistic circumstances in which the currency is always restricted some way or other, increased saving forms the basis for an easing of credit and therefore might mitigate the depression" (Myrdal, 1931, tr. 1939, p. 110). He also, and critically, drew attention to the consequences that would ensue if the downward process brought about a redistribution of income

> in favour of classes which save less at the expense of those which save more . . . [L]osses need not become as big as they must otherwise be in order to bring about the bookkeeping correspondence [i.e., *ex post* equality] between capital disposal and the value of real investments which is subse-

quently necessary. This means that the intensity of the depressive process is then not as great as it would otherwise be. (Myrdal 1931, tr. 1939, p. 119)

Passages such as this one in Myrdal's work and the remarks of Ohlin (1933, tr. 1978) referred to earlier are frequently cited in support of claims that they anticipated the arguments of Keynes (1936) that a real contraction would end in the economy settling down at an equilibrium level of output below the economy's productive potential. Patinkin (1982, pp. 36–57) has considered those claims in detail, and there is therefore no need to discuss them at length here. Suffice it to note that the emphasis in Swedish analysis was on *ongoing dynamic processes of contraction* in which price movements and their consequences for agents' expectations received at least as much attention as output and employment movements, which contrasts strongly with the *comparative static analysis of sticky-price unemployment equilibria* presented by the IS-LM model sketched in Chapter 1.

It is true that Brinley Thomas at one point characterized the end point of a downward cumulative process brought about by credit contraction as follows, attributing the result to Myrdal:

> . . . a new equilibrium would be reached with the following characteristics. A more or less unchanged price level of consumption goods, a fall in capital values corresponding to the rise in the rate of interest, lower wages, and a smaller output more particularly in the investment industries, a diminished rate of saving, a shorter average period of investment, and savings equal to investment. (Thomas 1936, p. 96)

However, that passage appeared after the publication of the *General Theory*. It is also interesting to note that Lundberg's 1937 monograph, which had assimilated multiplier analysis, used it not to determine an equilibrium level of income and employment but rather to produce elaborate "model sequences" based on its dynamic interaction with an accelerator mechanism.[16] All in all, it is difficult to resist the conclusion that members of the Stockholm School were not very interested in using comparative static methods in macroeconomics. Thus, to the extent that the IS-LM model is judged to be an appropriate vehicle for conveying the ideas of the *General Theory*, Patinkin's rejection of their claims to have anticipated that book seems to be well justified.

If, on the other hand, one follows George Shackle (1967) or, more recently, Allan Meltzer (1988) in arguing that IS-LM misses the point of Keynes's work, which rather lies in its emphasis on the central role of subjective

---

[16] See Lundberg (1937, pp. 197ff.). Note that Lundberg developed those sequences numerically rather than analytically. Analytic treatment of multiplier–accelerator interaction began in earnest with Samuelson (1939a,b), who was well aware of, and acknowledged, the relationship between his work and Lundberg's.

expectations in conditioning saving and investment decisions, as well as the effect of their volatility in rendering the economy's inter-temporal allocative mechanism capriciously unreliable, then the following quotation from Myrdal surely does present a clear anticipation of that message:

> The fact that the size of our current income available for purposes of consumption or saving is ... ultimately dependent upon our own subjective calculations, relating the present to the future periods by imputation, deserves increased attention in the explanations of booms and slumps. Thus it comes about that in certain conditions a sudden fall or rise in people's available incomes and consequently their consumptions and savings can occur, although the so-called objective circumstances do not justify the change. (Myrdal 1931, tr. 1939, p. 95)

Stabilization Policy

If the extent to which they anticipated Keynes in matters of theory is contentious, there can be no doubt that the members of the Stockholm School were very much advocates of what we nowadays think of (rightly or wrongly, though almost certainly the latter) as a ''Keynesian'' approach to stabilization policy. Their policy analysis started from exactly the same place as did that of the Austrians, though it was radically different in content.[17] The Austrians and the Stockholm School all accepted, to use Myrdal's words, ''the *value premise* that cyclical movements should be made less severe and the *factual premise* that this requires primarily the maintenance of the conditions of monetary equilibrium'' (Myrdal 1931, tr. 1939, p. 181, italics in original). The Swedish economists were, however, suspicious, and in Myrdal's case downright scornful, of an approach to business-cycle theory that represented ''a rationalization of economic liberalism, which erects its own fatalistic, negative attitude toward planned economic control into a doctrine'' (Myrdal 1931, tr. 1939, p. 201). Here Myrdal cited with approval a remark, which he attributed to Cassel, to the effect that

> perhaps the whole attitude was ultimately based upon a primitive puritanism; happiness is somehow evil, something immoral, which should be accompanied by a purifying misery now and then in order that those who have experienced it may be redeemed; and so it is only proper, right and natural that after the upswing, with all its sad mistakes, bad times should follow. (Myrdal 1931, tr. 1939, p. 202)

---

[17] It is important not to take for granted the validity of the ''value premise'' of the Stockholm School that cyclical fluctuations were undesirable. Modern ''real-business-cycle theory,'' in the spirit of Kydland and Prescott (1982), certainly does not lead to that result. More to the point here, the contemporary views of Schumpeter (1912) or Dennis Robertson (1915, 1926) did not lead to that result either. See Chapter 4, ''Innovation and Inter-temporal Allocation,'' for further discussion.

Monetary Policy

Nevertheless, despite the profound political, even ideological, differences between the groups evident in that remark, the Stockholm School's policy pragmatism was at least as well disciplined by economic theory as was the Austrians' nihilism. To begin with, as we have seen, their view that any behaviour on the part of the price level was, in principle, compatible with monetary equilibrium did not derive from some anti-market ideology. Rather, it followed from an important theoretical insight, namely, that forward-looking agents could, given enough notice, so arrange their affairs as to eliminate the real effects of any expected price-level fluctuations.[18] The practical implication for monetary policy that they deduced from that insight was that it should aim at a form of price stability, because if monetary measures were to be able to attain and/or sustain equilibrium, the public in general, and the business community in particular, would have to be aware of them and their likely consequences for prices.[19]

Hence, it followed that "publicly declared monetary policy can hardly serve its purpose if it is not stated in simple terms and in terms which are of direct importance to the anticipations of entrepreneurs" (Myrdal 1931, tr. 1939, p. 193). That consideration, in Myrdal's view, ruled out the idea that

> monetary policy should attempt to maintain the employment of the means of production at a maximum . . . a monetary policy with this aim as the only standard would either lead to certain general and cumulative price move-

---

[18] If any time path for the rate of interest is potentially compatible with monetary equilibrium, only given a term structure of inflation expectations, it is difficult to see how the Stockholm School intended to influence those expectations in the direction of price stability while simultaneously recommending that the rate of interest be used to maintain equilibrium, given expectations. That problem arose for them, whereas it does not for exponents of modern equilibrium modelling, because they were willing to entertain the possibility of disequilibrium occurring. Johan Myhrman (1993) has suggested that the Stockholm School's neglect of the quantity of money as a strategic economic variable, stemming from their reliance on Wicksell's model of a pure credit economy, rendered their analysis crucially incomplete, with that particular problem being a symptom of that incompleteness. A suggestion complementary to Myhrman's would be that that problem was symptomatic of their failure to produce a theory of the formation of forward-looking expectations. A more favourable account than Myhrman's of the Stockholm School's development of Wicksell's monetary theory has been given by Trautwein (1993).

[19] In practice, as Jonung (1979) has shown, the Stockholm School's chosen monetary-policy instrument was the interest rate, which, following Wicksell, they recommended raising in response to rising prices and lowering in response to falling prices. That policy did seem to work in practice. Indeed, Irving Fisher, that tireless advocate of *Stable Money* (1934), regarded that Swedish experiment as a prime example which illustrated both the feasibility and the effectiveness of a monetary policy devoted to the goal of price stability. See Fisher (1934, pp. 399–410). For further discussion of Fisher's advocacy of a price-stability rule for monetary policy, see Chapter 8, "A Price-Stability Rule for Monetary Policy."

ments . . . or else require quite extensive public regulations of markets. (Myrdal 1931, tr. 1939, p. 196)

Those statements seem at first sight to embody what we would nowadays term a very conservative conventional wisdom, but they need to be read in the context of the Stockholm School's overwhelmingly pragmatic attitude to economic policy. I referred earlier to *a form* of price-level stability as being the appropriate aim for monetary policy in the eyes of the Stockholm School, and it is important to be clear about just what that form was. The Swedish economists in general, but Myrdal in particular, took very seriously the idea that certain money prices in the economy were sticky, not just in the sense of being slow to respond to supply and demand, but in the deeper sense of following a time path heavily dependent on "different institutional circumstances – upon law, convention, consumption habits, methods of production, patterns of marketing, price policies, monopolistic elements of all sorts, and many other circumstances" (Myrdal 1931, tr. 1939, p. 135). Hence, if the maintenance of monetary equilibrium was desirable, but sticky prices were difficult to influence by monetary means, "a monetary policy aimed to preserve the equilibrium relations must . . . adapt the flexible prices to the absolute level of the sticky ones" (Myrdal 1931, tr. 1939, pp. 134–135, italics in original).[20] In turn, if sticky prices – money wages in particular – were subject to changes emanating from non-monetary sources, including variations over time in the balance of market power between buyers and sellers, then

> it is impossible . . . to specify monetary equilibrium merely by an expression of a price level or by the relation of price levels. . . .
>
> But at least [this quite negative result] can save us from an exaggerated faith in the possibility of stabilizing business by stabilizing the so-called general price level. (Myrdal 1931, tr. 1939, pp. 142–143)

More positively, it followed that

> maintaining a monetary equilibrium [is] a question not only of monetary policy but of economic policy as a whole, social policy and the institutions which rule the labour market, cartel legislation and all related factors. Various combinations of these heterogeneous things, more or less under political control, together with appropriate values of the standard combination of credit conditions, produce stable monetary equilibrium relations. (Myrdal 1931, tr. 1939, p. 184)

For Myrdal, then, and indeed for the Stockholm School in general, there existed a large "field of indifference" containing choices for the setting of policy instruments. The desirability of assigning monetary policy the task of

---

[20] Myrdal's treatment of sticky wages was there essentially identical with that in Keynes's *Treatise on Money* (see Chapter 6), though neither author cited the other in that context.

pursuing a particular time path for a particular price index depended critically upon a wide variety of considerations, including whatever other policy goals might be on the menu, not to mention the roles which the authorities might have assigned to other instruments in that pursuit. As Ohlin put it, ''what is a natural or an artificial policy can only be judged by examining to what extent the policy will bring within reach economic results which for one reason or another are considered desirable'' (Ohlin 1933, tr. 1978, p. 383).

Fiscal Policy

A particularly important element in that pragmatic and eclectic approach to policy, as far as the Stockholm School was concerned, was what we would now term ''fiscal policy.'' Arguments about the desirability of using government control over expenditures on ''public works'' and the methods whereby such expenditures might be financed in order to promote high levels of income and employment do, of course, have a history as old as economics itself. Keynes himself was at pains to point that out in the *General Theory*; but in the current context it is particularly relevant that arguments for public works were already fashionable when the Swedish economists took them up. As we shall see later, they can be found in British writings before World War I, and they made frequent appearances in both British and American debates in the 1920s.[21] Indeed, to the extent that it is appropriate to speak of academic orthodoxy on this issue during that period, it favoured such measures. The arguments offered in their support were, nevertheless, all too often assertive and logically vague, leaving them vulnerable to the challenge mounted by Austrian theorists at the beginning of the 1930s, not to mention more down-to-earth objections from cautious policy-makers.

The main factor differentiating Swedish contributions to those debates in the early 1930s from what had gone before was a political climate more open to innovative policy ideas than was the climate elsewhere. But the economic analysis with which the case for fiscal activism was supported in Sweden was also tighter, which is hardly surprising, as its principal exponents were the same economists whose theoretical innovations we have just been discussing. Their policy work was embodied mainly in studies carried out on behalf of the Committee on Unemployment, a Swedish government committee set up in 1927, whose members included senior academics, politicians, and industrialists.[22] That committee remained in existence until 1935, and with the onset

---

[21] These matters will be dealt with later. For references to British debates, see Chapter 4, and for American discussions, see Chapters 8 and 9.

[22] The work of that committee and its role in the development of Swedish economics have been described by Wadensjö (1993).

of the Great Depression it had become particularly concerned with seeking ways to alleviate the high and, as it was believed, cyclical unemployment rates that the depression brought with it. Even today, much of the work carried out under its auspices remains untranslated from Swedish, and some of it remains unpublished, but enough of the ideas which it generated have found their way into the literature available in English to permit their basic outlines to be discerned clearly.

Lindahl's brief essay "The Problem of Balancing the Budget" (1935, tr. 1939) was written in the form of a commentary on a 1934 study carried out by Myrdal for the Committee on Unemployment, and it referred extensively to that committee's two reports. It shows that the Swedish economists took what we would now think of as a conservative position on the choice of a long-run stance regarding fiscal policy.[23] They believed that secular considerations pointed to the desirability of not only a balanced budget but also, in the case of the national government, a surplus:

> The accepted standard of "financial soundness" in terms of Swedish financial traditions may be summed up by saying that the net assets (in the wider sense) of the State should in the long run be increased by the amount by which the value of new capital assets, not yielding a money income, exceeds the depreciation of old assets (of the same type), plus a certain amortization of public debt. (Lindahl 1935, tr. 1939, p. 355)

That aim was justified, however, at least by Lindahl, on quite radical grounds. He stressed the scope it would allow government ultimately to lighten the tax burden imposed on the working classes, and he noted that such a program would perhaps face opposition from the richer groups, whose taxes would, in the immediate future, have to contribute to the desired surplus. More important, Lindahl also noted that in the long run, "from the point of view of the labour market [i.e., from the point of view of employment policy] there do not seem to be any arguments for departing from a comparatively high standard of 'financial soundness'" (Lindahl 1935, tr. 1939, pp. 354–355). However, "the chief limitation to the principle [of financial soundness] is its reference to long periods of time; it is essential to modify it for the solution of the annual budget problem" (Lindahl 1935, tr. 1939, p. 355). The modifications which Lindahl discussed were nevertheless constrained by a requirement, again, by modern standards, rather conservative, that "government activities should not be expanded at the expense of

---

[23] A word of caution is in order here. Much Swedish work on this topic remains untranslated, and as both Assar Lindbeck and Michael Trautwein have warned me, Lindahl was, relatively speaking, conservative in his policy views. Hence the following few pages, based on his work, may somewhat understate the radical nature of Swedish views on fiscal policy. Lundberg (1996, pp. 23–34) has given a first-hand account of the relationship between the analysis and policy views of the Stockholm School during that period.

private enterprise," a principle to which, he noted, the members of the Committee on Unemployment, not to mention Myrdal, were strongly committed, and which "may be characterized as the *minimum* concerning which the various political parties in Sweden agree" (Lindahl 1935, tr. 1939, p. 356, italics in original).

The Relationship of Fiscal Policy and Monetary Policy

The modifications in question were also subject to a further important qualification, namely, that "the primary responsibility for trade cycle policy must . . . lie with the Central Bank" (Lindahl 1935, tr. 1939, p. 357). Those constraints nevertheless left ample room for counter-cyclical fiscal policy. Expansion of government activities was unobjectionable so long as it "takes place through the employment of productive resources that would otherwise have been (wholly or partly) idle" (Lindahl 1935, tr. 1939, p. 356), and so long as, in their planning, it was recognized that "public finance can . . . only be a supplementary instrument . . . if possible . . . co-ordinated with the policy pursued by the Central Bank" (Lindahl 1935, tr. 1939, p. 357).

Within those limits, the fiscal-policy regime which the Swedish economists envisaged went beyond merely offsetting the tendency of a balanced-budget fiscal regime "to intensify [cyclical] fluctuations" by maintaining, rather than curtailing, public-sector expenditures in the face of falling tax revenues during contractions, and increasing them during expansions. It also left scope for more actively counter-cyclical measures, whose implementation would be facilitated if appropriations for public-works expenditures could be made during booms, with the corresponding expenditures being postponed "until a reversal of the economic trend has taken place" (Lindahl 1935, tr. 1939, p. 360). That, it was recognized, would require a degree of centralization, with local-authority programs being brought more under state control, to take advantage of the greater budgetary flexibility available to the central government. It would also involve

> the organization in the depression of *additional public works*, which are not directly remunerative but which lead to increased employment of labour and other factors of production, and thus appear advantageous from the angle of an unemployment or expansionist policy. (Lindahl 1935, tr. 1939, p. 362, italics in original)

Now the idea that preservation of a full-employment monetary equilibrium required a smooth co-ordination of saving and investment was central to the macroeconomic theory of the Stockholm School, and they understood that the "over- and underbalancing" of the budget which such a counter-cyclical policy would involve would have an effect on the supply of savings available for private-sector investment. But they also understood that under such a policy,

> the supply [of saving] is reduced by "underbalancing" or current "deficits," when the public demands weigh heavily on the capital market, and increased in the opposite case. Since private demand for investment varies similarly, a better correspondence between these two factors is attained by the proposed policy. In this way, budgetary policy becomes a valuable aid to monetary policy in its task of *preserving equilibrium in the capital market.* (Lindahl 1935, tr. 1939, p. 363, italics in original)

In sum, the Stockholm School argued that three principles should govern budgetary policy. First: "The trade cycle should not be allowed to affect *normal public activities.*" Second: "Public *constructional work* . . . should . . . be concentrated in depression years." Third: "The *tax burden* should . . . be lighter during the depression and heavier during the boom" (Lindahl 1935, tr. 1939, pp. 364–365, italics in original). According to Lindahl (1935, tr. 1939, pp. 364), both Ohlin and Myrdal, not to mention the Committee on Unemployment itself, though they might differ concerning the details, all subscribed to those principles. And they also agreed that

> the degree of government "over or underbalancing" should be determined in consultation with the Central Bank . . . Budgetary policy will then influence the supply of savings available for private investment, and ensure a better correspondence with the variations in demand during the different phases of the trade cycle. (Lindahl 1935, tr. 1939, p. 365)

Open-Economy Considerations

Sweden had, of course, a relatively open economy, and although the theoretical analysis of the Stockholm School usually dealt with what we would now call closed-economy models, its members were well aware of the policy complications introduced by openness. Under a gold standard, "a small country like Sweden must for the most part adjust itself to international trade fluctuations" (Lindahl 1935, tr. 1939, p. 365), so that

> the rules of budgetary policy laid down above must . . . be applied with caution.
> In a country with a *free currency* [flexible exchange rate], on the other hand . . . the rules can be of greater importance . . . the crucial difference is that it remains possible to exercise a decisive influence on the future internal price level. The possibility of carrying out a financial programme of rational trade cycle policy is thereby substantially increased. (Lindahl 1935, tr. 1939, p. 366, italics in original)

On the other hand, Lindahl also conceded that under a flexible exchange rate,

> when monetary policy is skilfully managed and the great possibilities of a
> free currency in the stabilization of economic trends are judiciously utilized,
> the importance of certain portions of the budgetary programme outlined
> above is at the same time reduced. (Lindahl 1935, tr. 1939, p. 367)

Thus, though there can be no question that Swedish policy analysis accorded an important role to fiscal policy in stabilization, it was nevertheless to be a subordinate one.[24] Monetary policy, and specifically interest-rate policy, was the principal tool whereby high employment could be achieved and preserved. As we shall see in subsequent chapters, that was a policy vision which was widely shared elsewhere, not least in Britain and the United States.

The Distinctive Characteristics of Swedish Analysis

There is no defining theoretical core to the macroeconomic analysis of the Stockholm School. It was precisely the open-endedness of their "model sequences," the fact that the range of assumptions which they found permissible was wide enough to yield a wide variety of predictions, that most strongly differentiated the Swedish economists' work from that of their Austrian contemporaries. Even so, theirs was hardly a case of eclecticism for its own sake. On the contrary, it followed directly from certain theoretical preconceptions that all of the Stockholm School shared, preconceptions which decisively determined the direction that their development of the Wicksellian notion of monetary equilibrium was to take.

First and foremost was their approach to capital theory. Once capital was defined as the present value of an expected income stream, it was inevitable that psychological factors underlying the expectations in question would find a central place in the analysis of inter-temporal allocation. The Austrians had made an apparently objectively defined and difficult-to-vary time structure of production (an aggregate production function, to put it in modern terms) the fulcrum of their analysis. The Swedes, on the other hand, focused on inherently subjective and highly volatile expectations. Small wonder that their models pointed to so many possible ways of characterizing economic fluctuations. More generally, but closely related, the Stockholm School, and Myrdal in particular, attached great importance to the role of those expectations as factors conditioning the nature of the current price structure; and that meant that the state of full Walrasian equilibrium from which the Austrians usually started their conceptual experiments had no particular methodological signif-

---

[24] But recall that, as pointed out in footnote 23, Lindahl was relatively conservative in his views on those matters, and note also that the Swedish economists, like their contemporaries elsewhere, all came to place more emphasis on fiscal policies in the post-war years. See Lundberg (1996, pp. 39ff.).

icance for the Swedes. An equilibrium in which saving equalled investment could be characterized in Walrasian terms, as Lindahl had shown. Such an equilibrium was also desirable, and might be achieved and even maintained by the proper conduct of policy, but it would not necessarily arise of its own accord (as the Austrians believed) if policy were only to adopt an appropriately defined passivity. Hence, the Stockholm School was willing to ask questions about macrodynamic processes in which output and employment variations were of the essence, processes which might begin with unemployed resources rather than at full employment. Its policy activism followed naturally from that point.

In this chapter we have accepted Ohlin's *ex post* identification of a distinct Stockholm School of macroeconomics (Ohlin 1937) and have stressed its roots in the work of Wicksell, but it should be noted that Irving Fisher's development of capital theory was by no means the only non-Swedish work of which its members were aware. They were also very familiar with the work of their British contemporaries. As Eskil Wadensjö (1993, pp. 114–115) has noted, in 1932 Ohlin told the Committee on Unemployment of the existence of two approaches to business-cycle theory, Austrian and Anglo-Saxon, and warned that "the memoranda, prepared by Myrdal, Johansson, Hammarskjold and myself will be closely associated with [the latter]" (as translated and quoted by Wadensjö 1993, p. 115). He also identified the principal contributors to that approach as "Keynes, Robertson and Hawtrey" (as translated and quoted by Wadensjö, 1993, p. 115). In the next three chapters we shall consider the contributions made by those and other British economists to the theory of the cycle during the 1920s and early 1930s, showing how, despite a lack of familiarity with the details of Wicksell's work that was not remedied until quite late in the day, they developed the Marshallian tradition in monetary and cycle theory along lines that in important respects ran parallel to those followed by their Austrian and Swedish colleagues.

PART II

The Marshallian Tradition in Britain

CHAPTER 4

Cambridge Cycle Theory: Lavington, Pigou, and Robertson

Marshallian Foundations

It is evident from the names that Ohlin cited in 1932 – Keynes, Robertson, and Hawtrey – that the "Anglo-Saxon" tradition in business-cycle analysis to which he referred in 1932 was in fact the Marshallian Cambridge tradition, though he failed to mention two notable contributors to it, namely, Frederick Lavington, who had died in 1926, and, more important, Marshall's successor as Professor of Political Economy at Cambridge, Arthur C. Pigou.

Marshall's final book, *Money Credit and Commerce*, was published in 1923, when he was eighty years old and within a year of his death. The book was disjointed and repetitive, and though it expounded many important ideas, all of them had been developed much earlier. Indeed, many of the most memorable passages of *Money Credit and Commerce* were transcriptions, sometimes lightly edited and sometimes unchanged, of earlier writings. They included extensive quotations from evidence presented by Marshall to the Gold and Silver Commission of 1888–89 and to the Indian Currency Committee of 1899, as well as some passages dealing with the business cycle which dated back to the *Economics of Industry* of 1879, a book which Marshall had written in collaboration with his wife.[1] But if Marshall made no new contributions to monetary economics and cycle theory between the wars, his earlier work provided the foundations on which many others built during that period, and it is worth recalling just what its main characteristics were. Three items here were of particular importance to future developments: first, Marshall's reformulation of the quantity theory of money in stock-supply-and-demand terms; second, his account of the transmission mechanism linking money-supply changes and the price level; and third, his analysis of the roles of the interest rate, inflation expectations, and wage stickiness in the cycle.[2]

---

[1] For fuller accounts of Marshall's monetary theory, see Bridel (1987, ch. 3) and Laidler (1991, ch. 3). The basics of that theory were in fact worked out in unpublished notes which date back to the early 1870s (e.g., Marshall 1871), and some parts of *Money Credit and Commerce* (Marshall 1923), for example, Appendix D ("Diagrammatic Note on a Metallic Money"), also seem to be of that vintage. Evidence presented by Marshall to various Parliamentary committees and royal commissions has been reprinted (Marshall 1926).

[2] It is worth noting that Marshall and his Cambridge successors did not refer to themselves as quantity theorists. Rather, they thought of the quantity theory as one which related the

The Cash-Balance Approach to the Quantity Theory

Marshall's reformulation of the quantity theory of money in terms of the demand for and supply of a stock of currency, often referred to as the *cash-balance approach*, was essentially complete in the early 1870s, although its definitive exposition, by Pigou rather than by Marshall himself, did not appear in print until Pigou's classic *Quarterly Journal of Economics* article on "The Value of Money" (1917). Marshall, and Pigou too, paid considerable attention to the effects of institutional factors, particularly the development of banking, on the demand for currency, but they nevertheless emphasized that the great advantage of their approach was that it allowed monetary theory to be brought into direct contact with analysis of individual choice.

Even so, as Patinkin (1974) has argued, they left the choice-theoretic foundations of their analysis of the demand for money in what was, with benefit of hindsight, an unsatisfactory and incomplete state. For example, both Marshall and Pigou referred to the situation of individuals finding it convenient to hold a certain fraction of their "resources" in the form of cash, but they did not always make it clear whether that word referred to wealth or to income; and though those same individuals were portrayed as balancing the convenience of holding money against the income to be had by holding some alternative asset, the particular examples of those alternatives cited by Marshall – a horse, furniture, machinery, cattle – were highly indivisible. Only in 1923 did a financial asset, namely, a "stock exchange security" (Marshall 1923, p. 39), make an appearance in Marshall's discussion of that matter, and he never clearly formulated the money-holding decision as involving a marginal choice. Pigou sometimes did so, for example, in *Wealth and Welfare* (1912, p. 424), but he nevertheless put that insight to no particular use. He treated it more as an end product of his analysis than as an idea in its own right with further implications worth exploring.[3]

The Transmission Mechanism

Marshall's analysis of the transmission mechanism, whereby an increase in the quantity of currency would lead to a rise in the price level, was singled

---

behaviour of prices to that of the quantity of money and its velocity of circulation, with their own theory being one that in practice would yield essentially similar predictions. See Laidler (1991, ch. 3) for a comparison of their model with Irving Fisher's exposition of the quantity theory (Fisher 1911).

[3] That was one reason why Patinkin (1974) denied that Pigou had a properly formulated portfolio-choice theory of the demand for money. Patinkin was anxious to establish Keynes's priorities in that regard, and hence perhaps, by implication, also to establish a Keynesian pedigree for Milton Friedman's theory (1956) of the demand for money. Note that Patinkin did not cite Pigou (1912) in that context.

out by Keynes (1911) as having been a distinctive contribution of particular importance. Marshall first dealt with that matter in his evidence to the Gold and Silver Commission of 1888–89, taking, as had Cairnes and Mill before him, an inflow of gold from abroad as the starting point for the story; and the analysis in question reappeared in *Money Credit and Commerce* (pp. 255–256) with only minor and essentially cosmetic amendments. Such an inflow, Marshall argued, would be concentrated in the banking system, which would, as a result, become more willing to supply credit. Hence the rate of interest charged by the banks would fall, and borrowing would increase, so that "there is more capital in the hands of speculative investors, who come on the market for goods as buyers, and so raise prices" (Marshall 1923, p. 256). That rise in prices would in turn raise the demand for currency, which the newly imported gold would satisfy; a new equilibrium price level would in the end be established, and the interest rate would return to its old level.

That analysis contained elements that would later find a place in Wicksell's cumulative process, and Wicksell was indeed familiar enough with it to cite it in *Interest and Prices* (1898, p. 76). Certain things were missing, however. In particular, though Marshall's *Principles* (1890), a book dealing with what we would now call microeconomics, contained extensive discussions of the rate of interest as the price which would co-ordinate saving and investment decisions – he even raised the possibility that a configuration of thrift and productivity might arise at some future date which would require the rate to be negative – those essentially long-run real considerations were kept firmly in the background when, elsewhere in his writings, he discussed explicitly monetary questions.[4] In his analysis of interactions between the banks and their customers, in *Money Credit and Commerce* and elsewhere, Marshall emphasized the profit expectations of those customers, not some "natural" interest rate rooted in the economy's time structure of production. All of that was in obvious contrast to Wicksell's approach to the same matters.

The Cycle

Marshall had suggested to readers of the first and all subsequent editions of his *Principles* that a systematic treatment of the cycle would in due course be forthcoming from him, but that promise was never honoured. The discussion of the cycle in *Money Credit and Commerce* was fragmented, and parts of it dated back to the *Economics of Industry* (Marshall and Marshall, 1879). Here

---

[4] See Marshall (1890, 8th ed. 1920, bk. VI, ch. VI, fn. 3). It is interesting to note that Cassel (1903) explicitly took Marshall to task for that view, arguing that opportunities for productive investment were in fact so abundant that the rate of interest was bound to remain positive.

the influence of J. S. Mill (1871, pp. 542ff.) is evident, notably in those passages dealing with the role of bank credit creation in sustaining a boom. Something, "the opening out of foreign markets after a war, . . . a good harvest, . . . more often it arises from the mere passing away of old causes of distrust" (1923, p. 249) would lead to a rise in business confidence, an "improvement of credit" as Marshall called it. Borrowing from the banks would expand, a boom would gradually begin to gather momentum, and the price level would begin to rise, bringing with it further credit creation; and so on, in an ongoing sequence. That essentially descriptive account of the upswing was, however, supplemented with discussion of the distinction between the nominal rate and real rate of interest and the postulate that the nominal rate of interest charged by the banks would initially fail to keep pace with the price inflation that would mark a cyclical expansion. Marshall had first discussed those phenomena in "Remedies for Fluctuations of General Prices" (1887), where he had stressed the slow adjustment of the interest rate as being crucial in creating and sustaining an initially self-reinforcing spiral of credit expansion and rising prices.

That spiral would in due course come to an end, and indeed be reversed, although Marshall (again like Mill) was better at describing the relevant sequence of events than at explaining why they took place:

> . . . the demand for more loans raises the rate of interest very high. Distrust increases, those who have lent become eager to secure themselves: and refuse to renew their loans on easy or even on any terms. Some speculators have to sell goods in order to pay their debts. . . . As credit by growing makes itself grow, so when distrust has taken the place of confidence, failure and panic breed panic and failure. (Marshall 1923, p. 250)

Prices would then fall, and business failures cumulate, even among fundamentally sound enterprises. Moreover, as early as 1879, and ever after in his discussions of those matters, including that of 1923, Marshall stressed that money wages were sticky, particularly in a downward direction.[5] Hence he concluded that real wages would move counter-cyclically, ensuring that fluctuations in employment and output, amplified by inter-industry spillovers, would be an integral feature of the cycle.

Marshall's account of the cycle thus focused upon how a flexible price level for goods would interact with two sticky prices, namely, the nominal interest rate and the money wage. Therefore, for him, the key to eliminating cyclical fluctuations was maintenance of price-level stability, or, given that such a goal was hardly practical, widespread indexation of loan and wage

---

[5] That view of sticky wages dates back at least to Henry Thornton (1802), but it seems to have been Marshall and Marshall (1879) who first gave it a prominent role in mainstream discussions of the cycle. See Laidler (1991, pp. 95–100, 102–106) for a fuller discussion.

contracts. As we shall soon see, his Cambridge successors thought that matters were rather more complicated, but, as we shall also see, their work was nevertheless deeply marked by Marshall's vision of the cycle, which in turn had been derived from classical economics by way of Mill. Like Marshall, they treated the cycle as a cumulative phenomenon, involving some initial, probably non-monetary, disturbance setting in motion an ultimately unsustainable, but initially self-reinforcing, spiral of credit creation and demand expansion. Moreover, they extended Marshall's stock-supply-and-demand version of the quantity theory, ultimately turning it into the theory of liquidity preference, and they elaborated his treatment of the transmission mechanism along lines in some respects similar to those followed by Wicksell, though largely in ignorance of Wicksell's work.

Cambridge monetary economics and cycle theory in the 1920s were far from homogeneous, however. Different contributors stressed different issues, and some remained more closely wedded to Marshall's concerns than others. On balance, it was Pigou and Frederick Lavington who followed Marshall's lead most closely. It is convenient, then, to begin the discussion of inter-war Cambridge work with an account of their development of Marshall's ideas.

Pigou and Lavington on the Cycle

The speculative activity which Marshall, following Mill, had stressed as a central feature of the cycle was, by its very nature, forward-looking. That "prospectiveness," as Pigou (e.g., 1912, p. 456) was to call it, of business decisions was the starting point for his own particular development of Marshallian theory. *Wealth and Welfare* (Pigou 1912) had already provided a concise account of that development even before the war, though it was not until 1927, with *Industrial Fluctuations* (with a second edition appearing in 1929), that Pigou himself published a monograph solely devoted to the cycle.[6] The "leading ideas" of Frederick Lavington's brief primer on *The Trade Cycle* (1922) were, by his own account, "drawn from the writings of Dr. Marshall, Professor Pigou, Mr. D. H. Robertson," though he also acknowledged the influence of W. C. Mitchell (1913).[7]

---

[6] That work nevertheless included lengthy passages transcribed from Pigou (1912) without attribution to that earlier source. Note that the discussion of Pigou's work in this chapter mainly relies on the second revised edition of *Industrial Fluctuations* (1929). I do not believe that anything hinges on this matter here, but obviously a more detailed discussion of the evolution of Pigou's economic thought would have to pay attention to the changes made between 1927 and 1929, and also to what he had added to the discussions that first appeared in 1912.

[7] Even though Lavington had been Keynes's pupil, there is no mention of Keynes here or anywhere else in Lavington's writings, as far as I am aware. Keynes, in his turn, seems to have ignored Lavington just as completely. It would be interesting to know why.

The essential features of that branch of Cambridge cycle theory as it stood in the early 1920s were summarized by Lavington as follows:

> Among the characteristic features of modern organization are then these four: first, that the responsibility for production is assumed by a special class of business men, each acting on his own judgement and at his own risk; second, that, as production takes time, its present activity depends upon estimates of future conditions, on forecasts liable to error; third, that the market for the output of each firm is dependent on the output of all others; finally, that as business estimates are based not on prospective needs but on prospective prices, they are liable to further error from arbitrary variations in the price index. (Lavington 1922, pp. 26–27)

The upshot was that, in all likelihood, "the key to the causes of business fluctuations lies in the mind of the entrepreneur, in the influences which determine his confidence in the business future" (Lavington 1922, p. 28).

Prospectiveness and Error

The central factor at work in the cycle theory which Lavington set out in 1922, and of which Pigou was the major exponent, was encapsulated by the word *error*, which occurred twice in the foregoing quotation from Lavington. In Pigou's view, the forward-looking nature of investment decisions required that "expected facts are substituted for accomplished facts as the impulse to action" (Pigou 1929, p. 73), and that in turn would create scope for "errors of undue optimism or undue pessimism in . . . business forecasts" (Pigou 1929, p. 73). Those errors, moreover, were not random phenomena. Rather, their occurrence was highly correlated across agents and over time too.

Already in 1912, Pigou had asserted his belief that

> the forecasts made by business men are largely coloured by their present fortune. It follows that interdependence of fortune carries with it interdependence of forecasts, and, thus, allies itself with the psychology of crowds, as a force tending to promote action in droves. (Pigou 1912, pp. 461–462)

Pigou went on to draw attention to two features of a modern economy which he thought further exacerbated those tendencies. First, when businessmen had access to a banking system,

> an error of optimism once made by them is expanded to greater girth. They borrow more money, and, thereby, cause prices to rise still further. By this rise their fortunes are again improved, and, in consequence, the error of their forecasts is again expanded. (Pigou 1912, p. 463)

Second, the development of the joint stock company meant that the expectations underlying investment decisions were no longer only those of businessmen, who might be expected to have specialist knowledge of particular industries, but were those of market participants in general:

> Unfortunately, however, when the work of making operative forecasts about investment is thrown open to outsiders, it is not merely professional financiers who come into it. They are accompanied, on the contrary, by a large number of persons among the general public, who have no special knowledge or competence. (Pigou 1912, p. 458)

Pigou returned to that latter point in *Industrial Fluctuations*. He quoted Marshall to the effect that "one of the chief sources of disturbance is the action of the general public in providing funds for joint-stock companies" (Marshall 1923, p. 261) and argued that that was a consequence of the fact that "most members of the general public . . . are, if left to their own devices, quite incapable of giving any reasoned opinion upon the various propositions that are . . . put before them" (Pigou 1929, p. 75).[8]

Evidently, despite Ohlin's failure to mention them by name in 1932, Lavington's and Pigou's emphasis on the role of expectations in driving investment decisions, their insistence, to use Pigou's words, that "when . . . expected facts are substituted for accomplished facts as the impulse to action, the way is opened for . . . psychological causes" (Pigou 1929, p. 73) to dominate business decisions, marked them out as working along lines rather similar to those taken by members of the Stockholm School, who also stressed the forward-looking element in economic behaviour, as well as the uncertainty it generated. Thus, if the Stockholm School to some extent had anticipated Keynes (1936) in emphasizing those matters, and certainly they had, they had, in their turn, already been anticipated by Marshall's immediate successors at Cambridge.[9]

Furthermore, and also important in light of the stress that Keynes (1936) subsequently would place on the same point, Pigou and Lavington had little faith in the capacity of market mechanisms to co-ordinate successfully the inter-temporal allocation of resources, quite apart from any problems that the workings of the monetary system might create. Where individual decisions were based upon erroneous expectations, a harmonious outcome at the level of the economy as a whole was hardly to be expected. Lavington, indeed, thought that long-term investment was particularly prone to such problems:

> Inasmuch as optimism or pessimism naturally has greater influence on business judgements the less certain the basis on which those judgements rest, it is only to be expected that this influence should be most marked, and maladjustment of resources consequently most evident, in the output of new

---

[8] Keynes was equally sceptical about the capacity of ordinary individuals to make well-considered choices about investment decisions and in that respect was firmly in the Marshallian tradition, rather than being an innovator of any sort. See Chapter 10, "Expectations, Speculation, and Enterprise."

[9] Hicks (1936), Bertil Ohlin (1937), and Joan Robinson (1939) are among the earliest to have recognized the connection between Keynes' analysis and that of the Stockholm School. George Shackle (1967) would make much of that connection in the years after World War II.

capital plant designed to produce goods for very far-ahead and uncertain markets. (Lavington 1922, p. 91)

Lavington also took up that theme in the specific context of the upper turning-point of the cycle. Like Pigou, he thought of the downturn as coming about "when the bulk of the new capital equipment comes into operation" (Lavington 1922, p. 91), and he noted in particular that long-term investment would then fall off as a result of "the realization that the yield of the new equipment is likely to fall far short of the extravagant anticipations of those responsible for its creation" (Lavington 1922, p. 91).[10]

Inter-temporal Allocation and the Monetary System

Marshall had argued that price-level stabilization, or, failing that, indexation of both loan and wage contracts, would suffice to eliminate the cycle. Hence his analysis was open to the interpretation that cyclical fluctuations arose from a malfunction of the monetary system that could be corrected, rather than from any more fundamental flaw in market mechanisms.[11] One cannot interpret Pigou or Lavington in that way. They believed that much of the problem stemmed from the inability of markets properly to co-ordinate the choices made by individual agents, and though they thought that the workings of the monetary system exacerbated such difficulties, they did not think that those difficulties could be eliminated by any expedient as simple as generating price-level stability or introducing indexation. Such measures would help, but they would not provide anything approaching a complete cure.

Pigou, for example, was quite explicit that

> an important portion of the reactions which take place through the monetary and banking system during industrial fluctuations, and which are associated with changes in the stock of real capital held by business men, are merely mediating links, not causal factors . . . if the monetary and banking systems were eliminated, equal changes in the stock would be brought about in other ways. (Pigou 1929, p. 135)

Moreover, price-level stability, even if confidently expected by everyone, would not necessarily eliminate collective error on the part of the business community:[12]

---

[10] Thus there was a suggestion of an accelerator effect at work there, but Lavington did not develop that idea in the way that contemporary American economists such as J. M. Clark (1917), Mitchell et al. (1923), and Alvin Hansen (1927) did. See Chapter 8, "Mitchell and Hansen on the Cycle."

[11] Irving Fisher's view (1911) of the cycle was also very much along those lines. See Chapter 8, "The Quantity Theory and the Cycle," for a brief account, and Laidler (1991, pp. 89–100) for a fuller discussion of this matter. It was mainly for that reason that Fisher was, and remained, an ardent supporter of a price-stability rule for monetary policy.

[12] There Pigou clearly anticipated, if only in passing, Robert E. Lucas's notion of confusion between changes in relative prices and in the absolute price level (Lucas 1972).

> For, even though everybody is certain that the general level of prices is going to remain constant, everybody may also be convinced, without any internal inconsistency, that the price of his own particular product is going to rise or to fall. (Pigou 1929, p. 86)

Pigou even hazarded an estimate of how much of the amplitude of the cycle was due to errors unrelated to monetary disturbance, though he gave his readers no clue as to how he arrived at it:

> I hold that, if a policy of price stabilisation were successfully carried through, the amplitude of industrial fluctuations would be substantially reduced – it might be cut down to half of what it is at present – but considerable fluctuations would still remain. (Pigou 1929, p. 219)

That still left a considerable proportion of cyclical fluctuations to be accounted for by the workings of the monetary system, of course, and Pigou and Lavington both paid attention to analysing those matters. Not only did they follow Marshall's lead in drawing attention to the endogenous monetary expansions and contractions which amplified both upswing and downswing, paying particular attention to the propensity of commercial banks, "in response to offers of higher interest, to allow the ratio of their reserves to their liabilities to decrease" (Pigou 1929, p. 136) as the upswing of the cycle gathered momentum. They also discussed the role of cyclically induced variations in the velocity of circulation, with Lavington in particular making a contribution of lasting importance, and Pigou discussing the cyclical role of forced saving too.[13]

The Stock Demand for Money

Lavington's analysis of endogenous fluctuations of velocity was based upon a significant extension of the Marshall-Pigou cash-balance approach to the demand for money into what would later be called (by Keynes) liquidity preference theory, a contribution which received its fullest treatment in Lavington's study *The English Capital Market* (1921). That development, whose significance went far beyond the particular application to understanding pro-cyclical fluctuations in velocity that immediately concerns us here, was not properly appreciated until the 1930s.[14]

---

[13] Thus, though Pigou, along with Lavington, was sometimes characterized – for example, by Haberler (1937, ch. 6), who also put Keynes in that category – as an exponent of a mainly "psychological" explanation for the cycle, they paid sufficient attention to other factors, particularly monetary factors, that it is perhaps safer to classify them, and Pigou in particular, as eclectic. That was the view of Paul Douglas and Aaron Director (1931), who tended to bracket Pigou with Mitchell.

[14] Though Keynes never referred to Lavington, as noted in footnote 7, Dennis Robertson was aware of the significance of that particular contribution, which, crucially, he drew to the attention of John Hicks. See Hicks (1935, repr. 1982, p. 48, fn. 2; 1937, repr. 1982, p. 106, fn. 3). See also Bridel (1987, pp. 96ff.) for an appreciative discussion of the importance of that aspect of Lavington's work to the development of Cambridge monetary thought. It should

Arguing along the same lines as Pigou (1917) (including, unfortunately, his failure to distinguish properly between a flow of current consumption services and the stock which yields that flow), Lavington began by noting that for an individual,

> resources devoted to consumption supply an income of immediate satisfaction; those held as a stock of currency yield a return of convenience and security; those devoted to investment in the narrower sense of the term yield a return in the form of interest . . . the quantity of resources which he holds in the form of money will be such that the unit of resources which is just and only just worthwhile holding in this form yields . . . a return of convenience and security equal to the yield of satisfaction derived from the marginal unit spent on consumables, and equal also to the net rate of interest. (Lavington 1921, p. 30)

The clear statement with which that passage ends, that the rate of interest represented the opportunity cost of holding money, was remarkable enough for the time that it was written, but Lavington's contribution began, rather than ended, with that point.

He went on to point out that

> this distinction between the yield of convenience and security brings out the consideration that the stock of money held by a business man serves not only to effect his current payments but also as a first line of defence against the uncertain events of the future. (Lavington 1921, p. 30)

And he drew attention to

> the essential similarity between the distribution of resources by a business man and the distribution effected by a bank, where the two main considerations, the need to meet current and contingent demands and the need to earn a profit, are shown in clearer contrast. (Lavington 1921, pp. 30–31)

The upshot here was that to the extent that the businessman's demand for money derived not just from the need to finance current transactions but also from the need to satisfy the desire for liquidity that arose from "the degree of uncertainty in his business situation" (Lavington 1921, p. 31), it would vary with that degree of uncertainty.

Thus from the point of view of the business community in general,

> it seems reasonable . . . to regard this latter part of the aggregate money stock as a reserve whose size is regulated by the general level of confidence – a reservoir from which money flows into active circulation when times are good, and into which money flows from active circulation when times are bad. (Lavington 1921, p. 33)

----

nevertheless be noted that important elements of Lavington's formulation of the theory of the demand for money, along what we would now call "precautionary motive" lines, were anticipated by Francis Y. Edgeworth (1888), Carl Menger (1892), and Wicksell (1898). On Menger's contribution, see Erich Streissler (1973). On Edgeworth and Wicksell, see Laidler (1991, pp. 184–187 and 125–126, respectively).

Nor, Lavington went on to argue, should this be regarded as merely a process of hoarding and dishoarding: "the characteristic of a hoard is its uselessness, and the characteristic of a reserve lies in the fact that it does money work, though of a rather different kind from that of money in active circulation" (Lavington 1921, p. 33).

Forced Saving

Pigou and Lavington had, as we have seen, followed Marshall in paying attention to the banks' capacity for credit creation and destruction as an important factor underlying the monetary system's ability to amplify cyclical fluctuations, and Pigou in particular stressed the role played here by endogenous responses of the banks' reserve ratio to variations in the state of business confidence. In *Industrial Fluctuations* (1929, pp. 139ff.) Pigou went out of his way to rebut Edwin Cannan's "round assertion that the whole conception of bankers 'creating credit' is confused and fallacious," which Cannan had made, among other places, in an *Economica* paper (1921a).[15] The point of Pigou's argument about that matter, as he set it out in 1929, was not merely that induced variations in the volume of banking-system liabilities amplified cyclical variations in the price level but also that by putting new purchasing power into the hands of the business community, they led to an increase in "the stream of new capital" (Pigou 1929, p. 146) whose counterpart on the saving side was "the real levy made on the public" (Pigou 1929, p. 153).

For Pigou in 1929, that is to say, credit creation involved forced saving, just as it did for his Austrian contemporaries. That idea had appeared and reappeared in English classical monetary economics from Bentham and Thornton onwards, but it had never played more than a peripheral role in that tradition. Marshall, indeed, seems to have made no explicit mention of the phenomenon, though it is not difficult to read it into his analysis of the mechanisms linking a gold inflow to a price-level change, as discussed earlier in this chapter. The idea first appeared in Pigou's work in "Correctives of the Trade Cycle" (1924), where he briefly discussed the banking system's capacity to impose forced saving on the public.[16] Nevertheless, the new prominence accorded to the idea in his writings in the late 1920s seems to

---

[15] The notion of a bank credit multiplier had deep roots in the nineteenth-century literature, having been developed by, among others, Sir James Pennington (1829) and Sir Robert Giffen (1877). That notion remained sufficiently interesting that it was still being discussed in the journals as late as 1934. See James Meade (1934). Nevertheless, the only prominent academic figure who did not accept that analysis during the period of our interest seems to have been Edwin Cannan, professor of economics at the London School of Economics. Controversy about that matter played no role in the development of theories of the cycle and employment, except to the extent that Cannan kept raising the issue, and kept on being rebutted by other contributors.

[16] On this point, see Bridel (1987, pp. 100–101).

have been prompted not by the hints to be found in Marshall's work, nor by the spontaneous development of his own ideas, nor even by the Austrian cycle theory which was at that time already accessible to readers of German, but rather by the thorough treatment of the idea in the writings of Pigou's younger Cambridge colleague Dennis Robertson, particularly his study of *Banking Policy and the Price Level* (1926), to which Pigou explicitly referred in his own work.

Robertson's Cycle Theory

Robertson, though about the same age as Keynes, had been Keynes's pupil before the outbreak of war in 1914.[17] That intellectual pedigree thus placed him at the very centre of the Cambridge tradition, but his 1915 book, *A Study of Industrial Fluctuation*, made a considerable break with earlier Cambridge treatments of the cycle, not least that of Marshall himself, and that set out in Pigou's *Wealth and Welfare*. For Robertson, swings in output, rather than prices, were the cycle's principal feature, and under the acknowledged influence of Albert Aftalion (1913) he focused on indivisibilities in investment projects, the fact they take time to complete, and their durability once completed, as the crucial factors ensuring a cyclical response on the part of the industrial sector to the various real (as we would now call them) shocks which he believed provided the basic impulse for fluctuations.[18]

Innovation and Inter-temporal Allocation

Among such real shocks,

> one form in particular of lowered costs . . . seems to be of considerable importance both in inducing immediate prosperity and in stimulating the over-investment which sows the seeds of future depression; and that is a lowering of costs due to invention. (Robertson 1915, p. 66)

Robertson was at that time quite unaware of the work of Minnie England (e.g., 1912, 1913), Joseph Schumpeter (1912), and Wicksell (1907b) on the role of innovation as a force driving the cycle, but his ideas clearly had a

---

[17] The standard work on Robertson is, of course, by Presley (1978), and my failure to refer to that work at every turn of the argument in the following pages should not be taken to indicate a lack of awareness on my part of my indebtedness to it. Presley discussed the collaboration of Keynes and Robertson extensively, as he did in another paper (1989).

[18] Aftalion was also influential in the United States during that period, where his version of the accelerator mechanism was the acknowledged source of Alvin Hansen's (1927) enthusiasm for that device. See Chapter 8, "Mitchell and Hansen on the Cycle." It is interesting to note that in 1927 Aftalion published a summary of his cycle theory in English, in the *Review of Economic Statistics*.

good deal in common with theirs. Like them, he regarded some fluctuations in output as being integral to the process of economic growth and therefore, to use his adjective, *appropriate*; and considerable enthusiasm for cyclical fluctuations as necessary characteristics of economic progress would continue to mark his work throughout the inter-war years. Typically, such appropriate fluctuations involved bursts of investment in durable capital goods, whose long gestation period and durability explained why their output varied with greater amplitude than that of consumption goods.[19]

Desirable though they might be, however, periods of relatively rapid expansion were all too likely, in Robertson's view, to end in *overinvestment*, a state of affairs in which

> unless and until the consumable goods created by the new instruments appear in sufficient quantities . . . it will be physically impossible for the investment in construction goods to be maintained on the scale on which it has begun. The fundamental cause in such circumstances of the collapse of constructional enterprise is . . . the scarcity of real capital available for investment. (Robertson 1915, pp. 170–171)

Once we understand that the phrase "real capital" refers here to the working capital necessary to satisfy the consumption demands of workers engaged in completing fixed-investment projects, an essential similarity between this argument and the diagnosis offered by later Austrian analysis of the crisis phase of the cycle will be evident. Robertson's further observations that "the fundamental meaning of over-investment is failure to attain the ideal distribution of the community's income of consumable goods through time" (Robertson 1915, p. 180) and that "the temptations to over-investment may involve a general rupture between the sacrifice involved in postponing consumption and the future satisfaction procured by means of that sacrifice" (Robertson 1915, p. 200) strengthen that impression and more generally confirm the extent to which, at that early date, Robertson emphasized failure of the inter-temporal allocative mechanism as a key characteristic of the cycle.

The Monetary Element in Robertson's Analysis

Robertson's *A Study of Industrial Fluctuation* (1915) had much in common with later Austrian analysis, but there was one crucial difference between the two, namely, that Robertson did not at that time attribute, as the Austrians would later, the co-ordination failure which he diagnosed to the operations of the monetary system. In part, his neglect of that possibility may have reflected

---

[19] Thus there is a relationship between Robertson's cycle theory and modern research on "real business cycles" stemming from the work of Kydland and Prescott (1982). Charles Goodhart (1992) has discussed this matter.

nothing more than that at that stage of his career his mastery of monetary economics was anything but complete. Pigou's *Wealth and Welfare* (1912), a book which discussed the Marshallian analysis of the distorting effects of inflation on the real interest rate, was, by Robertson's own account (1949), "in my hands" when *A Study of Industrial Fluctuation* was being written; and that analysis could have provided him the means to integrate a discussion of monetary phenomena into his account of the disruption of the inter-temporal allocative mechanism that underlay the cycle. It is quite evident, however, that Robertson had not fully digested *Wealth and Welfare*, because in 1915 he still associated the monetary element in cycle theory with the hypothesis that monetary impulses were the primary (even the sole) cause of fluctuations.[20] Towards the end of his book, he noted, with evident satisfaction, that

> the fact that our long, complicated, and perhaps not unfruitful discussion has been conducted so far almost entirely without reference to specifically monetary phenomena relieves us of the necessity of a formal refutation of those who, like Clement Juglar and Mr. Hawtrey, find in monetary influences the sole and sufficient explanation of industrial fluctuation. (Robertson 1915, p. 211)

But there was perhaps a little more than youthful ignorance at work there. By the late 1920s Robertson had become an outstandingly accomplished monetary economist, and as the very title of his monograph *Banking Policy and the Price Level* (1926) indicates, he had moved much closer to the mainstream of the Marshallian tradition in according monetary factors an important role in cycle theory.[21] At the same time, however, his work continued to reveal considerable scepticism about the capacity of market mechanisms to co-ordinate inter-temporal choices in the absence of appropriate policy intervention. On that point he was evidently in complete accord with Lavington and Pigou, with their emphasis on the ubiquity of error in saving and investment decisions, but, just as evidently, he was a long way from his Austrian contemporaries.

Banking Policy and the Price Level was surely one of the most difficult books in the whole inter-war literature on business cycles. Its purpose was to

---

[20] Note that Hicks (1966, pp. 14–15) commented on the relative weakness of Robertson's grasp of monetary economics in the early 1920s, as well as the speed with which it strengthened during that decade.

[21] It is well known that Keynes had a strong influence on the writing of that book. Indeed, Presley (1978, ch. 3) went so far as to argue that Robertson's *Banking Policy and the Price Level* and his *Money*, along with Keynes's *Tract on Monetary Reform* (1923) and *Treatise on Money* (1930a), should all be regarded as having resulted from collaborative effort between their respective authors. See also Bridel (1987, ch. 6) for further discussion of Keynes's role in the writing of *Banking Policy*.

describe the outcome of Robertson's attempts to extend the analysis of *A Study of Industrial Fluctuation* to encompass monetary phenomena,

> to interweave with the mainly "non-monetary" argument of that work a discussion of the relation between saving, credit-creation and capital-growth ... a subject of whose difficulty I had become acutely aware in attempting to give an elementary account of the nature of banking in my book *Money* (1922). (Robertson 1949, p. vii)

Many of the difficulties with that book stemmed from the idiosyncratic vocabulary that Robertson used, which must have made it impenetrable to many readers, not least, and perhaps significantly, readers like Hayek, whose first language was not English. Fortunately, however, the essential ideas which it developed were also presented by Robertson, using a more conventional vocabulary, in the third edition of his widely read primer *Money* (1928a) and in a lecture subsequently published in *Economica* (1928b).[22] That fact, not to mention Pigou's incorporation of substantial parts of Robertson's analysis into his own *Industrial Fluctuations* (1927a), ensured that Robertson's ideas would quickly come to occupy an important position in the English-language literature on the cycle, even if the impenetrability of *Banking Policy and the Price Level* probably ensured that the readership of that book would remain rather narrow.

As Robertson told his readers in regard to four of the six substantive chapters of *Banking Policy and the Price Level*, "II, III, IV, and VII are in large part a restatement and development of part of the analytic framework of *[A] Study of Industrial Fluctuation*" (Robertson 1926, p. 5). The restatement, though, was highly condensed, and, significantly, it followed a different order. The major original theme of the earlier work, that the very process of economic development was likely to lead to "Appropriate Fluctuations of Output," was restated at the outset (in Chapter II, which bore that phrase as its title), but an account of "The Wage and Money Systems" (Chapter III) *preceded* Robertson's discussion of "Inappropriate Fluctuations in Output" (Chapter IV). As in *A Study of Industrial Fluctuation* (1915), he invoked conventional Marshallian wisdom about the tendency of money wages to lag behind prices and hence to induce counter-cyclical changes in real wages, as well as the tendency of "these changes [to] exert the same influence on the output policy of the employer as though they were ... changes in real cost" (Robertson 1926, p. 21); but also, and again as in *A Study of Industrial*

---

[22] The 1928 third edition of *Money* is sometimes referred to as the second edition, for the actual second edition was merely a reprint of the first. It is worth noting that though he may have collaborated in its writing, Keynes had considerable misgivings about *Banking Policy*, referring to it at one stage in its development, in a letter to his wife, as "Dennis's egg." See Hill and Keynes (1989, p. 327).

Fluctuation, he expressed very un-Marshallian doubts, which continued to mark his work well into the 1930s, about the universal desirability of stabilizing prices, and with them the cycle:

> I do not feel confident that a policy which, in the pursuit of stability of prices, output and employment, had nipped in the bud the English railway boom of the forties, or the American railway boom of 1869–71, or the German electrical boom of the nineties, would have been on the balance beneficial to the populations concerned. (Robertson 1926, p. 22)

Even so, monetary matters took on greater significance from having been being dealt with earlier in *Banking Policy and the Price Level* than they had been in *Industrial Fluctuation*. It is clear that by 1926, Robertson had come to think that the workings of the monetary system had a great deal to do with what he took to be an unarguable fact, namely, that "*actual* fluctuations in industrial output tend greatly to exceed the rational or appropriate fluctuations hitherto examined" (Robertson 1926, p. 34, italics in original), and that it therefore had a key role to play in the conduct of policy towards the cycle too:

> The aim of monetary policy should surely be not to prevent all fluctuations in the general price-level, but to permit those which are necessary to the establishment of appropriate alterations in output and to repress those which tend to carry the alterations in output beyond the appropriate point. The importance of this distinction will become still plainer when we come to examine more closely the *time*-element in production and the nature of a modern monetary system. To that task we must now turn. (Robertson 1926, p. 39, italics in original)

Forced Saving Again

The two chapters (Chapter V, "The Kinds of Saving," and Chapter VI, "Short Lacking and the Trade Cycle") which immediately followed the remark just quoted had no counterpart in *Industrial Fluctuation*, and it is worth noting that Robertson, who at that stage of his career worked closely with Keynes, remarked of them that "neither of us [himself and Keynes] now knows how much of the ideas therein contained is his and how much is mine" (Robertson 1926, p. 5). They developed an analysis of forced saving which, as we have already noted, quickly found its way into Pigou's writing and which, as we shall now see, anticipated, and in some respects went beyond, many of the theoretical results later to be found in Hayek's *Prices and Production*.[23] They did so using the idiosyncratic vocabulary noted ear-

---

[23] The fact that *Prices and Production* did not appear until 1931 does not, of course, alter the fact that Mises and Hayek had developed Austrian cycle theory during the 1920s, quite independently of Robertson's work.

lier (*lacking* was used to denote saving, *spontaneous and automatic lacking* were used to denote voluntary and forced saving, *real hoarding* was used to denote the quantity of real balances demanded, etc.), and it was fortunate that Robertson (1928a, 1928b) would soon set out his basic results in more accessible terms.

Robertson began from the institutional fact, relevant to the Britain of his day – less so for the United States, where, as Robertson was well aware (1928b, p. 41), consumer credit was already important – that the deposit liabilities of commercial banks represented the liability side of a balance sheet which displayed as its principal asset short-term commercial loans.[24] Hence the banking system had the task of co-ordinating the short-term saving of the public, *short lacking* as he called it, with firms' demand for working capital. But that system also created, as a by-product of its lending, deposits that functioned as means of exchange – *chequeries* in the colourful language of *Money* (1928a). By making loans and placing newly created money in the hands of firms, the banking system enabled them to carry through their investment plans with resources bid away from the production of consumption goods. In those circumstances, "the 'saving' which [the public] do is done under duress; and unlike ordinary saving it gives rise to no new fund of value in their possession which they can draw upon if they feel inclined to be extravagant at some future date" (Robertson 1928a, pp. 91–92).

Evidently Robertson's conception of the mechanics of forced saving was similar to that of the Austrians; and so was his understanding that forced saving could be imposed not only by inflation but also by the money creation necessary to hold prices stable in a growing economy, such as the United States of that day. There, he remarked, "in so far as the Federal System [*sic*] has not gone all out for stabilising the price of *labour*, it can not, I think, be wholly absolved from the charge of having burgled from the public in these years of rapidly advancing productivity" (Robertson 1928a, p. 144, italics in original). Though Robertson did not then proceed to forecast an inevitable American crisis, as the Austrians would do (cf. Robbins 1931, p. xii), he was clearly uneasy: "if that great country *should* ever become even temporarily saturated with fifty-storey buildings and motor cars, can we be certain that

---

[24] The fact that the distinction between long-term and short-term investments played an important role in Robertson's analysis, but was less central to Austrian cycle theory, presumably reflects the fact that the institutional framework lying in the background of the latter was German-style universal banking. Note also that the possibility of directing bank lending towards consumers as a means of offsetting forced saving was raised by Piero Sraffa in his 1932 review of *Prices and Production*, and Robertson, too, was aware of the possibilities there: "There is one more expedient at the disposal of banks – an expedient, to the Victorian mind, of an even more dubious kind. When you have pumped into the producer all the money he can absorb, you can try it on the consumer as well" (Robertson 1928a, p. 178).

any purely monetary policy would meet the needs of the situation?'' (Robertson 1928b, p. 41, italics in original).

Induced and Abortive Lacking

Even so, Robertson did not believe that forced saving was always dangerous. Like Lindahl and Ohlin a few years later, he found it possible to conceive of an equilibrating mechanism that would transform initially involuntary saving into a benign voluntary activity, though the specific mechanism he focused on was different from theirs: where the Swedes would look to induced changes in the income distribution to restore order to the inter-temporal allocative process, Robertson turned to a mechanism he called *induced lacking* which utilized the Marshallian idea of a stock demand for money.[25] That mechanism, as he explicitly acknowledged, was suggested to him by Keynes. He described it as follows:

> Induced Lacking occurs when, the same process that imposes Automatic Lacking on certain people having also reduced the real value of their money stocks, these people hold money off the market, and refrain from consuming the full value of their current output, in order to bring the real value of their money stocks up again to what they regard as an appropriate level. Thus Induced Lacking differs from Automatic Lacking in being voluntary and designed; but it resembles it, and differs from Spontaneous Lacking, in being the direct result of an increase in the stream of money directed on to the market. (Robertson 1926, p. 49)

Robertson's exposition of induced lacking included a lengthy algebraic appendix (Robertson 1926, pp. 59–70) that surely was the prototype, albeit an extremely clumsy one, for many a subsequent Swedish model sequence. To put it in modern terms, he showed that the phenomenon involved the banking system levying an inflation tax on agents' money holdings and redistributing the proceeds to firms, and Robertson's use of the Marshallian notion of a stock demand for money permitted the forced-saving mechanism to be brought into Cambridge cycle theory, without at the same time import-

---

[25] Harry Johnson (1974, p. 142) suggested that the concept of ''forced saving'' in the 1920s and 1930s was equivalent to the modern notion of the ''inflation tax.'' That was not a bad characterization of Robertson's treatment of the topic in the special case of ''induced lacking,'' but as a general proposition it badly oversimplified the issues at stake in discussions of that topic, particularly as it arose in Hayek's work, to which Johnson also referred. As Presley (1986a) has stressed, what Patinkin (1957) would later call the ''real balance effect'' lay behind the ''induced lacking'' mechanism – strong evidence that the effect was more widely understood among neo-classical economists than Patinkin (1957) was originally inclined to grant.

ing any theoretical basis for the policy nihilism that would later mark Austrian analysis.[26]

In any event, as has already been stressed, Robertson had no more faith than did any other Cambridge economist in the capacity of market mechanisms to co-ordinate saving and investment decisions without help from monetary policy. On the contrary, he thought that deliberate imposition of forced saving by the banking system, properly used, might sometimes be a stabilizing factor:

> the fundamental feature of the upward swing of a trade cycle is a large and discontinuous increase in the demand for Short Lacking [working capital], occurring as the essential preliminary to an expansion of output "justified" for one or more . . . reasons . . . [T]he supply of Short Lacking is not sufficiently elastic to cope with such pronounced and discontinuous increases in demand, and . . . the responsibility for meeting them rests almost entirely upon the banking system. (Robertson 1926, pp. 71–72)

Hence, it was his opinion, always delicately put – in "Theories of Banking Policy" (1928b, p. 40) he called it "my own private heresy" – but rather frequently repeated, that "I am not sure that a little forced saving now and again may not be the necessary price we have to pay for what we call progress" (Robertson 1928a, p. 145).[27]

Robertson's scepticism about the reliability of market mechanisms also underlay his analysis of *abortive lacking*, or hoarding. That phenomenon involved an increase in the public's demand for real balances, which, when unmatched by an increase in the quantity of nominal money, would cause the price level to fall. Perhaps under the influence of Lavington, whom he cited in the course of his discussion of that topic (Robertson 1926, pp. 52–53), Robertson assumed that extra money was demanded as a store of value pure and simple, so that the desire to add to cash balances stemmed from a desire to command more future goods. He then noted that agents' attempts to save by adding to their cash balances would not automatically result in provision

---

[26] His exposition, however, did not take account of the fall in the demand for real balances that ongoing inflation might induce, and it is of some interest to note that Pigou (1926) did fill that gap in the course of a paper largely devoted to a sympathetic exposition of Robertson's analysis of forced saving. It should also be pointed out that that particular effect was discussed at considerable length by Keynes (1923). See Chapter 5; "The Inflation Tax." Keynes stopped just short of developing an analysis of the revenue-maximizing inflation rate. Note that Cannan (1921b) provided a rather full analysis of the effect of inflation expectations on the demand for money, as did, in 1923–24, a number of German-speaking economists. See Laidler and Stadler (1998). The effects of the inflation rate on the demand for money were, that is to say, quite widely understood in the 1920s, and Robertson's omission is therefore a little surprising.

[27] It is worth noting that Ralph Hawtrey, who, as I shall argue in Chapter 5, did not believe inter-temporal allocative problems to be important, explicitly criticized that argument of Robertson's. See Hawtrey (1926, pp. 432–433).

for the production of more future goods.[28] Specifically, if the nominal value
of bank deposits remained constant, and agents succeeded in obtaining extra
real balances through a fall in the price level,

> they have achieved this object without any of the usual inconveniences of
> saving – without being obliged to refrain from the consumption of any
> desirable goods and services. . . . The intended thrift of the public has all
> gone to waste, and failed to benefit trade and industry in any way.
>   Now suppose in these circumstances the bank adds to its loans in such
> wise that the increased demand of those to whom the new loans are made
> just balances the reduced demand of the thrift-smitten depositors, and so
> prevents the shopkeepers from lowering prices. If it acts in this way the
> bank will be acting not as an oppressor but as a benefactor; it will not be
> imposing unsought burdens on the public, but merely enabling their thrifty
> intentions to bear fruit. (Robertson 1928a, p. 95)

Robertson would later devote the first substantive section of his "evidence-
in-chief" to the Macmillan Committee (1931b), which was then inquiring
into the working of the British monetary system, to that particular analysis.
Pigou (1931, para. 6597–6601) also discussed it in his evidence to the same
committee, arguing, like Robertson, that an increase in the demand for money
as a store of value would likely be concentrated on deposit accounts (time
deposits) rather than current accounts (demand deposits). He therefore also
followed Robertson in suggesting that the ratio of deposit accounts to current
accounts might be used as a "sign-post" by the banking system in the
conduct of its lending, with a high ratio signalling the need for expansionary
policy, and vice versa. Keynes's analysis (1930a) of the demand for deposit
accounts and current accounts as stemming from the "industrial" and "financial" circulations, respectively, and of their cyclical behaviour, which will be
discussed in Chapter 6, was also related to Robertson's treatment of "abortive
lacking." The latter therefore represented a key step in the evolution of the
Marshall/Pigou/Lavington theory of the demand for money into what Keynes
would call liquidity-preference theory, which would, in due course, provide
the basis for the LM side of the IS-LM model.

Robertson and the Marshallian Tradition

Now it is clear that Robertson's contributions were highly original when
viewed in the context of English economics, though perhaps somewhat less

---

[28] Robertson's analysis of abortive lacking thus bore some resemblance to Keynes's celebrated
parable of the thrift campaign in the banana plantation (1930a, vol. I, pp. 158–160). The fact
that Robertson treated the desire to hold more money as stemming from a desire to hold more
command over future goods is evidence that there were strong elements of liquidity-
preference theory in his analysis of that phenomenon. Robertson (1933) discussed the relationship between his own and Keynes's (1930a) analysis.

so when contemporary German contributions (Ellis 1934, pt. IV) are taken into account. For example, their first (1915) version injected a brand-new element – the concept of "appropriate" fluctuations driven by invention – into the Marshallian tradition. It is true that in 1929 Pigou argued firmly that industrial fluctuations as actually experienced were "social evils, in the sense that, if they could be mitigated without cost, economic welfare would be increased" (Pigou 1929, p. 239), and he applied that conclusion even to cycles in activity arising from waves of inventions. It is, however, also true that Pigou nevertheless opposed measures "to check the progress of invention" as undesirable: "whatever benefit might be secured in this way through diminishing industrial fluctuations would almost certainly be outweighed by the permanent loss of that economic power which inventions produce" (Pigou 1929, p. 250). And he also regarded the exercise of control "over the times at which the new inventions are exploited" (Pigou 1929, p. 250) as impractical.

Evidently, then, the Marshallian tradition, to the extent that Pigou may be taken to represent it, had largely accommodated Robertson's views on these matters by the end of the 1920s, and we have already noted the alacrity with which his analyses of forced saving and related matters were absorbed by Pigou. Nor should the degree of Robertson's own acceptance of the positive analysis of Pigou and Lavington be underestimated. He remarked as follows in *Banking Policy and the Price Level*:

> My differences with the dominant schools of thought are therefore partly differences of analysis and partly differences of emphasis. But I am anxious not to overstate these differences, and I have tried at appropriate points of my argument to indicate, even though briefly, my appreciation of the importance of Error, and of the partial Remediability of Error by monetary manipulation. (Robertson 1926, p. 3)

And when it came to normative analysis, he was, as we shall now see, entirely at one with them when he affirmed that

> I believe firmly in a policy of "credit control" as contrasted with a policy of *laissez-faire* in monetary affairs; but I conjecture that for a long while to come credit-control may prove a more difficult matter than some of its more ardent advocates would lead one to suppose, and that it may have to be envisaged ultimately not as an independent panacea but as one ingredient in a much more arduous and comprehensive programme of Stabilization. (Robertson 1926, p. 4)

Stabilization Policy

Pigou regarded cyclical fluctuations in economic activity as a prime example of market failure, and he explicitly linked the case for stabilization policy in particular to the more general case that he had developed in his *Economics of Welfare* for government intervention in the face of externalities.[29] He characterized the view that market mechanisms alone would accomplish all that could be accomplished in the way of ironing out fluctuations as a

> rigid doctrine . . . merely a particular application of the more general doctrine of maximum satisfaction . . . now known, like that more general doctrine itself, to be subject to large qualifications. The heart of the matter is that industrial fluctuations involve evil consequences of such a kind that, if an individual takes certain sorts of action to remove or lessen them, the social gain resulting from his action will not enter at full value into his private profit. (Pigou 1929, p. 247)

And he succinctly summarized their most socially destructive characteristics as follows:

> They involve fluctuations in the earnings and consumption of wage-earners as a body, and, in particular of the less fortunate among them. . . . [a]nd irregularity of employment and the lasting injury to which this often leads. . . . They also lead indirectly to a reduction in the aggregate of real income as against what would have been produced had industry been stable. (Pigou 1929, p. xiv)

It is hardly surprising, then, that very nearly half of Pigou's *Industrial Fluctuations* was devoted to discussing "remedies" for those fluctuations. As one would expect, prominent among the stabilization devices that he canvassed was the possibility of adopting "various devices for preventing errors – the official collection and publication of statistics and so on" (Pigou 1929, p. 250), noting that the cost-effectiveness of such measures would depend upon whether or not "successful attacks have . . . been made against the companion causes of disturbance, harvest variations and monetary instability" (Pigou 1929, p. 250).[30]

Pigou in fact discussed non-monetary factors in the cycle, such as harvest failures, only briefly, as a prelude to a far more elaborate treatment of monetary-policy issues. He argued for a long-run policy stance that would eliminate "forced levies and anti-levies" as secular phenomena, one that therefore would imply "a price level which is not stable but trends downward in a proportion inverse to that in which real income per head increases" (Pigou 1929, p. 254), and he explicitly cited Robertson's *Banking Policy and*

---

[29] There is strong evidence here that the so-called classical view of a smoothly functioning market economy was largely a figment of the imaginations of textbook writers after World War II. Keynes's Cambridge predecessors and colleagues were very much of an interventionist mind-set.

[30] Pigou's reference to the "collection and publication of statistics" probably reflected the influence of his American contemporaries, particularly Mitchell, to whose work he did, from time to time, refer, as did Lavington. On American discussions of those issues, see Chapter 8, "Stabilization Policies."

the Price Level as well as the 1928 edition of *Money* in support of that position. On that matter, then, Pigou and Robertson were in agreement with the Austrians, but on no other. Difficult though they thought it would be to arrange, the Austrians believed that avoidance of disturbances originating in the monetary system would be sufficient to ensure stability in the real economy. The Cambridge economists, however, lacked faith in the allocative efficiency of market mechanisms, so that against a background of secularly falling prices, they found ample scope for active counter-cyclical monetary policy. Pigou, who quoted extensively from Marshall on that point, also advocated indexation of long-term loan contracts (Pigou 1929, pt. 2, ch. IV).

Monetary Policy and Its Limitations

Referring to counter-cyclical monetary policy, Pigou pointed out that ''there are two forms of brake and stimulant available to the banking system, the method of rationing and the method of discount control, coupled, if necessary with open market operations'' (Pigou 1929, p. 265). Lavington had briefly discussed the use of credit rationing as a means of implementing monetary policy, without quite ruling it out (1922, pp. 108–109), but Pigou rejected it as essentially unworkable in Britain, and the bulk of his discussion of counter-cyclical monetary policy concentrated instead on the discount rate. That discussion was noteworthy in three ways. First, Pigou was careful to distinguish between traditional discount-rate policy, in the spirit of Walter Bagehot (1873), which had been aimed at defending the country's gold reserves, and what he called a ''stabilising discount policy'' designed to mitigate cyclical fluctuations. Second, and unusually for the 1920s, he paid some attention to problems posed by lags in the effect of policy: ''a small change applied in good time may well prove a stronger stabiliser than a large change applied later on when the forces tending to push prices up or down have gathered way'' (Pigou 1929, p. 285). Finally, Pigou discussed in considerable detail the compatibility of counter-cyclical monetary policy with the underlying monetary order, noting that

> if a stabilising discount policy is adopted in a whole hearted manner, the logical sequel as regards currency is neither the gold standard plan nor a plan on the Fisher [compensated dollar] model. It is a paper currency, the volume of which is not regulated by law, but is free to vary in response to whatever changes in the demand for it the stabilising discount policy allows. (Pigou 1929, p. 296)

That was very much in accord with views that we nowadays associate with Keynes from the early 1920s onwards. It is important to note, therefore, that Pigou was quick to add a qualification: ''This assumes, however, that the stabilising discount policy will in fact be loyally adhered to and that safeguards against human frailty are not required'' (Pigou 1929, p. 296). Thus, at the end of the day, though he was just as aware as Keynes of the potential for conflict between domestic stabilization goals and adherence to a gold standard, Pigou refused to come down on one side or the other of this issue.[31]

> Economic analysis can provide data for statesmen; but the attitude of public opinion and the current political and diplomatic situation are dominant factors in determining what, on the whole, it is best to do; and these lie beyond our range. (Pigou 1929, p. 305)

Pigou had been a member of the Cunliffe Committee, which in 1918 had urged Britain's speedy return to the gold standard at the 1914 parity, but in taking an agnostic position on such questions in 1929, he was well in the Cambridge mainstream. Robertson, for example, who in the first (1922) edition of *Money* had expressed his trepidation about what might happen if Britain did return to the gold standard at the 1914 parity, was nevertheless unwilling to advocate its abandonment in the third edition (1928a) of that book. Keynes, too, whatever his reputation might be nowadays, was ambiguous in his position on the gold standard over that same period. He criticized its restoration after the event, in ``The Economic Consequences of Mr. Churchill'' (1925); but he nevertheless treated the gold standard as a constraint on policy, rather than an obstacle to be removed, as late as 1931.[32]

Be that as it may, in Pigou's and Robertson's eyes, more than the gold standard stood in the way of achieving stabilization of the cycle by monetary measures. There was also the matter of their inherent unreliability in bringing about economic expansion. Pigou stressed that monetary policy, whether implemented by way of credit rationing or by use of the discount rate and open-market operations, would more likely be effective in slowing a boom than in promoting recovery from a slump:

> With regard to upward adjustments, however, both weapons are somewhat blunted, . . . in times of depression on neither plan can borrowing be expanded beyond a point. People do not want to borrow on any terms, and the banks cannot force them to do so. (Pigou 1929, p. 267)

Robertson, too, expressed the opinion that ``it is . . . unlikely that the monetary system will ever be able to cope unaided with a trade slump . . . as efficiently as with a trade boom'' (Robertson 1928a, p. 178).[33] Like Pigou,

---

[31] Note that the theme of conflict between the domestic goals of monetary policy and adherence to the rules of the gold standard was an old one in Cambridge economics. It long antedated World War I, having been broached by Marshall as early as 1887. See Laidler (1991, ch. 6) for a discussion of this and a number of related policy issues as they occurred in the literature before World War I.

[32] For a penetrating discussion of Keynes's shifting views on the gold standard, both before and after its 1925 restoration, see Barkai (1993). See also Chapters 6 and 7.

[33] That opinion was also widely held in the United States at that time among such commentators as Douglas and Director (1931) and Charles Hardy (1932) whose views will be discussed at greater length in Chapters 8 and 9.

however, he took comfort from the conventional wisdom of the period that if monetary policy could be used to moderate an upswing, that in itself would help reduce the severity of the subsequent contraction, though he also believed, again like Pigou, that dealing with a trade slump was "likely to require the assistance of a more powerful ally – the Government of the country itself" (Robertson 1928a, p. 178).

Public-Works Expenditures

What the government of the country could and should do by way of assistance, in the view of Pigou and Robertson, was implement a program of counter-cyclical public-works expenditures. In the late 1920s such proposals were already well established in the Cambridge tradition. Herbert Foxwell, Pigou's unsuccessful rival as successor to Marshall, had advocated such measures as early as 1882, and Lavington (1922, pp. 109–110) had also referred approvingly, albeit briefly, to such schemes. In *Wealth and Welfare* (1912) Pigou himself had argued their likely effectiveness, quoting with approval the *Report of the Royal Commissioners on the Poor Law*:[34]

> "This point has been well put by Professor Chapman, who suggests that, so far as the public authorities' demand for labour fluctuates, it is desirable to liberate such demand from the influences of good and bad trade and seasonality, and then deliberately to attempt to make it vary inversely with demand in the open market." (Pigou 1912, p. 481)

The section of *Wealth and Welfare* that includes the foregoing quotation was incorporated verbatim into *Industrial Fluctuations* (Pigou 1929, pp. 330ff.). And in the third edition of *Money*, Robertson argued as follows:

> What, after all, can be more sensible than that the Central Government should organise a collective demand for telephone equipment, or the local governments a collective demand for municipal lavatories, to take the place of an individual demand for ships or steel rails which has rightly and reasonably fallen temporarily away? If the public's desire to save is increasing so fast, or the processes of manufacture and salesmanship are being speeded up so rapidly, that private industry is left bothered and bewildered as to how to harness the productive forces thus released, what can be more sensible that [*sic*] the Government, using the monetary system as its handmaid, should intervene to turn them to good account, instead of allowing

---

[34] Perhaps I should note explicitly, lest I once again attract the wrath of Robert Dimand (1993b), that I am aware that various authorities have been recommending public-works expenditures at least since the days of Pericles. It is, however, important to an understanding of the evolution of twentieth-century economic thought to realize that their advocacy was widespread among mainstream economists from the late nineteenth century onwards and that it was in no way a product of the Keynesian revolution, as so much popular discussion would still have it.

them to leak away in the form of unlooked-for windfalls to some and undeserved ruin to others? (Robertson 1928a, pp. 178–179)

It should be noted that Robertson nevertheless took some notice of the implications of his own essentially Austrian view of the upper turning-point of the cycle for the design of such policies. Specifically, he warned readers of *Banking Policy and the Price Level* that "there is a limit to the extent to which it is wise to promote artificial revival in the constructional trades" (Robertson 1926, p. 95). However, not too much should be made of that, for Robertson's evidence to the Macmillan Committee showed that he meant no more than that there were reasons to be cautious about specific projects in specific circumstances. He told that committee that "anybody ought to have been able to see in 1920 that the world was so clogged with ships . . . that it would not . . . be a good or sensible use of the Trade Facilities Act to invoke it for the production of new ships" (Robertson 1931b, para. 11), and under questioning by the trade-union leader Ernest Bevin, he characterized that example as "an instance of the fact that an attempt to encourage capital construction, which I advocate, must be used with discretion" (Robertson 1931b, para. 4842).[35]

Concluding Comment

It is evident that in the late 1920s, Pigou and Robertson were exponents of an approach to business-cycle theory and of a view of counter-cyclical policy that in certain important respects resembled later Swedish analysis. In their emphasis on the role of expectations in driving investment decisions, in their scepticism about the efficiency of market mechanisms when it came to co-ordinating inter-temporal allocations of resources, and in their understanding that there might exist mechanisms which could transform forced saving into an equilibrium phenomenon the two groups had much in common, as they did also in their pragmatic attitude towards monetary policy and fiscal policy. And Robertson had also constructed a primitive but explicit model sequence, as the Swedes would later term it, in the course of analysing forced saving in *Banking Policy and the Price Level*. Ohlin was thus clearly correct when in 1932 he placed Swedish cycle theory in what he called the "Anglo-Saxon" tradition. But it will be recalled that Ohlin explicitly mentioned three contributors to that tradition – Hawtrey, Keynes, and Robertson. So far we have said nothing about Hawtrey, and we have mentioned Keynes only in passing. The following chapter will be largely devoted to their work on those issues during the 1920s.

---

[35] Bevin was, even at that time, a prominent figure in the Labour Party, and his distinguished political career culminated in his holding the office of foreign secretary in the post–World War II Attlee government.

CHAPTER 5

The Monetary Element in the Cambridge Tradition

The Monetary System and the Cycle

In the cycle theories of Pigou, Lavington, and Robertson, the monetary system provided an important channel through which essentially non-monetary impulses were both propagated and amplified. The system's workings were also seen as enabling the central bank to exert a significant, though by no means all-powerful, stabilizing influence on the economy. Even so, it would be inappropriate to label those economists as exponents of a purely monetary theory of the cycle in any usual sense of that phrase. For them, though the monetary element in the propagation of cyclical impulses was important, it fell far short of being all-important. The Cambridge tradition as it developed in the 1920s nevertheless included economists who treated monetary factors as far more central to macroeconomic issues, John Maynard Keynes and Ralph Hawtrey in particular.[1] In this chapter I shall deal first of all with Keynes's application of Marshallian monetary theory to post-war problems in his *Tract on Monetary Reform* (1923), paying particular attention to the rather fragmentary treatment of cyclical issues encountered during the course of its exposition, and I shall then turn to Hawtrey's much more fully developed analysis.

---

[1] Keynes's credentials as an intellectual heir of Marshall are impeccable and too well known to require any elaboration here. Suffice it to note that his father was a long-standing colleague and personal friend of Marshall, that Keynes himself was, from his childhood onwards, a frequent and welcome visitor to the Marshall home, and that he maintained close academic ties with Cambridge throughout the inter-war years. Moreover, his *Economic Consequences of the Peace* (1919) established him as a public figure, a position which he continued to occupy for the rest of his life. Though educated at Cambridge, Hawtrey's subject was (as with Keynes) mathematics, and such little training in economics as he received at that university came in the main from the economic historian Sir John Clapham, rather than from Marshall or any of his circle. Moreover, he made his career as a civil servant attached to the Treasury, where he learned much from Sir John Bradbury (Howson 1985). He held only one academic appointment during his lifetime, for one year at Harvard in 1928–29. Obviously, then, Hawtrey's direct claim to membership in any "Cambridge school" of economics is weaker than that of anyone else whose work is discussed in this and the preceding chapter; but, as we shall see, the components out of which Hawtrey constructed his monetary theory of the cycle were undoubtedly of Marshallian origin. See also Laidler (1991, pp. 100ff.).

Keynes as a Quantity Theorist: *A Tract on Monetary Reform*

In the early 1920s Keynes was a thoroughgoing exponent of the Marshallian version of the quantity theory of money, but he was already sensitive to problems of inter-temporal resource allocation and the importance of saving and investment being co-ordinated with one another if a market economy was to function smoothly. Even so, it is evident from his *Tract on Monetary Reform* (1923) that he was aware of no tension between those two elements of his economic thought. On the contrary, he regarded the quantity theory of money as an adequate guide to the policy problems raised by the co-ordination question, believing as he did, and, of course, as had Marshall, that cyclical fluctuations would essentially vanish if only the monetary system could generate price-level stability. Keynes expressed his views on those matters in the following terms in the opening sentences of the book's Preface:

> We leave saving to the private investor, and we encourage him to place his savings mainly in titles to money. We leave the responsibility for setting production in motion to the business man, who is mainly influenced by the profits which he expects to accrue to himself in terms of money. Those who are not in favour of drastic changes in the existing organisation of society believe that these arrangements, being in accord with human nature, have great advantages. But they cannot work properly if the money, which they assume as a stable measuring-rod, is undependable. Unemployment, the precarious life of the worker, the disappointment of expectation, the sudden loss of savings, the excessive windfalls to individuals, the speculator, the profiteer – all proceed, in large measure, from the instability of the standard of value. (Keynes 1923, p. xiv)

The *Tract on Monetary Reform* is not a scholarly monograph on economic theory. Rather, it is what its title says it is: a book about the immediately pressing monetary problems which in the early 1920s faced those countries which had been linked by the gold standard before 1914, and Britain in particular. Its overall theme is that between the goals of domestic price stability, on the one hand, and exchange-rate stability, on the other, domestic price stability should be given pride of place. In taking that position, its message ran somewhat counter to contemporary mainstream opinion, as embodied, for example, in the so-called Genoa Resolutions of 1922, in whose drafting Hawtrey, in his capacity as a representative of the British Treasury at the Genoa conference, played a major part.[2] Those resolutions called for a

---

[2] It should be noted that Keynes covered the Genoa Conference on behalf of the *Manchester Guardian*. See Skidelsky (1992, pp. 106–111). See Howson (1985) and Deutscher (1990, pp. 39–42) for more detailed discussions of Hawtrey's views on the gold standard. Howson noted his reluctance to change his views, even in the 1930s, and suggested that the decline in his influence during that decade owed something to that.

restoration of the gold standard in the international economy, coupled with co-ordination of domestic policies among individual countries to ensure that balance-of-payments constraints would not inhibit the restoration of domestic stability.

Those proposals went too far in the direction of exchange-rate fixity for Keynes:

> I doubt the wisdom of attempting a "managed" gold standard jointly with the United States, on the lines recommended by Mr. Hawtrey, because it retains too many of the disadvantages of the old system without its advantages, and because it would make us too dependent on the policy and on the wishes of the Federal Reserve Board. (Keynes 1923, p. 140)

Instead, Keynes envisaged a world divided into two fixed-exchange-rate blocks, one based on sterling and the other on the dollar. He was willing to countenance exchange-rate movement between the two blocks if that was necessary to reconcile the balance-of-payments effects of divergent domestic policies, although he did concede that "so long as the Federal Reserve Board was successful in keeping dollar prices steady the objective of keeping sterling prices steady would be identical with the objective of keeping the dollar–sterling exchange steady" (Keynes 1923, p. 147).

Be that as it may, though its main purpose was to set out a blueprint for post-war domestic and international monetary arrangements, the *Tract* had considerable theoretical content. For example, and not surprisingly given the policy issues it addressed, it provided a masterly account of the purchasing-power-parity doctrine and all the limitations to which it is subject, but to discuss that would take us beyond the scope of this book.[3] Its treatment of the influence of price-level movements on the level and distribution of income and its discussion of inflation considered as a tax on cash balances are also noteworthy, however, and those matters do require our attention here.

Price Stability as a Policy Goal

In the *Tract*, Keynes was, as I have noted, an advocate of price-level stability as the goal of monetary policy. As he argued, "inflation and deflation alike [have effects] in altering the *distribution* of wealth between different classes, inflation in this respect being the worse of the two. Each has also an effect in overstimulating or retarding the *production* of wealth, though here deflation is the more injurious" (Keynes 1923, p. 3, italics in original).

---

[3] See Keynes (1923, pp. 70–86). The leading exponent of the purchasing-power-parity doctrine in the second and third decades of this century was, of course, Gustav Cassel. See, for example, Cassel (1922). For a comprehensive survey of the development of international monetary economics in the period 1870–1960, see June Flanders (1989).

Like any good Marshallian, he drew "an instructive distinction between what are termed the 'money' rate of interest and the 'real' rate of interest'' (Keynes 1923, p. 19), and he recognized that "in so far as a rise of prices is foreseen, attempts to get advantage from this by increased borrowing force the money rates of interest to move upwards" (Keynes 1923, p. 20).[4] However, he did not then proceed to argue that in conditions of what we would now term a *fully anticipated* inflation or deflation, money would be *super-neutral*. Rather, he noted that

> it is not the *fact* of a given rise of prices, but the *expectation* of a rise compounded of the various possible price movements and the estimated probability of each, which affects money rates; and in countries where the currency has not collapsed completely, there has seldom or never existed a sufficient general confidence in a further rise or fall of prices to cause the short-money rate of interest to rise above 10 per cent per annum, or to fall below 1 per cent. A fluctuation of this order is not sufficient to balance a movement of prices, up or down, of more than (say) 5 per cent per annum – a rate which the actual price movement has frequently exceeded. (Keynes 1923, p. 20, italics in original)

For Keynes, then, inflation at moderate rates was unlikely to be fully anticipated, as we would now use the phrase.[5] It therefore "redistributes wealth in a manner very injurious to the investor, very beneficial to the business man, and probably, in modern industrial conditions, beneficial on the whole to the earner" (Keynes 1923, p. 29); and it also seemed to him to carry with it the risk that the savings incentives, on whose maintenance sustained capital accumulation ultimately depended, would be undermined. Keynes nevertheless viewed deflation as even more injurious, and once again he based his analysis on the presumption that it would not usually be fully anticipated. What he had to say on that issue is worth some attention. As we shall see in Chapter 8, the themes he raised also occurred in the American literature of the 1920s, with a particular, albeit aberrant, variation on them being central to the William Trufant Foster and Waddill Catchings version of underconsumptionism.

Keynes stressed that under what he called "modern methods of production" (Keynes 1923, p. 32), there would inevitably be a significant time lag

---

[4] That distinction is usually known as the "Fisher effect," after Irving Fisher, who first deployed it in 1896. However, the point in question had made sporadic appearances in the literature since the late eighteenth century, and it was Marshall (1887, 1890) who introduced it into the neo-classical literature. Fisher acknowledged those anticipations of his analysis. On this, see Laidler (1991, p. 44, fn. 10, and pp. 90–95).

[5] As the foregoing quotation demonstrates, Keynes's unwillingness to rely on a full Fisher effect stemmed not from any intellectual carelessness, but from a rather sophisticated (by contemporary standards) understanding of the way in which the calculus of probabilities might be used in modelling expectations – this is hardly surprising from the author of *A Treatise on Probability*.

between the incurring of production costs, on the one hand, and the realization of sales revenues, on the other. That lag had become more important with the passage of time, both because of the growing importance of international trade "involving great distances between the place of original production and the place of final consumption" (Keynes 1923, p. 32) and because of "the increased complication of the technical processes of manufacture" (Keynes 1923, p. 32). As a result, and over and above the risks arising from fluctuations in relative prices,

> during the lengthy process of production the business world is incurring outgoings in terms of *money* . . . in the expectation of recouping this outlay by disposing of the product for *money* at a later date . . . [and] . . . must always be in a position where it stands to gain by a rise of price and to lose by a fall of price. (Keynes 1923, p. 33, italics in original)

The upshot was that because "the *fact* of falling prices injures entrepreneurs . . . the *fear* of falling prices causes them to protect themselves by curtailing their operations" (Keynes 1923, p. 34, italics in original). Deflation, for Keynes, thus involved relatively depressed levels of output and higher rates of unemployment.[6]

If forced to choose between inflation and deflation, Keynes was clear that he would opt for inflation, "because it is worse, in an impoverished world, to provoke unemployment than to disappoint the *rentier*" (Keynes 1923, p. 36, italics in original), but he did not think that such a choice inevitably had to be faced. There was a third, and far preferable, policy option, namely, price-level stability, whose achievement would permit market mechanisms to co-ordinate saving and investment and enable the economy to function smoothly:

> The individualistic capitalism of today, precisely because it entrusts saving to the individual investor and production to the individual employer, *presumes* a stable measuring-rod of value, and cannot be efficient – perhaps cannot survive – without one. (Keynes 1923, p. 36, italics in original)

The right policy framework would not leave price-level behaviour to the vagaries of gold production and the like. Rather, it would allow "the regulation of the standard of value to be the subject of *deliberate decision*" (Keynes

---

[6] This analysis of Keynes is, as noted earlier, rather close to that of the American underconsumptionists Foster and Catchings (e.g., 1925). Keynes relied on the depressing effects of expectations about a future fall of prices in general, while in the underconsumptionist model it was expectations about the prices of consumer goods that mattered. The point is important for policy, because Keynes's quantity-theory-based analysis led only to the implication that the price level should be stabilized, whereas for Foster and Catchings and their followers the important thing was to put more purchasing power into the hands of households than their wage income alone would generate. See Chapter 8, "Underconsumptionism in America," and Chapter 9, "Paul Douglas and Underconsumptionism," for further discussion.

1923, p. 36, italics in original), so that "there shall never exist any confident expectation either that prices generally are going to fall or that they are going to rise" (Keynes 1923, p. 35).

> Even if such a policy were not wholly successful, either in counteracting expectations or in avoiding actual movements, it would be an improvement on the policy of sitting quietly by, whilst a standard of value, governed by chance causes and deliberately removed from central control, produces expectations which paralyse or intoxicate the government of production. (Keynes 1923, p. 35)

The Inflation Tax

It should be recalled that inflation was a very visible feature of the world of 1923, not least, but by no means solely, in the Weimar Republic. Keynes paid considerable attention to the phenomenon in the *Tract*, placing it firmly in the context of fiscal policy. His analysis of "inflation as a method of taxation," in Chapter 2 of that work, stops just short of developing the concept of a revenue-maximizing inflation rate based on the idea of expected inflation as the opportunity cost of holding real balances. Here we once again see the influence of the Marshallian approach to analysing the stock demand for money:[7]

> ... a government can get resources by a *continuous* practice of inflation, even when this is foreseen by the public generally. ... A government has to remember, however, that even if a tax is not prohibitive it may be unprofitable, and that a medium, rather than an extreme, imposition will yield the greatest gain. (Keynes 1923, p. 43, italics in original)

Even more fundamentally, Keynes invited the reader to consider inflation as one tool available to any state intent on preserving and promoting a liberal society in the wake of a war that had been financed by the accumulation of ruinous public debts. Noting that "there is a second way in which inflation helps a government to make both ends meet, namely by reducing the burden of its pre-existing liabilities in so far as they have been fixed in terms of money" (Keynes 1923, p. 53), Keynes presented it as one option available to a heavily indebted government, far inferior to the capital levy which he preferred, but perhaps superior to meeting the liabilities in question from the usual tax system.

---

[7] It should be noted that, as Laidler and Stadler (1998) have shown, in the contemporary German-language literature on the hyper-inflation, the Marshallian notion of a stock demand for money was also deployed, and inflation was treated as a cost of holding money, notably by L. Albert Hahn (1924b) and von Mises (1924). That Marshallian approach perhaps entered German-language monetary economics by way of Wicksell's analysis (1898, pp. 52ff.) of the "pure cash economy." On this issue, see Laidler (1991, pp. 125–127).

Nor can the fact that in time of war it is easier for the State to borrow than to tax, be allowed permanently to enslave the taxpayer to the bondholder. Those who insist that in these matters the State is in exactly the same position as the individual will, if they have their way, render impossible the continuance of an individualist society, which depends for its existence on moderation. (Keynes, 1923, p. 56)

Evidently Keynes's distaste for the bondholder, or, to use another word, the *rentier*, which so famously marks the *General Theory*, was already on display in 1923; more significantly, perhaps, so too was his view that economic policy had an important part to play in preserving a liberal political order.

The Cycle in the Tract

The case for discretionary monetary policy which Keynes made in the *Tract* was very much concerned with specific problems faced by the world in general and Britain in particular during the early 1920s, but a number of brief references to more general questions of counter-cyclical monetary policy were scattered through its exposition. Writing the Cambridge version of the quantity theory in the form

$$n = p(k + rk') \tag{5.1}$$

where n is the nominal stock of currency, p is the price level, k and k' are the public's demand for real balances of currency and deposits, and r is the banking system's reserve ratio, he expressed the view that "cyclical fluctuations are characterised, not primarily by changes in n or r, but by changes in k and k'" (Keynes 1923, p. 69), and he argued that

the business of stabilising the price level, not merely over long periods but so as also to avoid cyclical fluctuations, consists partly in exercising a stabilising influence over k and k', and, in so far as this fails or is impracticable, in deliberately varying n and r so as to *counterbalance* the movement of k and k'.

The usual method of exercising a stabilising influence over k and k', especially over k', is that of bank rate. A tendency of k' to increase may be somewhat counteracted by lowering the bank rate, because easy lending diminishes the advantage of keeping a margin for contingencies in cash. Cheap money also operates to *counterbalance* an increase in k', because, by encouraging borrowing from the banks, it prevents r from increasing or causes r to diminish. But it is doubtful whether bank rate by itself is always a powerful enough instrument, and, if we are to achieve stability, we must be prepared to vary n and r on occasion (Keynes 1923, p. 68, italics in original)

It should be evident from this passage that when it came to counter-cyclical policy, Keynes (1923) had very little to offer his readers that was not already to be found in the writings of Marshall. In particular, for Keynes, as for his mentor, the cycle was first and foremost a phenomenon of price-level fluctuations, albeit with systematic effects on real variables, and the *sine qua non* of stabilizing it was to achieve a stable time path for what we would now call MV. To that Keynes added the not very helpful observation that that could be brought about by the authorities varying, in some unspecified combination, the three instruments under their control, namely, the quantity of currency, the bank rate, and the reserve – deposit ratio imposed upon the commercial banks. And, as the reader will also note, in the course of making those points, Keynes displayed a rather uncertain grasp of the role of interest as an opportunity cost of holding money.

Perhaps Keynes's unoriginal treatment of specifically cyclical issues in the *Tract* should be attributed to the fact that the book was, after all, primarily devoted to other topics, some of which were, as we have seen, analysed with great insight. But it is difficult to resist the conclusion that in 1923, aware though he was of questions about the role of inter-temporal allocative mechanisms in economic fluctuations, Keynes was still very much constrained by intellectual limits imposed by Marshall's version of the quantity theory of money. As we shall see in due course, *A Treatise on Money* (Keynes 1930a), and particularly its first volume, *The Pure Theory of Money*, must be read as a systematic attempt to breach just those limits and to integrate the Marshallian quantity theory with a treatment of inter-temporal co-ordination issues along Wicksellian lines. Before we take up that matter, however, we must discuss yet another important and influential variant of the Marshallian tradition, namely, the cycle theory of Ralph Hawtrey.

Hawtrey's Monetary Theory of the Cycle

Ralph Hawtrey wrote prolifically and, as even his greatest admirers would have to admit, repetitively on the cycle throughout his long life; ideas expounded in his first book, *Good and Bad Trade* (1913), were still clearly visible in his 1958 evidence to the Radcliffe Committee. But among his writings, one book in particular stands out for its comprehensive exposition of his views, its visibility among his contemporaries, and its longevity, namely, *Currency and Credit*, which first appeared in 1919, was significantly revised in 1927, and saw its final edition in 1950.[8]

---

[8] As Howson (1985) noted, though the models of the cycle deployed in the two books were essentially the same, the institutional frameworks that lay in the background were rather different. In 1913 the gold standard was well established and taken for granted. In 1919 the framework was already more akin to that of the post-war world. Nevertheless, even in the 1920s some contemporary admirers of Hawtrey, such as Allyn Young, regarded *Good and Bad Trade* as a more accessible book than *Currency and Credit*. See Young (1920), as

It is important at the outset to be clear about the meaning of that book's title phrase and the more general significance of that meaning for Hawtrey's analysis. To him, the word "currency" signified just what it does nowadays, but he normally used the word "credit" to refer not to bank loans but to *commercial bank deposits*. Hawtrey, more often than not, used the word "money," which we would nowadays use to label the sum of these two, as a synonym for "currency." Such usage was not uncommon in the 1920s, but it was by no means universal, and semantic confusion between money and credit, and hence between bank liabilities and bank assets, was a common feature of the literature of the period, particularly the American literature.[9] Be that as it may, in modern terminology the title of Hawtrey's most important book would be *Currency and Chequable Deposits*, and there can be no stronger indication than this of the central role played by these monetary aggregates in his theory of the cycle.

The Role of the Quantity Theory

The quantity theory of money, in its Cambridge cash-balance version, was the starting point, but only the starting point, for the explanation of cyclical fluctuations that Hawtrey elaborated in *Currency and Credit*, and indeed elsewhere in his writings:[10]

> Scientific treatment of the subject of currency is impossible without some form of the quantity theory. . . . But the quantity theory by itself is inadequate, and it leads up to the method of treatment based on what I have called the consumers' income and the consumers' outlay – that is to say, simply the aggregates of individual incomes and individual expenditures. (Hawtrey 1919, p. v)

To Hawtrey, as to all his contemporaries, the phrase *quantity theory* signified a strictly proportional relationship between the price level and the quantity of money somehow defined, with causation running unidirectionally from money to prices. Its inadequacy for his purposes stemmed from its being an equilibrium relationship which held only in situations in which "the quantity of credit and money [i.e., demand deposits plus currency] in circulation is neither increasing nor decreasing" (Hawtrey 1919, p. 46), whereas

> in practice it seldom, perhaps never, happens that a state of equilibrium is actually reached. A period of expanding or contracting credit, when it comes

---

discussed by Deutscher (1990, pp. 195–196). On Hawtrey's evidence to the Radcliffe Committee, see Laidler (1989).

[9] Lauchlin Currie (1933a) provided a masterful account of the substantive confusion which such usage could produce when it came to the implementation of policy. See Chapter 9, footnote 25.

[10] Bridel (1987, pp. 61ff.) has provided an account of the role played by the Cambridge cash-balance approach in Hawtrey's analysis, as has Deutscher (1990, pp. 22ff.).

to an end, leaves behind it a legacy of adjustments, and before these are half completed a new movement has probably already set in. Therefore when drawing guidance from the quantity theory in the examination of actual conditions, we must beware of assuming too easily that, in a country where economic organisation has remained substantially unchanged, prices will go up and down in strict proportion to the quantity of purchasing power in circulation. Before making any such assumption we must first ascertain whether credit is expanding or contracting. (Hawtrey 1919, p. 46)

The Inherent Instability of Credit and the Unspent Margin

In Hawtrey's view, the behaviour of credit was prone to what he frequently called *inherent instability*, and he devoted the first dozen or so pages of *Currency and Credit* to showing why that was the case, along analytic lines that bore some resemblance to Wicksell's treatment (1898, ch. 9) of "the pure credit economy." Since Hawtrey was perhaps unaware of Wicksell's work at that time, that similarity presumably should be attributed to a common Marshallian influence on their work; and in any event it is by no means complete, as Keynes (1930a, vol. I, pp. 175ff.) was later to note. In particular, the rate of interest which borrowers were willing to pay in Hawtrey's analysis had nothing to do with the marginal productivity of fixed capital or any prospective yield on long-term investment. It was rather a short-term rate deriving from the profit expectations of wholesalers whose economic function was to hold inventories of finished goods.

Hawtrey first considered an economy whose only means of exchange was bank deposits. Those were created and destroyed as "wholesale merchants [who] fill a very important place in the trading system" (Hawtrey 1919, p. 8) extended or contracted the volume of their borrowing, which in turn was undertaken to finance their inventories. Within that framework, which captured certain essential features of British (and indeed American) commercial banking at the beginning of the twentieth century, but not of the Continental-style universal banking that lay in the background of Austrian and Swedish analysis, Hawtrey characterised the problem to be investigated as follows:

> If we are to prove that the monetary unit will be a stable standard of value, we must show that if exposed to any disturbing cause the unit will tend to *return* to its former value, or at any rate that it will arrive at a new and relatively stable value not differing much from the old. (Hawtrey 1919, p. 10)

He had no difficulty in showing that such stability would be absent. Any shock that set prices moving downwards would, for a given value of the nominal rate of interest, make it more expensive for merchants to hold inventories and would cause them to reduce their borrowing and hence the quantity of bank money in circulation, thus putting further downward pressure on prices, and so on; that process would come to an end only when bankers reduced the rate of interest. Any shock that set prices rising, on the other hand, would lead to an upward spiral, "and this movement is even more unlimited in scope" (Hawtrey 1919, p. 12), because

> in the case of the curtailment of credits the self interest of the bankers and the distress of the merchants [combine] to restore the creation of credits, though not to its pre-existing level. But in the case of the expansion of credits there is no such corrective influence at work. (Hawtrey 1919, p. 13)

At that point Hawtrey brought currency (money) into the picture, arguing, once more in the manner of Marshall, and, to a degree, of Wicksell too, that "[money] has to correct the instability of credit" (Hawtrey 1919, p. 15). But there again the resemblance between Wicksell and Hawtrey was far from complete: in Wicksell's analysis of the "cumulative process," the presence of currency, which played a dual role as bank reserve and means of exchange, ensured that the price level would move from one metastable equilibrium to another in response to some exogenous shock; in Hawtrey's model, the system, once disturbed and left to itself, was likely to oscillate perpetually.[11]

To understand the source of that difference, we must begin with Hawtrey's essentially Marshallian analysis of the level and composition of the public's holdings of currency and deposits, an aggregate to which he usually gave the label the *unspent margin* (e.g., Hawtrey 1919, p. 34). In discussing "the requirements of the community for reserves of purchasing power" (Hawtrey 1919, p. 38), Hawtrey distinguished between what we would now call households and firms. Also, and in strong contrast to Wicksell (not to mention his Swedish followers), he recognized the existence of a determinate stock demand for bank deposits which could be analysed in the same terms as the demand for currency:

> For each private individual the appropriate balance of credit and the appropriate balance of cash will bear a determinate proportion to his income. . . . For each business the appropriate balances will likewise be determined by convenience, but will be proportional rather to the gross transactions or turnover, than to the net income of the business. (Hawtrey 1919, p. 37)

The key players on the supply side were the banks, because, given the economy's stock of currency, it was they who would determine how much of that stock would be available to meet the demands of the non-bank public and what the volume of deposits would be. What mattered most for Haw-

---

[11] Note also that the key variable driving expenditure in Hawtrey's analysis was the quantity of money itself, which varied as a result of the credit-creation process. In Wicksell's analysis, the gap between the interest rate at which credit was on offer and the natural value of that variable was the strategic factor.

trey's cycle theory, however, was that *expansions and contractions* of bank credit would disturb, or prevent the establishment of, equilibrium between the supply and demand for "reserves of purchasing power." His treatment of that matter involved applying what were, by 1919, rather conventional cash-balance mechanics to the interaction of the stock supply and demand for money, albeit with a then-unconventional degree of emphasis on deposits rather than currency:

> The first thing that requires to be said . . . is that no one borrows money in order to keep it idle. The borrowing is done by people in business, who have deliberately relied on borrowing in order at other times to avoid keeping large idle balances. It follows that practically all the sums borrowed will be quickly paid away. . . .
> So we reach the conclusion that an acceleration or retardation of the creation of credit means an equal increase or decrease in people's incomes.
> An increase or decrease in people's incomes will lead to an increase or decrease in their expenditures. (Hawtrey 1919, p. 40)

At the beginning of an expansion, merchants who had borrowed to increase their inventories would be frustrated in their efforts; household expenditures, driven up by increased incomes, which were themselves the indirect consequence of those same merchants' borrowing, would reduce those inventories as fast as the merchants tried to build them up. Prices would therefore begin to rise, further borrowing would be induced, and the upswing would gather pace.

Effective Demand and Money-Wage Stickiness

The expenditure flows which Hawtrey thought were set in motion by money creation encompassed not just consumption spending but also saving, which, he took it for granted, would be transmuted into investment expenditure through the intermediation of a smoothly functioning capital market. Thus, when he used the phrase *effective demand* as a synonym for aggregate nominal expenditure in the economy, as he habitually did, the demand for investment goods of all varieties, as well as consumption goods, was included. Moreover, it was of the essence of his theory that fluctuations in effective demand were, to put it in modern terms, the consequence of cash-balance mechanics driven by discrepancies between the levels and rates of change of the stock of money and the demand for it.[12]

---

[12] On Hawtrey's use of the concept of effective demand, see Bigg (1987). The correspondence between Hawtrey and Keynes in the period leading up to the publication of the *General Theory* contained an exchange about the phrase "effective demand," with Keynes insisting that his immediate predecessors had never used it, and with Hawtrey pointing out that Marshall had once done so in a footnote. Hawtrey apparently was too self-effacing to mention that he himself had frequently used the phrase, and Keynes seems to have been quite unaware of that. See Keynes (1971–88, vol. XIII). See also footnote 4 in Chapter 10.

According to Hawtrey, three factors would interact to render his simple income–expenditure system's dynamics inherently cyclical. First, as we have seen already, credit expansion would be cumulative when the rate of interest charged by the banks on short-term loans lagged behind the expected profitability of borrowing. Second, during a boom, "it is only after a considerable interval that the prosperity of the manufacturer is reflected in an increase of *wages*" (Hawtrey 1919, p. 23, italics in original). Third, among the non-bank public, wage-earners would hold a relatively high proportion of their unspent margins in the form of currency. As a result, the drain of currency from the banks, which would provide them with the signal that their lending rates should be increased, would occur only after the boom had gathered considerable momentum and wages at last had begun to rise. That, in turn, would make it virtually certain that when lending rates were raised, they would be raised far enough not just to halt, but to *reverse*, the credit-expansion process. In the ensuing downswing, the same factors would work in the opposite direction. In the case of

> the depression of a prolonged credit contraction, . . . prices go on falling and the merchant repeatedly finds his profit turned into a loss, . . . the manufacturer cannot reduce quotations till he has reduced wages, . . . the workman dare not accept a reduction of wages which, interrupted as they are by periods of unemployment, seem already insufficient. (Hawtrey 1919, p. 356)

Eventually, falling incomes among wage-earners caused by the spread of unemployment and the wage reductions that inevitably would occur would generate an inflow of currency to the banks, interest rates would be cut, and the next upswing would begin.[13]

Note that the foregoing quotation describing the consequences of "a prolonged credit contraction" contains an ambiguity that is also, incidentally, to be found in *Good and Bad Trade* (1913). It simultaneously postulates *falling prices* and an *inability of manufacturers to reduce prices* because of wage stickiness. Hawtrey seems not to have noticed that ambiguity in 1913 or 1919, but by 1932 he was fully aware of the point, as the following passage shows:

> That deflation or a falling price level causes unemployment is generally accepted. But as to the precise manner and limits of this principle there is room for differences of opinion.
> One form in which the principle is sometimes enunciated is that as a fall

---

[13] That element of Hawtrey's analysis was also present in its 1913 version. Its emphasis on endogenous fluctuations in the public's currency–deposit ratio and banks' reserve ratios found its way into American monetary economics in the 1920s by way of the work of Allyn Young (1928) and thence in Lauchlin Currie's monetary explanation (1934a) of the Great Depression of 1929–32. Currie came closer than any of his contemporaries to anticipating the Friedman and Schwartz (1963) treatment of that topic. See Chapter 8, "Allyn Young and the Influence of Hawtrey," and Chapter 9, "Snyder and Currie on the Great Contraction."

of wages lags behind a fall of prices, profits are encroached on by costs, and some business, becoming unprofitable, is abandoned. The volume of production is thus diminished and part of the work-people are thrown out of employment. . . .

Another formulation of it is that the prospect of falling prices damps down enterprise, because it deters traders from holding stocks of goods. . . .

This is much nearer to an adequate account of the principle. And it brings out its relation to credit contraction. . . .

But I think the causation of unemployment by monetary contraction is best explained through the consumers' income and outlay. Suppose that anything occurs, whether a credit contraction, a decrease in velocity of circulation or anything else, to cause a reduction in the consumers' income. There will ensue a reduction of the consumers' outlay (not exactly equal, for consumers' balances may be drawn on). Thereby the total effective demand for commodities is curtailed. Dealers find their sales at existing prices falling off, and give smaller orders to the producers for the replenishment of their stocks. The diminished activity of the producers means a further diminution of the consumers' income and outlay. . . .

This process begins and may even continue for a time without any fall of prices. . . .

The fall of prices, so far as actually accomplished, is a relief; *it makes a given amount of money-demand absorb a greater amount of goods. The difficulty of reducing wages prolongs the depression, because it obstructs the fall of prices.* (Hawtrey 1932a, pp. 320–322, italics added)

This passage from 1932 is quoted because of its exemplary clarity, not because it marks the first appearance of the ideas it expresses in Hawtrey's work. Some years earlier he had come to understand that the influence of money-wage stickiness on the nominal price level provided a key link between effective demand and employment.[14] For example, the conceptual experiment which lay at the heart of his celebrated 1925 exposition of what later came to be called "the Treasury view" on the ineffectiveness of public-works expenditures concerned "a community in which there is unemployment. That means that at *the existing level of prices and wages* the consumers' outlay is only sufficient to employ a part of the productive resources of the country" (Hawtrey 1925, p. 40, italics added). The design of that experiment shows quite clearly that by then, Hawtrey already understood that the level of *nominal* effective demand in the economy, "*money*, offered by consumers in the market" (Hawtrey 1925, p. 39, italics in original), would, if *nominal* wages and prices were given, directly affect the *real* level of output. As he put it, "employment is given by producers. They produce in response to an effective demand for products" (Hawtrey, 1925, p. 39).

---

[14] That way of looking at things also appeared in Keynes's work in the mid-1920s, notably in "The Economic Consequences of Mr. Churchill." See Chapter 7 for further discussion.

Inter-temporal Co-ordination

Hawtrey's cycle theory was distinctive, in the literature of the 1920s, in paying relatively little attention to fluctuations in the rate of investment in fixed capital. He was well aware that, as an empirical matter, "the most important class of production which ebbs and flows with the contractions and expansions of credit is the production of fixed capital" (Hawtrey 1919, p. 91), and he was also aware of a need to explain that fact. In *Good and Bad Trade* (1913) he had done so in terms of what we would now call an accelerator mechanism, illustrated with an explicit numerical example.[15] Hawtrey did not, however, return to that particular line of analysis in *Currency and Credit*, though he did point out to its readers that "the construction of fixed capital is in most cases a lengthy process, and large capital commitments are therefore specially apt to overstrain credit when the turning point from expansion to contraction arrives" (Hawtrey 1919, p. 109).

Hawtrey cannot be accused, then, of ignoring fluctuations in the rate of fixed-capital formation, but there can be no doubt that to the extent that any type of investment was central to his explanation of the cycle, it was inventory investment on the part of merchants. Even so, we have seen that it was the interaction between variations in the rate of growth of money, particularly deposit money, and the non-bank public's stock demand for it that drove output fluctuations, in his view. Changes in merchants' *desired* inventories, prompted by changes in the relationship between their profit expectations and interest costs, provided the impetus to those variations in money growth. They did not, however, in and of themselves, constitute a significant *direct source* of output fluctuations. In Hawtrey's view of the world, household expenditure flows, generated by the money growth arising from merchants' borrowing, prevented those same merchants from actually attaining their desired levels of inventories.[16]

Hawtrey's relative neglect of fluctuations in the rate of investment in fixed capital as a force driving the cycle is symptomatic of a fundamental difference between his theoretical vision and that of many of his contempor-

---

[15] By the 1920s, Hawtrey had become rather critical of the accelerator mechanism as an important component in a theory of aggregate fluctuations. He noted, for example, that it would operate only when capital equipment was being used at full capacity, which was unlikely to hold true across the entire spectrum of industries at any particular time. See Hawtrey (1927).

[16] Hawtrey was no pioneer of the style of inventory cycle analysis developed much later by, for example, Lloyd Metzler (eg. 1941). Note also that Hawtrey's analysis was particularly criticized for putting too much emphasis on the short rate of interest and its influence on desired inventory investment, to the neglect of longer-term considerations (Haberler 1937, pp. 24–25). Even an admirer such as Allyn Young entertained doubts on that score. See Sandilands (1990b, pp. 82–83). So, too, did Lauchlin Currie (1931a, p. 217).

aries.[17] Though he would eventually write on capital theory and the inter-temporal allocation of resources in his book *Capital and Employment* (1937), he showed little interest in those matters in the 1920s and early 1930s, essentially taking it for granted, as Eric Davis (1980, p. 718) has noted, that the capital market did indeed function adequately. Thus, in a 1926 review of *Banking Policy and the Price Level*, he took Robertson to task for doubting (as we discussed in Chapter 4, footnote 27) the capacity of the capital market to supply working capital in sufficient quantities to keep long-term investment on track: "Mr. Robertson's problem of circulating capital is governed by the postulate that short lacking is unprocurable except through the agency of banks. . . . This assumption is erroneous" (Hawtrey 1926, pp. 432–433). And he went on to argue that

> a shortage of circulating capital does occur at a time of active trade, but that is merely because a credit expansion encroaches upon stocks of finished goods in the interval before prices are raised. . . .
> Inflation, which is proposed as a remedy for a shortage of circulating capital, is itself the most usual cause of the shortage. (Hawtrey 1926, p. 433)

Before 1937, however, Hawtrey did not provide his readers any closely argued analysis of the capacity of market mechanisms to co-ordinate the inter-temporal allocation of resources, and his relative neglect of those matters in the 1920s and early 1930s seems to have stemmed from reasons no more profound than a distrust of the practical value of abstract economic analysis. That distrust was displayed in the aforementioned review, for example, when Hawtrey expressed irritation with the style of Robertson's analysis, noting that much of it "depends on the behaviour of an extremely rarefied kind of economic man" (Hawtrey 1926, p. 417); and a few years later he complained about "the intolerably clumsy theory of capital" deployed in Hayek's *Prices and Production*, suggesting that "[Hayek] himself has been led by so ill chosen a method of analysis to conclusions which he would hardly have accepted if given a more straightforward method of expression" (Hawtrey 1932b, p. 125).

Even in 1937, when Hawtrey did write at some length about capital theory in the style of Böhm-Bawerk (though in his exposition he was inclined, not

---

[17] The Austrians and Robertson in particular. The fact is that capital-theory approaches to business-cycle theory are very difficult to reconcile with those that rely on fluctuations in the level of aggregate demand, for the simple reason that in the latter type of system, discrepancies between desired saving and investment occur only *ex ante*. *Ex post* they do not materialize, because output adjusts, and so future discrepancies between what consumers demand and what the structure of the economy's supply side can produce do not materialize. See Bridel (1987, ch. 9, particularly pp. 159–166) for a penetrating discussion of those issues as they arose in connection with the notion of "effective demand" as deployed in the *General Theory*.

without reason, to give more credit to Jevons for the basic framework), his ultimate impatience with such analysis remained quite evident. Having expounded the essential properties of that approach in a manner that left no doubt about his grasp of its basic characteristics, he concluded that

> there seems to be little advantage in seeking a measure in terms of the period of production at all. The practical points to be taken into consideration are always a capital outlay of a certain amount and a prospective yield or cost-saving capacity.
>
> The fact that capital can, subject to certain reservations, be expressed in terms of a lapse of time is of theoretical interest and importance. Without it the theory of capital would undoubtedly be incomplete. When we treat the passage of time as a factor of production, regulating the application of the advantages of protracted processes, we can link this lapse of time with the waiting to which economists have reduced the function of saving.
>
> But when economists go beyond this and attempt to express the ordinary operations of the investment market in terms of the period of production, they are simply introducing unnecessary difficulties. (Hawtrey 1937, pp. 28–29)

What mattered for Hawtrey was always the generation of income and expenditure, and current capital outlay was important to the extent that it contributed to effective demand. To go beyond that, and "instead of saying that a producer adds to the capital of his business, . . . [to] say that he extends the period of production of his output" was to cast the discussion in terms of "an abstraction not corresponding to any actual facts" (Hawtrey 1937, p. 29).

Hawtrey on Stabilization Policy

As we saw in Chapter 4, Pigou thought that using monetary policy to stabilize the price level, were that feasible, might reduce the amplitude of cyclical fluctuations by about one-half. Hawtrey, on the other hand, argued that, in principle at least, "if credit policy were based on stabilisation of the price level (suitably interpreted) instead of on gold reserves, cyclical fluctuations could be eliminated altogether" (Hawtrey 1929, p. 639). Marshall, who had held similar views, had not thought such stabilization of prices practicable, and so he had advocated widespread indexation as a means of protecting the economy against the real consequences of price-level fluctuations. Though Hawtrey certainly did not believe, as a practical matter, that complete elimination of cyclical fluctuations was feasible, he saw the difficulties here as stemming in the main from problems inherent in getting the timing of policy right.[18] He entertained few doubts about the effectiveness of monetary mea-

---

[18] This problem, in turn, stemmed from the cyclical pattern of commercial banks' holdings of excess reserves. On this matter, see Deutscher (1990, pp. 61–62).

sures in influencing aggregate demand, always provided, of course, that their implementation was not inhibited by international monetary considerations.

Possible conflicts between observing the rules of the gold standard and using monetary policy to pursue domestic stability had been much discussed from the 1880s onwards, not least by Marshall (e.g., 1887), and of course also by Fisher (e.g., 1911), and after World War I, the issue of domestic versus exchange-rate stability became central to debates about the reconstruction of the international monetary system. Keynes's views on those questions in 1923 have already been discussed, and it will suffice here to remind the reader of Hawtrey's position, largely embodied in the Genoa Resolutions of 1922, of which he was the principal architect. Hawtrey's preferred goal was to maintain (or rather restore) the gold standard, while simultaneously ensuring that the central banks of the world would co-ordinate their policies so as to stabilize prices internationally and eliminate conflicts between domestic and balance-of-payments goals. For such a solution to be feasible, the possibility of real shocks impinging differentially upon different economies, and requiring divergent monetary responses, would have to be absent, but in Hawtrey's analysis, and consistent with his view that aggregate fluctuations were always monetary in origin, that latter consideration went undiscussed. Even so, his advocacy of that scheme placed him closer to those who, like Keynes, and of course Fisher, gave priority to domestic price-level stabilization among the goals of monetary policy than to the more orthodox supporters of unilateral post-war restoration of the gold standard in Britain, such as the authors of the Cunliffe Report.

Bank Rate and Open-Market Operations

It is well known that Hawtrey was a firm advocate of using the central bank's discount rate – *bank rate*, as it is called in British terminology – as the principal instrument of monetary policy, and this might at first sight seem to place him in the tradition of Walter Bagehot.[19] However, Hawtrey's conception of the appropriate target for policy was very different from Bagehot's, and he was well aware of this difference. Bagehot had regarded the maintenance of gold convertibility as the *sine qua non* of monetary policy, and as Hawtrey told readers of his *Art of Central Banking*, "a central bank working the gold standard must rectify an outflow of gold by a restriction of credit,

---

[19] Bagehot (1873) was also an exponent of bank rate as the principal tool of monetary policy, but the goals at which policy was to be aimed were, first, the preservation of gold convertibility and, second, the avoidance of domestic financial crises that might threaten the existence of sound banks. He was in no sense an advocate of using bank rate for counter-cyclical purposes. For a discussion of this matter, see Laidler (1991, pp. 37–40, 180–182).

and an inflow of gold by a relaxation of credit'' (Hawtrey 1932a, p. 188). Under Hawtrey's preferred scheme, on the other hand,

> substantially the plan embodied in the currency resolutions adopted at the Genoa Conference in 1922, . . . the central banks of the world [would] regulate credit with a view to preventing undue fluctuations in the purchasing power of gold. (Hawtrey 1932a, p. 194)

More generally, he saw the task of central banking as being to mitigate that inherent instability of credit which was the driving force of economic fluctuations, by ensuring, as far as possible, that cumulative expansions and contractions of bank deposits were eliminated, or, failing that, when faced by depression, to bring about whatever degree of monetary expansion might be required to restore economic activity to a satisfactory level.

The array of policy instruments available to central banks had broadened somewhat since the 1870s, and though Hawtrey certainly followed Bagehot in emphasizing the importance of the bank rate, he was also an advocate of open-market operations. In 1919, he tended to see the latter as a supplementary device which would help to make the discount rate effective:

> By borrowing at the market rate [a central bank] can withdraw as much legal tender money as it pleases from the other banks, and they must either raise the market rate at least to a level with the bank rate, or else run the risk of having to borrow back at the bank rate what they have lent at a lower rate. (Hawtrey 1919, p. 51)

As the 1920s progressed, however, Hawtrey became more inclined to accord open-market operations an importance equal to that of the discount rate – ''[a central bank's] instruments for the restriction of credit are a rise of Bank rate and sales of securities, and for the relaxation a reduction of Bank rate and purchases of securities'' (Hawtrey 1932a, p. 188) – and in extreme circumstances he gave open-market operations pride of place.

By 1932, the Great Contraction was well under way in the United States. The cumulative collapse of confidence and borrowing which accompanied it was all too visible, and what Hawtrey termed a *credit deadlock* seemed to be firmly entrenched. Even so, and unlike the majority of contemporary observers, Hawtrey did not despair of the powers of monetary policy to deal with such a situation:

> But it may happen that demand is so contracted and markets are so unfavourable that traders, seeing no prospect of profit, abstain from enterprise and do not borrow. The reluctance of borrowers may cause a contraction of credit quite as effectively as the reluctance of lenders.
>
> When that happens, it seems to be the extreme of paradox to say that there is a shortage of money. . . .

> But the low rates [of interest] are merely the outward expression of the
> unprofitableness of business and the unwillingness of traders to borrow. . . .
> There is a deadlock which can best be broken by injecting money into the
> system.
>
> Now the central bank has the power of creating money. (Hawtrey 1932a,
> p. 172)

The tool to be used in those circumstances was open-market operations,
carried out not only in short-term debt, but if necessary in long-term securities
as well: "If . . . the bills offered and the suitable applications for advances
are inadequate and do not increase fast enough, the banks have the alternative
of buying long-term investments of a suitable marketable character" (Hawtrey 1932, p. 173). Such measures need only be pushed hard enough to
become effective:

> There must ultimately be a limit to the amount of money that the sellers
> will hold idle, and it follows that by this process the vicious circle of
> deflation can always be broken, however great the stagnation of business
> and the reluctance of borrowers may be. (Hawtrey 1932a, pp. 173–174)[20]

In arguing along the foregoing lines in *The Art of Central Banking* (1932a),
Hawtrey was reiterating a position which he had already articulated in his
1925 paper on "Public Expenditure and the Demand for Labour." There,
noting that "in a period of depression the rapidity of circulation is low"
(Hawtrey 1925, p. 43), he had gone so far as to concede that government
borrowing from the general public might be an effective means of increasing
the velocity of circulation, and that government borrowing from the banking
system, particularly from the central bank, might be "efficacious in stimulating an expansion of credit" (Hawtrey 1925, p. 45, fn. 1). Even so, he had
stated his general position in the following terms:

> . . . a low bank rate by itself might be found to be an insufficient restorative.
> But the effect of a low bank rate can be reinforced by purchase of securities
> on the part of the central bank in the open market. It is only when this
> remedy has been tried and has failed, that there is any case for having
> recourse to Government borrowing. Personally, I have no doubt that by the
> former method it is possible to find an escape from any depression, however
> severe. (Hawtrey 1925, p. 45)

---

[20] In light of that passage, written in 1932, I find it difficult to accept Frank Steindl's inclusion
of Hawtrey among the purveyors of "Misguided Monetary Messages" about the Great
Contraction (Steindl 1995, ch. 7). Hawtrey, it seems to me, was much more optimistic about
the expansionary powers of monetary policy than was conventional at that time, and he
deserves to be numbered among the intellectual forebears of Friedman and Schwartz (1963),
as I have argued elsewhere (Laidler 1993). Compare his views with those of Pigou or
Robertson in Britain, as discussed in Chapter 4, "Monetary Policy and Its Limitations," or
those of such American commentators as Hardy or Douglas and Director, as discussed in
Chapter 9. In 1930–31, moreover, Keynes still shared Hawtrey's optimism. See Chapter 6,
"Open-Market Operations and Their Limits."

Public-Works Expenditures, Money, and the Treasury View

Unlike the majority of his English (and, as we shall see in Chapter 9, American) contemporaries, Hawtrey thus had few doubts about the ultimate powers of conventional monetary policy to stimulate the economy, even in the most extremely depressed circumstances. In parallel with that belief, and again unlike most of his contemporaries, he was sceptical about the powers of government-expenditure programs to have any aggregate effects on income and employment, except to the extent that they were financed by money creation. Hawtrey was, in fact, the originator of the particular version of "the Treasury view" of those matters that Hicks (1937) would characterize in terms of a vertical-LM-curve version of the IS-LM framework.[21]

Hawtrey had presented at least the bare bones of that doctrine in *Good and Bad Trade* (1913), but his definitive exposition is to be found in his 1925 *Economica* paper. As has been noted, that exposition was cast in terms of a system in which, given the levels of money wages and prices, the levels of output and employment were determined by the aggregate rate of flow of nominal expenditure. In such a system, unless an increase in government expenditure on public works can be shown to imply an increase in the overall level of effective demand, the consequence must be an equal reduction in the expenditure of some other sector. If, however, the increase is implemented while holding the quantity of money constant, then, as Hawtrey put it,

> as soon as the people employed on the new public works begin to receive payment, they will begin to accumulate cash balances and bank balances. Their balances can only be provided at the expense of the people already receiving incomes. These latter will therefore become short of ready cash and will curtail their expenditure with a view to restoring their balances. An individual can increase his balance by curtailing his expenditure, but if the

---

[21] There was, of course, more to the "Treasury view" than Hawtrey's analysis. As readers of Peter Clarke (1988) will be aware, a policy debate in British political and bureaucratic circles concerning public-works expenditures ran parallel to the theoretical debates discussed in this book throughout the 1920s and into the 1930s, with overlapping lists of protagonists. Even so, it was Hawtrey's work which seems to have provided the intellectual core of the arguments deployed by the Treasury, particularly in the second half of the 1920s. But the Treasury deployed other arguments against public-works expenditures as well, arguments hinging on such matters as the practical difficulties of implementing such schemes and their potentially adverse effects on private-sector confidence, not to mention the fact that their impact might be limited to specific industries. See, for example, Sir Richard Hopkins's evidence to the Macmillan Committee (Hopkins 1931, para. 5,565). On the formation of the Treasury view in the late 1920s, and Hawtrey's role therein, see Clarke (1988, ch. 3). Arguments about confidence also found their way into American debates, notably in *The Economics of the Recovery Program* (Brown et al. 1934), a product of the Harvard Economics Department, which is discussed in Chapter 9. Dimand (1988, pp. 59ff.) has discussed the Treasury view in the context of the broad array of arguments that were advanced in Britain and the United States, in the early 1930s, against expansionary policy.

> unspent margin (that is to say, the total of all cash balances and bank balances) remains unchanged, he can only increase his balance at the expense of those of his neighbours. If all simultaneously try to increase their balances, they try in vain. . . . It is this limitation of the unspent margin that really prevents the new Government expenditure from creating employment. (Hawtrey 1925, pp. 41–42)

The logic there was impeccable, always provided that "the normal proportion between the consumers' income and the unspent margin" (Hawtrey 1925, p. 42), or, as one might nowadays put it, the income velocity of circulation, was held constant; but it was Hawtrey's view, held consistently over the years, that "it is only in exceptional circumstances that Government expenditure on public works will itself bring about an increase of velocity" (Hawtrey 1929, p. 637). That argument by Hawtrey deserves more respect than it is usually given. His conclusions do indeed follow from the money-growth-driven income–expenditure system with which he analysed the cycle. They also follow from an IS-LM model when the economy is operating where the interest sensitivity of the demand for money is negligible, so that what Hicks would later call "the classical theory" (Hicks 1937, p. 109) is relevant. If, with benefit of hindsight, Hawtrey might be convicted of over-generalizing from a special case, his analysis nevertheless made a significant contribution in demonstrating the dangers inherent in Pigou's practice (1912, pp. 147–148) of going "behind the distorting veil of money" in order to deal with such matters. Hawtrey's view, that the influence of public-works expenditures on the economy's overall rate of flow of money expenditures was crucial to their effects on employment, was surely valid.

The Role of the Banking System

It is true that the idea of a systematic interest sensitivity of the demand for money had been worked out by Lavington in the early 1920s, but it is also true that none of Hawtrey's critics, including Pigou, who took issue with him at considerable length about the effectiveness of public works, saw its critical relevance to this matter during that decade and into the next. Indeed, Hawtrey himself came as close as any of them did before 1936 to developing a more general, not to say correct, argument about the influence of the monetary system on the efficacy of public-works expenditures. In 1925 he conceded that

> when trade is slack, traders accumulate cash balances because the prospects of profit from any enterprise are slight, and the rate of interest from any investment is low. When trade is active, an idle balance is a more serious loss, and traders hasten to use all their resources in their business. (Hawtrey 1925, p. 42)

And he argued that *once an expansion got under way*, increased velocity would indeed accompany it. However, and crucially, he also insisted that "if no expansion of credit at all is allowed, the conditions which produce increased rapidity of circulation cannot begin to develop" (Hawtrey 1925, p. 42).

Hindsight, illuminated by an IS-LM diagram with an upward-sloping LM curve, shows that the last step of his argument was erroneous, but Hawtrey was not alone in holding such a position. The fact is that in the 1920s and early 1930s, many advocates of public-works expenditures were careful to note that their success would be contingent upon their being accommodated by appropriate monetary measures. For example, when Richard Kahn addressed that issue in his classic article on the employment multiplier, he argued as follows:[22]

> It is, however, important to realise that the intelligent co-operation of the banking system is being taken for granted. . . . If the increased circulation of notes and the increased demand for working capital that may result from increased employment are made the occasion for a restriction of credit, then any attempt to increase employment . . . may be rendered nugatory. (Kahn 1931, pp. 174–175)

Or, to cite another example, when the Polish economist Michal Kalecki offered an informal account of the "Mechanism of the Business Upswing" (1935), which he had developed mathematically in "Outline of a Theory" (1933), he noted an essential similarity among the effects of a private-sector investment increase prompted by a new invention, a program of public-investment expenditure, and government expenditure on "the payment of doles" (Kalecki 1935), before concluding that

> it must be added that the pre-condition of successful government intervention – and of the natural [i.e., private-investment-led] upswing as well – is the possibility of meeting the increased demand for credits by the banking system without increasing the rate of interest too much. Should the rate of interest increase to such an extent that private investment is curtailed by exactly the amount of government borrowing . . . then obviously no purchasing power would be created, but only a shift in its structure would take place. (Kalecki 1935, tr. 1966, p. 33)

Qualifications such as those clearly could have drawn no dissent from Hawtrey, though he would, of course, have preferred to interpret any resulting

---

[22] As Deutscher has noted, though surely aimed at Hawtrey, Kahn's article carefully avoided mentioning him by name. See Deutscher (1990, pp. 217–219) for a discussion of this and other matters related to the Treasury view. Bridel (1987, pp. 200–201, fn. 18) has also provided an interesting discussion of the relationship between Hawtrey's analysis of the cycle and his version of the Treasury view, which, however, does not mention Hawtrey's advocacy of open-market operations as a recovery-promoting policy tool.

increase in demand as being caused not by public works or other forms of government expenditure per se, but by the injection of newly created money into the system. He would have argued, and indeed did argue on a number of occasions, not least in 1925, that an equal amount of money creation *unaccompanied* by the government expenditure it was designed to accommodate would have had the same overall effect on output.[23]

> What has been shown is that expenditure on public works, if accompanied by a creation of credit, will give employment. But then the same reasoning shows that a creation of credit unaccompanied by any expenditure on public works would be equally effective in giving employment. (Hawtrey 1925, p. 44)

Even in

> the exceptional case where there is an extreme stagnation of balances . . . it is not the government expenditure that gives employment, but the government borrowing. The borrowing would have the same effect if it were to meet a deficit due to a remission of taxation. (Hawtrey 1925, pp. 44–45)

Nor did balance-of-payments considerations such as might impinge upon an open economy change Hawtrey's conclusions. He addressed those complications briefly in *Economica* (1925, pp. 45–47) and at greater length in his evidence to the Macmillan Committee (reprinted by Hawtrey 1932a). There he analysed the consequences for an open economy of public-works expenditures financed by a government borrowing operation that would divert funds from foreign lending and would therefore, given the workings of the gold standard, improve the balance of payments. He concluded, first, that "the amount of employment given is determined not by the numbers employed on the works that the Government undertakes, but by the increase in the consumers' income and outlay permitted by the change in the balance of payments" (Hawtrey 1932, p. 438), and, second, that "the desired end can be achieved by dropping out the expenditure on development works, and using the proceeds of the loan to extinguish Government floating debt in the hands of the banks and the money market" (Hawtrey 1932, p. 443).

Concluding Comment

It is quite evident from this and the preceding chapter that in the 1920s the Cambridge tradition encompassed a wide variety of viewpoints. On policy

---

[23] The similarity between that argument and the argument advanced by Friedman (1974) concerning the role of money finance in rendering fiscal policy effective is both obvious and striking. Here, then, is another reason, in addition to his monetary theory of the cycle, for regarding Hawtrey as a predecessor of the monetarism of the 1960s and 1970s. On this matter, and on the more general similarities between monetarism and the Cambridge economics discussed in this and the preceding chapter, see Presley (1986b).

issues, they ranged from scepticism about the powers of monetary measures to influence output and employment, such as Pigou and Robertson expressed, accompanied by a belief that public-works expenditures were highly desirable components of any policy package, all the way to Hawtrey's diametrically opposed position. And in the theoretical arena the contrast between the eclecticism of the former and the essentially monocausal monetary explanation of the latter was equally striking.

It is also evident that in 1923, Keynes was still closer to Marshall in his views than to any of his contemporaries. His stress on monetary factors differentiated his views strongly from those of Robertson and Pigou, but his emphasis on the critical importance of price-level behaviour per se rendered them just as distinct from those of Hawtrey, with his focus on the role of effective demand. Even in 1923, however, Keynes noted that real economic disturbances were closely related to dislocations of the inter-temporal allocative mechanism, though he did not delve deeply into those questions, being content to attribute the problems involved to price-level variations to whose explanation the Marshallian version of the quantity theory could be applied. The fact is that in 1923, if Keynes had read anything by Wicksell, he had failed to grasp the significance of Wicksell's message about the relationship between the monetary system and the processes of saving and investment. By 1930 it was a different matter, and the *Treatise on Money* was, as is well known, a systematic attempt to integrate Wicksell's insights with the Marshallian version of the quantity theory. That attempt, and certain reactions to it, notably on the part of Hayek, who was, as we have already seen, at that time in the process of developing a very different line of analysis, also grounded on Wicksell's insights, will provide the topics to be discussed in Chapter 6.

The *Treatise on Money* and Related Contributions

The Aim of the *Treatise*

No one could possibly deny the importance of Keynes's contributions to the policy debates of the 1920s, nor indeed the lasting significance of some of the theoretical insights that they contained. But that work stopped far short of being a systematic contribution to monetary theory per se, and no one was more aware of that than Keynes himself. Almost immediately after publication of the *Tract on Monetary Reform*, he set to work on what he hoped would be a definitive and comprehensive academic treatise on monetary theory.

Keynes did not withdraw from the public arena in order to make time for the completion of the work which he hoped would cement his academic reputation, and the *Treatise on Money* appeared only in 1930. At that time Keynes was a member of the Macmillan Committee, whose work involved a comprehensive review of the workings of monetary policy in post–World War I Britain, and to which he also gave evidence. Not surprisingly, much of the content of the *Treatise* found its way into that evidence, as it also did into three lectures which he delivered in early 1931 to a conference held at the University of Chicago under the auspices of the Harris Foundation. This chapter is mainly concerned with the analysis in question, which amounted to an alternative extension of the Cambridge monetary tradition to that developed by Hawtrey, and we shall discuss some immediate reactions to it on the part of Keynes's contemporaries.

Keynes intended the *Treatise* to deal with all aspects of monetary theory and its applications. In its Preface, he lamented that

> although my field of study is one which is being lectured upon in every university in the world, there exists, extraordinarily enough, no printed treatise in any language – so far as I am aware – which deals systematically and thoroughly with the theory and facts of representative money as it exists in the modern world. (Keynes 1930a, vol. I, p. xviii)

So much for Wicksell's *Lectures* and Mises's *Theory of Money and Credit*; and small wonder that some of his contemporaries, Hayek (1931b, 1932a) in particular, took Keynes to task for his neglect of the German-language literature!

The _Treatise_ was indeed extremely wide-ranging, but as we shall see in the course of this chapter, it ultimately amounted to something a little less than the sum of its parts. At its core lay a theoretical vision of the interaction of saving and investment and the influence of that interaction on prices, and hence on the course of the cycle, expressed in terms of analysis which may be fairly characterized as an attempt to succeed where, in Keynes's view, Wicksell had failed in "linking up his [Wicksell's] theory of bank rate to the quantity equation" (Keynes 1930a, vol. I, p. 167). The trouble with the _Treatise_, however, was that, though Keynes was acutely aware of the importance of explaining fluctuations in output and employment as part of the cycle, and though those phenomena figured prominently in the more discursive passages of the book, as they did also in his Macmillan Committee evidence and Harris Foundation lectures, he failed to integrate them systematically into the theoretical core of his analysis.[1]

The Fundamental Equations

Keynes set out much of his analysis in terms of two "fundamental equations" which he wrote as follows, with P the price level of consumption goods, R their real output, E the community's nominal income, O real output of consumption and investment goods, I' income earned in the investment-goods industries, I the value of new investment goods, S nominal saving, and π the price level of output as a whole:

$$P = (E/O) + [(I' - S)/R] \tag{6.1}$$

and

$$\pi = (E/O) + [(I - S)/O] \tag{6.2}$$

These equations were derived on pages 121–123 of the _Treatise_, and though he frequently lapsed into writing about them as if they were something more, they were nevertheless, in Keynes's own words, "purely formal; they are

---

[1] Keynes himself was unhappy with the _Treatise_, describing it as "an artistic failure" in a letter to his mother. On that, see Moggridge (1992, pp. 530–531). Richard Kahn (1984, pp. 109–110) detected a marked change in emphasis between the _Treatise_ and the Harris lectures, with the latter concentrating much more systematically on unemployment. It is true that relatively more space was devoted to discussing unemployment per se in those lectures, and, indeed, in Keynes's Macmillan Committee evidence too, than in the _Treatise_. It seems to me, however, that that reflected the fact that the _Treatise_ was meant to be a general academic treatment of monetary theory and policy, whereas the other two sources were aimed more directly at current policy questions. I have been able to detect no differences in the analyses per se among those three expositions. It is just that the analytic framework underlying Keynes's thought was laid out more explicitly and in more detail in the _Treatise_, so that its inadequacies are more visible there.

mere identities; truisms which tell us nothing in themselves. In this respect they resemble all other versions of the quantity theory of money" (Keynes 1930a, vol. I, p. 125).[2]

If for "quantity theory of money" we substitute "equation of exchange, in income-velocity form," we may accept that characterization of the equations; but we must also note that much of the difficulty we have in immediately recognizing that they amount to no more than a pair of somewhat eccentric variations on this well-known tautology arises from the fact that in defining money income E, Keynes *excluded* profits:

> We propose to mean identically the same thing by the three expressions: (1) *the community's money income*; (2) *the earnings of the factors of production*; and (3) *the cost of production*; and we reserve the term *profits* for the difference between the cost of production of the current output and its actual sale proceeds, so that profits are not part of the community's income as thus defined. (Keynes 1930a, vol. I, p. 111, italics in original)

Because *savings* was defined as "the sum of the differences between the money incomes of individuals and their money expenditure on current consumption" (Keynes 1930a, vol. I, p. 113), and the "value of investment [as] the value of the increment of capital during any period" (Keynes 1930a, vol. I, p. 114), it then followed that "the value of current investment . . . will be equal to the aggregate of savings and profits" (Keynes 1930a, vol. I, p. 114).

Saving and Investment

Keynes's odd definition of income was thus chosen so as to permit his measures of saving and investment to differ from one another, a characteristic which seemed desirable in a model designed to analyse a world where "the decisions which determine saving and investment respectively are taken by two different sets of people influenced by different sets of motives, each not paying very much attention to the other" (Keynes 1930a, vol. I, p. 250). The *ex ante–ex post* distinction, soon to be developed by the Stockholm School, was missing from his conceptual framework, and as Robertson (1949, pp. xi–xii) was later to note, Keynes was frequently prone to confusion about the analytic significance of the accounting identity between saving and investment when income was more conventionally defined.[3]

---

[2] For what is perhaps the clearest exposition of the relationship between the fundamental equations and the quantity theory of money, see Patinkin (1987). See also Bridel (1987, ch. 7) for a discussion of the relationship between the fundamental equations and Keynes's eccentric definitions of saving, investment, income, and profits, as well as the manner in which all of that related to the development of Cambridge analysis of saving–investment interaction.

[3] As pointed out in Chapter 3 (fn. 11), Joan Robinson (1939) would note the superiority of the Stockholm School's *ex ante–ex post* approach to the issue of reconciling the independence

Keynes's eccentric definitions were, however, of more than merely semantic importance. In combination with his occasional proclivity to attribute behavioural significance to the fundamental equations in which he embedded them, they misled him into making an important but fallacious claim about the substantive implications of any discrepancies between saving and investment – profits and losses, in his terminology – for the behaviour of the economy. Specifically, he argued, making explicit use of the first of his fundamental equations, equation (6.1), as a frame of reference, that in a situation where investment exceeded saving, so that profits were positive,

> if entrepreneurs choose to spend a portion of their profits on consumption
> . . . the effect is to *increase* the profit on the sale of . . . consumption goods
> by an amount exactly equal to the amount of profits which have been thus
> expended. This follows from our definitions, because such expenditure con
> stitutes a diminution of saving, and, therefore an increase in the difference
> between I and S. Thus, however much of their profits entrepreneurs spend
> on consumption, the increment of wealth belonging to entrepreneurs remains
> the same as before. Thus profits, as a source of capital increment for
> entrepreneurs, are a widow's cruse which remains undepleted however much
> of them may be devoted to riotous living. When, on the other hand, entre
> preneurs are making losses, and seek to recoup these losses by curtailing
> their normal expenditure on consumption, i.e. by saving more, the cruse
> becomes a Danaid jar which can never be filled up; for the effect of this
> reduced expenditure is to inflict on the producers of consumption goods a
> loss of an equal amount. (Keynes 1930a, vol. I, p. 125)

The Widow's Cruse Fallacy

Readers of the *Treatise*, not least Keynes's own younger colleagues at Cambridge, who constituted a self-styled "circus" of friendly critics of the book, soon noted a difficulty with that argument, to which one of them, namely, Joan Robinson, gave the label *widow's cruse fallacy*.[4] Dennis Robertson (1931a), who acknowledged the contribution of James Meade, another member of the circus, in "putting me on the right track here" (Robertson 1931a, p. 408, fn.), explained the problem to readers of the *Economic Journal* as follows:

---

of the investment and saving decisions with the existence of an accounting identity linking the two magnitudes. As we learned from Steiger (1971), Lindahl attempted to open a correspondence with Keynes on that issue in 1934, but with scant success. See footnote 6 in Chapter 10.

[4] For a first-hand account of the activities of the circus, see Austin Robinson (1977). Their role in the development of Keynes's own economic thought has been discussed, *inter alia*, by Skidelsky (1992, pp. 447–448), Moggridge (1992, pp. 532–533), Dimand (1988, pp. 87–88, 127–145), and Patinkin (1977, pp. 6–7).

... the quasi-magical peculiarity attributed to profits ... turns out ... to be only a special case of the general principle ... that all money must at any moment be somewhere; so that if we have ruled out (openly) the possibility that "costs" per unit of output can rise *and (tacitly) the possibility that output, and therefore aggregate costs, can be increased*, the money spent on any day by one entrepreneur must be found at nightfall in the bank balance of another. (Robertson 1931a, pp. 408–409, italics added, except for *aggregate*, which was italicized in the original)

Hayek, a less sympathetic critic than Robertson, pointed out to readers of *Economica* that some of Keynes's

most baffling conclusions, such as the famous analogy between profits and the widow's cruse and losses and the Danaid jar, are expressly based on the assumption "merely (*sic!*) that entrepreneurs were continuing to produce the same output as before." (Hayek 1932a, p. 31, italics in original)

And Hayek characterized Keynes's admission, in response to Robertson (Keynes 1931b, p. 412), "that he did not ... deal in detail 'with the train of events which ensues when, as a consequence of making losses, entrepreneurs reduce their output'" as "most surprising ... from an author who has set out to study the shifts between available and non-available output and wants to *prove* that saving will not lead to the necessary shifts" (Hayek 1932a, pp. 31–32, italics in original).[5]

One of Keynes's key theoretical propositions, namely, "that a boom is generated when investment exceeds saving and a slump is generated when saving exceeds investment" (Keynes 1931a, p. 21), thus applied in strict logic only to booms and slumps in the price level. Even so, Keynes, like all of his contemporaries, knew very well that fluctuations in output and employment were of the very essence of the cycle, and, again like most, if not quite all, of those same contemporaries, he believed those fluctuations to be the results of a failure of market mechanisms to harmonize saving and investment decisions. He was quite clear in his evidence to the Macmillan Committee, given in March 1930, that downward pressure on prices resulting from an excess of saving over investment brought on by contractionary monetary policy, for which an increase in bank rate was his shorthand expression, would in the first instance be exerted through a rise in unemployment:

That is the natural progress of causation. There is no way by which Bank rate brings down prices except through the increase of unemployment. It brings down prices by causing enterprisers to sell at a loss, but it does not

---

[5] As the reader will note, that criticism by Hayek stemmed from his own view that the effects of a current dislocation of saving and investment decisions would fall mainly on the time structures of future production and consumption rather than on the current level of output. In the vocabulary I adopted in Chapters 2 and 3, Keynes was very much a "demand-side" Wicksellian, in the same tradition as the Stockholm School.

> bring them down to the equilibrium price level except by operating through
> unemployment . . . putting on pressure for the price of labour to fall.
> (Keynes 1930b, pp. 49–50)

But the fact remains that in his attempts to come formally to grips with the
mechanisms discussed here, Keynes failed to integrate output and employment movements into his story.[6]

Serious though the aforementioned flaw was for the overall analytic coherence of the *Treatise on Money*, Keynes's particular vision of how independently taken saving and investment decisions were (or were not) co-ordinated
in a monetary economy by movements in interest rates in general, and bank
rate in particular, remained important. The *consequences* of co-ordination
failures for real variables were not properly worked out in the book, but it
nevertheless had many interesting things to say about *how co-ordination
failures arose*.

Keynes's Version of Monetary Equilibrium

There were echoes of Hawtrey in Keynes's treatment of the influence of the
rate of interest on saving and investment, but the investment decisions which
particularly concerned him were long-term ones, rather than those taken by
merchants with respect to their inventories, and that linked the theoretical
vision of the *Treatise* more closely to Wicksell than to Hawtrey, as Keynes
himself was aware:

> Whilst . . . Mr. Hawtrey has limited [the bank rate's] influence to one partic-
> ular kind of investment, namely investment by dealers in stocks of liquid
> goods, Wicksell . . . was closer to the fundamental conception of bank rate
> as affecting the relationship between investment and saving. (Keynes 1930a,
> vol. I, pp. 175–176)

The Natural Rate of Interest

Keynes's vision of the relationships among saving, investment, and interest
rates was essentially the same variation on Wicksell's vision that underlay

---

[6] It is interesting to note that, in the first volume of *The Theory of Prices*, Arthur Marget (1938–
41), in what was, overall, an extremely hostile commentary in the *Treatise*, was nevertheless
willing to concede that the book did contain a theory of output based upon the stickiness of
costs: ". . . such 'stickiness' was essential to the theory of output presented in the *Treatise*. It
is significant, however, that he [Keynes] tended to stress instances in which entrepreneurs . . .
subjected to out-of-pocket losses . . . would continue to make payments to the factors of
production at the abnormally high level of costs" (Marget 1938–41, vol. 1, p. 128). The main
thrust of Marget's book, however, which appeared too late to have any influence, was "criticism not of Mr. Keynes's positive analysis, but of his own criticism of received doctrine"
(vol. 1, p. vii). As such it is an obsessively wide-ranging documentation of Keynes's frequent
lack of generosity to his predecessors, which scores many accurate points of detail, but which
offers no alternative message to its readers.

the work of his Swedish contemporaries, particularly Lindahl and Myrdal, as described in Chapter 3, as a comparison of the following passage with the material presented there will make clear:[7]

> The attractiveness of investment depends on the prospective income which the entrepreneur anticipates from current investment relatively to the rate of interest which he has to pay in order to be able to finance its production; or, putting it the other way round, the value of capital goods depends on the rate of interest at which the prospective income from them is capitalised . . . [t]he rate of saving, on the other hand, is stimulated by a high rate of interest and discouraged by a low rate. It follows that an increase in the rate of interest tends – other things being equal – to make the rate of investment . . . decline relatively to the rate of saving . . . so that the price level tends to fall.
>
> Following Wicksell, it will be convenient to call the rate of interest which would cause the second term of our second fundamental equation [equation (6.2)] to be zero the *natural rate* of interest, and the rate which actually prevails the *market rate* of interest. Thus the natural rate of interest is the rate at which saving and the value of investment are exactly balanced, so that the price level of output as a whole . . . exactly corresponds to the money rate of the efficiency earnings of the factors of production. Every departure of the market rate from the natural rate tends, on the other hand, to set up a disturbance of the price level by causing the second term of the second fundamental equation to depart from zero. (Keynes 1930a, vol. I, pp. 138–139, italics in original)

Note in particular that, like the aforementioned Swedish economists, Keynes was treating the natural rate of interest not as some physical characteristic of the economy's production processes but rather as a discount rate at which "prospective income . . . is capitalised." However, whereas the Swedes had adopted that way of looking at things in the light of their knowledge of Cassel's and Fisher's analysis of the difficulties inherent in the Austrian alternative, there is no evidence to suggest that when he wrote the *Treatise*, Keynes was aware of the essentially Fisherine origins of his way of looking at things, or that, the occasional passing reference (e.g., Keynes 1930a, vol. I, p. 178) notwithstanding, he had thought deeply about the

---

[7] It seems to have been a visit by Bertil Ohlin to Cambridge in 1923–24 which first led the Cambridge economists to begin to appreciate the importance of Wicksell's monetary theory, an appreciation that led Keynes, in about 1930, to arrange for Richard Kahn to prepare the translation of *Interest and Prices* which appeared in 1936. On the matter of Wicksell's influence on the *Treatise*, see Bertil Ohlin's "Appendix 3" in the volume edited by Patinkin and Leith (1977), particularly pages 149–150. This is not to say that influence ran only one way from Sweden to Cambridge. On the contrary, there is good reason to believe that the Stockholm School's work during the early 1930s, particularly that bearing more directly on stabilization policy, was strongly influenced by Cambridge work, not least that by Keynes and Henderson (1929). The 1932 quotation from Ohlin (Chapter 3, "The Distinctive Characteristics of Swedish Analysis") would tend to bear that out. For a brief but to-the-point discussion of this issue, and references to relevant literature, see the contribution of Donald Winch (Patinkin and Leith 1977, p. 76).

Austrian alternative upon which Mises and Hayek had constructed their own theory of the cycle.[8]

Keynes believed that equality between the natural rate and the market rate of interest, though it involved equality between saving and investment, guaranteed nothing determinate about the behaviour of the price level other than that it would correspond to that of "the money rate of *efficiency earnings* of the factors of production" (Keynes 1930a, p. 139, italics added): that is, productivity-adjusted money wages in the case of labour, which Keynes usually treated as the only relevant input. Thus, Keynes solved those difficulties about how to characterize a Wicksellian monetary equilibrium in the presence of productivity change, which had so exercised the Austrians, by tucking them into a *ceteris paribus* clause and by tacitly assuming that wages dominated marginal-production costs to the extent that other components could be ignored.

Keynes furthermore believed, once again like the Swedes, particularly Myrdal, that money wages would be sticky in a market economy:[9]

> Under a socialist system the money rate of efficiency earnings of the factors of production might be suddenly altered by *fiat*. Theoretically, I suppose, it might change under a system of competitive individualism by an act of collective foresight on the part of entrepreneurs in anticipation of impending monetary changes, or by a *coup de main* on the part of trade unions. Practically . . . prices may be modified as the result of a spontaneous change in the actual rate of earnings relatively to efficiency, on account of a change either in the method of fixing wages or in the coefficient of efficiency. In existing circumstances, however, the most usual and important occasion of change will be the action of the entrepreneurs, under the influence of the actual enjoyment of positive or negative profits, in increasing or diminishing the volume of employment which they offer at the existing rates of remuneration of the factors of production, and so bringing about a raising or a lowering of these rates. (Keynes 1930a, vol. I, p. 141, italics in original)

As a practical matter, therefore, Keynes characterized situations of monetary equilibrium (in which profits, as he defined them, would be zero) as involving prices following a time path dominated by that of money wages, to which he,

---

[8] Keynes (1914) had reviewed the first (1912) edition of Mises's *Theory of Money and Credit* in the *Economic Journal* when it appeared, but the review was superficial, doing nothing to cast doubt upon its author's later denials of competence in German. In any event, Mises's cycle theory was more fully developed in the 1924 edition of his book, and there is no reason to suppose that Keynes had read that edition. I am indebted to Robert Dimand for useful discussion of this matter.

[9] For Myrdal's discussion (1931) of that matter, see Chapter 3, "Monetary Policy." Whether or not the Cambridge economists influenced the Swedes on that particular matter is not relevant to the discussion at hand, but see footnote 7 on the interaction of the two groups during that period. The reader's attention is drawn to the fact that in the following quotation, Keynes raised, and just as quickly dismissed, what in the 1970s and 1980s was to become an important hypothesis, namely, that money wages could be expected to respond without difficulty to anticipated policy changes.

like Myrdal, attributed "the ability . . . to have a trend of their own over long periods" (Keynes 1930a, vol. I, p. 83). That was also why, yet again like Myrdal, he argued that "we may do well in choosing our [monetary] standard to consider what will fit in best with whatever may be the natural tendencies of spontaneous change which characterise the earnings system as it actually is" (Keynes 1930a, vol. I, p. 152); though he was quick to add a rider: ". . . provided always that the rate of change in the price level is kept within narrow limits" (Keynes 1930a, vol. I, p. 153).

Money and the Interest Rate

Now an important aim of the *Treatise* was to provide a satisfactory link between what Keynes called the "theory of bank rate" and the quantity theory of money. He regarded earlier Cambridge analysis of those matters as inadequate. He pointed out, quite correctly, that such analysis had been grounded in a conception of "bank rate as acting directly on the quantity of bank credit and so on prices in accordance with the quantity equation" (Keynes 1930a, vol. I, p. 168). Hawtrey, he noted, had gone a little beyond that by taking account of the additional *direct* influence of bank rate on planned inventory investment, but it was Wicksell who had taken the decisive step in what Keynes regarded as the right direction, by being

> the first writer to make it clear that the influence of the rate of interest on the price level operates by its effect on the rate of investment, and that *investment* in this context means *investment* and not speculation. (Keynes 1930a, vol. I, p. 177, italics in original)

According to Keynes, even though Wicksell had been right in stressing the influence of the interest rate, he had nevertheless left the role of the quantity of bank money in the price-formation process unclear.[10] Keynes summarized his own view of the matter in following way:

> Given associated changes in the total quantity of money and in the effective level of bank rate respectively, it is via the latter that the ultimate modification in the purchasing power of money is generated, looking at the problem dynamically. The order of events is *not* that a change of bank rate affects the price level because, in order to make the new bank rate effective, the quantity of money has to be altered. It is, rather, the other way round. A change in the quantity of money affects the price level in the first instance, because . . . this means a bank rate which will change the market rate of interest relatively to the natural rate. . . .
> If we start from a position of equilibrium, then – provided that efficiency

---

[10]   Indeed, as was stressed in Chapter 3, "The Role of Expectations," Wicksell's neglect of that issue turned what should have been a matter of semantics into an important substantive issue and coloured much of the subsequent development of Swedish monetary economics.

earnings are stable – the condition for the continued stability of price levels is that the total volume of money should vary in such a way that the effect of the corresponding volume of bank lending on the market rate of interest is to keep the value of new investment at an equality with current saving. (Keynes 1930a, vol. I, p. 197)

Two questions arise here. First, how does bank rate influence the longer-term interest rates relevant to investment decisions? And second, what mechanisms enable the quantity of money to play its part in validating not only the stability of the price level that results from equality between the natural and market rates of interest, but also price-level changes, whose immediate cause is a discrepancy between these rates? Keynes answered the first of these questions by assumption in Volume I of the *Treatise*. He simply asserted the existence of a reliable link between bank rate and longer rates and referred his readers to Chapter 37 in Volume II for a detailed discussion of that link (Keynes 1930a, vol. I, p. 180). (See "Monetary Policy's Transmission Mechanism," later in this chapter.)

The Demand for Money

To deal with the second of the aforementioned questions, Keynes deployed a version of what, in the *General Theory*, he would call the theory of liquidity preference. Though, overall, his analysis here was by no means complete, not least because of its failure to consider changes in real output and their effects on the demand for money when the system was out of full equilibrium, his development of it was, in and of itself, of considerable interest. Indeed, Hayek characterized it as "in many respects, the most interesting part of his theoretical analysis . . . there is no doubt that he is here breaking new ground and that he has opened up new vistas" (Hayek 1932, pp. 34–35).

Keynes began by distinguishing between, on the one hand, what he called "*income deposits* and . . . *business deposits* [which] together make up what we shall call the *cash deposits*" (Keynes 1930a, vol. I, p. 31, italics in original), and, on the other, *savings deposits*. That distinction involved the motives underlying the demand for money. Specifically, cash deposits served the requirements of what he called "the industrial circulation," and savings deposits those of "the financial circulation."[11] But the distinction also in-

---

[11] It should be noted that the Italian economist Marco Fanno (1912) had similarly attempted to integrate the quantity theory with Wicksell's analysis along lines very similar to those later followed by Keynes, including development of an analysis of the demand for money that made use of a distinction between what Keynes would later call the industrial and financial circulations. Like Keynes's work also, Fanno's work dealt with a fully employed economy. The development of Italian monetary economics in the inter-war years clearly could bear a great deal more attention than it has so far received.

volved, at least approximately, the particular classes of bank liability that satisfied those competing requirements:

> A cash deposit roughly corresponds to what Americans call demand deposits and we call current accounts; and a savings deposit to what Americans call time deposits and we call deposit accounts. A savings deposit also corresponds to what used to be called in theories of money, which were stated with primary reference to a commodity money, the use of money as a "Store of Value." But the correspondence is not exact. (Keynes 1930a, vol. I, p. 32)

Keynes's analysis of the demand for cash deposits need not detain us, for it involved essentially the same minor extension of the Marshall-Pigou treatment of the demand for money that Hawtrey had deployed in *Currency and Credit*. His treatment of the demand for savings deposits, however, requires more attention.

To begin with, like Lavington (1921), whose clarity about this matter had been something of an anomaly in earlier Cambridge theorizing about the demand for money, but without citing him, Keynes treated the demand for savings deposits as involving the allocation of wealth: ". . . the decision as to holding bank deposits or securities relates, not only to the current increment to the wealth of individuals, but also to the whole block of their existing capital" (Keynes 1930a, vol. I, p. 127). Furthermore, the demand for savings deposits would vary systematically with the opportunity cost of holding them, which in turn was measured by the difference between the own rates of return on deposits and on securities.

> Now when an individual is more disposed than before to hold his wealth in the form of savings deposits and less . . . in other forms, this does not mean that he is determined to hold it in the form of savings deposits *at all costs*. It means that he favours savings deposits (for whatever reason) more than before at the existing price level of other securities. But his distaste for other securities is not absolute and depends on his expectations of the future return to be obtained from savings deposits and from other securities respectively, which is obviously affected by the price of the latter – and also by the rate of interest allowed on the former. (Keynes 1930a, vol. I, pp. 127–128, italics in original)

It will be noted that the experiment Keynes was discussing postulated *shifts* in the public's demand for savings deposits. To use Keynes's terms, an increase in "bullishness" would cause a shift out of deposits into securities, and in "bearishness" a shift in the opposite direction – this latter case being the one Robertson had analysed under the label "abortive lacking" in *Banking Policy and the Price Level*.[12] Thus, "it follows that the actual price level

---

[12] See Chapter 4 for a discussion of Robertson on "abortive lacking." Lavington's analysis of the demand for money is also discussed in Chapter 4.

of investments is the resultant of the sentiment of the public and the behaviour of the banking system'' (Keynes 1930a, vol. I, p. 128). It also follows that

> given the total quantity of money, only those combinations of the rate of earnings, the volume of output and the price level of securities are feasible which lead to the aggregate requirements of money being equal to the given total.
> This means, indeed, that in equilibrium . . . there is a unique relationship between the quantity of money and the price levels of consumption goods and of output as a whole, of such a character that if the quantity of money were double the price levels would be double also.
> *But this simple and direct quantitative relationship is a phenomenon only of equilibrium.* (Keynes 1930a, vol. I, p. 132, italics added)

That is, the relationship would hold only if, given the levels of output and prices, the rate of interest that equated the supply and demand for savings deposits also was equal to the natural rate of interest at which saving and investment were equal. The rate of interest thus had to bring about equilibrium on two margins simultaneously, but by what mechanisms that might occur, and what the implications of that would be for the behaviour of his system when it was not in full equilibrium, Keynes did not say. Discussion of that matter had to await the appearance of the *General Theory*.

A Digression: Hicks on the Demand for Money

What Hayek had termed the ''new vistas'' which the theory of the demand for money developed in the *Treatise* opened up were broader than those which Keynes himself would further survey a few years later. In particular, John Hicks's celebrated 1935 paper, ''A Suggestion for Simplifying the Theory of Money,'' amounted to a self-conscious call for ''a marginal revolution'' in monetary theory (Hicks 1935, p. 49).[13] Hicks explicitly recognized that the idea upon which such a revolution might be based

> emerges when Mr. Keynes begins to talk about the price-level of investment goods; when he shows that this price-level depends upon the relative preference of the investor – to hold bank deposits or to hold securities. Here at

---

[13] Hicks was not the only one to develop an analysis of the demand for money in the early 1930s along lines that would not bear fruit until the post-war years. In particular, the work of S. P. (Sir Paul) Chambers (1934) should be noted. In some respects, that work, which derived an explicit inventory theoretic model of the demand for transactions balances, and drew indifference curves between risk and return in the course of analysing what we would now call the precautionary demand for money, went beyond Hicks's much better known analysis, even though it antedated Hicks. On Chambers's paper, see J. C. Gilbert (1953) and Ivo Maes (1991).

last we have something which to a value theorist looks sensible and interesting! Here at last we have a choice at the margin! (Hicks 1935, p. 49)

Hicks went considerably beyond the *Treatise* with his own particular version of liquidity-preference theory. Referring to recent developments in consumer theory, to which he, along with Roy Allen, had been an important
contributor (e.g., Hicks and Allen 1934), his "suggestion [was] that monetary
theory needs to be based upon a similar analysis . . . not of an income account
but of a capital account, a balance sheet," and he carried that through,
developing an approach to the demand not just for deposit accounts, but for
money in general, in which, as he summarized it, "the amount of money
demanded depends upon three groups of factors: (1) the individual's subjective preference for holding money or other things; (2) his wealth; (3) his
anticipations of future prices and risks" (Hicks 1935, p. 50, fn. 7).[14]

Hicks's ideas on those matters were at least as much in the spirit of
Lavington's work as of the *Treatise*, and they formed an important link
between the inter-war literature and post-war literature on monetary economics, particularly that dealing with the microeconomics of the demand for
money. For developments in the inter-war period per se, the significance of
that 1935 paper was more limited, however. Hicks's argument "that it is
from this point [the analogy with value theory], not from velocity of circulation, natural rate of interest, or Saving and Investment, that we ought to start
constructing the theory of money" (Hicks 1935, p. 49) found no wide audience at that time. Instead of at once becoming the basis of a new approach to
monetary theory in general, his "Simplification" was seen as a development
parallel to Keynes's own further refinement of liquidity-preference theory, a
view which Hicks himself did much to encourage, not least by his own 1937
linking of Keynes's analysis, as set out in the *General Theory*, to the analyses
of Pigou and Lavington, while ignoring his own.[15]

The Cycle in the *Treatise*

It has already been noted that discrepancies between the market rate and
natural rate of interest, between saving and investment, and the occurrences
of abnormal profits or losses lay at the heart of Keynes's formal explanation
of price-level movements, and his informal explanation of output and employment changes too. By simple extension, then, what Keynes called "the
credit cycle" became, in the *Treatise*, an essentially disequilibrium phenom-

---

[14] The *locus classicus* for the approach to consumer theory with which Hicks here drew an
analogy was, of course, his own *Value and Capital* (1939, chs. 1–3).

[15] For Hicks's own acknowledgement of the relationship of his 1935 analysis to that of Lavington (1921), see Hicks (1935, repr. 1982, p. 48, fn. 2). For his later discussion, see Hicks
(1937, repr. 1982, pp. 132–133). It was probably Dennis Robertson who drew his attention to
Lavington's work. See footnote 11 in Chapter 12.

enon characterized by *movements* in the discrepancy between the market interest rate and its natural level. It was, furthermore, his empirical judgement, one which he shared with Wicksell, that movements in the natural rate were usually the initiating factors. Hence, and crucially, the cycle was presented as controllable by monetary policy, more specifically bank-rate policy, designed to eliminate, and then avoid the re-emergence of, such a discrepancy.

Keynes was wary of laying down any particular sequence of events as characteristic of cyclical fluctuations in general – "The possible varieties of the paths which a credit cycle can follow and its possible complications are so numerous that it is impracticable to outline all of them" (Keynes 1930a, vol. I, p. 253) – but nevertheless (and worth quoting at length),

> we may allow ourselves, by way of simplification, to pick out one path in particular which seems to us to be sufficiently frequented to deserve, perhaps, to be called the usual or normal course.
>
> Something happens – of a non-monetary character – to increase the attractions of investment. . . .
>
> The rise in the natural rate of interest, corresponding to the increased attractions of investment, is not held back by increased saving; and the expanding volume of investment is not restrained by an adequate rise in the market rate of interest.
>
> This acquiescence of the banking system in the increased volume of investment may involve it in allowing some increase in the total quantity of money; but at first the necessary increase is not likely to be great and may be taken up, almost unnoticed, out of the general slack of the system, or may be supplied by a falling off in the requirements of the financial circulation without any change in the total volume of money.
>
> At this stage the output and price of capital goods begin to rise. Employment improves and the wholesale index rises. The increased expenditure of the newly employed then raises the price of consumption goods and allows the producers of such goods to reap a windfall profit. By this time . . . all classes of entrepreneurs will be enjoying a profit. . . .
>
> . . . [A]fter a large proportion of the unemployed factors have been absorbed into employment, the entrepreneurs bidding against one another under the stimulus of high profits will begin to offer higher rates of remuneration.
>
> All the while, therefore, the requirements of the industrial circulation will be increasing. . . . A point will come, therefore, when the banking system is no longer able to supply the necessary volume of money consistently with its principles and traditions. . . .
>
> It may be . . . that the turning-point will come, not from the reluctance or the inability of the banking system to finance the increased earnings bill, but from one or more of three other causes. The turn may come from a faltering of financial sentiment. . . . If so, the growth of "bear" sentiment will . . . increase the requirements of the financial circulation . . . the tendency of the financial circulation to increase, on top of the increase in the industrial circulation, . . . will break the back of the banking system and

cause it at long last to impose a rate of interest, which is not only fully equal to the natural rate but, very likely in the changed circumstances, well above it.

Or it may be that the attractions of new investment will wear themselves out with time. . . .

Or, finally, . . . there is likely to be a sympathetic reaction . . . owing to the inevitable collapse in the prices of consumption goods below their higher level. (Keynes 1930a, vol. I, pp. 271–273)

Keynes and Cambridge Cycle Theory

Evidently, in 1930, there was a strong streak of eclecticism in Keynes's views on what impulses might get expansion going and on what factors might cause a downturn to begin; but the foregoing passage did identify certain features of the cycle as essential. Those, in turn, placed his work firmly in the Cambridge tradition as represented by Lavington and Pigou, and to a lesser extent, Robertson and Hawtrey as well.

To begin with, for Keynes, as for the first three of those theorists, fluctuations in the rate of investment in fixed capital were clearly the main components in fluctuations in the demand for output. Unlike Robertson, however, Keynes paid no attention to the consequences of those fluctuations for the structure of the economy's capital stock, and hence for its capacity to supply a particular mix of output, a characteristic of the analysis of the *Treatise* which, not surprisingly, came in for much criticism from Hayek (1931b, 1932a) in particular. Second, Keynes, like Lavington, postulated that the relationship between the *demand* for money and the rate of interest was sufficiently well determined to permit output and the price level to vary systematically and independently of the *supply* of money. Third, and for all of those elaborations, a rather Hawtreyan mechanism underlay the cycle as it was described in the *Treatise on Money*, namely, a market rate of interest which lagged behind its equilibrium level because of the workings of the monetary system, and then overshot that level as that system belatedly overreacted to the pressures thus created.[16]

All in all, it would be difficult to disagree with Hayek's designation of Keynes as a "purchasing-power theorist" (i.e., one who attributed cyclical fluctuations to variations in the aggregate rate of flow of expenditure in the economy) or with his verdict that

Mr Keynes' explanation of the cycle . . . [i]n essence . . . is not only relatively simple, but also much less different from the current explanations

---

[16] Nevertheless, Keynes's analysis there was by no means identical with that of Hawtrey. Indeed, Hawtrey's analysis of the role of shifts in the public's currency deposit ratio, stemming from the effects of wage stickiness on the distribution of income between wages and profits, made his treatment of that matter a good deal more precise than Keynes's. On Hawtrey's discussion, see Chapter 5.

than its author seems to think; though it is, of course, much more complicated in its details. (Hayek 1932a, p. 41)

Stabilization Policy

The justness of Hayek's designation is further confirmed by Keynes's treatment of stabilization policy in *A Treatise on Money*. Indeed, his discussion of those matters, not only in the book but also in his Macmillan Committee evidence and in his Harris Foundation lectures, demonstrated a continuing and strong affinity to that purely monetary branch of Cambridge cycle theory discussed in the preceding chapter, one to which he himself had contributed in the *Tract*. Though Keynes clearly disagreed with Hawtrey's "Treasury view" on the ineffectiveness of public-works expenditures, he was still, in the early 1930s, completely at one with Hawtrey in regarding *properly timed* bank-rate variations as sufficient to stabilize the economy under normal circumstances, and open-market operations as a weapon powerful enough to deal with deep depression, unless, as we shall see later, international complications inhibited their deployment.

Monetary Policy's Transmission Mechanism

Keynes's and Hawtrey's similar views on the effectiveness of monetary policy were nevertheless underpinned by rather different positive analyses of its transmission mechanism. Where Hawtrey stressed the importance of variations in the quantity of money – the unspent margin – as the principal influence on the rate of flow of nominal expenditure, and saw bank-rate policy and open-market operations as means of bringing about those variations in the quantity of money, Keynes saw causation as running mainly through the direct effects of interest-rate changes on expenditure, the critical relationship being between long-term interest rates and investment in fixed capital.[17] Though he conceded that short-term interest-rate variations might also influence planned inventory investment and money creation, he thought that that channel of causation played only a secondary role (Keynes 1930a, vol. II, pp. 326–327). The critical requirement for a depressed economy, then, was to stimulate investment by reducing the long-term rate of interest. As he put it in his Harris Foundation lectures,

> the central idea that I wish to leave with you is the vital necessity for a society, living in the phase in which we are living today, to bring down the

---

[17] In terms of a later vocabulary, Hawtrey stressed the importance of the "monetary channel" in the transmission of monetary policy, whereas Keynes stressed the "credit channel." In the latter respect, Keynes was following Wicksell, whose failure properly to appreciate that demand deposits could be analysed as a form of money led him to concentrate entirely on the credit channel.

> long-term rate of interest at a pace appropriate to the underlying facts. (Keynes 1931a, p. 366)

Monetary policy, however, involved, first of all, changes in short-term interest rates, and as we shall see in due course, the proposition that its powers over long rates were severely limited, particularly when the latter were already low, was to become a prominent feature of the analysis in the *General Theory*. In the early 1930s, however, Keynes held exactly contrary views on that point. At that time, he firmly believed that variations in short rates, and bank rate in particular, would have a systematic and reliable influence on long rates. He told the readers of the *Treatise* that "short-term rates influence long-term rates more than [they] might expect" (Keynes 1930a, vol. II, p. 324), albeit for reasons stemming from motives whose strict rationality

> I leave it to others to judge. They are best regarded . . . as an example of how sensitive – over-sensitive if you like – to the near future, about which we may think that we know a little, even the best informed must be, because, in truth, we know almost nothing about the more remote future. (Keynes 1930a, vol. II, p. 322)

And, he continued, elaborating a theme which, as we have seen, occurred in Pigou's work, and before that in Marshall's,[18]

> if this is true of the best-informed, the vast majority of those who are concerned with the buying and selling of securities know almost nothing whatever about what they are doing. They do not possess even the rudiments of what is required for a valid judgement, and are the prey of hopes and fears easily aroused by transient events and as easily dispelled. This is one of the odd characteristics of the capitalist system under which we live. (Keynes 1930a, vol. II, p. 323)

To the objection that "mob psychology" (Keynes 1930a, vol. II, p. 324) surely provided an unreliable foundation for monetary policy, Keynes had a ready, if perhaps glib, answer:

> Nor is it so precarious as might be supposed to depend upon these psycho-logical characteristics of the market. It is a case, indeed, of a homeopathic cure. For it is just these half-unreasonable characteristics of the market which are the source of many of the troubles which it is the object of management to remedy. If investors were capable of taking longer views, the fluctuations in the natural rate of interest would not be so great as they are. The real prospects do not suffer such large and quick changes as does the spirit of enterprise. The willingness to invest is stimulated and depressed by the immediate prospects. It is not unreasonable, therefore, to depend on

---

[18] For a discussion of Pigou's views on that issue, and their relationship to those of Marshall, see Chapter 4, "Prospectiveness and Error."

> short-period influences for counteracting a violent, and perhaps unreasoning, change in sentiment. (Keynes 1930a, vol. II, p. 324)

Keynes presented essentially the same arguments in his Harris Foundation lectures, albeit more briefly. As we have already seen, he stressed to his American audience that

> the task of adjusting the long-term rate of interest to the technical possibilities of our age so that the demand for new capital is as nearly as possible equal to the community's current volume of savings must be the prime object of financial statesmanship. It may not be easy and a large change may be needed, but there is no other way out. (Keynes 1931a, p. 365)

He also assured them that orthodox monetary policy carried out through the banking system's influence over short rates was ultimately capable of achieving that objective:

> In the course of time I see no insuperable difficulty. . . . [In] the long run the banking system can affect the long-term rate by obstinately adhering to the correct policy in regard to the short-term rate. (Keynes 1931a, pp. 365–366)

Open-Market Operations and Their Limits

Keynes did, however, concede that the desired effects might come through only rather slowly. In that event, if the "normal relation between the short-term rate of interest and the long-term" (1931a, p. 365) did not work fast enough in producing the desired consequences for the long rate, then the appearance of those effects could be speeded up "by means of open market operations" (p. 366). In the Harris Foundation lectures he pointed out that the speeding-up process could also be helped in two ways: first, by lowering deposit interest, still a feature of American banking in 1931, "to the vanishing-point" (p. 366), hence reducing the attractions of liquid assets relative to long-term securities; second, by enhancing "the attractions of non-liquid assets" as a result of "increasing confidence." The *Treatise* made it quite clear, however, that Keynes, like Hawtrey, gave pride of place to open-market operations as the most potent treatment for a depressed economy which was failing to respond to a low bank rate.[19] There, he put the point as follows:

> My remedy in the event of the obstinate persistence of a slump would consist, therefore, in the purchase of securities by the central bank until the long-term market rate of interest has been brought down to the limiting point, which we shall have to admit. (Keynes, 1930a, vol. II, p. 332)

---

[19] But Keynes saw the critical role of open-market operations as being to affect long-term interest rates. Hawtrey saw them as an alternative means of increasing the money supply. See the foregoing footnote 17.

That limiting point had three potential sources, none of which Keynes thought to be of particular relevance to the contemporary American situation, but one of which was important for Britain. The first was the possibility of an insufficient supply of securities of a type suitable for central-bank purchase, a contingency whose effects Keynes thought could be offset by reducing commercial-bank reserve requirements (Keynes 1930a, vol. II, p. 334). The second might come into play "when prices are falling, profits low, the future uncertain and financial sentiment depressed and alarmed" (Keynes 1930a, vol. II, p. 334). At such a time,

> the natural rate of interest may fall, for a short period, almost to nothing [but] the bond rate, far from falling towards nothing, may be expected – apart from the operations of the central bank – to be higher than normal. (Keynes 1930a, vol. II, p. 334)

Open-market purchases carried out in that situation, in order to drive the market rate down to "almost nothing," would expose the central bank to the risk of future losses when those purchases were reversed after the natural rate had recovered. In those hypothetical (as he then judged) circumstances,

> the choice may conceivably lie between assuming the burden of a prospective loss, allowing the slump to continue, and socialistic action [i.e., public-works expenditures] by which some official body steps into the shoes which the feet of the entrepreneurs are too cold to occupy. (Keynes 1930a, vol. II, p. 335)

The third source of difficulty, immediately relevant to Britain's circumstances in 1930 in Keynes's view, was the constraint placed by the gold standard upon the authorities of any single country intent on pursuing an independent monetary policy:

> ... if foreign borrowers are ready and eager, it will be impossible in a competitive open market to bring the rate down to the level appropriate to domestic investment. Thus the desired result can only be obtained through some method by which, in effect, the Government subsidises approved types of domestic investment or itself directs domestic schemes of capital development. (Keynes 1930a, vol. II, p. 337)

Public-Works Expenditures

In his Macmillan Committee evidence, Keynes also emphasized the constraints imposed upon Britain by the gold standard, and, consistent with the passage from the *Treatise* just quoted, he discussed the case for public-works expenditures in that context. Nevertheless, at the beginning of the 1930s he still regarded such policies as very much second-best measures. That was particularly evident in the *Treatise*'s discussion of "The Slump of 1930" (Keynes 1930a, vol. II, pp. 338–347), which made it clear that Keynes thought that the slump in question would best be dealt with by the Bank of England and the Federal Reserve System collaborating to pursue "bank-rate policy and open-market operations *à outrance*" (Keynes 1930a, vol. II, p. 347).

> Not until deliberate and vigorous action has been taken along such lines as these and has failed, need we, in the light of the argument of this treatise, admit that the banking system can *not*, on this occasion, control the rate of investment and, therefore, the level of prices. (Keynes 1930a, vol. II, p. 347, italics in original)

A few months after those lines were written, Keynes did concede to his Harris Foundation audience, with respect to public-works expenditures, that

> I am not sure that as time goes by we may not have to attempt to organise methods of direct government action along these lines more deliberately than hitherto, and that such action may play an increasingly important part in the economic life of the community. (Keynes 1931a, p. 364)

But even as the Depression gathered momentum in the United States, it is evident that Keynes still saw the need for such policies as lying in the future. He was not yet convinced of the immediate desirability of applying them.

Keynes's ambivalence about public-works expenditures in the early 1930s is interesting in light of the belief, commonly held among his Marshallian contemporaries (with Hawtrey the principal exception), that monetary policy was more reliable as a weapon against booms than against slumps, so that resort to public-works expenditures in bad times was quite appropriate.[20] Keynes was not averse to such measures on theoretical grounds. On the contrary, in his 1931 Harris Foundation lectures he explicitly said that "theoretically, it seems to me, there is everything to be said for action along these lines" (Keynes 1931a, p. 364); and passages from the *Treatise*, already cited, show that, again in theory, he entertained a role for them, particularly when a slump had been permitted to get out of hand and business confidence had become deeply depressed. In 1929, moreover, before the onset of the Depression in America, and with Britain still firmly committed to the gold standard, Keynes and Hubert Henderson had defended them as practical policy for Britain, in their pamphlet *Can Lloyd George Do It?* Henderson had shortly afterwards begun to doubt the feasibility of such policies, however, and Keynes seems to have had similar, albeit less pronounced, misgivings.[21] He expressed them succinctly to the Harris Foundation as follows:

---

[20] As we shall see in Chapters 8 and 9, the commonly held Cambridge belief about those matters was also influential in the United States at that time, not least at the University of Chicago. See, for example, Douglas and Director (1931).

[21] Henderson's misgivings were largely practical rather than theoretical. Indeed, Henderson does not, in general, seem to have had much time for economic theory per se. On that and related matters, see Moggridge (1992, pp. 502–506).

> The difficulty about government programmes seems to me to be essentially
> a practical one. It is not easy to devise at short notice schemes which are
> wisely and efficiently conceived and which can be put rapidly into operation
> on a really large scale. (Keynes 1931a, p. 364)

The Central Vision of the *Treatise*

In 1930–31 Keynes displayed great faith in the power of monetary policy to
correct slumps in general, as well as what was, by then, the rapidly developing Great Contraction, if only that policy was applied with sufficient vigour.
That faith did not arise from an empirical judgement about the relative
efficacies of monetary and fiscal tools, which in turn derived from a model in
which that was essentially an empirical matter. Rather, it stemmed from the
fundamental theoretical vision which underlay the *Treatise on Money*. In a
nutshell, if investment (as Keynes defined it) exceeded saving, profits would
be positive, prices would rise, and the economy would boom; if it fell short,
businesses would make losses, prices would fall, and the economy would be
depressed.

In the Harris Foundation lectures, he summarized his argument as follows:

> That is my secret, the clue to the scientific explanation of booms and slumps
> (and of much else, as I should claim) which I offer you. For you will
> perceive that when the rate of current investment increases (without a
> corresponding change in the rate of saving) business profits increase. More-
> over, the affair is cumulative. For when business profits are high, the
> financial machine facilitates increased orders for and purchases of capital
> goods, that is, it stimulates investment still further; which means that busi-
> ness profits are still greater; and so on. . . . And contrariwise when invest-
> ment falls off. For unless savings fall equally, which is not likely to be the
> case, the necessary result is that the profits of the business world fall away.
> (Keynes 1931a, p. 354)

Those discrepancies would persist, moreover, for just so long as the market
interest rate departed from its natural level. But to the extent that the market
interest rate could be controlled by the central bank, it followed that booms
and depressions could be eliminated by appropriate actions on its part. And
in 1930–31, Keynes had only a few doubts, mainly practical and having to
do with the workings of the gold standard, about the powers of the central
bank.

Enterprise, Thrift, Growth, and Inflation

The reference to the "cumulative" nature of the processes he was describing
and the suggestion that his analysis of them applied to "much else" gave the
foregoing passage something of an ambiguous overtone. They suggested that

Keynes believed the significance of the interaction of saving and investment to extend beyond the bounds of the cycle, which was the main topic of the Harris Foundation lectures and of the *Treatise* too; and indeed there are extensive passages in the latter, more discursive than analytic, to be sure, in which Keynes suggested that he thought the interaction in question to be the key to secular growth processes as well. Thus, the lengthy Chapter 30 of the *Treatise*, "Historical Illustrations," was concerned far more with secular issues than cyclical issues, and its theme was the contrast between the virtues of what Keynes called *enterprise* and the pitfalls of *thrift:*

> It is enterprise which builds and improves the world's possessions. Now just as the fruits of thrift may go to provide either capital accumulation or an enhanced value of money income for the consumer, so the outgoings of enterprise may be found either out of thrift or at the expense of the consumption of the average consumer. Worse still, not only may thrift exist without enterprise, but as soon as thrift gets ahead of enterprise, it positively discourages the recovery of enterprise and sets up a vicious circle by its adverse effect on profits. If enterprise is afoot, wealth accumulates whatever may be happening to thrift; and if enterprise is asleep, wealth decays whatever thrift may be doing.
>
> Thus, thrift may be the handmaid and nurse of enterprise. But equally she may not. And, perhaps, even usually she is not. For enterprise is connected with thrift not directly but at one remove; and the link which should join them is frequently missing. For the engine which drives enterprise is not thrift but profit. (Keynes 1930a, vol. II, pp. 132–133)

The reader will recognize here overtones of the "widow's cruse" and "Danaid jar" analogies; and another of the *Treatise*'s most striking parables, that of the "thrift campaign in a banana plantation" (Keynes 1930a, vol. I, pp. 158–160), with which Keynes also entertained the Macmillan Committee (1930b, pp. 76–80), bore directly on that issue. According to Keynes, the successful introduction of such a campaign into that mythical one-output economy raised saving above investment, inducing what he would call, in Chapter 30 of the book, a *profit deflation*, a downward spiral of prices, output, and employment in which

> there will be no position of equilibrium until either (a) all production ceases and the entire population starves to death; or (b) the thrift campaign is called off or peters out as a result of the growing poverty; or (c) investment is stimulated by some means or another so that its cost no longer lags behind the rate of saving. (Keynes 1930a, vol. I, p. 160)

That simple parable was, in Keynes's view, of considerable empirical relevance. "I am inclined to attribute the well-known correspondence between falling prices and bad trade to the influence of profit deflations rather than to strictly monetary influences" (Keynes 1930a, vol. II, p. 184), and that relevance certainly led him to flirt with the attractions of inflation-led growth.[22] He drew his reader's attention to what he believed to be "the extraordinary correspondence between periods of profit inflation and of profit deflation respective with those of national rise and decline" (Keynes 1930a, vol. II, p. 143) that European history seemed to display, and he suggested that

> the intervening profit inflation which created the modern world was surely worth while if we take a long view. Even today a tendency towards a modest profit inflation would accelerate our rate of progress, as compared with the results of a modest profit deflation. (Keynes 1930a, vol. II, p. 145)

Ultimately, however, Keynes's own expressed preference was for "a policy today which, whilst avoiding deflation at all costs, aims at the stability of purchasing power as its ideal objective" (Keynes 1930a, vol. II, p. 145); but he complained that among contemporary "monetary heretics [whose] theories of money and credit are alike in supposing that in some way the banks can furnish all the real resources which manufacture and trade can reasonably require without real cost to anyone" (Keynes 1930a, vol. II, p. 194) he had "gained . . . a better name than he deserves for being a sympathetic spirit" (p. 193). Perhaps Keynes had only himself to blame for that. Though his reputation in such circles had stemmed from his "writing a *Tract on Monetary Reform* and opposing the return to gold" (p. 193), there was not a little in the *Treatise on Money* to enhance it, at least among selective readers.

Saving, Investment, and Interest

It was Keynes's belief that discrepancies between saving and investment could arise independently of the workings of the monetary system and could persist for long periods of time, unless the authorities took specific action to eliminate them, that underlay his attraction to profit inflation and his fear of profit deflation. Not surprisingly, that belief attracted the hostile attention of Hayek, the leading exponent of the Austrian development of Wicksell's ideas. If such a discrepancy were to persist – Hayek took the deflationary example – that

> must mean that though the production of consumers' goods has become less profitable, and that though at the same time the rate of interest has fallen so that the production of investment goods has become relatively more attractive . . . yet entrepreneurs continue to produce the two types of goods in the same proportion as before. . . . I begin to wonder whether Mr. Keynes has

---

[22] It should nevertheless be noted that Keynes's flirtation with inflation was carried on only in a secular context. In Volume I of the *Treatise* (pp. 263–268) he disassociated himself from Robertson's opinion that in a cyclical context, a little inflation might from time to time be beneficial. In any event, Skidelsky's judgement (1992, p. 608) that it "would be too much to call [Keynes's views on long-term economic growth] a theory" was perhaps apt.

ever reflected upon the function of the rate of interest in a society where there is no banking system. (Hayek 1931b, p. 501)

And Hayek found support from Robertson for that line of criticism. The latter remarked, with specific reference to the banana-plantation parable, that

> the most fundamental answer to his dilemma . . . is to be found . . . along the Böhm-Bawerckian [sic] lines explored by Dr. Hayek. . . . The flood of savings will ultimately find its vent in facilitating the more roundabout methods of production made profitable by the accompanying fall in the rate of interest. I should not agree with Dr. Hayek that this solution has much relevance to the problem of cyclical depression; but then Mr. Keynes's legend seems to be not so much one of cyclical depression as secular decay. (Robertson 1931a, p. 399, fn. 1)

But just as Keynes did not altogether deserve the credit that monetary heretics accorded him, perhaps he did not altogether deserve that criticism either, for with regard to the behaviour of interest rates, he explicitly remarked that

> I think that the market rate of interest, as measured by the yield on long-dated securities, is very "sticky" in relation to the natural rate of interest. . . . [W]hen savings are abundant or deficient in relation to the demand for them for investment at the pre-existing level of interest, the rate does not adjust itself to the new situation quick enough to maintain equilibrium between savings and investment. (Keynes 1930a, vol. II, p. 182)

Keynes was thus aware of the role of the rate of interest in co-ordinating saving and investment, but he was dubious (rightly or wrongly is not the point here) of its capacity to play that role because of mistaken policies, albeit not in a world without money, but in the real world, and in particular the contemporary world:[23]

> the prospect for the next twenty years appears to be a stronger tendency for the natural rate of interest to fall, with a danger lest this consummation be delayed and much waste and depression unnecessarily created in the meanwhile by central banking policy preventing the market rate of interest from falling as fast as it should. (Keynes 1930a, vol. II, p. 186)

Keynes's Scepticism about the Efficacy of Market Mechanisms

In short, though the *Treatise* was mainly a book about the cycle, it also offered more than a glimpse of an economy threatened not just by a cyclical

---

[23] Note, however, that the opinion which Keynes was expressing about secular stagnation as the possible consequence of failure of the rate of interest to fall was not the same as the one he would later express in the *General Theory* (1936). In the latter work, the problem was said to arise from the essential nature of a money economy. In 1930 he saw it as a consequence of the behaviour of the banking system, and one that was susceptible to correction.

slump, but by something much closer to secular stagnation. The latter would be the result of investment being held back by falling profit expectations, a failure of market interest rates to fall far enough to offset that, and a failure of money wages to prove flexible enough to translate the consequences into a falling price level, rather than into a depression of real output and employment. It was not, then, as Hayek had more than hinted, that Keynes did not understand how the price mechanism was supposed to work in principle to co-ordinate economic activity, but rather that he doubted its capacity to do so in practice. That viewpoint, which permeated the *Treatise* and Keynes's related writings of the late 1920s and early 1930s, was hardly original within the Cambridge tradition, as we have seen. Scepticism about market mechanisms was deeply embedded in the work of Lavington, Pigou, and Robertson, as it had been in Marshall's writings too; but Keynes's extension of that scepticism beyond the bounds of the cycle and into the secular sphere did bring a new element into the story, at least as it was told by Cambridge economists.

Paradoxically, and more important, Keynes's failure to integrate the behaviour of output and employment changes into the analytic framework of the *Treatise* also proved seminal. As we have seen, the deficiency in question was particularly evident in the *Treatise*, so that the debates which followed its publication, among Keynes's allies as much as his opponents, focused far more attention on that gap in existing cycle theory than it had previously attracted. This is not to say that unemployment had not been studied, however. On the contrary, by 1930 there existed an extensive literature on that problem whose origins dated to well before the outbreak of World War I. We shall consider aspects of that literature in the next chapter.

CHAPTER 7

British Discussions of Unemployment

Beveridge and Pigou on Unemployment before World War I

It is impossible to fix any precise date at which unemployment emerged as a separate and distinct topic for economic analysis. Karl Marx (1867) was certainly ahead of his more orthodox contemporaries in identifying it as being not so much a sign of moral weakness on the part of those who happened to be unemployed as a chronic feature of the market economy which required an economic explanation; but the subject was widely discussed by neo-classical economists in the last two decades of the nineteenth century. On the eve of World War I, unemployment was already commonly being treated as "a problem of industry," to borrow the sub-title of William Beveridge's 1909 monograph on the subject, and a substantial British literature dealt with it in such terms. Indeed, the topic was of sufficiently wide interest by then that in 1913 Pigou contributed a short primer dealing with it to the Home University Library, a series aimed not at an academic audience but at a general readership.[1]

Labour-Market Frictions

Though Pigou and Beveridge differed on many details, their two books taken together are representative of the manner in which unemployment was ana-lysed by British economists at the beginning of the century. They used the tools of supply-and-demand analysis, rather than anything primarily derived from cycle theory; and they treated the cycle as a factor which alternatingly intensified and mitigated the effects on employment of forces that were always present in the labour market. Cyclical fluctuations in employment,

---

[1] For a discussion of the emergence of the perception that unemployment was an economic rather than a moral problem in the years before World War I, see Corry (1992). Note that in *Unemployment* (1913, e.g., p. 14) Pigou used the phrase "involuntary unemployment," but as Corry points out, what he meant by it was an excess supply of labour at the going wage, hence including unemployment that was the consequence of market frictions of one sort or another. Keynes would later classify such unemployment as voluntary.

155

like seasonal fluctuations, were thus understood in terms of particular variations on a more general Marshallian theme.[2]

As Beveridge put it, "the problem of unemployment is the problem of the adjustment of the supply of labour and the demand for labour" (Beveridge 1909, p. 4). Unemployment was not, in his view, a phenomenon to be "attributed to any general want of adjustment between the growth of the supply of labour and the growth of the demand" (Beveridge 1909, p. 11) or to "the idleness of the unemployable" (Beveridge 1909, p. 12), and it occurred despite the fact that "the forces which constantly tend to bring about this adjustment have not, either by excessive increase of the population or by the adoption of labour-saving devices, been brought to the limit of their power" (Beveridge 1909, p. 14). Rather, Beveridge emphasized the role of frictions within labour markets:

> ... there are specific imperfections of adjustment between the demand for labour and the supply of labour, and ... these give rise to a real and considerable problem of unemployment. The forces which constantly tend to adjust demand and supply work only in the long run. (Beveridge 1909, p. 14)

Pigou (1913) echoed Beveridge's emphasis on unemployment as a manifestation of market imperfections, albeit from a rather different perspective. Where Beveridge stressed the role of imperfect labour mobility and the like in slowing down the adjustment of *quantities*, Pigou saw the crucial frictions as being those which slowed the adjustment of *prices*, more specifically wages, to equilibrium.[3] He drew particular attention to

> ... the theoretical possibility that wage-rates at any moment and in every part of the industrial field can be so adjusted to the demand for labour of various grades that no unemployment whatever can exist. In other words ... unemployment is *wholly* caused by maladjustment between wage-rates and demand. (Pigou 1913, p. 51, italics in original)

Beveridge and Pigou took frictions and maladjustments seriously. Beveridge was always mindful that in the actual economy, the structure of industry changed over time and required redeployment of a labour force whose existing skills might not match up with the new pattern of demand. He noted that it took time to redeploy labour, even within a given line of work, and that led to an "irreducible minimum of unemployment in any trade [which] indicates the degree of friction in the movement of labour" (Beveridge 1909,

---

[2] Thus, to modern eyes, those early discussions of unemployment seem unremittingly ad hoc, inevitably involving departures from the supply-equals-demand equilibrium whose analysis the then-available theory permitted.

[3] Sticky money wages were given particular attention in discussions of cyclical unemployment. For a discussion, see Laidler (1991, pp. 95ff.).

p. 103). He therefore saw improving the informational efficiency of the labour market as the key to reducing unemployment; and he advocated setting up "known centres or offices or Exchanges, to which employers shall send or go when they want workpeople, to which workpeople shall go when they want employment" (Beveridge 1909, p. 198). He also urged the institution of some form of insurance against seasonal and cyclical unemployment and other "*minor* measures – the systematic distribution of public work [and] the steadying of the ordinary labour market by elasticity of wages" (Beveridge 1909, p. 230, italics added).

Wage Stickiness

The same themes appeared in Pigou's analysis, though the relative signifi-cance attributed to them was reversed. In particular, Pigou attached primary importance to the operations of trade unions and, more generally, a "spirit . . . that seeks, as far as it can, to establish throughout the country some sort of minimum wage for the lowest grade of workers, based upon current views concerning what constitutes a reasonable subsistence" (Pigou 1913, p. 65). Those factors tended, or so he thought, to maintain "the wages-rates of inferior workmen somewhat nearer to those of good workmen than their comparative efficiency warrants" (Pigou 1913, pp. 60–61).[4] He therefore argued that they would create unemployment, even in the absence of ongoing changes in the structure of the demand for labour, and that when structural changes occurred, they would, on balance, exacerbate the problem (Pigou 1913, pp. 76–77).

Pigou (1913) thus paid more attention to wage stickiness as a cause of unemployment than did Beveridge. For him, *money*-wage stickiness, attrib-utable to money illusion and the existence of nominal contracts that might be difficult to renegotiate, was what mattered.[5] Given that the cycle was charac-terized by fluctuations in the demand for labour, or, as Beveridge put it, "discontinuity in the growth of" (Beveridge 1909, p. 65) the demand for labour, a smoothly functioning labour market required pro-cyclical variations in real wages. Nominal wages moved more sluggishly than prices, and that produced counter-cyclical variations in real wages which amplified cyclical variations in unemployment. As we have already seen, that way of looking at things would continue to make frequent appearances in the post–World War I literature.

---

[4] The idea that "fairness" was involved in wage-formation processes, which Hicks would stress in Chapter 3 of *The Crisis in Keynesian Economics* (1979), and which he had discussed in his *Theory of Wages* (1934a), was thus present in the Cambridge tradition even before World War I.

[5] On this, see Laidler (1991, p. 98).

Pigou's suggested remedies for unemployment followed routinely from his analysis. Measures to promote price stability and to increase wage flexibility would help within the cycle, while public works would be useful too. In the longer term, to the extent that problems persisted, he stressed improvements in education, designed to raise the productivity of low-skilled workers to a point at which employers would be willing to pay them the wages which societal notions of fairness dictated, and he also followed Beveridge in advocating "the development of an organised network of Labour Exchanges" (Pigou 1913, p. 170) to enhance labour mobility.

Unemployment in the 1920s

The business-cycle literature discussed in the three preceding chapters had its roots firmly planted in pre–World War I experience: Hawtrey's *Currency and Credit* was written during the war, and it updated a theory of the cycle originally published in *Good and Bad Trade* (1913); Robertson's *Banking Policy and the Price Level* (1926) integrated the insights of *Industrial Fluctuation* (1915) with the essentially Marshallian analysis of banking contained in the first edition of *Money* (1922); and the main purpose of Keynes's *Treatise on Money* (1930a) was to integrate Wicksell's insights about saving and investment mechanisms, which dated back to 1898, with a Cambridge version of the quantity theory that was a product of the 1870s. Pigou, too, was quite explicit in telling readers of *Industrial Fluctuations* that "the conditions prevailing in the great post-war boom and subsequent depression have been so abnormal that I have not examined them here" (Pigou 1929, p. v), and virtually all the evidence presented in the course of that book's empirical discussions was for pre-war years.

The fact is that the behaviour of unemployment in Britain after 1921 seemed to contemporary observers to be without precedent in earlier times. Between 1922 and the outbreak of World War II, the unemployment rate among the country's insured labour force fell below 10 per cent in only one year (1927). Large-scale unemployment no longer seemed to be a temporary factor associated with the depression phase of the cycle, but a secular phenomenon. Cycles might still occur, to be sure, but after 1921 their elimination or mitigation seemed unlikely to ensure that such unemployment as persisted would be a fundamentally microeconomic problem associated with the way in which rather ill-defined frictions impinged upon particular segments of the labour market. After 1921, unemployment not directly associated with the cycle was no longer seen as a problem "of industry" but of the economy as a whole.

Even so, the tools commonly used to analyse the phenomenon in the 1920s were still those that had been deployed before the war, namely, a Marshallian supply-and-demand system supplemented by appeals to frictions of one sort or another. The same differences found in the pre-war literature, about just which frictions were critical, continued to mark post-war discussions. By and large, more theoretically inclined economists, such as Pigou, stressed wage stickiness as the principal problem, and, in particular, its persistence in the face of the price deflation imposed upon the economy first by the intended restoration and then, in 1925, by the actual restoration of gold convertibility at the pre-war parity.[6] Those who were less analytically oriented paid more attention to labour-mobility problems created, as they saw it, by a major restructuring of the world and British economies in the wake of the war.

The Level of Wages

Writing in the *Economic Journal* in 1927, Pigou succinctly stated his view of the contemporary unemployment problem. Before the war, he noted,

> it was nowhere suggested that the general body of wage-rates had been forced up too high relatively to the openings for employment, in such wise that, even had no industrial fluctuations taken place, a substantial number of healthy persons seeking employment must have been always unable to find it. In the post-war period, however, there is strong reason to believe that an important change has taken place in this respect; that, partly through direct State action, and partly through the added strength given to the workpeople's organisations engaged in wage bargaining by the development of unemployment insurance, wage-rates have, over a wide area, been set at a level which is too high in the above sense; and that the very large percentage of unemployment which has prevailed during the whole of the last six years is due in considerable measure to this new factor in our economic life. (Pigou 1927b, p. 355)

Now the wages that Pigou thought to be at too high a level were *real* wages, though he understood well enough that if real wages were to be lowered in a gold-standard economy, that would require driving down money wages. He was by no means insensitive to the distributional consequences of cutting real wages, suggesting, in the previously cited 1927 paper, that income-support measures (such as the payment of family allowances) might be needed to maintain the real incomes of low-paid workers and their families

---

[6] The reader should recall that the years following 1815 had also seen an economic slowdown associated with an effort to restore the sterling price of gold to a pre-war parity and that the participants in the debates of the 1920s were well aware of that earlier episode and the literature it had generated. See, for example, Bonar (1923) and Cannan's well-known introduction to the bullion report of 1810 (Cannan 1919). The measures finally introduced in 1925, inasmuch as they involved the introduction of convertible paper money, rather than the restoration of a gold coinage, were essentially those which had been first proposed by Ricardo (1816), but ultimately not enacted during that earlier episode.

in the wake of a wage cut. Pigou was, that is to say, aware of a problem to be stressed by Sir Henry Clay (1928) the following year, in a comment on Pigou's analysis, namely, that an examination of the distribution of British unemployment by region had revealed that "so far as 'high wages' are the explanation of the present unemployment, it is the low wage rates of the depressed industries that are 'too high', not the high wages of the prosperous industries" (Clay 1928, p. 9).

Maldistribution of Labour

That observation led Clay to echo Beveridge's pre-war analysis and conclude that a "maldistribution of labour" was a more fundamental cause of unemployment than wage stickiness per se. In that conclusion he was at one with Edwin Cannan, who asserted that

> the true remedy for long-term unemployment always applied throughout history, and always effectual, is neither rationalisation nor reduction of wages, but redistribution of labour-force between the different occupations [and] sometimes, as now certainly in the case of coal, the required redistribution is so great and sudden that it necessitates the transfer of some individuals from the depressed industry to others. (Cannan 1930, pp. 50–51)

For those two commentators, as for Pigou, unemployment insurance and the activities of trade unions had brought new friction to the post-war labour market, but the friction that Clay and Cannan stressed was not so much wage stickiness in the economy overall as reduced incentives to labour mobility among its sectors.[7] After 1925, Cannan, in particular, was sceptical about any attribution of unemployment to the price deflation associated with the restoration of the pre-war parity. Like Pigou, he had supported that measure, but unlike Pigou he had always been very much an optimist about the ease with which it could be implemented. In 1927 he was still of the opinion that

> in the case of Great Britain the cow of deflation had been swallowed in 1920–22, and the historian of "fifty years on" will not waste much time over the disappearance of the tail in 1925. . . . We may perhaps be permitted a hopeful doubt about the statement that "the conclusion that money wages are still too high is unescapable" (Cannan 1927, p. 83)[8]

---

[7] Here it is worth drawing attention to the work of Benjamin and Kochin (1979), whose efforts to rehabilitate, in the light of empirical evidence, the plausibility of such ideas were an important early manifestation of the new-classical reaction of the past quarter century against so-called Keynesian economics.

[8] That statement by Cannan is not quite as ridiculous as it looks in hindsight. In 1927, the unemployment rate among insured workers fell to 9.7 per cent from 12.5 per cent in the previous year. That, however, proved to be the last time the rate reached single digits before the outbreak of World War II. See Chick (1992, p. 4, table 1.1).

Keynes on Mr. Churchill

Keynes, as is well known, disagreed profoundly with that view. Although, as Barkai (1993) has shown, he had been extremely ambivalent about the 1925 return to gold before the event, he became the measure's severest critic once it had been implemented. His 1925 essay "The Economic Consequences of Mr. Churchill" is widely and correctly regarded as a powerful piece of economic-policy advocacy, but its power derives more from its literary style than from its analytic content. The latter was an uneasy mixture of Cambridge orthodoxy and unsupported assertion. The orthodox element in Keynes's case was its premise of downward wage stickiness and his expressed opinion that *if money wages could be reduced*, so could unemployment. In that one important respect his position was indistinguishable from Pigou's, though it should be noted explicitly that, unlike Pigou, Keynes did not advocate a policy of money-wage reduction. On the contrary, Keynes asserted the unorthodox view that the outcome of an across-the-board wage cut, were it feasible, would be higher employment with *no change* in *real* wages:

> As soon as the Government admit that the problem is primarily a monetary one, then they can say to Labour: This is not an attack on real wages. We have raised the value of sterling 10 percent. This means that money wages must fall 10 per cent. But it also means, when the adjustment is complete, that the cost of living will fall about 10 per cent. In this case there will have been no serious fall in real wages. Now there are two alternative ways of bringing about the reduction of money wages. One way is to apply economic pressure and to intensify unemployment by credit restriction, until wages are *forced down*. This is a hateful and disastrous way, because of its unequal effects on the stronger and on the weaker groups, and because of the economic and social waste whilst it is in progress. The other way is to effect a *uniform* reduction of wages by *agreement*, on the understanding that this shall not mean in the long run any fall in average real wages below what they were in the first quarter of this year. The practical difficulty is that money wages and the cost of living are interlocked. The cost of living cannot fall until *after* money wages have fallen. Money wages must fall *first*, in order to allow the cost of living to fall. (Keynes 1925, p. 228, italics in original)

Clearly, in 1925 Keynes was still firmly wedded to the pre-war orthodox Marshallian tradition in treating money-wage stickiness as the major cause of unemployment; but, equally clearly, he had begun to move away from that orthodoxy, as represented, say, by Pigou (1927b), in seeing the effects of money-wage stickiness working not through its influence on the real wage and thence to the demand for labour, but through a mark-up mechanism to the price level and thence to the demand for output.[9] For Keynes in 1925,

---

[9] Note that Keynes's treatment of that issue in 1925 differed from that in the *General Theory* in neglecting the fall in real wages that a declining marginal product of labour would bring

unemployment was primarily a monetary problem, not one centered on the labour market. As we have seen, those two views had coexisted uneasily in Hawtrey's writings since 1913, without the question of their logical compatibility initially being raised. The fact that Keynes, in 1925, chose to stress one at the expense of the other, as Hawtrey had also begun to do, did nothing to address the theoretical tensions that existed between them. The presence of the "widow's cruse" fallacy at the very heart of the *Treatise on Money was prima facie* evidence that those tensions remained unaddressed by Keynes five years later.

Pigou's *Theory of Unemployment*

If, during the 1920s, Keynes began to regard chronic unemployment as primarily a monetary matter, he offered no clear theoretical reason for doing so. Pigou, on the other hand, stuck to his belief that the problem was centered on the labour market and that excessively high *real* wages lay at its root. His *Theory of Unemployment* (1933) was intended to expound a systematic analytic basis for that view.[10] Pigou told readers of that book that it and *Industrial Fluctuations* (1927a) were "in some degree . . . complementary to one another" (Pigou 1933, p. vii). The earlier book had emphasized the dynamics of demand movements in generating the cycle, while the latter focused much more closely on the comparative static analysis of the determinants of unemployment. Pigou understood as well as any of his British contemporaries that the problem called for what we would now characterize as a general-equilibrium approach:

> It is possible to study the problem of unemployment either from the money end or from what I shall call, in contrast, the real end. The two studies, if made complete and carried through correctly, must necessarily come to the same thing, their analyses meeting in the middle. (Pigou 1933, p. v)

He thought, however, that the "money end" had been overstressed in recent discussions and that, as a result, "very important factors of a non-monetary character" (Pigou 1933, p. v) had been neglected.

The Real Wage and Wage Stickiness

The central proposition of Pigou's "real end" approach to explaining unemployment was Marshallian, namely, that the demand for labour, as measured

---

about. Though he did not quite deny some effect on real wages from an across-the-board money-wage cut, there was no sign in that essay of his having thought through the implications of his analysis with the aid of the marginal-productivity theory he would deploy in 1936.

[10] In an appendix to Chapter 19 of the *General Theory*, Keynes singled out that book for special, hostile, and not always accurate attention. For a recent exchange on the merits of his attack, see Cottrell (1994) and Brady (1994). In light of that attack, it is not too surprising that Pigou's review (1936) of the *General Theory* had an angry tone to it. See Chapter 11, "The Theory of Employment."

by employment plus unfilled vacancies, was an inverse function of the real wage. That proposition derived, in turn, from the relationship between the volume of employment and labour's marginal productivity. Though the relevant marginal-productivity schedule was a short-run one, in the sense that ''industrial equipment, both in form and quantity, may properly be regarded as more or less fixed'' (Pigou 1933, pp. 39–40), Pigou was nevertheless clear that even in the short run, allowance had to be made for the fact that

> as labour is withdrawn from work, bits of equipment are withdrawn also. In these circumstances there is, *a fortiori*, little reason for believing that variations in the quantity of labour employed, within the range intervening between something less than capacity output and a very deep depression will involve other than small variations in marginal productivity. (Pigou 1933, p. 51)

Thus, as a practical matter, Pigou thought that the demand for labour was highly elastic with respect to the real wage, even in the short run; but he also regarded the supply of labour as being essentially inelastic with respect to the real wage.[11] It was, he remarked, reasonable to take ''the number of would-be wage-earners in a given situation as a fixed datum, so that the quantity of unemployment and the quantity of employment are simple complements of one another'' (Pigou 1933, pp. 7–8). Moreover, though he believed that

> from a long-period point of view . . . *[w]ith perfectly free competition among workpeople and labour perfectly mobile* . . . [t]here will always be at work a strong tendency for wage-rates to be so related to demand that everybody is employed. (Pigou 1933, p. 252, italics added)

And though he used just such a concept of an equilibrium stable over the long term to anchor his analysis when monetary and cyclical factors were brought into the picture (in Part IV, pp. 185–246 of a 313-page book), the overall tone of the *Theory of Unemployment* made it quite clear that Pigou thought those assumptions of ''free competition'' and ''perfectly mobile'' labour to be seriously deficient from an empirical point of view.

As a practical matter, ''what is important to us is that wage-earners do in fact on some occasions make it an object of policy to 'keep real wages constant' or to 'prevent them from falling' '' (Pigou 1933, pp. 18–19). There were many reasons for that, all of which had already been widely canvassed in the literature discussed earlier in this chapter, and not least in Pigou's own paper ''Wage Policy and Unemployment'' (1927b): trade-union monopoly, the effects of unemployment insurance, not to mention the fact to which he

---

[11] Hawtrey (1937, p. 170) quite justifiably cited Pigou's views on that matter in rebuttal of Keynes's unfairness (1936) in attributing a belief in an upward-sloping supply curve for labour, derived from the increasing marginal disutility of work, to his ''Classical'' predecessors. See Chapter 11, footnote 2.

had drawn attention in 1913, namely, that "public opinion in a modern civilised State builds up for itself a rough estimate of what constitutes a reasonable living wage" (Pigou 1933, p. 255). All of those helped to put a floor under the real wages of the less productive members of the labour force. Moreover, in Britain, their influence had become much stronger since the war: "... the goal of long-run tendencies in recent times has been a wage level substantially above that proper to nil unemployment, and ... a substantial part of post-war unemployment is attributable to that fact" (Pigou 1933, p. 256). Pigou was there discussing not *money*-wage stickiness, but *real*-wage stickiness, a factor to which he had already begun to give more emphasis in his writings of the 1920s than he had in 1913. Thus, in 1927, he had remarked that "the very fact ... that the general public has come to think in terms of the cost of living instead of in terms of gold has tended to make wage policy, as regards *real* wages, somewhat more rigid than it used to be" (Pigou 1927b, p. 308).

In 1933 Pigou still noted the role of money-wage stickiness in amplifying employment fluctuations over the course of the cycle, just as he had done in 1913:

> These factors of inertia, which, in an economy where wage-rates were always contracted for in kind, would tend to keep real wages stable in the face of changing demand, in a money economy tend to keep money wages stable ... [T]he translation of inertia from real wage-rates to money wage-rates causes real rates to move in a manner not compensatory, but complementary, to movements in the real demand function ... and so the volume of employment, is substantially more variable than it would be, other things being equal, in an economy where wage-rates were being contracted for in kind. (Pigou 1933, pp. 294–296)

But in the post-war years, cyclical fluctuations were occurring against the background of a much higher average level of unemployment, which was, Pigou thought, the consequence of secular real-wage stickiness which had only recently become important. He believed that the labour market's departure from the frictionless competitive ideal had become chronic since the war and that market forces could, perhaps, no longer be relied on to put things right over any relevant time period. Therefore, "wage policy as a possible long-run determinant of unemployment calls ... at the present time, for closer study than would have been thought necessary twenty years ago" (Pigou 1933, p. 256).[12]

---

[12] It is worth drawing attention to the fact that, like Keynes in the *General Theory*, Pigou was treating wage determination as a matter for policy, rather than as something that could be safely left to market mechanisms.

General-Equilibrium Considerations

Much of the *Theory of Unemployment* analysed interactions among money wages, real wages, and the demand for labour in order to determine the elasticity of that last variable with respect to the first. We have already seen that Pigou believed the relevant short-run demand function for labour to be highly elastic with respect to the *real* wage – about minus 3 was his estimate of that parameter (Pigou 1933, p. 96) – but that still left the question of the elasticity of the real wage with respect to the money wage to be settled. Pigou was aware of what we would now call the general-equilibrium nature of that issue, even if his detailed handling of it was sometimes uncertain. He was also well aware of the pitfall of implicitly assuming full employment while trying to analyse variations in unemployment. That was why he rejected out of hand the argument that a cut in money wages would lead to an equiproportional fall in prices, no change in real wages, and hence no change in unemployment. That conclusion ''describes what would happen if money wage rates were reduced *and if the quantity of employment remained unaltered.* . . . The answer is assumed before the argument has begun'' (Pigou 1933, pp. 101–102, italics in original).

Pigou's intuitive grasp of the general-equilibrium nature of the problem of unemployment was evident from his arguments that in a money economy, following a cut in money wages, ''provided that any part of the population consists of non-wage-earners, either the real wage-rate is reduced, or the value of non-wage-goods relatively to wage-goods is increased . . . [a]dditional labour *must* be employed'' (Pigou 1933, p. 102, italics in original). It is even clearer from his observation that in order to know just how much extra employment would be involved, information about the nature of the monetary system would be required:

> What the value of . . . [the elasticity of demand for labour with respect to the money wage] . . . actually is in relation to . . . [its elasticity with respect to the real wage] . . . cannot be determined without reference to the nature of the monetary system that is established in the country. (Pigou 1933, p. 102)

The possible characteristics of the monetary system that Pigou considered lay between two extremes. On the one hand he considered a closed economy in which monetary policy would ensure that in the wake of a cut in money wages, the level of *nominal* national income would remain constant, and on the other hand, a small price-taking open economy on the gold standard. In the first economy, because prices would tend to fall as money wages moved downwards, output would have to increase. Prices would thus fall less than money wages, bringing about the decline in real wages required to induce employment to increase. Even so,

> a system in which (for short periods) the quantity of money income per unit of time grows as real income grows seems more natural and is more likely to be established. One reason for this is that, when real income grows because the real wage-rate asked for by labour is reduced, the real rate of interest on resources invested in working capital is increased; this tempts people to shift money out of passive into active balances, thus augmenting the volume of money income per unit of time, even though the stock of money is unchanged. (Pigou 1933, p. 104)[13]

Pigou, however, paid but fleeting attention to those complications stemming from an interest-sensitive demand for idle balances, moving on instead to the open economy, where we encounter his other limiting case, that of "a small country on the gold standard in a gold standard world [where] the monetary system is of such a sort that internal changes leave the price level substantially intact" (Pigou 1933, p. 105), and where, therefore, a money-wage cut would imply an equi-proportional cut in the real wage. He understood that a larger open economy would be less than a perfect price-taker and that it would be inappropriate to assume a given price level in that case. There the price level would tend to fall when money wages were cut, inducing a gold inflow and an increase in the quantity of money. Relative to the closed-economy case, the price decline would still be smaller, however, so a given cut in money wages would have a greater effect on employment. All in all, on the basis of that analysis, Pigou was inclined to believe that for an open economy such as Britain, "in times of deep depression . . . an all round cut of 10 per cent in money rates of wages would lead, *other things being equal*, to a more than 10 per cent expansion in the aggregate volume of labour demanded" (Pigou 1933, p. 106, italics in original).

Now the analysis we have been discussing in the preceding few paragraphs could, with benefit of sixty years' hindsight, be restated as a series of variations on a model featuring an aggregate supply-and-demand curve, with the latter relationship in turn underlain by the IS-LM system described in Chapter 1, modified where necessary for open-economy effects. Pigou did sometimes view his own analysis essentially in general-equilibrium terms. Anyone doubting that should consider the following passage:

> It is tempting at first sight to say that such and such an upward movement of real demand is associated with such and such a rise in the price level; that, the money rate of wage being given, this causes such and such a fall in the real rate of wage stipulated for; and that this, in turn, the elasticity of the real demand for labour being given, causes such and such a rise in the quantity of labour demanded, and so in the volume of employment. A chain sequence of this type does not, however, truly represent the facts. For when,

---

[13] Pigou was writing *after* the publication of the *Treatise on Money*, so we should not be surprised to find him postulating an interest-sensitive demand for idle balances.

in consequence of a given expansion of real demand, money demand expands by so much, the extent to which the price level rises itself depends on the extent to which employment and production are increased. . . . [W]hen inertia keeps the money rate of wage constant, the monetary factor does not affect the real rate of wage stipulated for in such and such a way and, through this, affect the aggregate quantity of labour demanded in such and such a way. Rather it affects the whole complex of balancing forces, and thereby brings it about that the real rate of wage stipulated for and the aggregate quantity of labour demanded are *both* modified. These movements, though bound together in a rigid nexus, are not successive links in a causal chain, but joint effects of a process that stands behind them. (Pigou 1933, pp. 296–297, italics in original)

Pigou did not, however, fully appreciate the analytic importance of that way of viewing matters, nor did he consistently think along such lines.[14] Instead, and in keeping with his intention of stressing the "real side" of things, he much more often than not (and, with benefit of the aforementioned hindsight, not always consistently) came back to an essentially partial-equilibrium focus on the effect of the real wage on the demand for labour when he analysed unemployment. That was true even of those sections of his book that explicitly dealt with monetary and cyclical issues against the background of the maintained assumption of an economy always tending to full employment.

The Role of Monetary Policy

In the context of the cycle, Pigou was dismissive of the idea of a "natural" level for the rate of interest (as recently deployed by Keynes in the *Treatise*). He thought that it added nothing to his own preferred (but essentially equivalent) notion of "the *proper* rate of bank interest" (Pigou 1933, p. 212, italics in original), which was that required to maintain what he called *the standard monetary system* in place. In turn,

> I define the standard monetary system as one so constructed that, for all sorts of movements in the real demand function for labour or in real rates of wages, whether they last for a long time or a short, the aggregate money income is increased or diminished by precisely the difference made to the number of workpeople (or other factors of production) at work multiplied by the original rate of money wages. (Pigou 1933, pp. 205–206, italics in original)

---

[14] Indeed, even after reading and reviewing the *General Theory*, Pigou still failed to see the point. As will be noted in Chapter 11, it was only in the course of his 1937–38 exchange with Nicholas Kaldor in the *Economic Journal* that, following the latter's deployment of an IS-LM diagram, he grasped the significance of a point which, as the passage quoted earlier in the text demonstrated, he himself had already made.

Pigou's concept of the "proper" rate of interest was thus one which would maintain equilibrium between the demand for and supply of labour while simultaneously keeping the money-wage level constant. In the short run, maintaining such an interest rate would require accommodating what Robertson (not explicitly referred to at that point) would have called appropriate fluctuations in output and employment. It would also lead to a "price level . . . not indeed absolutely, but fairly stable, so long as no marked improvements in productive efficiency occur; if such improvements occur, it will fall in a proportion not far from the inverse of that in which the improvements have caused output to increase" (Pigou 1933, p. 208). Quite how variations in the interest rate would act as a "controlling mechanism" which would "prevent money income from varying otherwise than in that precise manner which . . . the standard monetary system requires" (Pigou 1933, p. 211) was not, however, made clear; and, consistent with the analysis of his *Industrial Fluctuations*, Pigou conceded that deviations of the actual rate of interest from its "proper" level were inevitable under the existing institutional arrangements.

By 1933, Pigou's confidence in the stabilizing power of monetary policy, particularly when expansion was required, a confidence that had never been great, had further diminished. He was of the opinion that more than monetary policy might sometimes be needed to maintain equality between the actual rate and the proper rate of interest:

> The actual rate of bank interest cannot fall below nil. The weapon available to the banks for cancelling real factors that make for *contractions* in aggregate money income . . . may not be adequate to cancel them. It is, indeed, always possible for the Central Bank, by open market operations, to force out money into balances held by the public. But in times of deep depression . . . there may be *no* positive rate of money interest that will avail to get this money used. . . . In these circumstances attempts to uphold the standard monetary system, so long as reliance is placed on purely monetary defences, are bound to fail. If, however, at the same time that the banking system keeps money cheap the Government adopts a policy of public works, the risk of failure is greatly reduced. For this policy, providing, as it does, new openings for real investment, pushes up the *proper* rate of bank interest above what it would otherwise have been. (Pigou 1933, p. 213, italics in original)

In any event, if equilibrium between the supply of and demand for labour, and, equivalently, between the actual rate and the "proper" rate of interest, was to be maintained, that equilibrium first had to be established. As we have seen, Pigou believed that a disequilibrium ruled in the post-war British labour market and that it was neither a cyclical phenomenon nor merely a matter of a misallocated labour force; and he also had grave doubts about the capacity of market mechanisms, as they actually existed, to eliminate that disequilibrium at any reasonable pace. It is hardly surprising, then, that he kept returning to the policy conclusion that, as far as the "post-war period" was concerned, "to reduce unemployment from the side of wages it would have been necessary, after wage inequalities had been reduced and labour appropriately redistributed, *also* to reduce the average rate of real wages" (Pigou 1933, p. 270, italics in original).

Underconsumptionism in Britain

One common theme runs through the literature discussed so far in this chapter, namely, that a properly functioning market economy would generate an equilibrium situation in which the demand for labour would equal the supply. Though they often held different views about just which "frictions" were of critical importance, its contributors all agreed that frictions of one sort or another, in and of themselves inessential to the functioning of the economy, and hence curable, at least in principle, were responsible for unemployment. Thus they were writing in a tradition of economic analysis which stretched back to David Ricardo and Adam Smith. But there had always been dissenters from that particular orthodoxy, often known as Say's law, that demand creates its own supply. Ricardo's friend Malthus, Lord Lauderdale, the Swiss economist J. C. L. Simonde de Sismondi, and a host of lesser-known commentators had claimed, to the contrary, that the institutions of market exchange were fundamentally flawed and inherently prone to create a "general glut" of commodities, a state of chronic oversupply of goods, and as a corollary, of labour too.[15]

In Britain in the 1920s and early 1930s that tradition had a wide audience, not least in Labour Party circles, so much so that Evan Durbin, who was already well on the way to becoming a leading intellectual influence within the party, devoted much of his 1933 monograph, *Purchasing Power and Trade Depression*, to rebutting it. In the United States, the principal exponents of the doctrine were William T. Foster and Waddill Catchings, whose work will be discussed in the next chapter, and in Britain, John A. Hobson had long played that role.[16] The first of his many books on the topic, *The*

---

[15] For a penetrating account of British contributions to that tradition in the first half of the nineteenth century, and its relationship to classical orthodoxy, see Bernard Corry (1962).

[16] Hans Neisser (1934), on the other hand, related Hobson's work to a German Marxist tradition and dismissed Foster and Catchings's work as "more primitive" (p. 392). My own view, similar to that of Klein (1949, 2nd ed. 1966, p. 138), is that the latter two authors differed from Hobson in paying particular attention to the role of the monetary system in generating underconsumption (see Chapter 8). For a recent and helpful account of Hobson's work, see

Physiology of Industry, written jointly with A. F. Mummery, had appeared as early as 1889.

Mummery and Hobson

In Hobson's view of things, the market economy was prone to chronic "overproduction," or, equivalently, "underconsumption," whose essential character Mummery and he had described in the following terms:

> The object of production is to provide "utilities and conveniences" for consumers, and the process is a continuous one from the first handling of the raw material to the moment when it is finally consumed as a utility or a convenience. The only use of Capital being to aid the production of these utilities and conveniences, the total used will necessarily vary with the total of utilities and conveniences daily or weekly consumed. Now saving, while it increases the existing aggregate of Capital, simultaneously reduces the quantity of utilities and conveniences consumed; any undue exercise of this habit must, therefore, cause an accumulation of Capital in excess of that which is required for use, and this excess will exist in the form of general over-production. (Mummery and Hobson 1889, p. v)

The balance of their book was devoted to elaborating the difficulties of co-ordinating current decisions to save and invest with the future consumption behaviour of the community, and it included a fully worked out numerical illustration of the accelerator relationship (Mummery and Hobson 1889, pp. 85–86).[17] Mummery and Hobson argued that it was futile to rely on market mechanisms to achieve such co-ordination. In particular, they noted that "every increase in saving and in capital requires, in order to be effectual, a corresponding increase in immediately future consumption" so that "if people wish to save more now they must consent to spend more in the future" (Mummery and Hobson 1889, p. 37). Since "Production−Saving = Consumption" (Mummery and Hobson 1889, p. vii), and since "in the normal state of modern industrial Communities, consumption limits production and

---

Roger Backhouse (1995, ch. 5). Backhouse has noted the rather superficial nature of Hobson's treatment of specifically monetary issues. As we saw in Chapter 2, "Some Weaknesses" and "Contemporary Doubts," Durbin was a Hayekian, albeit a critical one, who nevertheless believed in the ultimate destructiveness of policies designed to stimulate the economy's overall level of aggregate demand. As we shall now see, such policies were essential corollaries of underconsumptionism. Hence Durbin treated the doctrines of Hobson, on the one hand, and Foster and Catchings, on the other, as essentially identical.

[17] It had been customary to give credit for originating the accelerator relationship to Aftalion (1913), Hawtrey (1913), or Bickerdike (1914). I fell into that error myself (Laidler 1991), and I am grateful to Roger Backhouse for drawing my attention to the priorities of Mummery and Hobson. Backhouse (1995, ch. 5, p. 81) has discussed that contribution, noting that it appeared only in *The Physiology of Industry* (Mummery and Hobson 1889) and not in any of Hobson's later writings. In terms of influencing others, however, it does seem as if Aftalion's work was crucial. It attracted the attention of Dennis Robertson and Alvin Hansen, among others.

not production consumption,'' an increase in saving per se would be self-defeating:

> If, owing to its desire to save, [the community] refrains from spending the whole of its money income, the whole of the consumable articles produced cannot be sold. Over-supply is, in consequence, caused, and prices and incomes continually fall until the production of consumable articles is reduced to the total actually consumed. (Mummery and Hobson 1889, pp. 98–99)

Hence their view that "depression in trade and excessive thrift are terms describing different phases of the same phenomenon" (Mummery and Hobson 1889, p. 98).

Hobson on Unemployment

Hobson was to continue to propagate those views, with little modification, well into the inter-war period, notably in his monograph *The Economics of Unemployment* (1923).[18] There, in answer to the orthodox economist's question – "The wants of man being expansible without limit, how is it possible that too much can be produced?" – he invoked "two related phenomena: first, the conservative character of the arts of consumption, or standards of living, as compared with the modern arts of production; second, the ways in which the current distribution of income confirms this conservatism of consumption" (Hobson 1923, p. 32). It followed that the ultimate cure for underconsumption was "a better distribution of income" (Hobson 1923, p. 116), by which Hobson meant a more nearly equal distribution. However, he saw little hope that such would be achieved under the prevailing economic arrangements:

> So far as the struggle is a purely economic one between organised labour and organised capital, it is not easy to see how the former can prevail, unless it can both obtain a normal basic wage which leaves little surplus profit and also stop the wage-lag which, assisted by speculative credit, is seen to be responsible for overproduction and consequent depression. . . . Labour can only defend itself effectively by political weapons, supposing it can get them and learn how to use them. (Hobson 1923, p. 116)

What was required, in Hobson's view, was the enforcement of strict minimum standards for wages and other conditions of employment throughout

---

[18] Hobson was a democratic socialist in his politics, and it is interesting to note that the Chicago economist Paul Douglas (1933) cited Hobson's *Economics of Unemployment* (1923) at a time when he, too, was embracing underconsumptionist doctrines as a component of a more general socialist approach to economic and social issues. On that aspect of Douglas's economic thought, see Chapter 9. Klein's account (1949, 2nd ed. 1966, pp. 135–138) of Hobson's underconsumptionism was also based on *The Economics of Unemployment* (Hobson 1923).

the economy, the taking into public ownership of "those essential services and industries which, left to private enterprise, exhibit a strongly monopolistic character" and the use of taxation "so as to secure for public consumption as much as possible of those surplus earnings that accrue from lucrative businesses which it is convenient to leave to private enterprise" (Hobson 1923, pp. 116–117). Those measures, in and of themselves merely redistributive, "if our analysis of the situation be correct . . . must be equally effective for the stimulation of enlarged production" for the simple reason that "we recognise the problem of greater productivity to be, in fact, inseparable from that of better distribution" (Hobson 1923, p. 117).

The Employment Multiplier

Quite evidently, and that part of Pigou's *Theory of Unemployment* dealing with the cycle notwithstanding, the analytic style of the orthodox post-war British literature dealing with unemployment per se was very different from the style of that dealing with the cycle. In the 1920s and 1930s, cycle theory was explicitly dynamic and dealt – more (e.g., Robertson) or less (e.g., Hawtrey) formally – with causative chains working themselves out over time in well-defined sequences. Orthodox employment theory, on the other hand, was primarily cast in comparative static terms. And yet, as far back as Bagehot (1873) and Marshall and Marshall (1879), perfunctory attempts had been made at a dynamic analysis of unemployment which sought to incorporate the same basic insight that underlay Hobson's underconsumptionism, namely, that the overall level of demand for goods and services prevailing in the economy might constrain output and employment to below feasible levels.

The lack of progress forthcoming in that regard was evident from the fact that the following quotation from the eighth (1920) edition of Marshall's *Principles* remained unchanged from the first (1890) and was, as its readers were explicitly informed, taken verbatim from Marshall and Marshall (1879):

> But though men have the power to purchase they may not choose to use it. For when confidence has been shaken by failures, capital cannot be got to start new companies or extend old ones . . . there is but little occupation in any of the trades which make fixed capital. Those whose skill and capital is specialized in these trades are earning little, and therefore buying little of the produce of other trades. Other trades, finding a poor market for their goods, produce less; they earn less, and therefore they buy less: the diminution of the demand for their wares makes them demand less of other trades. Thus commercial disorganization spreads: the disorganization of one trade throws others out of gear, and they react on it and increase its disorganization. (Marshall 1890, 8th ed. 1920, p. 491)

In the late 1920s and early 1930s, arguments along these lines appeared quite often, not only among professional outsiders such as Hobson but also, for example, in the writings of the Stockholm School, as they extended Wicksellian dynamics to "model sequences" in which money wages were sticky and output was not constrained to remain at a "full-employment" level. Hawtrey, too, by that time, had come to understand that output and employment contractions would characterize the downswing of his simple income – expenditure model if output prices were unable to fall because of wage stickiness. And as Patinkin (1982, ch. 7) has noted, Keynes himself (in collaboration with Hubert Henderson) in *Can Lloyd George Do It?* broached the idea (though not consistently so) that public-works expenditures could have a cumulative effect on employment.[19] Patinkin (1982, pp. 192–194) has also noted, however, that the Henderson-Keynes analysis relied on inter-industry spillovers that were more akin to modern input–output linkages than to a multiplier mechanism derived from a clear conception of the interaction of income and expenditure. Be that as it may, it was precisely Keynes's failure to integrate such spillover effects into the formal analysis of the *Treatise on Money* that had led him into the trap of attempting to explain cyclical swings in output with a model whose workings could be considered well defined only if output and employment were held constant.

Kahn's Contribution

If the phenomena first noted by Bagehot and the Marshalls were again attracting attention among the orthodox by the end of the 1920s, nevertheless their insights still were not being much extended. It is one thing to note that unemployment in one sector of the economy will have consequences for the demand for the output of others, and hence for unemployment therein too, but quite another to be able to say anything about the orders of magnitude of the spillovers in question, about whether their consequences will be explosive or self-limiting, and about what properties of the economic system need to be understood in order to answer such questions. That crucial gap was soon to be filled, with Richard Kahn (1931) taking the first all-important step.[20]

---

[19] It should be noted that the pamphlet was prepared on behalf of the Liberal Party, which was advocating public-works expenditures as part of its 1929 general-election platform. Patinkin's discussion (1982, pp. 191–196) places the pamphlet in its historical context. See also Mog-gridge (1992, pp. 460–464) and Skidelsky (1992, pp. 303–306).

[20] It would be more accurate, perhaps, to say that Kahn's was the first step to attain widespread and permanent visibility among mainstream economists. Both Klein (1949, 2nd ed. 1966, pp. 143–147) and Patinkin (1982, ch. 7, p. 191) noted that the German-American businessman and economist Nicholas Johannsen (1908) developed a doctrine of the effects of what he called "impair saving" and used the term "multiplying principle" in discussing the effects of investment expenditure on economic activity. Keynes (1930a, vol. II, p. 90) mentioned – "brushed off" was Klein's characterization (Klein 1949, 2nd ed. 1966, p. 147) – Johann-sen's work on that matter in the *Treatise*, but does not seem to have referred to it subse-quently. Johannsen's work dealt within the overall workings of the monetary system and its

Kahn's 1931 article "The Relation of Home Investment to Unemployment" is rightly regarded as a classic. Its main purpose was to show that the so-called Treasury view of the difficulty of financing public-works expenditures, and their likely ineffectiveness, was misconceived. As was pointed out earlier, Kahn in fact circumvented Hawtrey's version of that latter doctrine by assuming "the intelligent co-operation of the banking system" (Kahn 1931, p. 174). But it was nevertheless the case that the role of monetary policy in his analysis had nothing in common with Hawtrey's special case, in which public-works expenditures *appeared* to be effective precisely because and *only* because money was created in order to finance them. Monetary factors were purely permissive in Kahn's story.

His analysis, as is well known, rested on the proposition that the inception of an expenditure program would create "primary employment" among otherwise idle workers, and extra income that they would spend. As a consequence, "to meet the increased expenditure of wages and profits that is associated with the primary employment, the production of consumption-goods is increased. Here again wages and profits are increased, and the effect will be passed on, though with *diminished intensity*" (Kahn 1931, p. 173, italics added).

The sequence of secondary expenditures generated in that way could be written as a geometric progression with a finite sum, whose relationship to the original injection of public-works expenditure would depend upon the rate at which the intensity of secondary expenditures diminished, or, to put it more precisely, on a parameter k determining the fraction of newly generated income that, at each stage in the process, was spent on consumption goods. Ultimately, "the ratio of secondary employment to primary employment is $k/(1 - k)$" (Kahn 1931, p. 183).

Now Kahn in fact stressed two factors in particular as being important in keeping k below unity. He told his readers that "the secondary employment is smaller the greater are the saving on the dole, the increase in imports, and the other alleviations that accompany a unit increase in employment" (Kahn 1931, p. 179). He also pointed out that supply-side considerations were important: "At normal times, when productive resources are fully employed . . . [the] building of roads carries with it little secondary employment and causes a large rise in prices. But at times of intense depression . . . [the] amount of secondary employment is then large and the rise in prices is small" (Kahn 1931, p. 182). It is, furthermore, worth noting that he related his analysis of that matter explicitly to that of the *Treatise on Money*. Specifically, he showed that its correspondence to Keynes's work was closest when full

---

interaction with the real economy. For a comprehensive discussion, see Hagemann and Rühl (1990).

employment prevailed, so that price-level movements rather than output variations had to absorb the impact of injections of expenditure.

As late as 1933, in his *Theory of Unemployment*, Pigou was to ridicule employment-multiplier analysis of that type, though he did not refer explicitly to Kahn in that context:[21]

> It is often argued that, if . . . the number of men employed in road-making, or other sorts of capital construction, is increased, without offsetting reductions in other non-wage-good industries, a large mass of further employment will be created in the industries that make wage-goods by the expenditure of the newly employed men. . . . The people set to work on road-making, or whatever it may be, have, *pro tanto*, more money to spend; they spend it, and so set to work more makers of the wage-goods that they buy; these, by spending their money, set to work more makers of the wage-goods *they* buy; and so on indefinitely. Indeed, according to this argument, it is only because some of the wage-earners' goods are bought from abroad that the setting of a single new man to work on road-making does not cause an infinite number of men to obtain employment in making wage-goods! (Pigou 1933, pp. 74–75, italics in original)

Given the way Kahn set out his argument, one can have a certain amount of sympathy with that objection. It *is* discomfiting to be faced with an argument that appears to become ridiculous when moved from the context of an open economy to a closed economy; and Kahn's other main leakage, "savings on the dole" (not taken up by Pigou), depended for its existence on a particular institutional detail, namely, a publicly funded unemployment-benefit system under which payments to individuals would cease when they became employed, so there could be no comfort there either.

Warming's Clarification

Pigou was, nevertheless, being unfair, because Kahn had referred to "other alleviations," and among those were savings made not out of employment income but out of profits. To be sure, it would have required an argument about the likely magnitude of distributional effects, along the lines pursued,

---

[21] Kahn evidently was already familiar with the line of criticism in 1931 (Patinkin 1982, ch. 7, p. 197). It is difficult to see why Pigou would have allowed a comment of that sort to stand in a work that was not published until fully two years after Kahn's essay, or indeed why he failed to refer to Kahn's work. In light of Kahn's efforts to relate his analysis of the multiplier to the *Treatise on Money*, it is interesting to note that it was in the course of commenting to Keynes on the *Treatise* that Hawtrey developed an analysis of how output might respond to changes in investment, which comes close to the multiplier. Hawtrey, however, did not incorporate that analysis, of which he provided an algebraic version (Hawtrey 1932a, pp. 351–352), into his monetary theory of the cycle, because he believed that changes in the volume of saving would in fact influence the rate of investment. See Deutscher (1990, pp. 103–104). See also Eric Davis (1980, p. 719). See also footnote 23.

for example, by Lindahl (1930) or Ohlin (1933) (see Chapter 3), to make the mechanism at work there precise, and Kahn did not provide such an argument. But in a comment on Kahn's paper that appeared in the *Economic Journal* in June 1932, and therefore nearly a year before Pigou's book went to press, Jens Warming, a Danish statistician, provided exactly the modification to Kahn's multiplier analysis needed to make it proof against such suspicions of fragility.[22] Warming is worth quoting at length on that matter:

> I agree with Mr. Kahn in his interest in public works, in his emphasising the international difficulties, and in his calculations about secondary employment; but as this last problem has also been discussed in this country [presumably Denmark], I have something to add.
>
> If (*ceteris paribus*) we invest 100 mill., this amount will be paid out as direct or indirect wages, interest, profit, etc.; the receivers will increase their consumption and thus create employment for a new set of unemployed factors, and so on, only with "diminished intensity" (Kahn). As to the cause of this diminished intensity, Mr. Kahn only considers the fact that a share of the employment goes abroad, while he expressly supposes that the new income (or rather the profit) is devoted to consumption in its entirety. It is here that I have something to add, as the saving from this income is a very important by-product to the secondary employment, and is just as capable of financing the activity.
>
> The sum of this saving can be calculated by aid of the same mathematical formula which Mr. Kahn employs for the secondary effects. . . . If we . . . consider a closed system, where nothing is lost abroad, but where 25 per cent. is lost to saving, the first set of secondary employment is 75 per cent., the next 56.25 per cent., etc. With 0.75 as k in the formula we then find 0.75/0.25 or 3, which, together with the original investment, gives 4. For the investment of 100 mill. we thus get a total employment of 400 mill., and of this 100 mill. will be saved, just covering the investment. (Warming 1932, pp. 214–215)

Though Warming was not correct in suggesting that Kahn had ignored saving, particularly from profits, a point which Kahn himself stressed in his reply to Warming (Kahn 1932), his analysis nevertheless represented a considerable step forward. It grounded leakages from the multiplier process in a well-defined behavioural relationship that might be expected to hold in either a closed or an open economy (and the bulk of Warming's paper was concerned with the latter) and to be independent of the institutional details of unemployment relief.[23] It is small wonder, then, that, as Skidelsky (1992,

---

[22] Kaergaard, Andersen, and Topp (1996) have provided an interesting account of that and Warming's other (considerable) contributions to resource economics and to analysis of the identification problem.

[23] As Eric Davis (1980) has shown, Hawtrey understood the analytic significance of leakages into saving as early as 1930 or 1931, but his discussion of those issues did not postulate a stable marginal propensity to save, but merely that an increase in income was likely to be

pp. 451–452) has pointed out, Keynes, who had been making use of Kahn's analysis in his work with the Committee of Economists of the Economic Advisory Council to the British government, adopted Warming's formulation (albeit without acknowledgement of Warming as its source) almost immediately upon its publication.

Concluding Comments

Certain features of the analysis discussed in this chapter are worth stressing. To begin with, it has been shown that the problem of unemployment at the level of the aggregate economy had come to be regarded as a secular one in post-war Britain. Cyclical factors were still seen as exacerbating economy-wide unemployment, to be sure, but they were no longer treated as its principal causes as they had been before World War I. Closely related, the approach usually taken to analysing the phenomenon was comparative static rather than dynamic. Also, even though the full implications of doing so were not fully appreciated, it was understood that economy-wide unemployment needed to be approached from a general-equilibrium perspective and that the interaction of the monetary system with the labour market needed to be analysed if it was to be understood. We have, moreover, seen that unemployment was also the focus of an underconsumptionist critique of the market economy. Also, we have noted that Kahn's analysis of a cumulative process involving unemployment, rather than prices, was made precise by Warming's postulate that a stable fraction of the income generated by an injection of public-works expenditure would be saved. Finally, and crucially, that postulate was understood to render the cumulative process in question reliably self-limiting.

But, rich though it was, the literature on unemployment was above all diverse, with many themes, not always mutually consistent, running through it. As we shall see in due course, it was through the medium of Keynes's *General Theory of Employment, Interest and Money* (1936) that a selection

---

divided between consumption and saving, which was not quite the same thing. In his algebraic exposition (1932a, pp. 351–352), Hawtrey referred to income being divided between consumption and saving in the ratio k to $(1-k)$. Even there, however, the behavioural significance he attached to those fractions was not quite clear. Deutscher (1990, p. 104) went no further than to argue that k "looks very much like the marginal propensity to consume." Hence, and in light of the fact that Hawtrey himself did not accord the analysis in question more than peripheral significance in his own cycle theory, he perhaps should not be accorded an important place among early exponents of the multiplier. For further discussion, see the recent exchange between Dimand (1997) and Darity and Young (1997). Note that Neville Cain (1979) argued persuasively for Warming's influence on Keynes's analysis of the multiplier, as Skidelsky has acknowledged. Furthermore, as Dimand (1988, p. 145) has noted, Kahn (1985) agreed that Warming's contribution did help clarify his own, and James Meade's, thinking about the multiplier.

of those features of the literature on unemployment were brought into contact with others drawn from cycle theory to help produce the IS-LM framework. But before we can take up those matters, the American experience and the economic ideas that it produced in the inter-war years need to be discussed. It is to these matters that we now turn.

PART III

American Analysis of Money and the Cycle

CHAPTER 8

American Macroeconomics between World War I and the Depression

The Economic Background

In the 1920s and early 1930s there existed a vigorous and diverse American literature dealing with monetary theory and policy, as well as the business cycle, which was anything but provincial. Contributors to that literature drew freely upon European sources, and Europeans in turn drew freely upon American contributions. The distinctiveness of that literature was partly a matter of the originality of individual contributors, but in the macroeconomic field, in particular, it also stemmed from the fact that in the 1920s the economic climate in the United States was very different from that prevailing in Europe.

World War I had created much less economic trauma for the United States than for Europe, even though a large-scale military commitment to a European conflict had marked a political turning point of enormous significance. For the United States, the war had lasted less than two years and had been managed without continuing adherence to the gold standard ever coming into question. The United States' economy had, to be sure, shared in the instability of the immediate post-war years, but recovery from the severe contraction of 1920–21 had been rapid in most sectors of the economy. Agriculture was an important exception, however, and recurrent problems for banks in agricultural areas were associated with that sector's continuing weakness. Even so, the serious secular unemployment that plagued Britain throughout the 1920s had no parallel in the United States. All of that would in due course change with the onset of the Great Depression in 1929, but what in Europe looked like the worsening of a secular problem of a decade's standing would at first be treated in the United States as an unusually bad cyclical downturn.

The United States had done without a central bank until 1913, and, perhaps related to that fact, financial crises associated with the upper turning-point of the cycle were much fresher in the memory there. Indeed, according to Sprague (1910), ad hoc responses to crisis in the banking system by such bodies as the New York Clearing House Association had been markedly less adept in 1907 than on a number of earlier occasions, and the severity of that particular crisis had been a powerful impetus towards the creation of the Federal Reserve System. In Britain, by way of comparison, financial panic and bank failures at the onset of a cyclical downturn had last been encountered on a large scale in the 1860s, and the Bank of England's handling of the Baring Crisis of 1893 had established, once and for all, its credibility as a lender of last resort. In Britain, therefore, by the 1920s, financial panic was nothing more than a distant memory associated with a long-ago-superseded policy regime.

Policy Questions

There was considerable continuity in the policy problems that faced the United States before and after World War I. The cycle remained an issue, as did the role that could be played by a newly established central bank in coping with it. Questions about whether or not to restore the pre-war parity, and if so, how, and about how to deal with an apparently new phenomenon of high secular unemployment simply did not arise there in the 1920s. The war had injected two new elements into the economic environment, however. First, as Barber (1985) has recounted, management of the war effort had provided an example of large-scale and effective government organization of economic life, which had led to rather optimistic discussions of the possibilities for activist policies, and particularly stabilization policies, during the 1920s. Second, the United States had emerged as the world's leading creditor nation and as the repository of a significant fraction of its monetary gold stock. In the 1920s, international constraints on the conduct of monetary policy were as loose in the United States as they were tight elsewhere in the world, and discussions of domestic monetary policy could proceed almost as if the economy were closed. As W. Randolph Burgess of the Federal Reserve Bank of New York put it in 1927,

> I think you would have to look through many pages of banking history to find a period in which a bank of issue in an important country has been in the position of the Federal Reserve System, with a reserve ratio so high that it could be neglected in the determination of credit policy. (Burgess 1927b, p. 140)

American economists did not take it for granted that the Federal Reserve System should be merely a Bagehotian defender of gold convertibility and lender of last resort; they also debated the possibilities of giving that institution a much more ambitious role as a major instrument of counter-cyclical policy. There was nothing new about such a conception of central banking. As I have discussed elsewhere (Laidler 1991), such possibilities had been widely discussed in the neo-classical literature from the 1880s onwards, a literature to which American economists had contributed and with which, in the 1920s, they were still thoroughly familiar. However, in the United States of the 1920s, such possibilities were matters of practical politics in a way that they were not elsewhere. It is hardly surprising, then, to find that Irving Fisher, whose contributions to the pre-war literature had been of the first order of importance, was deeply involved in debates about the cycle and the conduct of monetary policy in the 1920s.

The Quantity Theory and the Cycle

Immediately before the war, Irving Fisher's *The Purchasing Power of Money* (1911) had done much to rescue the quantity theory of money from the disrepute that its association with inflationary policy proposals had brought upon it in the final two decades of the nineteenth century. That book, like related contributions (e.g., Kemmerer 1909), had been mainly concerned with explaining the secular behaviour of the price level and with putting that explanation on a firm empirical basis, but it had contained one chapter (Chapter 4, ''Transition Periods'') dealing with the cycle, expanding ideas which had first appeared in Fisher's monograph ''Appreciation and Interest'' (1896).

Central to Fisher's pre-war analysis of the cycle had been the distinction between real and nominal interest rates and the hypothesis that expectations regarding inflation adapted to experience at differing speeds on the two sides of the market for bank loans, with business borrowers adjusting more rapidly than lenders; and that analysis also allowed for feedbacks from inflation to monetary expansion through the market for bank credit. Specifically, any shock, to the quantity of currency, say, that set the price level rising would put in motion a cumulative process of expanding bank lending, deposit creation, and hence further price increases. It would do so because the more rapid response of the business community's expectations to rising prices would create a perception of increased profit opportunities on projects financed by bank lending, a perception that would persist so long as bank interest rates failed to adjust fully to inflation. That process would eventually come to an end, however: inflation would erode the value of part of the collateral held by banks against business loans, and those institutions would, in any event, begin to encounter reserve shortages. Hence lending rates would in due course rise and indeed run ahead of expectations of further profit opportunities. When that occurred, a downswing would begin, driven by exactly the same mechanisms working in reverse.[1]

---

[1] Note, however, that the cycle described by Fisher (1911) was predominantly a cycle in the price level. On that matter, see Laidler (1991, pp. 93–95). It was only after World War I that American quantity theorists began systematically to consider fluctuations in real variables as

A "Dance of the Dollar"

The title of Fisher's essay "The Business Cycle Largely a 'Dance of the Dollar' " (1923) is nowadays better known than its contents. The paper itself was mainly statistical; it presented the results of correlating the rate of price inflation in the United States with "The Business Barometer of the American Telephone and Telegraph Company" (Fisher 1923, p. 1026) over the 1914–22 period, and it found that "this one element, *rapidity of price movement*, during the period 1914–1922 seems to account, almost completely, for the ups and downs of business" (Fisher 1923, p. 1027, italics in original). Less well known, but more revealing of the views that Fisher came to hold during the 1920s, is the title of a slightly later paper: "Our Unstable Dollar and the So-called Business Cycle" (Fisher 1925). The results presented there were very similar to those of the earlier paper, but Warren Persons' "Index of Trade" was used as the dependent variable, and the period studied was 1915–23.

As Wesley C. Mitchell (1927, pp. 35, 465) noted at the time, Fisher interpreted those results as showing that the cycle was, in essence, a myth, as the following passage from Fisher (1925), quoted by Mitchell, demonstrated:

> . . . if by the business cycle is meant merely the statistical fact that business does *fluctuate* above and below its average trend, there is no denying the existence of a cycle – and not only in business but in any statistical series whatsoever! If we draw any smooth curve to represent the general trend of population, the actual population figures must necessarily rise sometimes above and sometimes below this mean trend line. . . . In the same way weather conditions necessarily fluctuate about their own means; so does the luck at Monte Carlo. Must we then speak of "the population cycle," "the weather cycle" and "the Monte Carlo cycle"?
>
> I see no more reason to believe in "the" business cycle. It is simply the fluctuation about its own mean. And yet the cycle idea is supposed to have more content than mere variability. It implies a regular succession of *similar* fluctuations, constituting a sort of *recurrence*, so that, as in the case of the phases of the moon, the tides of the sea, wave motion, or pendulum swing,

---

the main characteristics of the cycle. That will be clear, in the case of Fisher, from the discussion that follows in the text. But that was also true, to some extent, of Kemmerer (1921, pp. 62–63), who canvassed the possibility that unemployment would be one inevitable consequence of post-war deflation. That analysis by Fisher bore a superficial resemblance to Wicksell's cumulative process (e.g., 1898), but it was in fact much more closely related to, though by no means identical with, contemporary English monetary theories of the cycle, notably that of Hawtrey (e.g., 1913, 1919). That was because, as I have recounted elsewhere (Laidler 1991), Fisher's work and Hawtrey's developed within the same neo-classical tradition in monetary economics. Indeed, Fisher's *Purchasing Power of Money* (1911) was the only work cited in the entirety of Hawtrey's 1913 monograph. Unlike Wicksell's work, that branch of the neo-classical tradition stressed the importance of endogenously caused changes in the quantity of bank money as the primary cause of subsequent variations in expenditure.

we can forecast the future on the basis of a pattern worked out from past experience, and which we have reason to think will be copied in the future. We certainly cannot do that in predicting the weather, or Monte Carlo luck. Can we do so as to business? Not so long as business is dominated by changes in the price level! (Fisher 1925, pp. 191–192, as quoted by Mitchell 1927, pp. 465–466, italics in original)

By the 1920s, Fisher's views of business fluctuations thus differed in a number of important respects from those of Hawtrey, who was by then recognized in his own right, not least in the United States, as a leading exponent of an exclusively monetary explanation of the phenomenon. First, as is apparent from the foregoing quotation, Fisher regarded price-level behaviour per se as the key link in the causative chain running from money to economic activity. Hawtrey, on the other hand, stressed flows of money income and expenditure which in turn induced real fluctuations in the presence of, and indeed because of, wage and price-level stickiness. Second, Fisher regarded price-level stabilization as not merely helpful, but sufficient, for the stabilization of business activity in general. Third, and quite crucially, Fisher believed that price-level stabilization was feasible, whereas Hawtrey was more modest in his belief about what monetary policy could accomplish in practice.

Hawtrey located the cycle's cause in exactly the same cumulative processes of money and credit creation and destruction as did Fisher, but he thought that central banks lacked the information needed to act so as to iron them out, and the phrase "inherent instability of credit" was ubiquitous in his writings.[2] As far as Fisher was concerned, there was nothing "inherent" about it. The fact is that by the early 1920s, Fisher was already beginning to display that simplicity and rigidity of viewpoint that would in due course earn him a reputation as something of a crank.

A Price-Stability Rule for Monetary Policy

In the 1920s, the Stable Money Association (originally the Stable Money League and then the National Monetary Association), whose organization had owed a great deal to Fisher's efforts, actively promoted legislation to subject the conduct of monetary policy to a simple rule. Fisher (1934, ch. V) outlined the history of those efforts, which involved a series of attempts to have Congress adopt resolutions or pass bills urging or mandating the Federal Reserve System to adopt price-level stabilization as a policy goal. Three bills introduced into the House of Representatives attracted particular attention:

---

[2] This is not to say that Hawtrey thought that central banks were powerless to influence the economy. On the contrary, he was to argue in 1932 that sufficiently vigorous open-market operations could have significant effects on the depressed American economy.

the Goldsborough bill of 1922 and two Strong bills of 1926 and 1928, named for the congressmen who introduced them. The first of those would have implemented Fisher's ''compensated-dollar'' plan, and the latter two would have required the Federal Reserve System actively to pursue a price-stability target by more conventional methods.[3] The first Strong bill would, for example, have amended the Federal Reserve Act so that, in addition to ''accommodating commerce,'' as the system's initial mandate required, discount policy would thereafter also be *''promoting a stable price level for commodities in general. All of the powers of the Federal Reserve system shall be used for promoting stability in the price level''* (69 Cong. 1 sess. H.R. 7895, as quoted by Hardy 1932, p. 201, italics in original). That first Strong bill contained no provision for any changes in the system's powers or organization, nor any recognition, even a purely ritual one, that its ability to control the price level might in any way be circumscribed. Not surprisingly, the bill failed, as indeed did its successor, which was ''much less precise . . . as to the specific nature of the responsibilities to be laid on the Federal Reserve authorities'' (Hardy 1932, p. 202), as a result of attempts to deal with the fact that the system's ability to control the price level was limited.

Other Guidelines for Monetary Policy

Even so, a policy position with deep roots in the quantity theory of money, one that would make price stability monetary policy's principal aim, was, beyond doubt, popular in the 1920s, and that popularity led to serious discussion, far beyond the immediate debate surrounding the Strong bills, about how that aim could be achieved. Systematic empirical work, which had long been a prominent feature of American monetary economics, played an important part in that discussion, not least in the contribution made to it by Carl Snyder of the Federal Reserve Bank of New York. In 1924 he published a short paper setting out the results of an application of Fisher's transactions version of the quantity theory of money to recent United States data (Snyder 1924).

The results in question were striking, for they appeared to show that fluctuations in the volume of transactions associated with the business cycle were essentially entirely accommodated by variations in the velocity of circu-

---

[3] Fisher's ''compensated-dollar'' scheme involved regular alterations in the dollar price of gold in order to offset variations in the gold price of goods. For a discussion, see Laidler (1991, pp. 176–177). On the 1922 Goldsborough bill, see Barber (1985, pp. 24–26). The Strong bills attracted some formidable academic support, and not only from within the United States: Gustav Cassel, for example, testified in their favour. Moreover, a few years later, in the early 1930s, the recommendations of Keynes's *Treatise on Money* on the use of bank rate as a tool for price-level stabilization, and hence business-cycle stabilization, seemed to put him in the same camp as their supporters, as Hardy (1932, pp. 199–200) was to point out. The following account draws heavily on Hardy (1932, ch. X, pp. 199–226).

lation around a trend value that was to all intents and purposes constant. It followed from that, however, that in order to stabilize the price level over time, it would suffice to keep the money supply expanding at the economy's long-run rate of growth. Because Snyder did not propose that the Federal Reserve System be given a *legislated mandate* to that end, he should not be regarded as a proponent of a money-supply growth *rule*, but he could make a strong claim as an early supporter of at least a money-growth *guideline*.[4]

He elaborated and extended his empirical work further in a 1927 monograph, where he noted that "it seems probable also that the trend of prices has a real influence on the amplitude and duration of business cycles. In the period of falling general prices through the '70's and '90's depressions were more severe, and of longer duration, than in the following period of rising prices" (Snyder 1927, p. 204). That result, which originated in a study by Willard Thorp (1926), was much noted in the American literature of the period (cf. Mitchell 1927, pp. 407–412; Douglas and Director 1931, pp. 182–183), and it gave added strength to the case for maintaining secular price stability, or at least avoiding even slow secular deflation.[5]

In the 1920s, exponents of stable money growth regarded it not as a desirable alternative to self-conscious pursuit of price stability, but rather as the best practicable means of achieving that end and, along with it, an automatic damping, though perhaps not total elimination, of the cycle as well. Harold Reed, who acknowledged Snyder's priority in advocating stable money growth (Reed 1930, p. 199), expressed matters as follows:

> In our examination of special periods we have concluded that mistakes have usually been later admitted whenever the aggregate credit supply of the country has been permitted to undergo pronounced fluctuations for any extended period of time. The stabilization of business seems to be very largely a matter of avoiding serious departures from a rate of credit enlargement corresponding roughly to the physical growth of the country's trade. (Reed 1930, p. 198)

Lionel Edie was extremely doubtful about the feasibility of using the rate of interest as the principal tool of stabilization policy, "for the reason that the elasticity of credit demand behaves in an unstable and often unpredictable

---

[4] That was the opinion of Thomas Humphrey (1971, repr. 1993, p. 106) and George Garvey (1978). Note, however, that Tavlas (1982, pp. 97–98) argued that Alexander Del Mar (1885) had a prior claim on that idea. Tavlas and Aschheim (1985) gave an interesting overview of Del Mar's contribution to monetary economics. It is also worth noting that Snyder (e.g., 1935) was later to be an exponent of a monetary explanation for the Great Depression, though Lauchlin Currie (e.g., 1934a,b) developed that explanation with more thoroughness.

[5] Recall that Keynes (1923, pp. 32–34) presented a theoretical argument as to why deflation would depress real activity, based upon the idea that with falling prices, firms would have difficulty in selling output at a price that would cover earlier-incurred production costs. He did not ignore the effect of expectations on interest rates in that book, but rather questioned their ability to adjust sufficiently to eliminate problems of that sort. See Chapter 5, "Price Stability as a Policy Goal," for a more detailed discussion.

manner'' (Edie 1931, p. 102) – essentially the same reason Hawtrey gave for believing credit to be "inherently unstable."[6] He therefore went a little further than Snyder or Reed in specifying just how money growth might be regulated and advocated what we would nowadays call "base control":

> Central Banks should aim at so regulating the reserves of the banking system that the outstanding credit built upon those reserves will expand at the same rate as the long-term growth of production. There is enough credit when the curves of credit growth and production growth parallel each other. More than this is too much; less than this is too little. (Edie 1931, p. 117, original in italics)

Monetary guidelines of any type, however, were very much a minority taste at that time, particularly among practitioners of monetary policy, as Edie explicitly pointed out:

> A symposium of central bank opinion in various countries revolves about such maxims as: "Artificial interference with the natural commercial demand for credit is dangerous and unwarranted"; "It is impossible to strike a blow at speculative excesses without at the same time cutting off the credit supply to meet the legitimate needs of trade"; "We can make money easy but we cannot force people to borrow it. One can lead a horse to water but one cannot make him drink." (Edie 1931, pp. 91–92)

Nowhere were ideas such as those more prevalent than in the Federal Reserve System itself, more particularly at the Federal Reserve Board, and among some of its close associates in the American banking and academic communities.

The Banking School Element in American Monetary Economics

The Federal Reserve System had been created in 1913, at a time when the gold standard was apparently at its zenith, largely in order to provide lender-of-last-resort facilities to a banking system which, it was taken for granted, would operate against a background of gold convertibility. The mainstream of neo-classical monetary economics had, by then, long since moved beyond the point of regarding the price level in terms of gold as being determined independently of the configuration and operation of the monetary system.

---

[6] The word "credit" is used by Reed and Edie rather than "money." It is nevertheless the case that both Reed and Edie were concerned with the behaviour of the banking system's liabilities rather than assets, though they used data on the time path of assets to gauge that of liabilities. We have seen in Chapter 5 that Hawtrey typically used the word "credit" to denote "deposit money," and it was not, in fact until the appearance of an article by Lauchlin Currie (1933a), as discussed in Chapter 9, footnote 25, that semantic clarity began to characterize discussion of those issues. See also the discussion later in footnote 11 of this chapter.

Even so, the belief that under the gold standard the price level would largely take care of itself, so long as the central banks of the world observed the "rules of the game," was still rather widely held. For that reason, even though gold convertibility no longer placed any systematic constraint on Federal Reserve policy in the 1920s, discussions of monetary policy, in which price-level behaviour was a subsidiary issue, were still common at that time, particularly in the aforementioned circles.[7]

The provision of lender-of-last-resort facilities had not, however, been the only aim of the founders of the Federal Reserve System. As one of its principal architects, H. Parker Willis, who in the 1920s and 1930s held a professorship at the Columbia University School of Business, had noted in 1915, "the Federal reserve system is . . . not simply an insurance against panic, but a regular working part of the banking mechanism of the country with given functions to be steadily and continuously performed" (Willis 1915, p. 24). Among those given (and rather modest) functions, the system was required "to furnish an elastic currency" and "to afford means of rediscounting commercial paper" (digest of the Federal Reserve Act, as reprinted by Willis 1915, p. 315). Nothing as ambitious as stabilization of the price level, let alone the real economy, was expected of the system. There was, in fact, a rather strong overtone of what can properly be called a British Banking School viewpoint built into the Federal Reserve Act.

Reverse Causation between Money and Prices

Those who espoused such views, notably Willis and Benjamin Anderson, who in the 1920s was chief economist of the Chase Bank and an influential contributor to monetary debates, were hostile to Fisher's version of the quantity theory. In that, and many other respects too, their work reflected the influence of Willis's mentor, James Laurence Laughlin of the University of Chicago. For example, the Anderson treatise *The Value of Money* (1917), published when he held an academic position at Harvard, should be read as a systematic attempt to rebut claims made on behalf of the quantity theory in Fisher's *Purchasing Power of Money*.[8] In that work, the following argument appeared:

---

[7] In this regard, it is interesting to note that in what we would now call a collection of readings for undergraduates on *Principles of Money and Banking*, which ran to 495 pages, Harold Moulton (1916), of the University of Chicago, included precisely one page and three lines of material discussing "The Relation of Money and Prices" as a topic in its own right. That collection evidently was fairly widely used, for it saw its fourth printing in 1920.

[8] The viewpoint represented by Laughlin and those whom he influenced treated the price level as largely exogenous to the behaviour of the banking system, and the cycle as mainly a consequence of real shocks of one sort or another; and for some of its exponents it also encompassed what Lloyd Mints (1945) would later call the "real-bills doctrine." Its exponents

> The quantity theory is that, while particular prices may rise from causes affecting them, as compared with other prices, without a change in money, velocities, etc., still there cannot be a rise in the general average, because other prices will be obliged to go down to compensate. The issue is as to the possibility of a rise in particular prices, uncompensated by a corresponding fall in other particular prices, without a *prior* increase in money, or velocities, or decrease in trade. . . . I shall maintain that particular prices can, and do, rise, without a *prior* increase in money or bank-deposits, or change in the volume of trade, or in velocity of money or deposits and also without compensating fall in other particular prices. Putting it in terms of Fisher's equation, I shall maintain, as against Fisher, that P can rise through the direct action of factors *outside* the equation of exchange, that *as a consequence of such rise* the other factors readjust themselves, and that a new equilibrium is reached which, in the absence of new disturbances from causes outside the equation, tends to be as permanent and stable as the old equilibrium was. (Anderson 1917, p. 293, italics in original)

Now some of the examples with which Anderson went on to illustrate that contention should in fact be acceptable to exponents of the quantity theory, even in the form Fisher gave it, and to that extent they represented something of a straw man. They hinged on the effect of a rise in world prices on the price level in a small open economy, implicitly assumed to be on the gold standard or some other fixed-exchange-rate arrangement.[9] In such circumstances, Anderson argued, domestic prices would also rise, and the balance of payments would improve for so long as was necessary to bring the money supply up to a level that would validate that change (Anderson 1917, pp. 296–300). Other examples Anderson offered were less convincing, however, because, following Laughlin (whom he cited in his own support on that point), he was of the opinion that

> the trouble with Fisher's notion comes in his definition of the value of money in purely relative terms as the *reciprocal of the price-level*, and his contention that the study of the value of money is identical with the study of price-levels. Value is not a mere exchange relation. Rather, every exchange relation involves *two* values, the values of the two objects exchanged. These two values *causally* determine that exchange relation. In the case of particular prices, then, we must consider not only the value of goods,

---

were well aware of its origins in the Banking School literature, as their relatively frequent references to those earlier writings make quite clear. On the debate between Laughlin and Fisher, see Laidler (1991, pp. 75–76). For accounts of Laughlin's work, see Girton and Roper (1978) and Skaggs (1995). Note that Laughlin remained intellectually active into the 1930s, publishing a major monograph in 1931. His views, however, remained essentially as they had been in the 1880s.

[9] Fisher himself considered that case (1911, p. 91), arguing that it was sometimes convenient to treat the price level in an open economy as determined exogenously, just as it was sometimes convenient to describe the level of water in a lagoon as determined by that of the sea. He was not always consistent on that matter, however.

but also the value of money. (Anderson 1917, pp. 312–313, italics in original)

Anderson also followed Laughlin in arguing that the value of paper money derived from the prospect of its redemption in gold.[10] As he told readers of the *Chase Economic Bulletin* of March 23, 1925,

> if the market believes that redemption is certain and is merely deferred for a very short time, the discount [on paper relative to gold] will be slight. If the market believes that redemption is uncertain or that the time of redemption is remote, the discount will be great. (Anderson 1925, pp. 15–16)

Money and the Real Economy

There is no need to mount an elaborate critique of those doctrines here. What is important is that, erroneous though the first of them surely is (unless one maintains some variant of the labour or cost-of-production theory of value), and extreme though the second may be in the way in which it implicitly assumes that money is nothing but a store of value, they formed part of the theoretical basis for a view of monetary policy that was extremely influential in the United States in the 1920s. Though Anderson explicitly left open the possibility that some fluctuations in the price level might originate on the side of money, as had Laughlin before him (Anderson 1917, pp. 313, 389–390), the overall tone of his argument was that their source was more commonly to be found in the real economy and that in those circumstances, if the quantity of money did not validate them, then velocity would adapt instead. In Anderson's words, " 'velocity of circulation' is a blanket name for a complex and heterogenous set of activities of men. . . . The safest generalization possible concerning it is that it varies with the volume of trade and with prices" (Anderson 1917, p. 394). Nor was that necessarily undesirable: ". . . the business cycle is not, by any means, an unmitigated evil, and the important thing is to prevent the extreme fluctuations rather than to try and keep industry and prices on a dead level at all times, even if this were possible" (Anderson 1927, p. 121).

In any event, the views of those who ". . . see the whole explanation of the business cycle in the . . . movements of the general average of commodity prices, and . . . of the movements in the average of commodity prices in the phenomena of expanding and contracting money and bank credit" (Anderson 1927, p. 121) were "unsound." Anderson believed that the quantity theory was superficial and that monetary theory needed to move beyond questions about the interrelations between money and the price level to those involving

---

[10] In that matter, Anderson was closer to Adam Smith (1776, bk. II, ch. 2) than to Thomas Tooke and the Banking School.

the influence of monetary arrangements in general, but banking in particular, on real variables:

> Production waits on trade. The problem of marketing in the modern world is often more important than the problems of production in the narrower sense. . . . "Volume of trade," far from being dependent on "physical capacities and technique," is almost indefinitely flexible, with changing tone of the market, with changing values, and with other changes, including changes in the volume of money and credit. (Anderson 1917, p. 393)

To gear monetary policy to the pursuit of a price-level target required one to assume that the price level was, as Anderson termed it, "passive" and that the volume of transactions was independent of the quantity of money. Since he believed neither postulate to be true, it is hardly surprising that he also argued that "the proposal that the Federal Reserve Banks should stabilize commodity prices by varying their rediscount rates . . . is thoroughly vicious and unsound" (Hepburn and Anderson 1921, p. 35). Nor is it surprising that with specific reference to Keynes's proposals, in the *Tract on Monetary Reform*, to put domestic price stabilization ahead of exchange-rate stability, he remarked that "these theories are dangerous as well as false. They represent a refined and subtle form of Greenbackism or fiat money doctrine. They are hard to confute if the quantity theory on which they rest is true" (Anderson 1925, p. 4).

Anderson, however, held a view of the essential role played by "money and credit" in economic life quite different from anything offered by the quantity theory.

The Quality of Credit and the Needs of Trade

The phrase "money and credit" requires some attention at this point. Anderson's European contemporaries usually used the word "money" to mean currency, reserving "credit" for the chequable liabilities of commercial banks. Sometimes Anderson, and other Americans such as Willis, also used the word "credit" that way, but they frequently used it to denote the assets that lay on the other side of the banking system's balance sheet; and they paid a great deal of attention to the types of assets that commercial banks held, or to the *quality* of bank credit, as the usage of the time had it.[11] For

---

[11] Of course, in a banking system in which lending was confined to short-term commercial loans, the volume of bank credit granted in that way would move closely with the volume of the system's deposit liabilities. That was why such commentators as Reed (1930) and Edie (1931) used measures of bank credit as proxies for bank deposits. Nevertheless, semantic carelessness implicit in the ambiguous use of the word "credit" to refer interchangeably to both sides of the balance sheet could and sometimes did lead to outright confusion when propositions about the influence of the deposit liabilities of the banking system were wrongly

them, that *quality* of credit was far more important for the conduct of monetary policy than was the *quantity* of money, and meeting the needs of trade for means of exchange was a far more important policy goal than stabilizing the price level.

Just what "meeting the needs of trade" did and, equally important, did not involve was made clear by Willis:

> ... a main function of banking is to enable persons who have debts to pay to get the funds with which to meet them. ... banking is a process of equalizing the supply of fluid funds among those who require them. The Federal reserve system is intended to provide just this means of liquefying and equalizing resources. It is not a method of supplying capital to borrowers for investment. (Willis 1915, p. 190)

For Willis, as for Anderson, bank lending that facilitated trade in goods and services made an indirect, but appropriate, contribution to the economy's productivity by helping to maintain an equilibrium structure of relative prices. The central role of commercial banks was to provide the means of exchange necessary to facilitate trade, and, in normal times, it was believed that such provision would be close to automatic. Anderson warned, however, that

> in a period when idle bank funds are seeking employment, and when bankers must compete with one another for the opportunity to place their funds in capital uses ... there is obvious danger of substantial diversion of loanable funds from productive to speculative uses. (Anderson 1926, p. 27)

There is no need here to do more than note the difficulties involved in giving operational content to such distinctions among the qualities of bank assets, in tracing the proceeds of particular loans through the financial system from their primary lender to ultimate user, and in deciding whether their ultimate use has been productive or speculative. The important point is that the influential economists whose work we are here discussing believed that such distinctions could become a basis for practical policy guidelines. Willis, writing in collaboration with George W. Edwards, may again be allowed to speak for them on the matter:

> ... banking tends to create a condition of exchange in which it is easier to dispose of goods, or in which goods are enabled to command the widest possible market ... the effect of banking is to bring about an equalization of the demand for and supply of goods. ... If banking credit be freely extended to borrowers the effect of it is that of rendering the borrowers' wealth, whatever it might be, more readily available as purchasing power. ... When banks are overconfident in their estimates of future value and

---

applied in discussing the effects of bank lending per se. See Currie (1933a) for a masterly contemporary account of that matter.

> grant to each applicant an undue proportion of credit . . . they place in the hands of the borrowers purchasing power which the latter are not entitled to – that is to say, purchasing power which [they] really do not possess. In this case the borrowers are given a control over the commodities of others which they ought not to have, and if they exercise or apply it they are able to make an artificial demand for the commodities of others. The effect of such action . . . is to raise prices, and the resulting condition is called inflation. (Willis and Edwards 1926, pp. 492–494)

Willis and Edwards went on to note that "this danger is limited or largely avoided if banks are constantly compelled to redeem their outstanding credits in money" (Willis and Edwards 1926, p. 494).[12] A drain of reserves into circulation would, under such circumstances, eventually prompt credit contraction.

In the absence of convertibility, however,

> bank credit becomes an independent factor in the equation.
>
> The question properly to be asked in this connection relates to the standards or measures which banks can or should apply in determining whether the credit extensions they make are likely to have the moderating influence already spoken of or the disturbing influence. It seems to be assumed by some writers that there is no definite means by which the banker can assure himself of the effect of the credit he grants, so that as a matter of fact he can never be certain of the social influence produced by his work. This is an erroneous view of the situation. There is one perfectly safe and reliable guide which can almost invariably be applied by the banker. If the credit that he grants is for a period not longer on the average than the period of commercial credit in his community, his extension of credit will tend to bring about a steadier, smoother flow of goods from producer to consumer, and so will tend to "even up" prices. If, on the other hand, the period of credit allowed by the banker is much longer than that which is necessary to bring about the transfer of goods from producer to consumer, the banker is practically supplying the producer with capital, or in other words is enabling him to keep turning over his operations. In this case the counter effect of credit already spoken of sets in. (Willis and Edwards 1926, pp. 494–495)

Here we have an absolutely clear-cut statement of the "real-bills doctrine": the proposition that, even in the absence of convertibility, a banking system which confines itself to lending on the security of good-quality short-term commercial loans will automatically act so as to stabilize the price level.[13]

---

[12] There was therefore some resemblance between the views of Willis and Anderson and those that underpinned Austrian business-cycle theory, as epitomized by, for example, Hayek (1931a). However, the resemblance was far from complete, since those Americans showed no particular interest in the abstract capital theory on which Hayek based his analysis.

[13] Note that what I am here, following Mints (1945), calling the real-bills doctrine was a proposition about the consequences for the price level of a particular rule for bank lending. Sar-

The fact that the doctrine in question had been exposed as fallacious as early as 1802 by Henry Thornton, and that in writing about the early 1800s Bagehot (1873, p. 86) had described statements of it by certain directors of the Bank of England as "almost classic in their nonsense," quite evidently did nothing to prevent it from being espoused by some very influential monetary economists in America during the first two decades of the Federal Reserve System's operation.

Advocates of Stabilization Policy

This is not to say that so clear-cut a version of the doctrine as we find in Willis's writings was an undisputed touchstone for American monetary policy in the 1920s, let alone that the Strong bills were rejected on its basis. Matters were more complicated, even ambiguous, than that. The intellectual space that separated the advocates of monetary rules such as were embodied in those bills from the exponents of Banking School ideas was well occupied. Its occupants did not, however, form a well-defined school holding a common set of specific beliefs, beyond perhaps a modest faith in the stabilizing powers of discretionary monetary policy.

The Burgess-Riefler View

Charles O. Hardy quoted from pages 34–35 of the 1923 annual report of the Federal Reserve Board as follows:

> Administratively, therefore, the solution of the economic problem of keeping the volume of credit issuing from the Federal Reserve Banks from becoming either excessive or deficient is found in maintaining it in due relation to the volume of credit needs as these needs are derived from the operating requirements of agriculture, industry, and trade, and the prevention of the uses of Federal Reserve credit for purposes not warranted by the terms or spirit of the Federal Reserve Act. (Hardy 1932, p. 78)

He went on to note that that argument, which was essentially the same as that of Willis and Edwards (1926) just quoted, seemed to imply that the system should not engage in stabilization policies, "but merely . . . adapt itself to conditions as it finds them" (Hardy 1932, p. 79). As Hardy then pointed out, "the logical outcome of this policy would be to make stability of interest rates the primary test of policy" (Hardy 1932, p. 79, fn. 5).

---

gent and Wallace (1982) used the phrase to describe the rule itself, but correctly did not claim (unlike Willis and other advocates of its adoption) that if it were followed, price-level stability would be guaranteed.

However, Hardy also quoted another passage from the same report which led in another direction, and he concluded that

> the view, that it is the business of the Reserve system to work against the extremes either of deflation or inflation and not merely to adapt itself passively to the ups and downs of business, nor to confine itself to guarding against the inflow of credit into non-productive uses, is the view which in general has seemed to dominate Reserve system policy. (Hardy 1932, p. 80)

Hardy attributed that moderate position, which lay between the extremes espoused by, say, Willis on the one hand and Fisher on the other, to no individual in particular, but it was certainly held by Burgess (1927b) of the Federal Reserve Bank of New York, who actually managed to subsume such activities under the rubric of "meeting the needs of trade." Burgess (1927a) also produced a widely read monograph on the Federal Reserve System in which he argued that it should pursue policy along the lines later described by Hardy. To that end, he advocated counter-cyclical use of the discount rate, supplemented by open-market operations, whose main influence, he thought, would be on the degree of bank indebtedness to the Federal Reserve.

There was some resemblance between the views of Burgess, which were representative of those held at the Federal Reserve Bank of New York where he held an appointment, and those of Hawtrey, but they were by no means identical. As both Karl Brunner (1968) and Allan Meltzer (1995) have noted, Burgess, like Winfield Riefler (1930), who held a position at the Federal Reserve Board in Washington, and with whom they coupled Burgess, thought that monetary policy worked through its effects on bank lending rates in particular and credit conditions in general, rather than by way of its influence on money balances, or the "unspent margin" as Hawtrey termed it. As E. A. Goldenweiser (1930), director of research at the Federal Reserve Board, put it in an introduction to the book by Riefler (1930), in which he summarized Riefler's work,

> in modern money economy the all-important vital force is the flow of money, and the nerve center of the economic organism is the money market, where money is the article of trade and where its price [i.e., short-term interest rates] is determined. . . .
>
> [Riefler] arrives at the conclusion that open-market operations of the Federal reserve banks, because they are reflected in changes of member bank indebtedness, are fully as important as changes in discount rates in determining *the level of money rates in the market*. (Goldenweiser, 1930, pp. vii–viii, italics added)

Allyn Young and the Influence of Hawtrey

An important place among American commentators on monetary policy in the 1920s was occupied by Allyn Young. His significance was greater than his current reputation would suggest, and he was strongly influenced by Hawtrey.[14] Until 1927, Young was a professor of economics at Harvard, where, according to his obituarist Oskar Morgenstern (1929, p. 488), his ideas had become "a matter of oral tradition just as [had] – according to Keynes – Marshall's theory of money in Cambridge." He was also an advisor to Governor Benjamin Strong of the Federal Reserve Bank of New York, albeit perhaps not so influential there as was his colleague at Harvard, Oliver Sprague.[15] It was Young's position that

> no central bank could assume its necessary responsibilities and pursue a purely passive policy. If it did, sooner or later its reserves would be drained dry by gold exports or by a flow of currency into hand-to-hand circulation. There are two ways in which it can protect itself. First, by advancing its discount rate. . . . Second . . . by selling some of its earning assets. . . . Under different conditions, of course, the central bank may safely adopt the opposite policy, reducing its rates and increasing the amount of its cash liabilities, so as to permit a general expansion of credit. (Young 1927, p. 79)

And he noted with approval that

> since the war new importance has been attached to the effects which the operations of central banks have on the general condition of business, and it is quite generally held that their policies should be determined with primary reference to the securing of the maximum practicable degree of business stability. (Young 1927, p. 80)

On the evidence of his 1927 essay, then, Young's attitude towards monetary policy was very different from those of Anderson, Willis, or indeed any other exponent of the real-bills doctrine, and in the emphasis he placed on the volume of the Federal Reserve's cash liabilities and the expansion of credit (which should here be read as referring to bank money), he was also somewhat closer to Hawtrey than were Burgess and Riefler. Young was also

---

[14] Young, whose students included Frank H. Knight, Edwin Chamberlin, Harold Reed, Arthur Marget, James Angell, and Lauchlin Currie, has recently been the subject of a long-overdue biographical study by Charles Blitch (1996). His monetary economics has been thoroughly and perceptively discussed by Mehrling (1996), who has stressed the importance he attached to finding a coherent "middle-ground" position between the extremes of Fisher's quantity approach to monetary policy and that of Anderson, Willis, and others. See also Laidler (1993) for a briefer discussion, on which the following few paragraphs draw.

[15] It is well known that many of the difficulties encountered by the United States monetary authorities in the late 1920s and early 1930s stemmed from conflicts between the Federal Reserve Board in Washington and the Federal Reserve Bank of New York. It is a good first approximation to describe that conflict as one stemming from the different views on monetary theory propounded by Willis and Anderson, on the one hand, and Sprague and Young, on the other, with Burgess and Riefler, who did not subscribe to the real-bills doctrine, but attached no particular significance to the quantity of money either, poised between them. Sprague, however, was less influenced by Hawtrey and therefore was also less optimistic than Young about monetary policy's stabilizing capacity. My discussion of these issues owes much to correspondence with Allan Meltzer.

opposed to subjecting the Federal Reserve System to any legislated rule, such as that embodied in the Strong bills. When it came to laying down criteria for central-bank behaviour, he was adamant that "we can be certain that reliance upon any simple rule or set of rules would be dangerous" (Young 1927, p. 81). On the contrary, "what the Federal Reserve Banks need most . . . is not more power or less power, or doctrinaire formulations of what their policy ought to be, but merely an opportunity to develop a sound tradition, and to establish it firmly" (Young 1927, p. 82).

The foregoing quotations from Young were, as has been noted, reminiscent of Hawtrey. They canvassed the possibilities of discount-rate policy and open-market operations as instruments of counter-cyclical policy, they were cautious about what could be expected from such measures, and they stressed that central banking was an "art" whose practice could not be codified in simple legislated rules. That resemblance was no accident. Though he took an altogether more eclectic approach to cycle theory than had Hawtrey, Young was nevertheless a great admirer of Hawtrey's work and had reviewed *Currency and Credit* twice in the early 1920s, calling it "one of the most significant – possibly *the* most significant – of modern treatises on money" (Young 1924, p. 349, italics in original). He utilized the book extensively in his teaching at Harvard and was also instrumental in arranging Hawtrey's only academic appointment, as a visitor at Harvard in 1928–29.[16]

Young was also the author of a monograph, essentially a sophisticated exercise in descriptive statistics, entitled *An Analysis of Bank Statistics for the United States* (1928), which was first published as a series of four articles in the *Review of Economic Statistics*. Although those articles used data for national banks only, and only the last of them dealt with post-1914 data (1915–26 to be precise), they nevertheless documented those pronounced seasonal movements of currency out of New York in the autumn that, when combined with the propensity of New York banks to hold call loans to financial markets as secondary reserves, did much to contribute to the fragility of the National Banking System; and they also documented New York's central place in what (perhaps with the exception of California) had become an integrated nationwide monetary system even before 1914. Significantly in the current context, Young remarked, with respect to the movements of funds

---

[16] Thus, though Young recommended *Good and Bad Trade* (Hawtrey 1913) to readers of Ely's *Outlines of Economics* (1923), whose chapter dealing with the business cycle he prepared, he also recommended Lavington (1922), among other works. His views on counter-cyclical policy were also more eclectic than Hawtrey's, as discussed later in this chapter. The influence of Hawtrey's views on Young, and on Lauchlin Currie too, and the relationship of their analysis to what is often called "the Chicago tradition" in monetary economics have been explored elsewhere (Laidler 1993).

into New York banks from the hinterland, and thence through financial markets and out to the hinterland again, and the fluctuations in reserve-and-currency/deposit ratios that accompanied them, that ''I have little doubt but that relations such as we are now considering lie at the very heart of the problem of the instability of the modern mechanism of bank credit and of those business activities which depend upon credit'' (Young 1928, p. 28), and to that remark he appended a footnote: ''I know of no better analysis of the essential instability of the volume of bank credit than is to be found in R. G. Hawtrey's work, *Currency and Credit*'' (Young 1928, p. 28, fn. 1).

Hawtrey quite evidently exercised considerable influence on the middle ground of American monetary economics in the 1920s, as such diverse commentators as Schumpeter (1954), Deutscher (1990), and Mehrling (1996) have pointed out; but, as Mehrling has particularly stressed, there was a good deal more to that middle ground than simple adaptation of Hawtrey's ideas to local conditions. Young was, as has been noted, no adherent of a purely monetary theory of the cycle, and he was also, and quite unlike Hawtrey, a supporter of using public-works expenditures for stabilization purposes. His views on those matters reflected the fact that, as Mehrling has also noted, his work derived from the American institutionalist tradition.[17] The business-cycle theory which that tradition generated in the 1920s found its most influential exponent in Wesley C. Mitchell, but Alvin Hansen, who was later to become America's leading exponent of Keynes's *General Theory*, also made an important contribution to that body of literature in the 1920s.

Mitchell and Hansen on the Cycle

It was no accident that Fisher's scepticism, discussed earlier, about the existence of a systematic phenomenon that could be referred to as *the business cycle* should have attracted the attention of Mitchell. That scepticism, as Fisher expressed it in 1925, was in large measure directed at Mitchell's own research agenda, which had already received a comprehensive statement in his 1913 monograph *Business Cycles*, written in California just prior to his move to Columbia University in New York, where, in 1920, he would assume the directorship of the National Bureau of Economic Research (NBER).

---

[17] The American institutionalist tradition was not entirely home-grown, having been influenced by the German Historical School. However, by the 1920s its influence was being re-exported to Europe, not least to Germany, under the auspices of the Rockefeller Foundation. On that matter, see Earlene Craver (1986). The Oxford Institute of Statistics was also a Rockefeller Foundation enterprise. The objective was to encourage systematic empirical work on European economies.

Mitchell's Systematic Empiricism

Mitchell's work on business cycles is nowadays usually thought of as primarily descriptive – "measurement without theory," to borrow a famous phrase from Tjalling Koopmans (1947), a later critic of the NBER approach which Mitchell pioneered – but that is unfair, as Mary Morgan (1990, pp. 44–48) and Mark Perlman (1996, ch. 4, p. 84, fn. 2) have argued. Mitchell was certainly an empiricist, but he was well aware, as Backhouse (1995, ch. 7, pp. 106ff.) has also pointed out, that one needed theory in order to select and organize the facts to be studied. That was why his 1927 NBER book on the topic, *Business Cycles: The Problem and Its Setting*, began with a lengthy (over 40 pages) survey of then-current theoretical explanations for the cycle, which he motivated in the following terms:

> It is not advisable to attack the statistical data until we have made this survey of theories. For while the statistics will come to seem scanty as our demands develop, they are sufficiently abundant and diverse, susceptible of enough transformations and combinations, to make hopeless a purely empirical investigation. At every turn, we shall need working hypotheses to guide our selection of data, and to suggest ways of analyzing and combining them. Our survey of theories will provide us with the most promising hypotheses which have been invented. Not until we are thus equipped can we begin constructive work upon the problem of business cycles, confident that we are not overlooking elements already proved to be important. (Mitchell 1927, p. 3)

What Mitchell found uncongenial, that is to say, was not theory, but rather monocausal theorizing about the cycle, uninformed by careful empirical investigation of the phenomenon. Thus, though it would be possible to "take up the theories one by one, make a critical examination of the evidence offered in support of each, at need devise new tests, and treat conclusions regarding the validity of each theory as our main objective" (Mitchell 1927, p. 58). Mitchell preferred instead to study, one by one, the successive phases of the cycle (revival, prosperity, crisis, depression, revival, etc., to use his 1923 vocabulary), making "conclusions regarding the fluctuations our main objective, treating verdicts upon the theories as by-products to be turned out when convenient" (Mitchell 1927, p. 58).

Mitchell's method thus required that close attention be given to empirical evidence, and he paid a great deal of attention to the individual features of specific cycles. Nevertheless, and unlike Fisher, Mitchell regarded each one as an example of a general phenomenon. As he put it in 1923, "instead of a 'normal' state of business interrupted by occasional crises, men look for a continually changing state of business – continually changing in a *fairly regular* way'' (Mitchell 1923, p. 6, italics added).[18] Furthermore, though he was eclectic, Mitchell was anything but agnostic when it came to theory. The very fact that he regarded the cycle as a recurring phenomenon whose analysis could ''start with any phase . . . we choose'' (Mitchell 1923, p. 7) set him apart from those theorists who saw some essentially exogenous shock, perhaps one which, once discovered, could be removed, as the source of fluctuations: Fisher, with his ''dance of the dollar,'' provided a clear example of that alternative approach.

Money and the Accelerator

Mitchell had an extremely clear idea of where the vital link in the mechanism which kept the cycle in motion was to be found:

> To keep from getting lost in a maze of complications, it is necessary to follow constantly the chief clue to business transactions. Every business establishment is supposed to aim primarily at making money. When the prospects of profits improve, business becomes more active. When these prospects grow darker, business becomes dull. (Mitchell 1923, p. 6)

He returned to the same theme, which had also figured prominently in Thorstein Veblen's pre-war writings on the cycle (e.g., 1904), in 1927 (e.g., pp. 105–107).[19] There he made it clear that the emphasis on profits also implied

> that an account of economic fluctuations in a business economy must deal primarily . . . with the pecuniary aspect of economic activity. This conclusion runs counter to one of the traditions of economic theory. . . . The classical masters and the masters of utility analysis thought that they were delving deeper into the secrets of behaviour when, with scarcely a glance at the ''money surface of things,'' they took up the labor and commodities, or the sacrifices and utilities, which they held to be the controlling factors. When followed in the present field of study, this practice diverts attention from the way in which business cycles come about, and concentrates attention upon alleged non-business causes of fluctuation. (Mitchell 1927, pp. 106–107)[20]

---

[18] On this point, but only on this point, I am inclined to differ with Morgan (1990, pp. 44–48). I think that Mitchell saw a little more uniformity among individual cycles than she is willing to concede.

[19] Mitchell did, of course, receive his graduate education at the University of Chicago, where, however, he was primarily a student of J. Laurence Laughlin, rather than Veblen. Nevertheless, it is worth noting that, unlike, say, Henry Parker Willis, he had moved away from Laughlin's anti-quantity-theory position by the 1920s. Veblen's influence on Mitchell was more durable.

[20] The non-business causes to which Mitchell referred – ''changes in crops, and in methods of manufacturing, storing, shipping and distributing goods – as well as . . . changes in politics, fashion, education, recreation and health'' (Mitchell 1927, p. 107) did have a role to play in

For Mitchell, then, the monetary element was critically important to any satisfactory account of the cycle, but it was far from being all-important as it was in Fisher's (or indeed Hawtrey's) analysis. One matter which attracted particular attention from him, for example, was the accelerator mechanism, particularly in his 1923 essay, where it was the main topic of a complete section entitled "How Prosperity Breeds a Crisis" (Mitchell 1923, pp. 10–15).[21] Mitchell illustrated the operation of that relationship with an explicit numerical example showing how

> during depression and early revival the equipment-building trades get little business except what is provided by the replacement demand. When the demand for products has reached the stage where it promises soon to exceed the capacity of existing facilities, however, the equipment trades experience a sudden and intense boom. But their business falls off again before prosperity has reached its maximum, provided the *increase* in the physical quantity of products slackens before it stops. Hence the seeming anomalies pointed out by J. Maurice Clark [1917]:
>
> "The demand for equipment may decrease . . . even though the demand for the finished product is still growing. The total demand for [equipment] tends to vary more sharply than the demand for finished products. . . . The maximum and minimum points in the demand for [equipment] tend to precede the maximum and minimum points in the demand for finished products, the effect being that the change may appear to precede its own cause." (Mitchell 1923, p. 13, italics, and all deletions and additions, in original)

Mitchell nevertheless regarded the accelerator mechanism as only one factor at work during the cycle's upswing and at its upper turning-point. The same 1923 essay from which the foregoing quotation is taken gives overall pride of place to the role of the monetary system. Mitchell emphasized the influence of monetary expansion on the profitability of business during the upswing, and its subsequent tightening at the upper turning-point, and he noted that as far as capital-goods industries were concerned, that general tendency "intensifies the check which [they have] already begun to suffer from an earlier-acting cause" (Mitchell 1923, p. 12), namely, the accelerator.

All in all, Mitchell's view of business cycles defies any simple summary. This is hardly surprising, given that his overall research agenda was empirical, and given the importance he attached to guarding "against the besetting sin of theorists in this field – neglecting phenomena which do not fit neatly into preconceived schemes" (Mitchell 1927, pp. 48–49). And yet an empha-

---

driving the cycle, in his view, but only to the extent that they "affect[ed] the prospects of making money" (Mitchell 1927, p. 107).

[21] Mitchell based his account of the accelerator on the work of J. M. Clark (1917). He did not refer to such European contributors as Aftalion (1913), Bickerdike (1914), and Mummery and Hobson (1889).

sis on profit-seeking behaviour, within an economic system in which money was a good deal more than a veil, was a central theme of his eclecticism.

Alvin Hansen in the 1920s

The aforementioned stress on money, as we shall now see, was not unique to Mitchell's work. It also occupied a prominent place in Alvin Hansen's exposition (1927) of business-cycle theory, where it was, as in Mitchell's work, supplemented by careful consideration of the accelerator mechanism, in the analysis of which Hansen stressed the purely technical links, between the rate of flow of current production and the stocks of capital goods required to sustain it, that underlay the relationship in question:[22]

> But we must not blame the thermometer – price and profits – too much. Even though these were abolished by a socialistic or communistic order, there would still remain the difficulty of adjusting the capitalistic, or round-about, process of production to social wants. . . . It is the *need* itself which misleads and deludes the producers. It is doubtful if leaders in any régime would be able to make a more satisfactory adjustment than entrepreneurs make in the individualistic order.
>
> Now an increase in the demand for consumer's goods gives rise to far greater fluctuations in the demand for fixed capital. (Hansen 1927, p. 111, italics in original)

The accelerator, however, was not the only factor driving the cycle. It supplemented the workings of the monetary system in Hansen's 1927 analysis, very much as it did in Mitchell's. The basic principle at work as far as the monetary element in the cycle was concerned

> may be stated as follows: If for any reason the prospective profit rate deviates from the rate of interest charged in the loan market, the discrepancy between them tends to develop into an expansion or contraction of business, depending upon whether the profit rate is above or below the loan rate. (Hansen 1927, p. 191)

---

[22] That similarity between Hansen's approach and that of Mitchell was surely due to the fact that Hansen was very much a product of that same American institutionalist tradition in cycle theory whose leading exponent was Mitchell. It is worth noting, nevertheless, that in a 1921 monograph, Hansen had come down firmly on the side of a purely monetary explanation of the cycle, similar in broad outline to that of Hawtrey, though apparently at that time he was unaware of Hawtrey's work. He had, to be sure, considered the accelerator as a central feature of the cycle in that study, but had rejected its significance after considering evidence on the cyclical behaviour not of *volumes* of consumption and investment but of the *prices* of investment and consumption goods. The fact that the rate of change of the latter did not systematically lead the level of the former had seemed to him inconsistent with the accelerator's operation. Mehrling (1995) has provided a perceptive overview of Hansen's contributions to macroeconomics, stressing the extent to which his emphasis on the accelerator in the 1920s derived from the influence of such continental European writers as Aftalion.

That mechanism, supplemented by the effects of a lag in production costs behind prices, and the accelerator, served to ensure that the consequences of exogenous shocks to the system stemming from "changes in the arts, changes in consumers' demand, and changes in the bounties of nature" (Hansen 1927, p. 192) would initially be cumulative, but eventually cyclical, in nature, as what he termed "limiting or restraining forces" (e.g., Hansen 1927, p. 194) came into play. Among the latter were a variety of resource constraints on the level of economic activity, a tendency for the rate of growth of consumption to slow down, inducing a fall in investment, as well as the tendency of interest rates to catch up with profits as the upswing progressed.

It is worth noting that in 1927, Hansen explicitly denied that the cycle was inherently self-generating and self-perpetuating. One reason was that "were there no new disturbing factors business men would gradually learn to adjust themselves to the situation in such a manner that, bit by bit, the oscillations would tone down" (Hansen 1927, p. 198). He agreed, referring explicitly to technical accelerator and monetary mechanisms, that such learning processes would be slow and unreliable:

> In an individualistic, competitive economy there is good ground for believing, with Aftalion and Hawtrey, that society cannot adjust itself to the time lags inherent in our capitalistic and money economy, and so the oscillations, once started, tend to perpetuate themselves. (Hansen 1927, p. 200)

But, ultimately, he argued, they would die away in the absence of new shocks:

> If we pull a twig and let it snap back, we set up a swaying movement back and forth; but the twig, once deflected and then left to itself, soon stops swaying. Friction brings it to rest. So in business: we must assume that the effect of any initial disturbance would soon wear off after a very few oscillations of rapidly diminishing amplitude. (Hansen 1927, pp. 202–203)

Stabilization Policies

Because he believed that the cycle was inherently damped, Hansen also believed that new exogenous shocks were needed to keep it going, and that made him optimistic about the future prospects for economic stability. New resource discoveries and technical innovations were, he thought, unlikely to be as significant in the future as they had been in the past; agricultural output was less susceptible to weather conditions than it had been; and once "the whole world is brought into the industrial system, when economic imperialism has run its course" (Hansen 1927, p. 205), wars would be less likely too. Moreover, and perhaps crucially, business men are gradually accumulating experiences which help them to meet and evade the disturbing factors inherent in the modern system of production. The organization of industry, says Spiethoff, will more and more fit itself to the requirements of the capitalistic manner of industry. The modern means of gaining information, the growing publicity with respect to new opportunities, make for better insight into and control over economic conditions. . . . Social control, trade associations, and Kartells [sic], and the control exercised by centralized banking systems are illustrations of an increasing social adjustment to the capitalistic method of production and the money economy. Laissez-faire is gradually being displaced more and more by purposeful and scientific control, not only with respect to discount policies but also with respect to trade competition and intertrade relations. Voluntary associations, even more than governmental regulations, are working in the direction of greater business stability. (Hansen 1927, p. 205)

Though the specifically cited inspiration for the foregoing passage of Hansen's was the German economist Arthur Spiethoff, there was nothing about its tone to place it outside the mainstream of the American business-cycle literature of the 1920s.[23] A similarly pragmatic tone, based on guarded optimism about the likely fruits of increasing knowledge, was the hallmark of the economics of the "new era," discussed by Barber (1985), that developed in the United States in the wake of World War I. Such a tone permeated the volume by Mitchell et al. (1923) and was clearly present in *Business Cycles* (Mitchell 1927). It was also explicitly expressed in the Foreword to the volume by Mitchell et al. (1923), written by Herbert Hoover, then secretary of commerce, who was very much a political patron of such views.[24] Hoover pointed out that in addition to making "constructive suggestions" about the use of public-works expenditures to stabilize employment over the cycle, the contributors to that volume had concluded that

---

[23] Spiethoff had been heavily influenced by the German Historical School, and his 1933 entry in the *Encyclopaedia of the Social Sciences* on "Overproduction" shows him to have been an exponent of a rather eclectic and empirically oriented analysis of the cycle, similar in spirit to that of Mitchell. It is not, therefore, surprising to find a sympathetic citation of his views in Hansen's work. See Ingo Barens (1987) for a brief account of his work.

[24] It should be noted that the views of Hoover and the economists associated with him were by no means radical by the standards prevailing in the United States at that time. For example, Rexford Tugwell, then at Columbia University, was an altogether more enthusiastic exponent of economic planning, and according to Barber (1985, pp. 44–46) he found the Hooverites "insufficiently bold." Tugwell would hold a number of important appointments in the Roosevelt administration, including under-secretary of agriculture. His 1925 textbook *American Economic Life*, written jointly with T. Munro and R. E. Stryker, and his 1933 monograph *The Industrial Discipline and the Governmental Arts*, among other works, made a case for comprehensive involvement of government in economic life. It is worth noting that Tugwell's advocacy of economic planning owed little directly to contemporary European economic thought, but a great deal to the Veblenite tradition within American institutionalism. On that tradition, see Malcolm Rutherford (1994, pp. 146–148).

> the strategic point of attack [on the cycle] is ... mainly through the provision for such current economic information as will show the signs of danger, and its more general understanding and use by producers, distributors, and banks, including more constructive and safer policies. (Hoover 1923, p. vi)

Allyn Young, who, as we have seen, occupied an important place in the middle ground of American debates about the stabilizing capacity of monetary policy in the 1920s, shared that pragmatic confidence about the cycle. It was he who prepared the chapter on "Business Cycles" for the 1923 edition of Richard T. Ely's widely used textbook *Outlines of Economics*; that chapter, in addition to endorsing public-works policies and judicious use of monetary policies, particularly at cyclical extremes, also suggested that

> methods of *forecasting* the probable movement of business conditions have already become important and promise to acquire yet greater importance ... With the further perfecting and increasing use of such methods, the major oscillations of the business cycle are likely to be anticipated and discounted. Paradoxically, anticipating such fluctuations will tend to diminish them.
>
> Individual firms and, in some measure, trade associations in different industries, are giving increased attention to the scientific analysis of the particular conditions that particularly affect their own industries. The federal government, also, has made praiseworthy beginning in the work of collecting, publishing, and supplying to bankers and business men some of the fundamental current economic facts upon which intelligent business planning must be based. (Ely 1923, p. 336)

Though none of those authors, Hansen included, looked forward to immediate elimination of the cycle, the overall tone of their contributions to the American literature of the 1920s was one of optimism about the prospects for significantly mitigating it. Improved public policies, increasing knowledge, and, based upon that knowledge, modified private-sector behaviour, too, seemed likely to make things better in the future than they had been in the past.

Underconsumptionism in America

Not every American economist writing in the 1920s was optimistic about the future prospects for smooth functioning of the economy. Just as in England at that time J. A. Hobson (e.g., 1923) was keeping alive the so-called underconsumptionist critique of orthodox economic analysis, so in America too did that theme find articulate exponents in William Trufant Foster and Waddill Catchings. Their particular version of underconsumptionism differed from Hobson's, inasmuch as they stressed the workings of the monetary system, rather than the mechanisms driving the distribution of income, as the source of the basic flaw in the operations of the market economy, but their analysis was nevertheless clearly in the same tradition as his. Indeed, in his critique of underconsumptionist doctrine, Durbin (1933, pp. 20–38) treated Foster and Catchings and Hobson as expounding essentially a single "central thesis."

Foster and Catchings were neither academics nor bankers, but published their work under the auspices of the privately sponsored Pollak Foundation for Economic Research. The seriousness of purpose that marked that foundation's work, however, can be gauged from the fact that its first publication was no less a work than Irving Fisher's *The Making of Index Numbers* (1922); and, as Meir Kohn (1987) has recorded, a wide academic readership for Foster and Catchings's own work was further guaranteed by the foundation's offer, in 1926, of a prize of $5,000 for the best essay criticizing their ideas, which were developed at considerable length in their books *Money* (1923), *Profits* (1925), and *The Road to Plenty* (1928), as well as a 1927 collection of more popular essays, *Business Without a Buyer*.

The Monetary System and Underconsumption

The central theme to which Foster and Catchings returned again and again was that

> our modern economic life is founded on money. Our whole industrial order is based on production of goods for sale at a money profit. The economic value of virtually everything, except consumers' goods already in the hands of consumers, is based on the expectation that it can be sold for money, or will have a part in producing something that can be sold for money. (Foster and Catchings 1923, p. 5)

The trouble was, they thought, that there existed a flaw in the mechanism of monetary exchange which, in the absence of appropriate policy, made it impossible for those expectations systematically to be realized in an economy that simultaneously realized its full productive potential. The incomes of consumers, on which the demand for goods depended, originated in the incomes paid out to them in their capacity as producers of those same goods. But because firms would retain some of their earnings, and because households would devote part of their income to saving, consumption expenditure was bound to fall short of the amount necessary to purchase current output at a price sufficient to yield a profit to producers.[25] Therefore,

---

[25] Thus there was some resemblance between Foster and Catchings's underconsumptionism and the analysis of Keynes (1923) discussed earlier in footnote 5. Unlike them, however, Keynes did not single out consumption-goods industries for special attention. It is nevertheless all too easy to confuse, as did Tavlas (1976, 1977, 1982) and Tavlas and Aschheim (1981), their analysis with treatments based upon the quantity theory. Klein (1949) correctly noted a close relationship between the Foster and Catchings work and certain basic ideas of Keynes's *General Theory*.

periodic business depressions, with the inevitable accompaniment of unemployment, reduced production, and lower standards of living, are caused fundamentally by the failure of consumers' income to keep pace with output. (Foster and Catchings 1925, p. 350)

The theoretical basis of that message was worked out in *Money*, with the aid of an early version of a diagram of the circular flow of income and expenditure, and it was further developed in terms of numerous special-case examples, illustrated with copious statistics, in *Profits*.[26] The details of those examples need not concern us, for they added nothing to Foster and Catchings's central message that thrift was potentially destructive, that, in their colourful phrase, "a penny saved is sometimes a penny lost" (Foster and Catchings 1925, p. 400); nor were they necessary for an understanding of the broad policy implications of their theory, which were developed at greatest length in *The Road to Plenty*, namely, that the key to high employment lay in maintaining an adequate level of consumer expenditure. There was, of course, nothing particularly new or original in that broad message: As Alvin Hansen (1927) pointed out, it followed the theoretical tradition, as discussed in Chapter 7, dating back to Malthus, Lauderdale, and Sismondi, to which Hobson in England and Veblen in the United States had more recently contributed.[27]

Public Works and Money Creation

Unlike the vast majority of their contemporaries, both American and British, Foster and Catchings saw little help to be had from public-works programs, if those involved merely changing the timing of an otherwise given outlay in order to give it a counter-cyclical bias, or if they were either debt-or tax-financed:

---

[26] Don Patinkin (1981, ch. 2, pp. 61–63) has discussed that diagram and suggested that it may have derived, indirectly by way of the work of M. C. Rorty, from a similar diagram deployed by Nicholas Johannsen (1908), whose role as a pioneer of the multiplier notion was briefly discussed in Chapter 7 (footnote 20). Foster and Catchings, however, did not refer to Johannsen.

[27] *Business-Cycle Theory* (Hansen 1927) was initially written as an entry to the Pollak Foundation competition for the best critique of Foster and Catchings's ideas, which was why those ideas occupied such a prominent place in its pages. It should be pointed out that, unlike Veblen in particular, Foster and Catchings did not see their work as forming part of a comprehensive dissenting critique of the nature of modern capitalism. Their dismissal of Veblen's attack on conspicuous consumption made that abundantly clear: "So when Thorstein Veblen lashes, with all the thongs of his far-flung vocabulary, the conspicuous waste of the leisure class . . . we should bear in mind, however tempted we may be to join in the flaying, that every consumer is the sole judge of what he really wants" (Foster and Catchings 1925, pp. 201–202). Consumption of any kind was, in their view, desirable so long as it was sustained at an adequate aggregate level.

> Merely adjusting Government expenditures to business fluctuations . . . , although it tends toward stability, does not permanently increase consumer purchasing power. Since it merely distributes a given outlay more evenly over a series of years, it does not in the long run offset deficiencies in demand. (Foster and Catchings 1925, p. 340)

Moreover, "Government loans, as well as taxes, in so far as they cause no changes in the volume of money in circulation, can neither offset a deficiency in consumer demand nor create one" (Foster and Catchings 1925, p. 338). That sounds very much like Hawtrey, but it is important to recall that for the latter, *any* change in the quantity of money, or its velocity of circulation, would, given a modicum of price stickiness, affect income and employment. Not so for Foster and Catchings: For them, the point in the circular flow of money income and expenditure at which new money was injected was all-important:

> The chief economic need, therefore, is a flow of money to consumers sufficient to provide for the necessary growth in their savings, and yet enable them to buy and to continue to buy at an approximately stable price level, all the goods that are *actually* ready for final consumption. (Foster and Catchings 1925, p. 364, italics in original)

Bank lending to business would not inject new money in the right place, and indeed, in their 1923 and 1925 books Foster and Catchings remained remarkably, albeit self-consciously, vague about how that central policy issue might be solved in practice: "What is the way out? . . . most readers . . . will be disappointed, no doubt, because we do not offer a definite answer" (Foster and Catchings 1925, p. vi). But even at that early date they did give one tantalizing hint in the course of their discussion of deficit finance:

> When . . . the money wherewith to buy government securities is obtained by means of the expansion of bank credit, the result is an increase on the consumer side of the volume of money in circulation. This is what happened during the World War. In fact, the slogan of the Liberty Bond campaigns was "Borrow and Buy Bonds"; and the use of the bonds themselves, as security for bank loans wherewith to buy more bonds, caused an expansion of money which was first used to take goods off the markets. This would have helped to offset deficiencies in demand had there been any deficiencies; but since at that time demand was outrunning supply, the result was a rising price-level.
>
> It should be observed, incidentally, that it makes no difference to the annual equation how effectively the Government spends the money which it receives as loans and taxes. All we have said so far applies as well to money usefully employed by governments as to money wasted. . . . What we have said does not apply, however, to that exceedingly small proportion of Government expenditure which actually brings about an increase in the volume of goods which are sold to consumers. (Foster and Catchings 1925, pp. 338–339)

In short, the important thing was to increase the quantity of money flowing through the hands of consumers without increasing the quantity of consumer goods being offered for sale. In *The Road to Plenty* (1928) they developed a well-articulated case for using public-works expenditures as a means to that end and proposed (1928, sect. XV) that a new federal agency, analogous to the Federal Reserve Board, be set up to gather "the data best adapted to show the adequacy of the flow of consumer income" (Foster and Catchings, 1928, p. 192) and then to administer an ongoing program of public-works expenditures designed to maintain its adequacy.

That analysis by Foster and Catchings attracted an important supporter in the 1920s, one who was to continue to propagate a version of it well into the 1930s, namely, Paul Douglas of the University of Chicago. Indeed, it was he, rather than Foster and Catchings, who first published a reasonably fully developed account of its implications for public-works policies in 1927. Pointing out that J. B. Say had long ago argued that "since ultimately goods are exchanged for goods, . . . to increase production is merely to give producers more commodities with which they may barter" (Douglas 1927, pp. 36–37), and that "this reasoning [ever since] has been accepted in the main by economists of the orthodox tradition," Douglas went on to credit Foster and Catchings with detecting "an extraordinary error of logic" in that position in their "brilliant and suggestive writings" (Douglas 1927, p. 37). He then proceeded to elaborate on the policy measures which might ensure that "monetary purchasing power [would] be augmented sufficiently to prevent prices from falling," the key factor in avoiding contractions in Foster and Catchings's view (and in his own view), and he concluded that

> perhaps the best way would be for the government to expend purchasing power for the construction of public works which would thus give purchasing power to the workers and stabilize the price level. Since the services of these public works would later largely be offered gratuitously to the public, they would not enter into the volume of commodities offered for sale and hence would not cause a fall in the price level. (Douglas 1927, p. 41)

Douglas considered a variety of ways for financing such expenditure, including government borrowing from the banks, but

> if proper safeguards could be provided to prevent inflation instead of such borrowing, I would personally favor an issue of paper money on the part of the government to pay for the materials and the labor utilized. In this way society could get needed public works constructed without any added cost to itself. Labor which would otherwise be largely unemployed would be used instead to construct needed roads, buildings, playgrounds, etc.
>   . . . the issue should be so limited as: (1) to prevent the index of unemployment . . . from rising above, let us say five per cent; (2) to prevent the general price level from rising by more than two or three per cent; (3) to prevent the foreign exchanges from being dislocated. (Douglas 1927, p. 42)

Such proposals were to become popular, not to say immediately relevant, in the 1930s; but in the 1920s, even though Foster and Catchings received considerable attention from commentators other than Douglas, including Mitchell (1927) and Hansen (1927), the type of unequivocal support which he gave to their position was somewhat unusual.[28] Contributors to the academic mainstream of American business-cycle analysis shared Foster and Catchings's conviction that the institutional fact of monetary exchange was central to the nature of economic fluctuations, but they were also eclectic when it came to the details of the mechanisms at work in both generating and perpetuating them. The monocausal nature of the Foster and Catchings analysis was too much for them to swallow. Hansen (1927) was perhaps representative in characterizing Foster and Catchings's analysis of "the conditions necessary for economic equilibrium [as] satisfactory as far as it goes, but . . . too simple for an adequate analysis of the complex forces at work in the business cycle" (Hansen 1927, p. 57).

Concluding Comment

It was remarked at the outset of this chapter that in the 1920s there existed a vigorous, diverse, and distinctly American literature dealing with monetary economics and the business cycle. That has surely now been amply demonstrated. By the 1940s, however, so-called Keynesian macroeconomics was well on its way to becoming dominant in the United States. In the usual story, that doctrine was an import from Britain, welcomed with open arms by a younger generation of American economists desperate to understand the Great Depression, an event which inherited wisdom was utterly unable to explain, and for which it was equally unable to prescribe a cure. It should already be clear from this chapter that there was something radically wrong with that usual story.

Already in the 1920s, as Barber (1985) has extensively documented, some strands in the American literature, and particularly those dealing with the cycle, were displaying certain features which later came to be called (obviously inaccurately) "Keynesian": on the theoretical side, the insistence that any useful analysis of the workings of the economy as a whole should put

---

[28] George Tavlas (1977) has argued that Douglas was an important pioneer of the Chicago tradition out of which Milton Friedman's work in due course developed. I find that argument unconvincing in light of Douglas's underconsumptionism, which, after going into abeyance during his collaboration with Aaron Director (Douglas and Director 1931), re-emerged as a prominent feature of his work in the 1930s (e.g., Douglas 1933, 1935). Tavlas presumably treated Douglas in that way because he also classified Foster and Catchings as quantity theorists. See, e.g., Tavlas (1976, 1997). That latter classification seems quite indefensible in light of the textual evidence. Douglas's work of the 1930s will be discussed in Chapter 9.

the monetary system at the centre of things, and the amount of attention paid to the accelerator relationship; on the policy side, a proclivity to pragmatic activism of various sorts, not to mention widespread faith in the stabilizing powers of counter-cyclical public-works expenditures. But American economics in the 1920s was also rather optimistic about the economic future, in a way that, with benefit of hindsight, seems to have been extraordinarily naive. How the onset of the depression affected its development over the next few years and enabled what have been termed its "Keynesian" features to develop further are among the topics to be addressed in the following chapter.

CHAPTER 9

American Macroeconomics in the Early 1930s

The Great Contraction

The stock-market crash of October 1929 was not the cause of the Great Contraction. It was not even the contraction's first event, for output had in fact begun to turn down in the summer of that year. The crash did, however, give a very public signal that things were about to go badly wrong with the American economy. The story of subsequent events is well known and needs no detailed retelling here. Between 1929 and 1933, when United States adherence to the gold standard was suspended, money income fell by 53 per cent, real income fell by 36 per cent, unemployment rose to 25 per cent of the labour force, and a series of bank failures culminating in the "bank holiday" of March 1933 made a major contribution to a 33 per cent fall in the money supply.[1]

In a little over three years, that is to say, the prosperity of the 1920s had vanished and deep depression had become the central policy problem confronting the United States. The severity of the contraction was all too evident long before it had run its course, and the focus of American economics had already begun to shift dramatically by 1931. Although the influence of European thought, both Austrian and in the Cambridge tradition, became somewhat stronger in the early 1930s than it had been earlier, it is important not to exaggerate that factor. The change in American macroeconomics that came with the Great Contraction was mainly driven by new and pressing problems, rather than by newly imported analytic tools.[2]

Pessimism in the Wake of the Contraction

At the end of Chapter 8, attention was drawn to the optimism that marked a good deal of American writing on economics in the 1920s, but it was also noted that such optimism and the belief in policy activism that underpinned it were not universally shared. In particular, such commentators as Anderson

---

[1] These data come from Friedman and Schwartz (1963, pp. 301–302). The money-stock data refer to their preferred M2 aggregate.
[2] The reaction of American economists to the contraction has been discussed by Barber (1985, chs. 4–9).

and Willis had, throughout the 1920s, expressed grave doubts about the appropriateness of using monetary policy as an active tool of stabilization policy. For them, the banking system was fulfilling its role so long as it met the "needs of trade," something that it would accomplish more or less automatically, provided that commercial-bank lending was confined to short-term loans secured on good-quality commercial paper. Nothing that happened after 1929 changed their views on those matters. Their scepticism about the stabilizing powers of monetary policy, and their pessimism about the prospects for using it to mitigate the depression, moreover, came to be shared by some economists who had held more optimistic views in the previous decade, as we shall see.

The "Banking School" Reaction

According to Willis, writing in 1933 with John M. Chapman and Ralph M. Robey, the growth of bank credit in the United States after 1924 had been "out of proportion . . . to any corresponding need for media of exchange that was showing itself in connection with the volume of exchanges of goods" (Willis, Chapman, and Robey 1933, p. 740). Instead, "much of the new volume of credit was being used to purchase investments and long-term paper and was apparently getting into a 'frozen' condition" (Willis, Chapman, and Robey 1933, p. 740), and those tendencies had been contrary to the principles of "sound banking," namely "that type of management which results in adjusting bank assets closely to liabilities according to maturity" (Willis, Chapman, and Robey 1933, p. 752). The growth of credit had taken place against a background of stable, rather than rising, prices, but it had nevertheless had two adverse consequences. First, there had been created "a progressively greater brittleness on the part of the banking and credit system of the United States" (Willis, Chapman, and Robey 1933, p. 740), and that had set the stage for the massive bank failures of the early 1930s. Second, in the industries which had been recipients of bank credit, "overproduction" had occurred, a phenomenon which was "the result of undue concentration of capital and productive power in [those] industries" (Willis, Chapman, and Robey 1933, p. 754). As Willis and his co-authors put it,

> there can . . . be no doubt that the free credit enjoyed by such industries, prior to the collapse of 1929, tended to promote unemployment and to intensify the suffering caused by it after the breakdown had occurred. (Willis, Chapman, and Robey 1933, p. 749)[3]

---

[3] Of course, such doubts were not confined to Willis and his associates nor even to the United States. We saw in Chapter 4, "Forced Saving Again," that Dennis Robertson was expressing such concerns before the event in 1928, as were the Austrians (Chapter 2, "Hayek's Accelerationism").

On that analysis, then, though more prudent behaviour on the part of the banking system before 1929 might have prevented the contraction before the event,

> where no . . . check is applied by banks to the advancement of credit, surpluses of goods become unmanageable and unemployment is the result. When this condition is fully developed there is little that banks can do to check it. They must await the general development of consumption and the gradual readjustment of different elements in supply of goods. (Willis, Chapman, and Robey 1933, p. 754)

Indeed, Willis and his collaborators expressed considerable scepticism about the likely effectiveness of efforts to stimulate the American economy by the application of "the pre-panic or 'new era' philosophy of banking [involving] '[e]asy money,' large doses of artificial bank credit and effort to avoid writing off losses" (Willis, Chapman, and Robey 1933, p. 754).[4] In taking that position, as in much else, they were completely in accord with Benjamin Anderson, who in September 1930 had argued that "it is definitely undesirable that we should employ this costly [cheap money] method of buying temporary prosperity again. The world's business is not a moribund invalid that needs galvanising by an artificial stimulant" (Anderson 1930, p. 19).

Willis, too, writing in early 1932, had argued against expansionary monetary policy along similar lines. It would "simply mean an aggravation of existing difficulties, due to the fact that we are already overburdened with construction work and fixed capital that are not likely soon to be employed" (Willis 1932, p. 105), and it might threaten the maintenance of gold convertibility into the bargain.

> The truth of the matter is that inflation [of credit] is never a remedy for anything, and that it is more harmful when allowed to hurt and weaken bank portfolios than at any other time or than when released in any other way. (Willis 1932, p. 106)

Austrian Influences

Now all this has something of an "Austrian" tone to it, although the American heirs to the Banking School did not base their policy doctrines on any explicitly worked out microeconomic theory of the inter-temporal allocation of resources as did Mises, Hayek, and their associates.[5] The differences here,

---

[4] Note the phrase "new era," which referred to the optimistic policy activism associated with, though not exclusive to, Herbert Hoover and his associates. See Barber (1985) for discussion of that usage.

[5] The relationship between the policy pessimism of Willis and Anderson and their associates and that of the Austrians was somewhat similar to that linking the pessimism of their British contemporary Sir Theodore Gregory to Austrian ideas, as discussed in Chapter 2. It is perhaps not entirely coincidental that Gregory (1928) was the author of a lengthy, albeit not uncritical,

as well as the similarities, will be readily apparent to anyone comparing Willis's 1932 paper to another delivered at the same Harris Foundation conference, namely, Gottfried von Haberler's "Money and the Business Cycle." Haberler, who was a visitor at Harvard in 1931–32, with due acknowledgement to Hayek, offered an "explanation of the slump" in terms of the capital theory set out by the latter in *Prices and Production* (Hayek 1931a). His typically Austrian exposition of the allocative problems posed by the roundabout nature of production had no close parallel in Willis's paper. His equally typically Austrian conclusions about the likely ineffectiveness, indeed counterproductiveness, of expansionary monetary policies were, however, essentially identical with those of Willis:

> . . . we must lose confidence in all the economic and monetary quacks who are going around these days preaching inflationary measures which would bring almost instant relief. If we accept the proposition that the productive apparatus is out of gear, that great shifts of labor and capital are necessary to restore equilibrium, then it is emphatically not true that the business cycle is a purely monetary phenomenon, as Mr. Hawtrey would have it; this is not true, although monetary forces have brought about the whole trouble. Such a dislocation of real physical capital, as distinguished from purely monetary changes, can in no case be cured in a very short time. (Haberler 1932, p. 70)

Although Austrian cycle theory was very much a minority taste among American economists, as indeed, albeit to a lesser extent, were the Banking School doctrines of Willis and Anderson, scepticism about the desirability, and even the feasibility, of countering the contraction with monetary measures was much more widespread. It was shared, for example, by Alvin Hansen, who in the early 1930s fell for a while under the influence of Joseph Schumpeter.[6] Hansen's 1932 monograph, *Economic Stabilization in an Unbalanced World*, placed the United States contraction in an international context and explained it in terms of the interaction of forces which produce long waves of advance and decline in economic activity of the type proposed by Nicolai Kondratieff, the decennial cycle as analysed by Clément Juglar,

---

commentary on the work of Thomas Tooke, the leading exponent of the Banking School ideas that underlay the work of Willis and Anderson. This matter would bear further investigation.

[6] The views of Schumpeter to which Hansen referred (in the quotations to follow) were exposed to an American audience at the 1930 American Economics Association meetings, in a session at which Hansen served as Schumpeter's discussant. See Schumpeter (1931). A longer and more accessible account of Schumpeter's analysis of those questions is available (Schumpeter 1935). Though he was Austrian by origin, Schumpeter's analysis of the depression differed from that of Hayek or Haberler, as we shall now see. However, in according no role to monetary contraction in bringing the depression about, and in his pessimism about, indeed opposition to, expansionary measures to hasten its end, he did have an important policy position in common with them. For a study of the views of Hayek and Schumpeter on the depression, see Klausinger (1995).

and the shorter (roughly 40-month) fluctuation documented by Warren Persons and Mitchell:

> Now the year 1930, as Professor Josef Schumpeter has pointed out, fell not only in the downswing of the long cycle (Kondratieff), but also formed part of the down grade of the major cycle (Juglar), and at the same time a part of it (probably the second half) fell in the trough of the minor forty-month cycle (Persons-Mitchell). The convergence of all three cycles upon the years 1930–31 accounts in part for the severity of this depression. (Hansen 1932, p. 95)

Underlying all of that was what seemed to Hansen to be a downward secular trend in the price level. Referring to work by Mitchell and Willard Thorp (specific citations were not given, but compare Mitchell 1927, pp. 407ff., and Thorp 1926), he expressed the belief that "in such periods depressions are long and severe." Hansen attributed the secular decline in world prices to the insufficiency of the world's gold stock to support prices at their post-war levels, not to mention the concentration of existing gold stocks in France and the United States.[7] Therefore, on the premise that the gold standard in some shape or form would remain in place, he concluded that

> we shall not succeed in solving the depression through the soothing and agreeable device of inflation. We shall come out of it only through hard work, and readjustments that are painful. There is no other alternative. And we shall have to face the probability of having to repeat the process in future, since, on balance, a downward trend in prices is likely.
>
> Inflation is not a sound remedy, since it carries within it the seeds of subsequent maladjustments. It is quite a different matter, however, to urge international banking coöperation [sic] looking toward the prevention of a further fall in prices. Unfortunately, one cannot help being skeptical that anything really effective will be done.
>
> Under the lash of dire necessity and greater efficiency, a higher standard of living can eventually be achieved. But this entails unemployment and suffering while the readjustment is going on. In the depression period society suffers the birth pangs of an improved production technique that paves the way for higher material standards. (Hansen 1932, p. 378)

Harvard Economists on The Economics of the Recovery Program

The echo of Schumpeter in the foregoing quotation from Hansen is clear, and indeed, in a contribution to the 1934 volume *The Economics of the Recovery*

---

[7] The problem of secular deflation would carry over into Hansen's later work on the stagnation thesis. Though influenced by Schumpeter in the early 1930s, he remained intellectually independent. Barber (1985, pp. 101–102) has discussed the influence of Schumpeter on Hansen at that time, while a major theme for Mehrling (1995) was the eclectic independent-mindedness that marked his work from beginning to end.

Program (Brown et al. 1934), put together by a group of economists drawn from Harvard University's Economics Department, Schumpeter himself argued, with respect to the contemporary American situation, that

> recovery is sound only if it does come of itself. For any revival which is merely due to artificial stimulus leaves part of the work of depressions undone and adds, to an undigested remnant of maladjustment, new maladjustment. . . . Particularly, our story provides a *presumption* against remedial measures which work through money and credit. (Schumpeter 1934, p. 20, italics in original)

The pessimism of Schumpeter, and Hansen too, about the powers of monetary policy to deal with the depression had at least the virtue of deriving from a coherent theoretical base, which is more than can be said for that displayed by two of Schumpeter's Harvard colleagues who also contributed essays on that issue to the same volume. Seymour Harris began his essay, entitled "Higher Prices," with the observation that

> in recent years, there has been a growing demand for monetary measures as the means of improving the economic situation. The explanation is simple: Non-interference leaves private enterprise with the responsibility of getting its house in order, and the process is painful. (Harris 1934, p. 90)

Forty-four pages later, he began his "Conclusions" by noting that three monetary-policy tools were available to induce higher prices: "Reserves may be increased by devaluating [*sic*], by issuing greenbacks or by undertaking large open market operations" (Harris 1934, p. 134). He then warned his readers that "all these methods . . . set the stage for excessive expansion in the future, which may very well bring a crisis and serious maladjustment later" (Harris 1934, pp. 134–135). The intervening discussion, which had dealt with public works as well as monetary policy per se, had been no more definite: Monetary measures of one sort or another might affect expenditure and prices, or they might not, depending upon their influence on costs and/or confidence; to the extent that increased government intervention in the economy increased government borrowing, "private business is made unprofitable and therefore investors desert private security markets, while at the same time the appeals for Government intervention become more frequent" (Harris 1934, p. 110); but still, "expenditures on public works are to be heartily approved unless they stimulate production of capital goods relative to consumption goods for which a new demand is now induced to such an extent as to cause unhealthy increases in the price of consumption goods" (Harris 1934, p. 116); and so on.

Edward Chamberlin, writing on "Purchasing Power," was, if anything, less coherent. Noting that "it is obvious that the available supply of money and bank credit has been used very slowly during the depression" (Chamberlin 1934, p. 25), he asked ''could not something be done to put this money into more rapid circulation?'' (Chamberlin 1934, p. 25), and then expressed doubts about the feasibility of doing so, in the following terms:

> To the extent that increased spending can be brought about it will either raise prices or expand business activity, or both. An expansion of business (or using up of accumulated stocks) proportional to the increased spending would obviously leave prices exactly where they were. In fact, a rise in prices is an index of the extent to which the revival of business has fallen short of the revival in spending. Dollars are buying less, and those whose money incomes have not changed have less real purchasing power than before. As for those newly employed, the rise in prices indicates that goods are not being produced for their consumption. They get a share of the available supply only because the consumption of others is diminished. (Chamberlin 1934, pp. 25–26)

It is not surprising that commentators such as those, who so clearly lacked a coherent analytic framework, should be bewildered by the depression and would share the scepticism of such as Willis, Haberler, Hansen, and Schumpeter about the powers of monetary measures to deal with it; but that scepticism also infected some of those who in the 1920s had been more confident about the stabilizing powers of monetary policy.[8]

Other Pessimists

The 1936 edition of W. R. Burgess's *The Reserve Banks and the Money Market*, first published in 1927, had been significantly revised. It took the position that monetary policy had been tried and found wanting as a significant tool for counter-cyclical policy, summarizing that conclusion as follows: ''During the depression, the Reserve System has exerted great pressure towards easy money and freely available credit, but . . . its efforts were relatively ineffective'' (Burgess 1936, p. 293). Charles Hardy, like Burgess, was no exponent of Banking School ideas, being more inclined to be ''in complete accord with the [Austrian] neutral money principle'' (Hardy 1932, p. 319), though he also thought that, in practice, variations in velocity made it very difficult to apply (Hardy 1932, pp. 319–325). He, too, found ''little in the experience of Federal Reserve control in the years from 1922 to 1931 to create optimism as to the possibility of stabilizing business through credit control'' (Hardy 1932, p. 89), and he concluded that

[8] The scepticism in question extended to fiscal policy too. As Barber (1985, pp. 132–138) has shown, the fiscal deficits produced by the contraction were far greater than exponents of counter-cyclical public-works policies had contemplated when discussing those matters in the 1920s, and those financing problems, along with the sheer speed with which events evolved, underlay much of the incoherence of the Hoover administration's response to the contraction. See Barber (1985, esp. pp. 132–138).

> the Reserve system's control of rediscount rates and its open market operations constitute a crude and circuitous technique for controlling the state of the money markets, and through them the pace of business activity. It would be unjustifiable to impute to the Reserve system primary responsibility either for the prosperity which the country enjoyed during the major portion of the period under review [1922–31] or for the disasters with which the decade closed. (Hardy 1932, p. 239)

Another student of Federal Reserve policy in the 1920s, Harold L. Reed (1930), attributed more influence to monetary factors in the 1920s than did Hardy. He was also critical of the idea that stock-market speculation in 1928–29 had deprived the rest of the economy of access to credit, an argument popular among adherents of Banking School views. Furthermore, he denied that the stock-market crash had a crucial causative role in bringing on the subsequent contraction:

> It is not difficult . . . to find evidence that the business depression was born largely of causes independent of the stock-market crash. In the first place, most indices of the physical volume of trade and production began their descent from the high point of 1929 several months before the crash. (Reed 1930, p. 195)

As we saw earlier, Reed was an advocate of steady money growth, so it is not surprising that he drew attention to the fact that "the rate of credit expansion in 1928 and 1929, if not nil, was at least unusually low" (Reed 1930, p. 174), thus raising the possibility that the onset of the Great Depression might have been monetary in origin. Despite all that, however, Reed ultimately became as sceptical as Hardy about the powers of monetary policy to counter the contraction once it had taken hold. In 1935, he put the point as follows:

> Under certain conditions, I believe that central banks can easily push more credit into effective use. . . . When reverse conditions obtain, as I believe they were after 1929, forcing policies may be devoid of efficacy. Is not the art of central banking that of keeping always in a position to make effective use of available powers? (Reed 1935, p. 616)

Mitchell in the Early 1930s

In the early 1930s, Wesley C. Mitchell's comments on the depression were, as Barber (1985, p. 100) has noted, "sparse and guarded." It was his view that the main problem was to explain not so much the occurrence but rather the severity of the downturn, and Mitchell thought that that could be accounted for, in Barber's words, by the "coincidence of a number of random shocks" (1985, p. 101). All in all, Mitchell seems to have been puzzled, at

least at first, by the events of the early 1930s, and on one occasion he even
flirted with Austrian ideas.[9]

We get the clearest view of Mitchell's overall position on the nature of the
depression, and what might be done about it, from his 1935 paper, "The
Social Sciences and National Planning." There he expressed not just his
long-held opinion that "the frequent recurrence of economic crises and depressions is evidence that the automatic functioning of our business system is
defective" (Mitchell 1935b, p. 91) but also the view that recent experience
showed that "the difficulty of maintaining the necessary equilibrium among
different factors in the enormously complicated mechanism is becoming
greater rather than less" (Mitchell 1935b, p. 91). Mitchell noted the increased
share in output of "semidurable goods which people can stop buying for a
time if times are bad" (Mitchell 1935b, p. 91), the increased urbanization of
the population, and the reduced self-sufficiency of the agricultural sector that
went with it, as well as an increasing reluctance of large firms to cut prices
in the face of falling demand, and an accompanying proclivity to cut back on
output and employment. All those factors, he thought, were operating simultaneously to make downturns more serious when they occurred and "recovery . . . a far slower and more halting process than it was when all prices were
flexible in much the same degree" (Mitchell 1935b, p. 92).

Thus, by 1935, the severity of the depression was no longer, for Mitchell,
merely the outcome of a series of unfortunate coincidences, nor even the
result of overexpansionary monetary policy in the 1920s and an over-built
capital stock, as the Austrians had it. Rather, it was a symptom of a more
general, and increasing, incapacity of an economy organized on laissez-faire
principles to function efficiently. That made him pessimistic about relying on
the economy's own inherent tendencies towards recovery to restore prosperity
quickly, but moderately hopeful about what could be achieved by greater
reliance on "national planning." Mitchell regarded "the movement toward
business combinations [as] largely a businessman's remedy for uncertainty"
(Mitchell 1935b, p. 91), although an inadequate one, because "combination
by one group of enterprises increases the hazards for other enterprises"
(Mitchell 1935b, p. 91). Hence he was not surprised that "with growing
frequency businessmen have turned to the government for aid" (Mitchell
1935b, p. 91). Indeed, he found such a tendency well-justified, not just among

---

[9] In a review of Lionel Robbins's book *The Great Depression* (1934), while expressing grave
doubts about Robbins's characteristically Austrian faith in the efficacy of market mechanisms,
and suggesting that some of his discussions of empirical issues, notably the role of interest
rates, paid insufficient attention to the complexities of the real-world financial system, Mitchell
nevertheless remarked, with respect to Robbins's explanation of the onset and persistence of
the depression as the inevitable consequence of excessive capital accumulation over the 1926–
29 period, that "much of this analysis seems to me sound" (Mitchell 1935a, p. 505).

the business community, but among the labour force too, and he clearly expected it to bear political fruit in due course. Even so, Mitchell's guarded optimism about what national planning might accomplish was not based upon any careful specification of what it might involve; nor did he go into detail about how it might be carried out, beyond urging the provision of counter-cyclical public-works expenditures and the dissemination of information and forecasts about the economy, measures that he had already promoted in the 1920s.

Paul Douglas and Underconsumptionism

Paul Douglas, who was a more vigorous proponent of a planned economy than was Mitchell in the early 1930s (Douglas 1932), provided altogether more detail about what such a program might entail, not least its monetary-policy and fiscal-policy components which concern us here. We have seen that in 1927, Douglas had enthusiastically embraced the underconsumptionist doctrines of Foster and Catchings. His underconsumptionism went into temporary abeyance, however, in a 1931 book, *The Problem of Unemployment* (Douglas and Director 1931), written in conjunction with his research assistant Aaron Director, but Douglas's scepticism about the powers of orthodox monetary policy, and his preference for public-works expenditures, preferably financed by money creation, was just as evident in 1931 as it had been in 1927, or was to be later in the 1930s after his underconsumptionism had re-emerged.[10]

Douglas and Director on Unemployment

Douglas and Director's book *The Problem of Unemployment* was, as its title suggests, a comprehensive survey of the current state of knowledge on that topic. It dealt with unemployment's extent and costs, its potential seasonal and technological causes, and such policy measures as the creation of "Public Employment Offices" and "Unemployment Insurance." It also contained a

---

[10] That book was written not at Chicago, but at Swarthmore, while Douglas was on leave there. The fact that Director was Douglas's research assistant, rather than an independent co-author, accounts for his name being placed out of alphabetical order. It is an interesting speculation that Director might have had some influence on the absence of underconsumptionism from that book, but I know of no evidence that would support or contradict such speculation. It is clear, however, from Douglas's memoirs (1972) that at that time he was preoccupied with the breakdown of his marriage. It was that, rather than the opportunity to write *The Problem of Unemployment*, that provided the main motive for his visit to Swarthmore. It is interesting to note that J. Ronnie Davis (1971), in a book devoted to establishing the priorities of American, and particularly Chicago, economists as pioneers of what came to be called "the new economics" (i.e., Keynesian policy doctrine), did not mention that book.

lengthy discussion of cyclical unemployment (1931, pp. 167–251). The cycle theory presented by Douglas and Director was eclectic, very much in the spirit of Mitchell (1913, 1927) and Pigou (1927a), who, they argued, had been inappropriately classified as merely an exponent of "the Psychological or Emotional school of business cycle theory" (Douglas and Director 1931, p. 168, fn. 3).[11] Their closest approach to an underconsumptionist theme, in the tradition of Foster and Catchings, occurred when they discussed the effects of secularly falling prices on the severity of cyclical downturns. Citing the study by Willard Thorp (1926) concerning the apparent relationship between those phenomena, to which Mitchell (1927) had drawn attention, and to which Hansen (1932) would also refer, Douglas and Director noted that

> there is one way in which technical improvements and savings do at times help to cause and to prolong business depressions and consequently to create unemployment. This is when they cause the volume of goods produced in society as a whole to increase faster than the supply of money and credit and therefore cause an inevitable fall in the general price level. (Douglas and Director 1931, p. 181)

They did not suggest "that this is the sole cause of business depressions but it is a factor which can initiate a period of depression and accentuate one initiated by other factors" (Douglas and Director 1931, p. 182). The problem stemmed from the facts that production took time and that deflation inevitably led to depressed profits and greater fragility of business. That analysis ultimately was closer to the ideas of Keynes (1923) than to those of Foster and Catchings, however, and it led Douglas and Director to argue as follows:

> If the supply of money and credit were to increase commensurately with the increase in production, the price level would be held constant and the goods produced would be sold at prices which would permit industry to go on with undiminished profits and without curtailment of activity. (Douglas and Director 1931, p. 183)

Nothing was said about the specific importance of putting money into the hands of consumers, and that passage may well have been the first from Chicago authors extolling the virtues of stable money growth, on the basis of arguments deriving from a version of the quantity theory of money.[12]

---

[11] The works of Pigou (1927a) and Mitchell (1927) that influenced Douglas and Director were discussed in Chapters 4 and 8. Note that it was the first edition of Pigou's *Industrial Fluctuations* (1927a) upon which they drew, rather than the second (1929) edition, which is the basis of my own discussion.

[12] Unless one is willing to follow Tavlas (1977) in according that priority to Douglas (1927). In my view, the unrelenting underconsumptionist stance of the latter paper makes it unhelpful to classify it in that way. It is worth noting that the quantity-theory tradition to which Douglas and Director's policy proposal related was the Cambridge version, as developed by Keynes (1923), rather than Fisher's variant.

Consistent with their view that secular deflation was only one factor impinging upon depressions, however, Douglas and Director, like Hardy and Reed, and like Pigou (1927a), to whose views on that matter they explicitly referred (Douglas and Director 1931, p. 230), went on to express a very limited faith in the counter-cyclical powers of monetary policy. According to them, both discount-rate policy and open-market operations would be more effective in checking a cyclical rise in prices than a fall, because, "while business men will be attracted by the lower rate of interest which results from the abundance of credit, they will also be deterred by the general shrinkage in prices and the declining volume of sales" (Douglas and Director, 1931, p. 243). Indeed, they thought that those problems might even hamper monetary policy in its efforts to offset secular deflation as well.[13]

Douglas and Director's preferred remedy for cyclical unemployment, therefore, was public-works expenditure, to which a full third (pp. 192–221) of their discussion of that problem was devoted. They surveyed the theoretical and empirical literature on the topic, including Hawtrey's views on the ineffectiveness of such expenditures except as a means of putting new money into circulation, and concluded that such expenditures would be effective for increasing the rate of employment no matter how they were financed. They noted, nevertheless, that tax or bond financing would reduce their impact relative to what could be expected from financing by money creation: ". . . it is possible for government to increase the demand for labor without a corresponding contraction of private demand, and . . . this is particularly the case when fresh monetary purchasing power is created to finance the construction work" (Douglas and Director 1931, pp. 210–211). Here again we have a theme which Douglas had sounded in 1927, but the specific connection between public-works expenditure and the possibility of stimulating consumption by placing purchasing power in the hands of consumers, which he had then stressed, was no longer raised.

Douglas and Director showed considerable sensitivity to the practical problems involved in implementing public-works expenditure programs. Those arose from the difficulties of forecasting the cycle – "the possibilities of employment increase as the work advances, and the chief addition to labor demand may not come until after the depression period is well over" (Doug-

---

[13] The overall sceptical stance on the powers of discount-rate policy and open-market operations expressed by Douglas and Director was so pronounced, and so conventional for its time, that I believe it is a mistake to treat that book, as does Tavlas (1997), as an important building block in the so-called Chicago tradition from which Milton Friedman's ideas are thought to derive, its advocacy of steady money growth notwithstanding. As with their views on the unreliability of counter-cyclical monetary policy, there is also nothing to distinguish Douglas and Director's position on public-works policies from those held by such contemporaries as Pigou, Robertson, or Mitchell.

las and Director 1931, p. 214) – from difficulties in ensuring that the projects undertaken actually would be socially useful – "When the time comes to fill in the gap, needs may have changed" (Douglas and Director 1931, p. 215) – and from the lack of an appropriate administrative framework – "In the United States any very large degree of centralization is inconceivable; . . . The lack of centralized authority within the municipalities, states, and federal government is even more serious than that between them" (Douglas and Director 1931, pp. 215–216).

Even so, their ultimate conclusion was as follows:

> Our analysis so far, indefinite as it is, permits us to conclude that over a period of time it is possible, through the use of public expenditures, to reduce somewhat the extreme fluctuations in employment.
>
> In the long run, however, we may expect more than this. We may actually expect a reduction in the average level of unemployment. (Douglas and Director 1931, p. 219)

Evidently, by 1931, those American economists had reached a position on the matter of public-works expenditures that was, in most practical respects, similar to those which many of their British and Swedish contemporaries were simultaneously reaching – and that at a time, moreover, when Keynes (1930a, 1931a) was still advocating such measures only for an economy such as that of Britain, which he thought faced severe balance-of-payments constraints under the gold standard, while recommending that the United States should rely on monetary policy alone to fight the depression.[14]

Douglas's Underconsumptionism

As the depression deepened, Douglas continued to write on those problems, though no longer in collaboration with Director.[15] He did so at greatest length in his 1935 monograph *Controlling Depressions*, but the essential content of that book had already been set out in a 1933 pamphlet, *Collapse or Cycle?*, whose title hints at, and whose contents reveal, a distinct reversion to his theoretical perspective of 1927. From being an exponent of an eclectic cycle theory in the spirit of Mitchell and Pigou, Douglas re-emerged as an under-consumptionist in the tradition of Foster and Catchings, though he no longer

---

[14] Thus, as Davis (1971, p. 122) noted, when Keynes delivered his lectures on unemployment in Chicago in early 1931, stressing the importance of monetary policy, his views seemed "uninspiring and disappointing" to some of his audience, for many of whom the advantages of public-works expenditures were already clear. See Davis (1971, pp. 107–124) for an account of the discussion that took place at that conference, and note also that there was no constituency among its participants for wage cuts as a cure for unemployment.

[15] For a useful account of Director's solo work on those questions, see Tavlas (1997).

cited those authors, preferring to refer to J. A. Hobson's *Economics of Unemployment* (1923) as an example of work in that vein.[16]

In Douglas's 1933 view, the depression had started because, by the end of the 1920s, as at the end of any boom period, "more goods than [could] be sold at a given price level" were being produced. At such times, "it only requires a slight fall in prices to produce a great fall in profits and in some cases an outright loss," and "when [business] starts on the down-grade, it tends, unless checked by other forces, to move cumulatively downhill" (Douglas 1933, p. 4). Douglas noted that "there are those like Dr. Wesley Mitchell . . . who maintain that after a time a depression inevitably creates of itself a revival" (Douglas 1933, p. 9) but, he went on, "there is at least one crucial flaw in this cheerful theory. It assumes not only that people *want* to buy more food, clothing, furniture, etc., but that they have the money to pay for it" (Douglas 1933, p. 9, italics in original). To the contrary, and referring to conditions then prevailing, he argued that

> the effective purchasing power of the great masses of urban and rural workers has therefore been so greatly reduced that although there is a strong desire to buy, the means to do so are largely lacking. It is therefore very difficult to see how this unexpected wave of buying by the consumers is really going to set in by itself without stimulus from the outside. (Douglas 1933, p. 9)

---

[16] Let it be stressed that my characterization of Douglas's work of that period is not solely a matter of my own *ex post* judgement. Erik Lundberg visited the United States as a graduate student under the auspices of the Rockefeller Foundation in 1931–33, spending the first eleven months at Chicago. In his report to the foundation, he remarked that "in the field of business cycle theory the University of Chicago had very little to offer. Professor Mints touched on some of the problems in his lectures on monetary theories, while Douglas offered a very simple overproduction and underconsumption theory" (Lundberg 1934, repr. 1995, p. 51). Joseph Reeve (1943, p. 224, fn. 60), who acknowledged considerable help and encouragement from Douglas, also noted that Douglas's advocacy of what he termed "fiscal inflation," i.e., the use of budget deficits to increase the money supply, was based on underconsumptionist analysis. He cited Douglas (1935, pp. 53–78) in support of that judgement. Davis (1971, pp. 47–60) discussed Douglas's views extensively, also relying mainly on *Controlling Depressions* (1935), but failed to discern the underconsumptionist basis of its analysis. It is interesting to note that in *Prosperity and Depression* (1937), Gottfried von Haberler made no mention of Douglas, relying instead on Foster and Catchings (1923, 1925, 1928) and Arthur D. Gayer (1935a) as American representatives of the underconsumptionist approach. See Haberler (1937, p. 131). Though Haberler (1937, p. 115) suggested that Foster and Catchings, along with J. A. Hobson, had presented the "best reasoned form" of that doctrine, he did not discuss the work of the former in any detail. Gayer (1935a, pp. 113–135) did indeed provide, as Haberler suggested, an explanation for the depression in terms of the failure of consumption expenditure to keep pace with output during the 1920s, but his advocacy of public-works expenditures was based more on their potential effects on investment expenditure per se, supplemented by multiplier effects, than on their capacity to put purchasing power in the hands of consumers, though he did mention the latter effect. All in all, Gayer's policy views were closer to those set out by Douglas and Director (1931) than those by Douglas (1935). See also Gayer (1935b, esp. ch. XIV).

Orthodox monetary policy alone would not provide such a stimulus, in Douglas's opinion.[17] He believed that open-market operations had already been tried in 1932 and found wanting:

> The expectation was that the banks would be so choked with cash that they would have to increase their loans.
>
> The hoped for results did not occur. It is not enough to give banks the power to create more credit. It is necessary that the loans should actually be made in large quantities. That did not happen because in a period of depression businessmen are afraid to borrow and banks are afraid to lend. (Douglas 1933, p. 10)

Rather, and clearly in the spirit of Foster and Catchings, Douglas argued that "the chain of revival runs primarily from the increased purchasing power of the consumers and greater demand by consumers to increased borrowings and bank loans." What was called for, therefore, was large-scale government expenditures on relief, to satisfy both "actual human needs and the necessity for stimulating increased purchasing by consumers," as well as "larger expenditures for public works" (Douglas 1933, pp. 10–11). Referring to Keynes's recently published *Means to Prosperity* (1933), Douglas also went on to note that "each dollar spent on public works would . . . have a multiplicative effect in stimulating business" (Douglas 1933, p. 12).[18] As to the finance of such expenditures, Douglas preferred money creation to government borrowing, just as he had in 1927: "if the issuance of money can be controlled, this would seem to be by far the more economical way" (Douglas 1933, p. 13).

By the time Douglas's 1933 pamphlet was written, the United States had temporarily left the gold standard, as a preliminary to raising significantly the dollar price of gold, while forbidding private holdings of the metal. The authorities were therefore much freer to pursue independent monetary and fiscal policies than before. That was no bad thing in Douglas's view, for

---

[17] As we have already seen, Douglas's pessimism about orthodox monetary policy long predated the events of 1932 and ultimately had derived from his underconsumptionist views. Even in *The Problem of Unemployment* (Douglas and Director 1931), when his underconsumptionism went into temporary abeyance, that pessimism remained. Steindl (1995, pp. 93–94) has discussed Douglas's relationship to the "Chicago tradition," as discussed later, and has concluded that "Douglas did not have a systematic, coherent monetary interpretation" (Steindl 1995, p. 94) of the Great Contraction.

[18] As Barber (1985, p. 16) has pointed out, the potentially "multiplying effects" of public-works expenditures had been touted in U.S. discussions in the early 1920s, though the theoretical basis for expecting them was, to put it mildly, crude. Richard Kahn had, of course, visited the United States in 1932 and had published a paper applying his 1931 analysis to the conditions of the more nearly closed U.S. economy (Kahn 1933). J. M. Clark also developed the multiplier notion at about that time, suggesting that he had become aware of Kahn's analysis only after he had worked the matter out independently (Clark 1934, p. 85, fn. 15). Reeve nevertheless cited Kahn and Keynes as the originators of "the most persuasive analysis during this period of the cumulative effects of deficit expenditures" (Reeve 1943, p. 220).

though the gold standard had at times inhibited "uncontrolled inflation" in some nations, it had also "held back other nations from sanely expanding workers' purchasing power to put men back to work." Douglas entertained the ultimate desirability of an "internationally managed currency," but he expressed a clear preference for a "nationally managed currency" relative to "an internationally unmanaged currency such as gold" (Douglas 1933, p. 18).

Douglas's preference for national autonomy in monetary policy was not just an expedient response to the current economic situation. He looked forward to a time when, the task of getting out of the depression having been accomplished, "the next is to prevent our falling into another" (Douglas 1933, p. 18). For that purpose, Douglas advocated a monetary policy designed to ensure that "the monetary purchasing power in the hands of the consumers" would increase at the economy's long-run growth rate, and he envisaged that ". . . 'prosperity dividends' distributed to consumers through the familiar creation of monetary purchasing power" (Douglas 1933, p. 19) might be needed to achieve that. Such a policy, moreover, probably would be best implemented through a reformed

> banking system which will prevent the banks from lending more to individuals than the amount of money created by the federal government and which will therefore do away with the creation of purchasing power by private banks in the form of bank credit. (Douglas 1933, p. 19)

The Quantity Theory in the 1930s

Douglas held a professorship in economics at the University of Chicago throughout the period under discussion here. Nowadays we are accustomed to thinking of that institution as the home, in the early 1930s, of an intellectual tradition, based on the quantity theory of money, that advanced a monetary explanation for the cycle in general and the Great Contraction in particular, took a rather optimistic view of the powers of orthodox monetary policy to deal with that contraction, was strongly committed to governing monetary policy by rules, and came to advocate a monetary system based upon 100 per cent reserve requirements against those banking-system liabilities that functioned as means of exchange.[19] Though Douglas subscribed to the last two elements of that body of doctrine, he opposed the rest of it, and he was, quite evidently, an underconsumptionist, not a quantity theorist. The fact is that

---

[19] The idea of a Chicago tradition, largely oral, was first broached by Friedman (1956). Both its content and its uniqueness have been sporadically debated ever since, by, among others, Patinkin (1969, 1974), Humphrey (1971), Friedman (1974), Laidler (1993, 1998), Steindl (1995), and Tavlas (1997). My own views on these questions are discussed in the following pages.

there was more agreement among Chicago economists concerning what should be done about the depression than concerning why it should be done. Moreover, advocacy of what Joseph Reeve (1943) would term "Monetary Expansion via the Banking System" and "Fiscal Inflation," by which he meant money-financed budget deficits, as means for restoring prosperity, though well represented at Chicago, was rather widespread among American economists.

Irving Fisher on the Great Contraction

In the 1920s, Irving Fisher had been, as we have seen, an exponent of a monocausal explanation for variations in real income and employment as consequences of fluctuations in the price level, and he had also been a leading advocate of subjecting monetary policy to a price-stability rule. In the early years of the depression he was a tireless public advocate for a variety of policies designed, first, to drive up the price level to the height it had attained in the 1920s, which he saw as the key to restoring prosperity, and thereafter to stabilize it as a means of preserving that prosperity. As Joseph Reeve (1943, ch. 11), in a book which derived from a 1939 Chicago Ph.D. thesis (Patinkin 1973, pp. 279–281), has recounted, at various times in the years 1932–34 Fisher was successively an advocate of the 1932 Goldsborough bill, which sought to mandate the Federal Reserve System to engineer reflation followed by price-level stability, of the issuance of stamp-scrip money, and of proposals, mainly associated at that time with the Cornell University agricultural economist George F. Warren, to raise the dollar price of gold as a means of forcing up the price level.[20]

Fisher's policy proposals all derived from an analysis of the depression as a monetary phenomenon, which, as Frank Steindl (1995, ch. 6) has shown, was shared by his sometime students and collaborators James H. Rogers and Harry G. Brown. That analysis, in turn, was grounded in his earlier view of the cycle as a "dance of the dollar," which, as Dimand (1993a) has shown,

---

[20] Among the many monetary reformers who came into and faded from popular view in the United States in 1930s, Fisher, along with Father Charles E. Coughlin, the "radio priest," and Senator Elmer Thomas, a leading advocate of massive increases in the note issue, was one of the three whom Joseph Reeve thought important enough to merit a separate chapter devoted to his views and activities in his monograph *Monetary Reform Movements* (1943). Because Fisher had publicly expressed his faith in the durability of the stock-market boom in September 1929, had persisted in pronouncing the market's subsequent collapse temporary well into 1930, and had also found time in 1930 to publish a defence of Prohibition (Fisher 1930b), it is not surprising that he found himself thus placed in the company of monetary cranks. But Reeve was nevertheless respectful of Fisher's stature as a monetary theorist, noting that "in terms both of the effectiveness of his monetary reform crusades and of the calibre of his economic analysis, Professor Fisher presents a striking contrast to Father Coughlin and to Senator Thomas" (Reeve 1943, p. 184).

underwent considerable elaboration in the early 1930s. As Fisher put it himself in the Preface to *Booms and Depressions* (1932), which he dedicated to Mitchell, "the vast field of 'business cycles' is one on which I had scarcely ever entered before, and I had never attempted to analyse it as a whole" (Fisher 1932, p. vii). That monograph, and a subsequent 1933 *Econometrica* paper, set out the results of that analysis.

In 1933, Fisher still asserted, as he had in 1923, that "the old and apparently still persistent notion of 'the' business cycle as a single, simple, self-generating cycle . . . and as actually realized historically in regularly recurring crises, is a myth" (Fisher 1933, p. 338). However, his qualification to the effect that "it is as absurd to assume that, for any long period of time, the variables in the economic organization, or any part of them, will 'stay put' in perfect equilibrium, as to assume that the Atlantic Ocean can ever be without a wave" (Fisher 1933, p. 339) by then carried much more weight, because it was linked to theoretical arguments about the proclivity of inflation expectations to behave asymmetrically between borrowers and lenders and also to lag systematically behind experience as prices rose and fell. After *The Purchasing Power of Money* (1911, ch. 4), he had not emphasized those theoretical arguments in his writings on the cycle, though he had, of course, treated them at some length in his 1928 monograph *The Money Illusion*, as well as in *The Theory of Interest* (1930a, ch. 19).

Furthermore, Fisher had added an important new element to his analysis, as the title of his 1933 article makes plain, namely, "The Debt-Deflation Theory of Great Depressions." The basis for that particular theory was simple enough, and hardly original, having played a role in Veblen's 1904 explanation of fluctuations. The theory was that debts were usually denominated in nominal terms, so that when prices fell, the real burden that they implied increased.[21] Fisher's new variation on that theme came with two insights: first, that as that burden increased, agents would attempt to liquidate assets in order to lighten it; second, that

> *the very effort of individuals to lessen their burden of debts increases it, because of the mass effect of the stampede to liquidate in swelling each dollar owed.* Then we have the great paradox which, I submit, is the chief secret of most, if not all, great depressions: *The more the debtors pay, the more they owe.* The more the economic boat tips, the more it tends to tip. It

---

[21] That debt-deflation theory of Fisher's would be rejected by Chicago quantity theorists: "In general, we maintain that the cycle problem is a problem of cost-price maladjustments (or the inertia of operating costs), on the one hand, and of the short-run changes in the quantity and velocity of effective money which aggravate these maladjustments. *It follows as a corollary, incidentally, that the problem of unemployment is not, to an important extent, a problem of debt*" (Simons et al. 1933, app. p. 6, italics added). Note the essentially Hawtreyan character of the preferred view of Simons and associates.

is not tending to right itself, but is capsizing. (Fisher 1933, p. 344, italics in original)

Given the stress that Fisher placed on price-level behaviour as the key to mitigating the depression, and on the quantity of money as its determinant, it is not surprising that in 1935 we find him a vigorous supporter of the same plan that attracted Douglas, the plan for imposing a 100 per cent reserve requirement against the monetary liabilities of commercial banks as a means of increasing the Federal Reserve's control over the money supply, nor is it surprising that one label that is often given to the scheme was bestowed on it by Fisher: *100 per cent. Money* (1935). Another label for the same scheme, originating in that same year, was, of course A. G. Hart's "the Chicago plan," and as was noted earlier, one version of that plan did indeed originate at the University of Chicago. Much of the support which it received, there and elsewhere, was based neither on underconsumptionism nor on debt-deflation theory, however, but rather on a more traditional monetary analysis, of the cycle in general and the Great Contraction in particular, that derived from the quantity theory of money.

The Chicago Tradition

In 1974, Milton Friedman described a "Chicago tradition" as it had appeared to him in the early 1930s and drew attention to two documents surviving from those years which seemed to him to represent its basic characteristics (Friedman 1974). The first was the proceedings of the January 1932 Harris Foundation conference, held at the University of Chicago (at which Willis and Haberler had presented papers, as cited earlier in this chapter), and the second was an unsigned and unpublished manuscript dating from November 1933 on "Banking and Currency Reform" which, it is generally agreed, was mainly the work of Henry Simons.

The Harris Foundation conference produced a manifesto for transmission to President Hoover which bore the signatures of twenty-four economists (Willis and Haberler were not among them, nor was Paul Douglas), twelve of whom held appointments at Chicago. It advocated an essentially monetary approach to fighting the contraction. Specifically, its key proposals were as follows: first, that administrative and legislative measures be taken to create "an important defense against the consequences of gold withdrawals" by "increasing the free gold of the Federal Reserve System"; second, that "the Federal Reserve banks systematically pursue open-market operations with the double aim of facilitating necessary government financing and increasing the liquidity of the banking structure" (Wright 1932, p. 162); third, that existing public-works programs be kept in place while the federal government co-operated with state and local governments in the "maintenance of adequate unemployment relief" (Wright 1932, p. 162).

As to the 1933 manuscript by Simons and co-workers, an appendix attached to it, entitled "Banking and Business Cycles," sketched an essentially monetary explanation of the cycle:[22]

> In any money economy there will be some tendency toward cumulative maladjustment over periods of a few years, largely because of two circumstances:
> (a) The relative inflexibility of those prices which largely govern operating costs of production;
> (b) The sensitiveness or responsiveness of money "circulation" to changes of business earnings. (Simons et al. 1933, app. 1)

The latter "sensitiveness" was presented as an inherent property of a monetary system based upon commercial banks. During a cyclical upswing,

> a considerable expansion of bank loans and, thereby, of the community's effective money is likely to occur before any automatic checks become operative.
> Once a crisis has developed, and once earnings have begun to decline, the process is even more chaotic . . . in a country where wages and freight rates . . . are as inflexible as they are in the United States, there is no limit, in the absence of drastic federal interference, to the deflation which may ensue. (Simons et al. 1933, app. p. 5)

Now Simons and associates did not attribute the existence of the cycle solely to the operation of banking. They were, in fact, silent on that fundamental question. But there can be no questioning that it was their belief that the severity of the ongoing contraction was to be laid at the door of the monetary system: ". . . if some malevolent genius had sought to aggravate the affliction of business and employment cycles, he could hardly have done better than to establish a system of private deposit banks in the present form" (Simons et al. 1933, app. p. 3).

Thus, there is no question that views about the role of monetary factors in the depression, very much like those which we nowadays associate with Chicago, did have currency there in the early 1930s, nor is there any question that the Chicago signatories of the 1932 manifesto did indeed support measures of a type which Friedman and Schwartz (1963) later argued would have done much to mitigate that contraction, if pursued with sufficient vigour.

---

[22] The main purpose of that 1933 document, however, was to set out what came to be called the Chicago plan for 100 per cent reserve banking. Barber (1996) has listed Director and Douglas, among others, as sponsors of the plan. The essentially monetary theory of the cycle contained in the appendix to the document under discussion here is not compatible with Douglas's underconsumptionist arguments published in the same year, and it is difficult to believe that he had anything to do with the preparation of that appendix, as opposed to the main document. Douglas's support for the 100 per cent money plan is not, that is to say, in question.

Even so, though a "Chicago tradition" such as Friedman described in 1974 certainly had existed from early 1932 onwards, its characteristic views were not uniquely held by Chicago economists, nor indeed did they find their earliest or most extensive development in their writings, as we shall now see.

Snyder and Currie on the Great Contraction

As early as 1931, Carl Snyder of the Federal Reserve Bank of New York, whose empirical work on the secular and cyclical behaviour of the transactions velocity of circulation (e.g., 1924) was discussed in Chapter 8, presented an extensive empirical study of the hypothesis that the downturn of 1929 had its origins in a previous bout of "overproduction" (Snyder 1931b). As we have seen, that view had Austrian advocates, but more important, it was the explanation favoured by many in the financial community, including the Federal Reserve System itself. Snyder, however, concluded that there was no evidence to support it, and he hinted instead at a monetary explanation of the event, as he also did in a shorter presentation to the American Economics Association (Snyder 1931a).

In 1935 he reiterated his conclusion at greater length, arguing, in rebuttal of views similar to those of Anderson and Willis, but without specifically citing those authors, that "the spectacular period from 1922 to '29" had produced no serious real distortions in the economy, and he therefore concluded that "the problem of economic (and social) stability seems now clearly revealed as essentially a problem of Credit Control" (Snyder 1935, p. 203). As to the stock-market crash, he remarked that "*unless there is a violent contraction of credit,* i.e., purchasing power, as a consequence, even the wildest speculation need not necessarily prelude a prolonged general prostration" (Snyder 1935, p. 204, italics added). Those unequivocal views led Harold Reed, who, as we have seen, believed that the Federal Reserve System was essentially powerless after 1929, to remark, accurately but not approvingly, that "Snyder is compelled to hold that the unexplained rigor of the existing depression must be attributed to the one fact that our reserve banks permitted the outstanding credit volume to collapse" (Reed 1935, p. 618).

Snyder was not alone in his views, even outside of the University of Chicago. In fact, by far the most systematic attempt to develop a monetary explanation for the contraction was the work of a Harvard instructor, Lauchlin Currie.[23] As a graduate student, Currie had been a protégé of Allyn Young,

---

[23] On Currie's explanation and the extent to which it anticipated that of Friedman and Schwartz, see Brunner (1968), Humphrey (1971), Roger Sandilands (1990a, pp. 31–38), Laidler (1993), and Frank Steindl (1995, ch. 4). My own views on this contentious issue emerge in the following pages.

and he was also Ralph Hawtrey's teaching assistant during the latter's year at Harvard in 1928–29. Currie's work of the early 1930s, particularly his Ph.D. thesis, "Bank Assets and Banking Theory" (1931a), and the monograph *The Supply and Control of Money in the United States* (1934b), which grew out of the thesis, was deeply influenced by both Hawtrey and Young, particularly the latter, to whose memory the 1934 monograph was explicitly dedicated.

It was Young's *Analysis of Bank Statistics for the United States*, discussed in Chapter 8, which most influenced Currie. His monetary analysis of the onset of the Great Contraction used Young's systematic empirical approach to show how a version of Hawtrey's cycle theory could be used to explain the evolution of events in the United States over the 1921–30 period.[24] Currie was critical of Hawtrey on some points, in particular taking him to task for overemphasizing the role of short-term commercial lending in generating monetary instability; but, Currie concluded, "Hawtrey's theory does not rest solely on the movement of commercial loans. He only uses the wholesaler's and the merchant's demand for loans as a means of bringing about an expansion of credit which is the essential thing in his theory" (Currie 1931a, p. 217).[25] And Currie summarized that theory in the following terms:

> . . . effective demand . . . may fall short of the supply of goods, *at a price.* . . . The effective demand for goods is conditioned by the amount of consumers' outlays, which in turn is determined by their incomes plus or minus a decrease or increase in their deposit balances, the unspent margin. . . . Assuming for the moment that the rate of flow [velocity of deposits] remains constant, an expansion of deposits would cause an increase in consumer's incomes, outlays and the demand for goods; a decrease in deposits would

---

[24] That was completely clear in the original version of his Ph.D. thesis (Currie 1931a), submitted for the degree in early 1931, but less so in his subsequent writings, where, without changing the substance of his theoretical arguments, he seems to have taken considerable pains to downplay their Hawtreyan origin. For example, the final substantive chapter of the thesis, "Bank Assets and the Business Cycle," began with an eleven-page account of Hawtrey's theory, which was deleted from the version he submitted in an unsuccessful bid for the Harvard department's Wells Prize in 1932. I am indebted to Roger Sandilands for drawing my attention to that later version of Currie's dissertation. Why Currie would have made that deletion is mysterious.

[25] Attention was drawn in Chapter 8 to the ambiguities inherent in the word "credit" in the literature of that time, and Currie was particularly sensitive to them. See, in particular, "Treatment of Credit in Contemporary Monetary Theory" (Currie 1933a), which is a slightly revised chapter from his 1931 thesis that also appeared as a chapter in *The Supply and Control of Money* (1934b). In the latter he pointed out that "the term was in the way of acquiring, among monetary writers, a fairly precise connotation: means of payment represented by demand deposits" (Currie 1934b, p. 48), and he cited Hawtrey and Young, among others, as authorities for that usage. But, as he also noted, "particularly in America, [the term] has become increasingly identified with something else – loans of all kinds, and particularly bank loans and investments" (Currie 1934b, p. 48). By 1934, when Currie meant "demand deposits," that is what he wrote; thus, in the passage dealing with Hawtrey, dating from early 1931, that is how the word "credit" should be read too.

cause a diminished demand for goods. (Currie 1931a, p. 212, italics in original)

Currie's interpretation of the Great Depression thus involved an application of Hawtrey's monetary theory of the cycle to that particular event, with fluctuations in the quantity of money playing a central role.[26]

In the 1934 monograph, Currie significantly extended his Ph.D. thesis. There he argued that most of his contemporaries paid too little attention to the behaviour of the money stock:

> ... in the past an altogether disproportionate amount of importance was attached to variations in the supply of money. In consequence of the almost universal abandonment of the quantity theory of money, however, there is danger that the pendulum may swing too far in the opposite direction so that the effect of variations in the supply of money may be unduly minimized. (Currie 1934b, p. 3)

Furthermore, his data on the behaviour of the United States economy's means of payment – he paid particular attention to demand deposits, a narrower aggregate than the liabilities matching the "loans and investments" which commentators such as Reed used to track the behaviour of the quantity of money – showed a more marked tightening of policy in 1928–29 than did a time series created at about the same time by another of Young's former students, James Angell (1936).[27] The monetary contraction in question had, in Currie's view, been the consequence of a deliberate and erroneous policy choice based on what I have earlier termed Banking School ideas, but which he called "The Commercial Loan Theory of Banking." The authorities' intention had been to curb stock-market speculation by cutting back on bank lending for financial transactions, while attempting to maintain the availability of credit for commercial borrowers. Currie argued that, though successful in its own terms, that policy had led to a fall in what we would now call the narrow money supply. That, in turn, had precipitated an initial downturn, whose subsequent transformation into a serious depression he also laid at the door of the Federal Reserve System.

---

[26] It is interesting to note that Gardiner Means (1935), best known as a pioneer of the theory of "administered prices," also attributed the depression to output being forced to contract because prices were unable to fall. However, Means attributed the initial fall in demand for goods to an increase in the demand for money, and he advocated an accommodative monetary-policy regime, very similar to that supported by exponents of the "needs-of-trade" doctrine. I am grateful to Fred Lee for drawing my attention to that paper.

[27] Currie (1936) reviewed Angell's book and was rather critical of the latter's data, particularly as far as his method of estimating the division of demand deposits from time deposits among non-member banks was concerned. Note that Clark Warburton (1946, p. 82), whose work provided an important stepping-stone from the research under discussion here to the later research of Friedman and Schwartz (1963), argued that Angell's own data suggested a more important causative role for the quantity of money in the early years of the Great Contraction than Angell himself was willing to allow.

As early as the winter of 1931 Currie had expressed the view that "a much greater expansion of credit might have been brought about after the downturn in business in 1929 than did in fact take place" (Currie 1931a, p. 237). The thesis in which he developed that position at some length remained unpublished, but he presented a brief outline of the position in question in a review of Reed (1930) in the *American Economic Review* (Currie 1931b). In 1934 he elaborated it as follows, quite contrary to the views of Douglas, or indeed the views of more orthodox critics of monetary policy such as Burgess or even Reed:

> Some writers have even argued as follows: It has been held that security purchases by a central bank in the downswing of business will bring about an expansion of money. In 1932 the reserve banks bought an unprecedented amount of bonds and money did not expand. Therefore open market operations cannot bring about expansion in periods of depression. The answer to this line of argument is, of course, that the major premise as stated is incomplete. The assumption is that the purchases will result in an actual increase in member bank reserves. The open market policy of 1932 was offset by an outflow of gold and the liquidation of member bank indebtedness to the reserve banks so that only a comparatively small increase in reserves occurred. . . .
>
> Much of the current belief in the powerlessness of the reserve banks appears to arise from a complete misreading of the monetary history of 1929–32. It is generally held that the reserve administration strove energetically to bring about expansion throughout the depression but that contraction continued despite its efforts. Actually the reserve administration's policy was one of almost complete passivity and quiescence. (Currie 1934b, pp. 146–147)

Currie thus dealt specifically, and as readers of Mints (1946, p. 62) and Friedman and Schwartz (1963, pp. 345–350), none of whom acknowledged his priority in that matter, will recognize, in essentially the same way as they would later do, with what was widely believed to have been the failure of open-market operations to bring about monetary expansion in 1932, an outcome which was widely treated as clear evidence of the futility of orthodox monetary measures, and to which Keynes was to draw specific attention, as an example of the liquidity trap at work, in the *General Theory*.[28]

A Chicago–Harvard Connection

Currie, a Harvard instructor, clearly argued from early 1931 onwards that the Federal Reserve System had mismanaged things in the late 1920s and early

---

[28] As did Alvin Hansen, too, in his *Guide to Keynes* (1954). That episode clearly was a key one in the history of economic thought, with the critical counter-factual question being, What would have happened had the Federal Reserve System pushed its open-market operations even further than it did?

1930s. He also located the origins of that mismanagement in the prevalence of Banking School ideas within the system, and particularly at the Federal Reserve Board in Washington. Nowadays we associate such views with Friedman's Chicago tradition, and similar ideas were indeed to be found in contemporary Chicago writings, though none of them were completed as early as Currie's works (1931a, b). In a paper for the same 1932 Harris Foundation conference to which extensive reference has already been made, Jacob Viner, then at the University of Chicago, noted that

> while the New York Federal Reserve Bank has made more effort than any other central banking institution to develop a program and a technique of credit control with a view to stabilization, it has at critical moments found itself at cross-purposes with, and inhibited from action by, a Federal Reserve Board with an attitude towards its functions resembling with almost miraculous closeness that of the Bank of England during its worst period. (Viner 1932, p. 28)

Thus he reiterated a theme which was prominent in Currie's work and which, it might be noted, Allyn Young had sounded well before the depression had begun, as I have discussed elsewhere (Laidler 1993, p. 1082).

Others at Chicago presumably held similar views in early 1932, for, as has already been noted, in addition to Viner, eleven other economists from that university signed the manifesto that emerged from the 1932 Harris Foundation conference; but his was nevertheless the only paper by a Chicago author to be presented at that conference. Viner was, moreover, somewhat hesitant about how much might be achieved by the use of orthodox expansionary monetary policy, not least because its implementation would jeopardize the United States' continued adherence to the gold standard.[29] He conceded that "for over a century writers have pleaded for the abandonment of the gold standard and the substitution of a managed paper currency" (Viner 1932, p. 35), but he nevertheless expressed "an individual view, [that] we know too little as yet of the possibilities of stabilization to take immediately any major steps in that direction" (Viner 1932, p. 37). The most he would concede was that

> we could soon learn a great deal more than is now known of the possibilities of comprehensive stabilization, if some country now off the gold standard were to attempt by credit control or otherwise to raise its price level somewhat above its present level, and then were to regulate the volume of bank credit so as to approximate a constant level in some significant index of prices. (Viner 1932, p. 38)

---

[29] Note that until passage of the Glass-Steagall Act of 1932, which relaxed the gold-reserve requirements to which the Federal Reserve System was subject, there was widespread concern that the system's ability to pursue expansionary policy was severely circumscribed by the possibility of international repercussions.

Another participant in the same Harris Foundation conference was a little less hesitant. John Williams of Harvard, one of those who drafted the conference manifesto, also prepared a paper on behalf of its signatories to explain the motivation underlying it; he put matters as follows:

> Granting . . . the dangers of expecting too much from credit management, and granting also the deficiencies of our understanding, it is safe to say that both our ability to control and our knowledge of why to control considerably outrun our performance. . . .
> . . . The immediate problem is to restore normal conditions. The greatest single help, internally, would be a vigorous open-market policy designed to reduce rediscounts of member banks and to increase the supply of purchasing power. (Williams 1932, pp. 156–157)

Williams acknowledged, as did Viner, a potential conflict between the policy goals of internal and external monetary stability and thought that its eventual resolution was to be found in "closer co-operation of central banks looking towards some form or degree of supernational management" (Williams 1932, p. 158). Though Williams cited neither of them in his paper, it is difficult to believe that the views he expressed in it did not owe something to Currie, whose Ph.D. thesis he had recently finished supervising, and, particularly with reference to international complications and how they should be handled, to Hawtrey, who had recently been his colleague.[30]

Even so, the differences between Williams and Viner were much more matters of emphasis than of substance, and should not be overstated. As George Tavlas (1997) has pointed out, Viner's relative pessimism about the powers of monetary policy stemmed from two sources: first, the constraints imposed by the gold standard, and second, doubts about the effectiveness of discount-rate policy and open-market operations under depression conditions. One element in his colleague Douglas's underconsumptionism was the claim that money-financed deficit spending on the part of the government, on public works and relief, would be an effective means of increasing the purchasing power of consumers. Once convertibility constraints had been relaxed by the passage of the Glass-Steagall Act of 1932, and removed altogether by the subsequent abandonment of the gold standard in 1933, Viner, along with some of his Chicago colleagues, took up a variation on that theme and defended money-financed deficit expenditures as a means for reliably increasing the money supply when more orthodox means seemed likely to fail in the face of reluctance on the part of the private sector to borrow from the banking system. That variation, "fiscal inflationism," as Reeve (1943) would call it,

---

[30] Tavlas (1997) has been rather condescending towards Williams's work, particularly that of the later 1930s. That had no bearing on the role played by Williams at the Harris Foundation conference, which is a simple matter of fact, nor on the content of the paper he presented there, which is a matter of published record.

would in due course become a staple of teaching at Chicago as the 1930s progressed, though it did not receive a definitive statement in the academic literature until the appearance of an article by Mints (1946).[31]

Even so, the monetary explanation for the depression, which we nowadays associate with Chicago alone, is best regarded as having originated in a Harvard–Chicago interaction which continued until late 1934. In addition to the evidence of that interaction already cited, two important papers by Currie were published in 1933 and 1934, under Viner's editorship, in the *Journal of Political Economy*. The first of those (Currie 1933b) was a version of the chapter from his doctoral dissertation (1931a) in which he discussed the confusion of money with credit that lay at the heart of the "commercial-loan" theory of banking upon which Federal Reserve policy had been largely based; and the second (Currie 1934a) bore a title which even today speaks for itself: "The Failure of Monetary Policy to Prevent the Depression of 1929–32." Finally, it is worth pointing out that when, in the summer of 1934, Viner organized the "Freshman Brains Trust" to work on economic-policy issues on behalf of President Roosevelt, Currie, whom Viner characterized as "too good for Harvard," was one of its members. In light of that university's subsequent refusal to extend Currie's leave while he continued to work in Washington, and of the mediocrity of that product of its economics department, the 1934 *Economics of the Recovery Program* discussed earlier in this chapter, it is difficult to disagree with that judgement. But none of that can alter the fact of an important Harvard–Chicago link in the development of a monetary analysis of the Great Contraction, and through that link a connection to the work of Hawtrey and, posthumously, to that of Allyn Young as well.[32]

100 Per Cent Money and Monetary-Policy Rules

We have seen that Douglas (1933, pp. 19–20) briefly canvassed the establishment of 100 per cent reserve requirements against the monetary liabilities of

---

[31] One must wonder about the depth of Viner's commitment to that point of view. It made no appearance in his 1936 review of Keynes's *General Theory*, for example, nor, incidentally, did it appear in Frank Knight's review (1937) of the same book. Reeve (1943, p. 210) noted that Viner's commitment to fiscal inflation was rather short-lived and that he "apparently later did not favour the continuance of deficits." Steindl (1995, ch. 5) has provided an account of the views of Chicago economists in the 1930s which documents their support for fiscal deficits as a means of expanding the money supply in the early 1930s. His account of Mints's views (pp. 88–93) is particularly useful.

[32] However, as Milton Friedman has pointed out to me, Hawtrey's *Currency and Credit* was on Lloyd Mints's reading list at Chicago in the early 1930s, and the fact that Douglas and Director (1931) discussed his views on fiscal policy also attests to the fact that members of the Chicago department were familiar with his work. Nevertheless, the fact remains that in the 1920s, Young had been Hawtrey's most visible supporter in American academic circles.

commercial banks. Currie independently made a similar proposal in his 1934 book. Though he was of the opinion that the experience of 1929–32 "should not be cited as evidence of the *inability* of a central bank to arrest contraction of money and bring about expansion" (Currie 1934b, p. 148, italics in original), he nevertheless believed in the desirability of a better system of monetary control "in which expansions and contractions of the supply of money could be brought about easily and quickly to any required extent" (Currie 1934b, p. 151). Specifically, he argued that "it appears to the writer that the most perfect control could be achieved by direct government issue of all money, both notes and deposits subject to check" (Currie 1934b, p. 151).

The Chicago Plan

Currie's independently developed proposal notwithstanding, *100 per cent. Money*, as Irving Fisher (1935) would call it, is usually, following Albert G. Hart (1935), labelled "the Chicago plan," and with considerable justice, if we set aside the claims of Frederick Soddy (1926), whose work was known to Frank Knight (Daly 1980). Douglas (1933) undoubtedly based his brief discussion of the idea on the unpublished memorandum on the matter by Simons et al. (1933), to which Hart drew Currie's attention as his monograph (Currie 1934b) was going to press. Furthermore, Douglas's much longer 1935 account of the issues involved in such a scheme began with the following words: "The ablest proposal in this direction is, in my opinion, that which a group of my colleagues at the University of Chicago under the leadership of Mr. H. C. Simons have set forth" (Douglas 1935, p. 184).

Hart stressed that " 'the 100 per cent system' [was] an effective remedy for the weaknesses of the banking system which now unfit it *either for automatic functioning or for use as an instrument of monetary management*" (Hart (1935, repr. 1952, p. 444, italics added). That was important, because Currie, to whose "masterly account" of the way in which "conversion of chequing deposits into cash or *vice versa* influences the total quantity of both in existence" (Hart 1935, repr. 1952, p. 444) Hart paid tribute, very clearly advocated it for the latter purpose.[33] As he had remarked in 1933, echoing the views of Hawtrey and Young,

> in such a delicate and difficult task as the determination of proper central banking policy it would appear to be a safe generalization that automatic rules render more difficult the task of central bankers, while discretionary powers facilitate it. (Currie 1933a, p. 356)

---

[33] Though at Chicago in 1935, Hart had earlier been Currie's undergraduate student at Harvard. See Sandilands (1990a, p. 25).

Simons, on the other hand, was of the opinion that "managed currency without definite, stable, legislative rules is one of the most dangerous forms of 'planning' " (Simons 1935, p. 558), and the importance which he attached to that point may be gauged from the fact that though that quotation is drawn from a review of Currie (1934a), almost the same phrases are to be found in Simons et al. (1933, pp. 4–5), Simons (1934, p. 24), and Simons (1936a, repr. 1952, p. 339). For Simons, therefore, in stark contrast to Currie, 100 per cent money was a means for implementing a monetary-policy rule that would eliminate the discretionary powers of central bankers.

A Price-Stability Rule

The rule advocated by Simons et al. (1933), after whatever reflation might be needed to reverse the effects of the recent contraction, was maintenance of a constant money supply. In that memorandum, and again the next year in Simons's well-known pamphlet *A Positive Program for Laissez-Faire*, the merits of a range of policy rules were discussed: "At one extreme is the rule of fixing the quantity (M) or the total turnover (MV); at the other is the rule of stabilizing some index of commodity prices" (Simons 1934, pp. 24–25). In the 1933 memorandum, the last of those, which had, of course, been the centrepiece of Fisher's long-standing advocacy of monetary-policy rules, was rejected:

> It is sadly lacking in definiteness as a rule of long-run management. Thus it leaves too much room for administrative discretion and political manipulation. (This will be clear immediately to anyone familiar with the technical, statistical problems of price-level measurement over long periods.) (Simons et al. 1933, suppl. p. 7)

Stabilizing MV – the neutral money principle – would not do either, because of the difficulties in establishing procedures for offsetting changes in V

> ... without in effect granting to the monetary authority large freedom for discretionary action[.] Moreover, if we be not alarmed by the thought of some discretionary action, is there any feasible way of permitting discretionary measures in the short-run and still assuring realization of the long-run objectives? (Simons et al. 1933, suppl. p. 4)

In any event, because "some of us are inclined to feel that the disturbances occasioned merely by changes of velocity are unlikely to be of serious magnitude" (Simons et al. 1933, suppl. p. 3), a constant-money-supply rule would in practice suffice to stabilize the level of input prices, and money wages in particular, which Simons believed to be sticky. Such a rule, moreover, combined with 100 per cent money, would also imply a balanced-budget rule for fiscal policy, a desirable outcome in its own right:

> One may well question the expediency of permitting Congress to spend more funds than it provides through the imposition of taxes. The financing of expenditures merely by increase of the Reserve Banks' circulation is so easy and attractive from the legislator's point of view that even moderate resort to the expedient threatens abuse. (Simons et al. 1933, suppl. pp. 4–5)

It is nevertheless interesting to note that in his 1934 discussion of those matters, Simons no longer expressed a preference among alternative monetary rules and that by 1936 he had come to favour a price-level stabilization rule essentially identical with that which Fisher and his associates had long advocated, and which had been embodied in the Strong bills of 1926 and 1928, as well as the Goldsborough bill of 1932, among other pieces of draft legislation. Simons's change of mind on that question stemmed from an appreciation of the importance of what we would now call "the Lucas critique." By 1936, he had come to fear that

> the fixing of the quantity of the circulating media might merely serve to increase the perverse variability in the amounts of "near-moneys" and in the degree of their general acceptability, just as the restrictions on the issue of bank notes presumably served to hasten the development of deposit (checking-account) banking. (Simons 1936a, repr. 1952, p. 341)[34]

If Simons's position on the appropriate goal for monetary policy had thus converged on that to which Irving Fisher had long been committed, so, too, did Fisher adopt as one of his own causes the Chicago plan of "100 per cent. money" as a means for attaining that goal. But it was only on matters of monetary-policy prescription that the views of Fisher and Simons (as well as Paul Douglas) converged. There were, as we have seen, large differences among the theoretical analyses from which their individual support for those measures derived.

Concluding Comments

There can be no neat summary of the complex literature which the Great Contraction engendered in the United States. It is difficult to think of any explanation for the event itself, or any policy position regarding how to cope

---

[34] The reference there was almost certainly to the effects that Sir Robert Peel's 1844 Bank Charter Act, which created a Bank of England monopoly over the note issue, had on the subsequent development of deposit banking in England. Simons's colleague Viner was well aware of those effects, as readers of his *Studies in the Theory of International Trade* (1937) will be aware. Thus, Friedman's argument (1967) that Simons would have supported a money-growth rule, had he been aware of the monetary facts of the depression, cannot be sustained. Indeed, Simons, as a reviewer of Currie (1934b), must have been well aware of those facts (Simons 1935).

with it, that did not have its adherents. Moreover, virtually every theme appearing in the European debates which preceded the publication of Keynes's *General Theory* found an echo somewhere in American discussions. And yet the emphases accorded various problems and viewpoints differed on the two sides of the Atlantic by more than enough to give the American literature its own distinctive character. First, and notably, less attention was paid by American economists than by their European contemporaries to formal theoretical discussions of the role of the capital market in co-ordinating intertemporal choices, at least as far as the analysis of economic fluctuations was concerned. Explicitly Austrian ideas, such as Haberler imported to Harvard in the early 1930s, did not catch on in America to the extent that they did, for example, in Britain at about the same time. There was no American equivalent to Lionel Robbins, an established senior figure in an important department of economics who adopted and promoted them.

That is surely why, outside of the Anderson-Willis group, there was no organized opposition as a matter of principle among American academic economists to expansionary monetary policy or public-works expenditures. There was, nevertheless, as we have seen, considerable, albeit pragmatic, scepticism about their likely effectiveness, and among some rather distinguished commentators – Schumpeter and Hansen, to name but two. There was also considerable confusion, notably among some of the contributors to *The Economics of the Recovery Program*. The balance of opinion in America, on the specific question of the capacity of monetary policy to combat the contraction, was much as it was in regard to analogous questions in Europe. American economists who put great faith in orthodox monetary policy were in a minority, just as were their European counterparts.

Among that latter group, Lauchlin Currie was outstanding, and he quickly acquired great influence after following Viner to Washington in 1934, becoming a senior adviser to Marriner Eccles at the Federal Reserve Board and, in due course, the first economic adviser on the White House staff. Though Currie's views on what had caused the depression and what might have been done to offset it during 1929–32 did not change with the passage of time, his opinion on what monetary policy was capable of achieving in dealing with contemporary circumstances did change, and radically so, as the 1930s progressed. It was not Currie, but rather Clark Warburton (1966; Bordo and Schwartz 1979) who was to keep the monetary interpretation of the depression alive from the late 1930s onwards, until Friedman and Schwartz (1963) took it up. After 1934, Currie became a vigorous proponent of income redistribution as a means for bringing about increased consumer expenditure, and of fiscal deficits as a means of providing a ready supply of securities for the banking system to purchase, thereby mobilizing their large and steadily growing stock of excess reserves.[35] The first set of measures would in due course become associated with Keynesian economics, and so to a degree would the second, though it is worth noting that Currie's particular version of the case for deficit finance bore a closer resemblance to the possibility which Hawtrey (1925) had broached, albeit briefly and purely hypothetically, as a means for breaking a credit deadlock that would not succumb to open-market operations, than to anything that Keynes would propose in the 1930s.

Perhaps the most distinctive American contribution to the monetary-policy literature of the 1920s and early 1930s was the extensive discussion of monetary-policy rules which it contained, along with accompanying proposals for 100 per cent money.[36] The circumstances of the 1930s, however, robbed those proposals of immediate relevance. They were, after all, prescriptions for staying out of trouble, not for getting out of it, as their proponents well understood. The literature which discussed such rules was to have considerable influence on post–World War II debates, but it was either irrelevant to the immediate concerns of the 1930s or, to the extent that it also discussed the means whereby stability might first be restored, not really distinct from a much wider body of work. As we have seen, by 1935 or thereabouts, Currie, Douglas, Fisher, and Simons all favoured 100 per cent money, and the latter three also supported a price-stability rule, but their views on why such measures were desirable, on what had caused the depression, and on how it might be cured prior to the implementation of their proposals for monetary policy, were very different indeed. The fact is that the single most salient feature of American writing on money and the cycle between 1929 and 1936 was the absence of any kind of theoretical consensus to underpin its widespread (though by no means universal) advocacy of monetary and fiscal expansion.

---

[35] For a discussion of the evolution of Currie's thought after 1934, see Currie (1978) and Sandilands (1990a, ch. 3). As Sandilands (1990a, p. 91) noted, Currie had introduced arguments for fiscal deficits into his teaching while still at Harvard, evidently to the annoyance of his superiors. However, those arguments did not appear in his written work until after 1934. Indeed, even in 1935, after his arrival in Washington, Currie defended his 1934 monograph in some detail against a scathing but, in light of the latter's views, quite predictable attack by Benjamin Anderson. See Anderson (1935) and Currie (1935). Davis (1971) made no mention of Currie in his book on American pioneers of the "new economics."

[36] The reader is, however, reminded that Currie, too, was an advocate of 100 per cent money. Once in Washington in 1934, he presented a plan for implementation of the proposal to Henry Morgenthau, then secretary of the Treasury. That plan was reprinted in the 1968 edition of *The Supply and Control of Money* (Currie 1934b). By 1935, Currie, as adviser to Marriner Eccles, was deeply involved in preparing the Federal Reserve System's draft version of what eventually became the Banking Act of 1935. As Ronnie J. Phillips has shown, though Currie, a key sympathizer with the "Chicago Plan," was very much an influential insider in the preparation of that legislation, 100 per cent money failed to be incorporated into it, not because that proposal was found intellectually wanting, but "as a matter of pure political expediency" (Phillips 1993, p. 19).

PART IV

Keynes, the Classics, and IS-LM

CHAPTER 10

The *General Theory*

The Nature of the Book

More has been written about the *General Theory* than about any other work in twentieth-century economics. That it is a contentious book is beyond question, but its reputation for being difficult to read is less obviously justified. Much depends on how close a reading it is given. Anyone paying careful attention to the book's every word certainly runs into many obscurities of detail, particularly in its later chapters, but the *General Theory*'s overall structure is clear and is reflected with great precision in its title. Keynes promised his readers *The General Theory of Employment, Interest and Money*, and that is what he delivered, with the component parts of the theory in question initially being taken up in just that order.

The book's "main purpose is to deal with difficult questions of theory, and only in the second place with the applications of this theory to practice" (Keynes 1936, p. xxi); it was "primarily a study of the forces which determine changes in the scale of output and employment as a whole" (Keynes 1936, p. xxii); and its central conclusion was that "a monetary economy . . . is essentially one in which changing views about the future are capable of influencing the quantity of employment and not merely its direction" (Keynes 1936, p. xxii). But though the role of money was essential to the book's argument, the nature of that argument was such that "technical monetary detail falls into the background" (Keynes 1936, p. xxii), which perhaps explains why, in contrast to the *Treatise*, questions of the determination of the money supply simply were not discussed.

The Theory of Employment

The *Treatise on Money* (1930a) lacked a satisfactory account of endogenous fluctuations in output and employment. As Keynes himself put it,

> my so-called "fundamental equations" were an instantaneous picture taken on the assumption of a given output. They attempted to show how, assuming the given output, forces could develop which involved a profit-disequilibrium, and thus required a change in the level of output. But the dynamic development, as distinct from the instantaneous picture, was left incomplete and extremely confused. (Keynes 1936, p. xxii)

From the standpoint of the *Treatise*, it would have been natural to incorporate any extension of its analysis along such lines into a theory of the cycle; but the *General Theory* is not primarily about the cycle.[1] Though the framework it provides does have obvious applications to that area, which Keynes took up in Chapter 22 of the book, it is more immediately a contribution to the literature discussed earlier in Chapter 7, on secular unemployment.

Keynes's Version of Classical Theory

The book begins with an account of what Keynes called the "Classical" theory of employment, to which his "general" theory was to be contrasted, an essentially Marshallian Framework featuring the supply of and demand for labour as functions of the real wage. That "Classical" theory, said Keynes, was

> compatible with what may be called "frictional" unemployment . . . also
> . . . with "voluntary" unemployment due to the refusal or inability of a unit
> of labour, as a result of legislation or social practices or of combination for
> collective bargaining or of slow response to change or of mere human
> obstinacy, to accept a reward corresponding to the value of the product
> attributable to its marginal productivity. (Keynes 1936, p. 6)

Application of the theory in question was, in his view, complicated, to an extent not always appreciated by its exponents, by the fact that wage bargaining was in fact carried out in money terms rather than real terms. Simply to postulate money-wage stickiness did not suffice to overcome the problems involved. There were empirical difficulties:

> . . . the contention that the unemployment which characterises a depression
> is due to a refusal by labour to accept a reduction of money-wages is not
> clearly supported by the facts. It is not very plausible to assert that unem-
> ployment in the United States in 1932 was due either to labour obstinately
> refusing to accept a reduction in money wages or to its obstinately demand-
> ing a real wage beyond what the productivity of the economic machine was
> capable of furnishing. (Keynes 1936, p. 9)

But also, and crucially, Keynes saw theoretical difficulties too: "There may exist no expedient by which labour as a whole can reduce its *real* wage to a given figure by making revised *money* bargains with the entrepreneurs. This

---

[1] I would draw the reader's attention to the extensive literature dealing with the evolution of Keynes's economic thought between the publication of the *Treatise* (1930) and the *General Theory* (1936), which is not dealt with here. See, for example, Patinkin and Leith (1977), Kahn (1985), Rymes (1989), Clarke (1988, ch. 11), Dimand (1988), Moggridge (1992, ch. 21), and Skidelsky (1992, ch. 15). Harry Johnson's 1977 contribution to the Patinkin and Leith volume is a fascinating attempt at reconstruction of the socio-intellectual milieu at Cambridge at that time.

will be our contention'' (Keynes 1936, p. 13, italics in original). Note the phrase ''labour as a whole'' here. As we have seen, Pigou (1933) had earlier shown himself to be aware of the fact that the determination of money wages and real wages, as well as employment, at the level of the economy as a whole involved general-equilibrium mechanisms; but he had presented those issues as complicating the application of his Marshallian framework.[2]

Involuntary Unemployment

Keynes, on the other hand, argued that those issues fundamentally changed the nature of the problem; for him, a new and general theory of employment was required to take account of them, one which would explain not just the frictional and voluntary unemployment with which ''Classical'' theory could deal, but which could also, and crucially, deal with involuntary unemployment, which he defined as follows:

> *Men are involuntarily unemployed if, in the event of a small rise in the price of wage-goods relatively to the money-wage, both the aggregate supply of labour willing to work for the current money-wage and the aggregate demand for it at that wage would be greater than the existing volume of employment.* (Keynes 1936, p. 15, italics in original)

In Keynes's view of the world, that is to say, workers could remain unemployed and the real wage rate could remain too high not just because of various institutional rigidities and other frictions particular to the labour market but because the workings of a monetary economy may (not must) prevent the real wage from coming into equality with labour's full-employment level of marginal productivity through any wage-bargaining process. Keynes's theory of employment was thus to be *general* precisely in the sense that it permitted that possibility (in his view, the empirically typical one, as we shall see) to be analysed along with the others.

Keynes did not for one moment deny the existence or empirical importance of labour-market rigidities. When he referred to wage flexibility in the *General Theory* he usually characterized it as a ''policy,'' that is to say, something to be brought about by government action, rather than as a phenomenon likely to occur naturally in any actual labour market; and, for much of the book, he adopted the working assumption that

> the money-wage and other factor costs are constant per unit of labour employed. But this simplification, with which we shall dispense later, is introduced solely to facilitate the exposition. The essential character of the argument is precisely the same whether or not money-wages, etc., are liable to change. (Keynes 1936, p. 27)

---

[2] For discussion, see Chapter 7, ''General-Equilibrium Considerations.''

That last conclusion followed because the "essential character" of Keynes's theory of employment was that "given what we shall call the community's propensity to consume, the equilibrium level of employment . . . will depend on the amount of current investment" (Keynes 1936, p. 27), and that had nothing, or next to nothing, to do with the labour market. It did, however, have everything to do with "views about the future," as he had warned readers in his Preface, and as he elaborated in Chapter 5 of the book itself, "Expectation as Determining Output and Employment."

Expectations and the Determinants of Effective Demand

We have already seen that in the inter-war years, appreciation of the importance of expectations far outran economists' abilities to analyse the phenomena associated with them, and Keynes's manner of finessing that problem is worth explicit attention.[3] He divided expectations into short-term and long-term, treating the former as determined, and accurately so, by immediately past experience, and the latter (usually) as exogenous. Current employment decisions depended proximately upon short-term expectations, which were "concerned with the price which a manufacturer can expect to get for his 'finished' output at the time when he commits himself to starting the process which will produce it" (Keynes 1936, p. 46).

Because, however,

> it would be too complicated to work out the expectations *de novo* whenever a productive process was being started . . . it is sensible for producers to base their expectations on the assumption that the most recently realised results will continue, except in so far as there are definite reasons for expecting a change. Thus in practice there is a large overlap between the effects on employment of the realised sale-proceeds of recent output and those of the sale-proceeds expected from current input; and producers' forecasts are more often gradually modified in the light of results than in anticipation of prospective changes. (Keynes 1936, p. 51)

Current output decisions, that is to say, though taken to meet *expected* sales volume, or *effective demand*, as Keynes, borrowing, though without attribution, a phrase which Hawtrey had regularly been using for more than twenty years, called that aggregate (cf. Keynes 1936, p. 55, and Hawtrey 1913, pp. 4, 78, and 224, for his earliest usages), were assumed in fact to depend on the *recently realized* value of that variable. Short-term expectations were thus pushed well into the background, and, operationally speaking, Keynes's concept of effective demand became indistinguishable from Hawtrey's, though

---

[3] The Stockholm School economists, in particular, were important in that respect, not least for the problems they encountered in trying to make expectations endogenous. For a discussion, see Chapter 3, "The Role of Expectations."

his separate analyses of consumption and investment as the key components of the demand for output as a whole have no parallel in the latter's writings.[4]

Consumption and the Multiplier

Keynes discussed many factors which might influence what he called the "propensity to consume," including consumers' income expectations, but he nevertheless ended up asserting that

> the fundamental psychological law, upon which we are entitled to depend with great confidence both *a priori* from our knowledge of human nature and from the detailed facts of experience, is that men are disposed, as a rule and on the average, to increase their consumption as their income increases, but not by as much as the increase in their income. (Keynes 1936, p. 96)

Quite typically, he cited no source in which the "detailed facts of experience" were documented. However, the "psychological law" which he invoked clearly was a qualitative version of the relationship between income and consumption expenditure postulated by Warming (1932) in his comment on Kahn's analysis of the employment multiplier.[5] In Warming's numerical example, 75 per cent of an increment to income was spent, and 25 per cent was "lost to saving," so that the static multiplier was equal to four. Keynes derived the algebraic formula linking the static income multiplier and what he called the "marginal propensity to consume," though confusingly he used the symbol k to signify the multiplier, and $(1 - 1/k)$ the marginal propensity to consume, whereas Warming, following the style of Kahn, used k to designate the marginal propensity to consume (without, of course, using that phrase).

Keynes's theory of employment nevertheless amounted to a great deal more than a minor variation upon the results from a couple of articles by

---

[4] Hawtrey objected to Keynes's use of the phrase "effective demand" to refer to an "expected magnitude," in a letter of June 1935 (Keynes 1971–88, vol. XIII, pp. 567–568) and in another of November 7, 1935 (Keynes 1971–88, vol. XIII, pp. 596–597). Keynes's reply of November 8, 1935, claimed that the term "effective demand" had gone out of use in modern economics, telling Hawtrey that "effective demand always reflects the current expectation of actual demand whether it is arrived at by a careful attempt at elaborate foresight on the part of entrepreneurs, or merely by revision at short intervals on the basis of trial and error" (Keynes 1971–88, vol. XIII, p. 603). Hawtrey's response of November 20, 1935 (Keynes 1971–88, vol. XIII, pp. 610–611) was remarkable in that he did not draw Keynes's attention to his own frequent use of the term, but pointed out, correctly in my view, that "hypothetical expected demand is not really useful or material to your exposition. Practically the only cause determining employment that you deal with is actual sales" (Keynes 1971–88, vol. XIII, p. 611). That, of course, made Keynes's concept identical with that long deployed by Hawtrey. Once more Hawtrey was too polite to draw attention to that fact.

[5] See Chapter 7, "Warming's Clarification," for a discussion of this matter and for Keynes's possible, but never acknowledged, debt to Warming.

Kahn and Warming concerning the impact of public-works expenditures on employment and output. He used the multiplier to link shifts in the long-term expectations of investors to variations in output and therefore employment, and there was no parallel in their analyses to Keynes's treatment of those expectations:

> . . . in the case of durable goods, the producer's short-term expectations are based on the current long-term expectations of the investor [and] it is of the nature of long-term expectations that they cannot be checked at short intervals in the light of realized results. Moreover . . . they are liable to sudden revision. Thus the factor of current long-term expectations cannot be even approximately eliminated or replaced by realised results. (Keynes 1936, p. 51)

That emphasis on the forward-looking nature of investment decisions brought the multiplier into direct contact with the central theoretical question of the inter-temporal allocation of resources. The decisions to save and invest were taken independently of one another, by different agents: ''. . . the amount of saving is an outcome of the collective behaviour of individual consumers and the amount of investment of the collective behaviour of individual entrepreneurs'' (Keynes 1936, p. 63), but the aggregate outcomes of those decisions had to be equal to one another, and multiplier-driven changes in output and employment, rather than variations in the rate of interest, provided the mechanism whereby that was achieved.

Keynes's exposition of that particular matter was, nevertheless, both confused and confusing. The helpful Swedish distinction between *ex ante* and *ex post* was not part of his intellectual equipment, and having abandoned the eccentric definitions of ''income'' and ''saving'' which he had deployed in the *Treatise*, he often wrote as if equality between saving and investment stemmed purely from the conventional definitions of those terms, which definitions he had by then adopted, thus presenting what we would now call the static multiplier as something looking very like a tautological relationship.[6] Thus he argued that ''the logical theory of the multiplier . . . holds good continuously, without time lag, at all moments in time'' (Keynes 1936, p. 122), though he also allowed that

> an unforeseen, or imperfectly foreseen, expansion in the capital-goods industries does not have an instantaneous effect of equal amount on the

----

[6] Note that Lindahl had written to Keynes in 1934, drawing Keynes's attention to his own paper on ''the dynamic pricing problem'' (Lindahl 1934) and to the distinction between planned and realized values of saving and investment he there deployed, noting its relationship to the analysis of the *Treatise*. Keynes's response to Lindahl, in a letter of December 8, 1934, can best be described as polite but uncomprehending. On all of that, see Steiger (1971, pp. 204ff.). I am grateful to Michael Trautwein for drawing my attention to that exchange.

aggregate of investment but causes a gradual increase of the latter; and . . . may cause a temporary departure of the marginal propensity to consume away from its nominal value, followed, however, by a gradual return to it. (Keynes 1936, p. 123)

That Keynes did indeed grasp that an equilibrating mechanism was at work was nevertheless apparent from the following passage:

> The reconciliation of the identity between saving and investment with the apparent "free-will" of the individual to save what he chooses irrespective of what he or others may be investing . . . is closely analogous with the proposition which harmonises the liberty, which every individual possesses, to change, whenever he chooses, the amount of money he holds, with the necessity for the total amount of money, which individual balances add up to, to be exactly equal to the amount of cash which the banking system has created. (Keynes 1936, p. 84)

Keynes's analysis of inter-temporal co-ordination issues differed from that of the Austrians most obviously in emphasizing that it was income and employment, rather than the rate of interest, that moved to reconcile saving and investment decisions. But that difference reflected another, which arguably was more fundamental. The Austrians thought of saving and investment plans as the outcomes of calculated maximizing behaviour on the part of savers and investors, but Keynes did not think of either activity as an expression of any kind of optimizing behaviour. For the Austrians, a failure of the capital market to co-ordinate those plans, stemming from the operations of the monetary system, was the source of economic fluctuations, and an appropriate redesign of those operations was a potential remedy for the problem. Keynes certainly doubted the capacity of the rate of interest to co-ordinate saving and investment in a monetary economy, but for him the problem arose not from the conduct of monetary policy but from the very nature of the decisions themselves and the nature of the economy in which they were made.

The Marginal Efficiency of Capital

We have already seen that for Keynes, the volume of saving resulted from the working of a "fundamental psychological law," and as we shall now see, he was, even more than other Cambridge economists, utterly sceptical about what we might term the "rationality" of investment decisions. Though Keynes did not usually follow Lavington, Pigou, and even Robertson in using the word "error" in that context, he clearly believed that the phenomenon to which they had given that label was pervasive and was so deeply rooted in the way in which individual agents made their decisions as to render a significant degree of collectivization necessary for smooth functioning of the economy.[7]

The central concept in Keynes's theory of investment was what he called the *marginal efficiency of capital*: "that rate of discount which would make the present value of the series of annuities given by the returns expected from the capital-asset during its life just equal to its supply price" (Keynes 1936, p. 135). He acknowledged that that concept was identical with Fisher's "rate of return over cost" (1930a) and, moreover, that he was using it for the same purpose (Keynes 1936, pp. 140–141). If the marginal efficiency of capital exceeded (fell short of) the rate of interest, investment would (not) be profitable and therefore would (not) be undertaken. Crucially, however, Keynes took great pains to point out that the marginal efficiency of capital was defined in terms of "the *expectation* of yield . . . of the capital-asset" (Keynes 1936, p. 136, italics in original). That forward-looking theme was every bit as central to his analysis as it was to the analyses of those other economists who followed Fisher's lead in the theory of capital, namely, the Stockholm School, just as was its implication that long-term expectations about the future had consequences for the present:

> It is by reason of the existence of durable equipment that the economic future is linked to the present. It is, therefore, consonant with, and agreeable to, our broad principles of thought, that the expectation of the future should affect the present through the demand price for durable equipment. (Keynes 1936, p. 146)

Expectations, Speculation, and Enterprise

Keynes's own variation on Cambridge scepticism about the capacity of individual agents to deal with the problems inherent in forming long-term expectations, and about the consequences of that for the working of market mechanisms, came into full play at that point:

> The outstanding fact is the extreme precariousness of the basis of knowledge on which our estimates of prospective yield have to be made. Our knowledge of the factors which will govern the yield of an investment some years hence is usually very slight and often negligible. . . . In fact, those who seriously attempt to make any such estimate are often so much in the minority that their behaviour does not govern the market. (Keynes 1936, pp. 149–150)

---

[7] The analyses of Lavington and Pigou were discussed in Chapter 4. They did not explicitly recommend a significant degree of collectivization for economic life, but the general tone of their argument was sceptical of the capacity of a market economy to function smoothly if left to itself.

The problem there, he thought, like Marshall and Pigou before him, was greatly exacerbated by the existence of organized stock markets. They rendered investments which were quite illiquid from the point of view of the economy as a whole liquid for the individual, and in the inevitable absence of information about their true prospects for profitability, the valuation of those investments at any moment became a matter of a *convention*, whose essence "lies in assuming that the existing state of affairs will continue indefinitely, except in so far as we have reasons to expect a change" (Keynes 1936, p. 152). Moreover, and crucially,

> it might have been supposed that competition between expert professionals, possessing judgement and knowledge beyond that of the average private investor, would correct the vagaries of the ignorant individual left to himself. It happens, however, . . . most of these persons are, in fact, largely concerned, not with making superior long-term forecasts of the probable yield of an investment over its whole life, but with foreseeing changes in the conventional basis of valuation a short time ahead of the general public. (Keynes 1936, p. 154)

Thus, Keynes argued, the expectations upon which the marginal efficiency of capital depended were largely divorced from those long-term prospects which nowadays we call *fundamentals*, and the informational problems inherent in making rational investment decisions, far from being mitigated by the workings of market mechanisms, were exacerbated by their failure:[8]

> The social object of skilled investment should be to defeat the dark forces of time and ignorance which envelope our future. The actual, private object of the most skilled investment to-day is "to beat the gun," as the Americans so well express it, to outwit the crowd, and to pass the bad, or depreciating, half-crown to the other fellow. (Keynes 1936, p. 155)

Keynes also believed that those problems were becoming worse with the passage of time. Using "the term *speculation* for the activity of forecasting the psychology of the market, and the term *enterprise* for the activity of forecasting the prospective yield of assets over their whole life," he conceded that "it is by no means always the case that speculation predominates over enterprise," but he also argued that "as the organisation of investment markets improves, the risk of the predominance of speculation does, however, increase" (Keynes 1936, p. 158, italics in original). He cited Wall Street, in

---

[8] Karl Brunner (1987) and Allan Meltzer (1988) both stressed the importance of that aspect of Keynes's analysis, and both treated it as an empirical hypothesis which, if true, would support Keynes's policy conclusions. The differences of those "monetarists" from Keynes on matters of policy were thus based on a difference of opinion about how long-term investment decisions were actually taken in a market economy, rather than on some *a priori* ideological preference for laissez-faire.

particular, as an example of that unfortunate tendency.[9] That market's success in directing "new investment into the most profitable channels in terms of future yield, cannot be claimed as one of the outstanding triumphs of *laissez-faire* capitalism" (Keynes 1936, p. 159).

"Even apart from the instability due to speculation," he saw other problems arising from the inherently forward-looking nature of investment decisions:

> Most, probably, of our decisions to do something positive, the full consequences of which will be drawn out over many days to come, can only be taken as a result of animal spirits – of a spontaneous urge to action rather than inaction, and not as the outcome of a weighted average of quantitative benefits multiplied by quantitative probabilities. (Keynes 1936, p. 161)

Moreover, when animal spirits were "dimmed . . . enterprise will fade and die; – though fears of loss may have a basis no more reasonable than hopes of profit had before" (Keynes 1936, p. 162). Though Keynes did not believe that those considerations rendered investment behaviour completely insensitive to rates of interest, they did not leave him with much faith in the stability or reliability of the relationship between those variables.

The Role of the Rate of Interest

The *General Theory*'s treatment of interest theory rests upon the observation that if the interaction of saving and investment determines the levels of income and employment, it cannot simultaneously determine the interest rate:

> But the notion that the rate of interest is the balancing factor which brings the demand for saving in the shape of new investment forthcoming at a given rate of interest into equality with the supply of saving which results at that rate of interest from the community's psychological propensity to save, breaks down as soon as we perceive that it is impossible to deduce the rate of interest merely from a knowledge of these two factors. (Keynes 1936, p. 165)

Liquidity Preference

Keynes's response to the puzzle implied there followed immediately, and it is worth quoting at some length:

---

[9] Note that "enterprise" was being used in a rather narrower sense than in the *Treatise*, where it was contrasted with "thrift" and seemed to refer to investment decisions taken for whatever reason. In the foregoing quotation it was being contrasted with "speculation" and hence focused a little more narrowly on long-term investment.

The psychological time-preferences of an individual require two distinct sets of decisions to carry them out completely. The first is concerned with that aspect of time-preference which I have called the *propensity to consume*. . . .

But this [saving] decision having been made, there is a further decision which awaits him, namely, in *what form* he will hold the command over future consumption which he has reserved, whether out of his current income or from previous savings. . . . In other words, what is the degree of his *liquidity-preference* – where an individual's liquidity-preference is given by a schedule of the amounts of his resources, valued in terms of money or of wage units, which he will wish to retain in the form of money in different sets of circumstances?

We shall find that the mistake in the accepted theories of the rate of interest lies in their attempting to derive the rate of interest from the first of these two constituents of psychological time-preference to the neglect of the second. . . .

. . . the rate of interest at any time, being the reward for parting with liquidity, is a measure of the unwillingness of those who possess money to part with their liquid control over it. The rate of interest is not the "price" which brings into equilibrium the demand for resources to invest with the readiness to abstain from present consumption. It is the "price" which equilibrates the desire to hold wealth in the form of cash with the available quantity of cash. (Keynes 1936, pp. 166–167, italics in original)

An essential feature of Keynes's theory of "liquidity-preference" was its invocation of "the ancient distinction between the use of money for the transaction of current business and its use as a store of wealth" (Keynes 1936, p. 168).[10] That non-interest-bearing money would be held for the former purpose, as a result of what he termed "transactions" and "precautionary" motives, even if other interest-bearing assets were available, presented no problem, because "it is obvious that up to a point it is worth while to sacrifice a certain amount of interest for the convenience of liquidity" (Keynes 1936, p. 168), but when it came to holding money as a store of wealth, it was a different matter:

But, given that the rate of interest is never negative, why should anyone prefer to hold his wealth in a form which yields little or no interest to holding it in a form which yields interest. . . . There is . . . a necessary condition failing which the existence of a liquidity-preference for money as a means of holding wealth could not exist.

This necessary condition is the existence of *uncertainty* as to the future of the rate of interest. (Keynes 1936, p. 168, italics in original)

---

[10] Keynes gave no reference to any ancient source for that allegedly ancient distinction, which is not surprising, since it was in fact rather a new one. On the absence of money's store-of-value role from nineteenth-century discussions of money's functions, see Laidler (1991, pp. 8ff.).

Uncertainty and the Demand for Money

Two things would follow from such uncertainty: First, because the value of future rates of interest was uncertain, agents would demand a risk premium for holding bonds that might yield a loss should they have to be liquidated before maturity: "The actuarial profit or mathematical expectation of gain calculated in accordance with the existing probabilities – if it can be so calculated, which is doubtful – must be sufficient to compensate for the risk of disappointment" (Keynes 1936, p. 169). Second, given the existence of "an organised market for dealing in debts" (Keynes 1936, p. 169), there would exist the possibility of making a profit from betting against prevailing market sentiment as to the future value of the rate of interest:

> Just as we found that the marginal efficiency of capital is fixed, not by the "best" opinion, but by the market valuation as determined by mass psychology, so also expectations as to the future of the rate of interest as fixed by mass psychology have their reactions on liquidity preference; – but with this addition that the individual, who believes that future rates of interest will be above the rates assumed by the market, has a reason for keeping actual liquid cash, whilst the individual who differs from the market in the other direction will have a motive for borrowing money for short periods in order to purchase debts of longer term. The market price will be fixed at the point at which the sales of the "bears" and the purchases of the "bulls" are balanced. (Keynes 1936, p. 170)

That use of the terms "bull" and "bear" was an explicit reminder that Keynes's latest analysis of the demand for money as a store of value was essentially the one he had deployed in the *Treatise*. One should note, however, that the stickiness of expectations about future interest rates that was there postulated was exactly contrary to the sensitivity of those expectations to current rates that he had assumed in the course of his defence of the powers of monetary policy in the earlier work.[11] The new postulate, for which Keynes offered no empirical evidence, was nevertheless to become the stuff of a generation of textbooks, yielding, as a special case, the "liquidity-trap" doctrine which later orthodoxy would express in terms of the LM curve becoming horizontal at some low level of the rate of interest.

Keynes himself was ambiguous about the empirical relevance of that last possibility:

> As a rule, we can suppose that the schedule of liquidity-preference relating the quantity of money to the rate of interest is given by a smooth curve which shows the rate of interest falling as the quantity of money is increased. (Keynes 1936, p. 171)

---

[11] On this point, see Chapter 6, "Monetary Policy's Transmission Mechanism."

That general result was heavily

> dependent on the existence of a *variety* of opinion about what is uncertain.
> . . . [If] we are to control the activity of the economic system by changing
> the quantity of money, it is important that opinions [about the future value
> of the rate of interest] should differ. (Keynes 1936, p. 172)

If, however, circumstances arose in which there was something approaching
unanimity about that future value, then "even a large increase in the quantity
of money may exert a comparatively small influence on the rate of interest
. . . a small change in present rates may cause a mass movement into cash"
(Keynes 1936, p. 172). In such a situation, attempts at controlling the level
of economic activity through variations in the money supply would become
less effective, a state of affairs more likely to occur "in the United States,
where everyone tends to hold the same opinion at the same time, than in
England where differences of opinion are more usual" (Keynes 1936,
p. 172).

   That reference to the United States was not merely gratuitous, for although,
a little later in the *General Theory*, Keynes claimed that he knew "of no
example, . . . hitherto" of "liquidity-preference [becoming] virtually absolute" (Keynes 1936, p. 207), he immediately went on to discuss "examples
of a complete breakdown of stability in the rate of interest, due to the liquidity
function flattening out in one direction *or the other*" (Keynes 1936, p. 207,
italics added). The discussion in question was brief, and, to be sure, it dealt
mainly with a flattening-out of the function relative to the vertical axis in
conditions of what we would now call hyperinflation. But Keynes did give
one example of the curve flattening out in the other direction, albeit under
"very abnormal circumstances": ". . . in the United States at certain dates in
1932 there was a . . . crisis of liquidation, when scarcely anyone could be
induced to part with holdings of money on any reasonable terms" (Keynes
1936, pp. 207–208).[12]

Wage Flexibility

Chapter 19 of the *General Theory* bears the title "Changes in Money Wages"
and begins with an exposition of Keynes's interpretation of what he called
the "Classical Theory" of the influence of money-wage flexibility on employment:

---

[12] Recall the disagreements among Paul Douglas (1933) and W. R. Burgess (1936) and Lauchlin
Currie (1934b) regarding that episode, as discussed in Chapter 9. It clearly provided one of
the key "stylized facts" underlying the evolution of monetary economics in the 1930s and
1940s, and the interpretation that Keynes was offering for it was the conventionally accepted
one. That was why Friedman and Schwartz's revival (1963) of Currie's view was initially so
controversial and ultimately so influential.

The argument simply is that a reduction in money wages will *cet. par.* stimulate demand by diminishing the price of the finished product, and will therefore increase output and employment up to the point where the reduction which labour has agreed to accept in its money-wages is just offset by the diminishing marginal efficiency of labour as output (from a given equipment) is increased. (Keynes 1936, p. 257)

Keynes was of the opinion that the application of that argument to the economy as a whole rested on what amounted to a fallacy of composition:

This conception is then transferred without substantial modification to industry as a whole; and it is supposed, by a parity of reasoning, that we have a demand schedule for labour in industry as a whole relating the quantity of employment to different levels of wages. . . .

If this is the groundwork of the argument . . . surely it is fallacious. For the demand schedules for particular industries can only be constructed on some fixed assumption as to the nature of the demand and supply schedules of other industries and as to the amount of the aggregate effective demand. . . . whilst no one would wish to deny the proposition that a reduction in money-wages *accompanied by the same aggregate effective demand as before* will be associated with an increase in employment, the precise question at issue is whether the reduction in money-wages will or will not be accompanied by the same aggregate effective demand as before measured in money, or, at any rate, by an aggregate effective demand which is not reduced in full proportion to the reduction in money-wages. (Keynes 1936, pp. 259–260, italics in original)

It is quite evident from our earlier discussion in Chapter 7, "General-Equilibrium Considerations," that Pigou (1933), for one, was well aware of that problem and discussed it at some length, but Keynes either chose to ignore that fact or was unable to make a connection between Pigou's approach and his own.[13]

Money Wages and Effective Demand

The critical mechanisms requiring analysis, as far as Keynes was concerned, were those underlying the influence (if any) of money-wage cuts on the factors determining effective demand, "on the propensity to consume for the community as a whole, or on the schedule of marginal efficiencies of capital,

---

[13] One could, however, make the case that Keynes's characterization of that "classical" position could have applied to many expositions before the publication of Pigou (1933), including that of Marshall and Marshall (1879), which more than any other work brought wage stickiness into the picture as a key to explaining why the cycle involved fluctuations in employment. Their argument did posit flexible prices, sticky money wages, and hence a counter-cyclical movement of real wages, and it did not systematically investigate feedbacks from lower employment to the demand for output, and related variables.

or on the rate of interest'' (Keynes 1936, p. 262). Keynes did not expect much in the way of effects operating through the propensity to consume, and he dealt with them only briefly. Such effects as might occur would hinge on the redistributive consequences of a fall in money wages and of its repercussions on prices. Those would favour the recipients of fixed-nominal-interest incomes, *rentiers*, in Keynes's vocabulary, at the expense of wage-earners and entrepreneurs, and to the extent that that group was relatively rich, the overall effect was ''more likely to be adverse than favourable'' (Keynes 1936, p. 262).

With potential effects on consumption pushed firmly into the background, Keynes turned to the marginal efficiency of capital, noting that what would happen there would be crucially dependent upon the influence of a current cut in money wages on expectations about their future behaviour. The argument was reminiscent of the analysis of the depressing effects of deflation in the *Tract on Monetary Reform*: A downward drift of money wages that was expected to continue into the future would be equivalent in its effects to an increase in the rate of interest and hence would depress the marginal efficiency of capital.[14] He conceded that ''a sudden large reduction of money-wages to a level so low that no one believes in its indefinite continuance would be the event most favourable to a strengthening of effective demand'' (Keynes 1936, p. 265), but he also argued that such a scheme ''is scarcely practical politics under a system of free wage-bargaining'' (Keynes 1936, p. 265). Hence, so far as effects on the marginal efficiency of capital were concerned, ''it is more expedient to aim at a rigid money-wage policy than at a flexible policy responding by easy stages to changes in the amount of unemployment; . . . But is this conclusion upset when we turn to the rate of interest?'' (Keynes 1936, p. 266). Keynes's answer to that question was a qualified no. The qualification in question was analytically important, however:

> It is . . . on the effect of a falling wage- and price-level on the demand for money that those who believe in the self-adjusting quality of the economic system must rest the weight of their argument; though I am not aware that they have done so. If the quantity of money is itself a function of the wage- and price-level, there is indeed, nothing to hope in this direction. But if the quantity of money is virtually fixed, it is evident that its quantity in terms of wage-units can be indefinitely increased by a sufficient reduction in money-wages; and that its quantity in proportion to incomes generally can be largely increased. . . .
> We can, therefore, theoretically at least, produce precisely the same ef-

---

[14] The argument also was not far removed from the underconsumptionist analysis of Foster and Catchings (e.g., 1923). See Chapter 8 for a discussion.

fects on the rate of interest by reducing wages, whilst leaving the quantity of money unchanged, that we can produce by increasing the quantity of money whilst leaving the level of wages unchanged. (Keynes 1936, p. 266)[15]

Keynes therefore concluded that "a flexible wage policy and a flexible money policy come, analytically, to the same thing," but he also took great pains to stress that "in other respects there is, of course, a world of difference between them" (Keynes 1936, p. 267). And it was those other respects that he thought to be empirically, as opposed to merely theoretically, important.

To begin with, though increasing the quantity of money was feasible, engineering an across-the-board money-wage cut was not. "Except in a socialised community where wage-policy is settled by decree, there is no means of securing uniform wage reductions for every class of labour" (Keynes 1936, p. 267). Such a policy would also be unfair, for there were other groups in society, such as *rentiers* and recipients of fixed nominal salaries, who would gain in real terms from a wage cut, but not from an increase in the quantity of money: ". . . it can only be an unjust person who would prefer a flexible wage policy to a flexible money policy" (Keynes 1936, p. 268). The two policies would, furthermore, have opposite effects on the burden carried by debtors, and "it can only be an inexperienced person" (Keynes 1936, p. 269) who would prefer to increase that burden by forcing down money wages and prices. Finally, as Keynes had already pointed out, "if a sagging rate of interest has to be brought about by a sagging wage level, there is . . . a double drag on the marginal efficiency of capital and a double reason for putting off investment and thus postponing recovery" (Keynes 1936, p. 269). All in all, Keynes believed that

> the chief result of this policy [of money-wage flexibility] would be to cause a great instability of prices, so violent perhaps as to make business calculations futile in an economic society functioning after the manner of that in which we live. To suppose that a flexible wage policy is a right and proper adjunct of a system which on the whole is one of *laissez-faire*, is the opposite of the truth. (Keynes 1936, p. 269, italics in original)

When it came to very long run considerations, however, where the fact of productivity growth forced a choice between money-wage stability and price-level stability, he did express a preference for the latter, and hence for a secularly rising money-wage level, though he thought that "no essential point of principle is involved" (Keynes 1936, p. 271) in the choice in question.[16]

---

[15] The argument harks back to that of "The Economic Consequences of Mr. Churchill" (1925) and to Hawtrey's contemporary treatment of the same issues. See Chapters 5 and 7.

[16] That was essentially the position that Keynes had taken in the *Tract*. Note also that for Austrian theory, an all-important point of principle was at stake, for they would have argued that money-wage stabilization was the *sine qua non* of a neutral money policy.

The Rate of Interest and Chronic Unemployment

If we read the *General Theory* in the context of the inter-war British debate on the causes of, and possible cures for, chronic unemployment, then its contribution was to call into question, from a theoretical perspective, both the attribution of the problem to excessively high real wages and the advocacy of money-wage cuts as a remedy. The fundamental problem was instead presented as stemming from a deficiency of effective demand, which an expansionary monetary policy probably would more reliably relieve than would money-wage cuts, and without the baleful side-effects of the latter policy. To stop here would be to give a misleadingly incomplete account of Keynes's views, however, because he was extremely pessimistic about the powers of monetary policy to exert sufficient influence on investment to ensure full employment.[17] He had doubts that there was any positive rate of interest low enough to induce sufficient investment to fill the gap between full-employment output and consumption, and he also believed that there existed a floor to the rate of interest at a value significantly above zero.

An Interest-Rate Floor

It is important to recall that Keynes gave two sets of theoretical reasons for that latter belief. The first involved short-term speculation on the margin between money and bonds in the light of current expectations about the future value of the rate of interest, and it was destined to become the staple of subsequent textbook discussions of the ''liquidity trap,'' even though, as we have seen, Keynes himself was of two minds about its empirical relevance. The other had to do with the influence of uncertainty about future yields on capital assets. Such uncertainty ensured that if those assets were to be held, their expected rate of return would always have to include a premium over and above the zero own rate of return to be had from holding money as a store of value. Keynes entertained no doubts about the empirical relevance of that latter postulate, which helped underpin his view that chronic secular unemployment was likely to be a prominent feature of any modern market economy. He developed that theme at considerable length in Chapters 16 and 17 of the *General Theory*.[18]

---

[17] That represented a very large shift from the position that Keynes had taken in the *Treatise* and in his 1931 Chicago lectures. It did, however belatedly, bring his views into line with those held by the majority of his contemporaries. See Chapter 6, ''Open-Market Operations and Their Limits.''

[18] Many passages in those chapters, particularly Chapter 17, were obscure or even totally opaque, but the title of the latter, ''Essential Properties of Interest and Money,'' makes it

Keynes succinctly summarized the central message of Chapter 17 at its very outset in the following terms: "It seems, then, that the *rate of interest on money* plays a peculiar part in setting a limit to the level of employment, since it sets a standard to [*sic*] which the marginal efficiency of a capital-asset must attain if it is to be newly produced" (Keynes 1936, p. 222, italics in original). The answer Keynes gave to what he believed to be the puzzle posed by that fact stemmed ultimately from the interaction between money's capacity to function as a store of value and its role as a unit of account: "The convenience of holding assets in the same standard as that in which future liabilities may fall due and in a standard in terms of which the future cost of living is expected to be relatively stable, is obvious" (Keynes 1936, pp. 236–237).

The important point there was not merely that wages and prices were set in terms of money. It was rather that, as an empirical matter, wages in particular displayed stability in terms of that unit of account, and that, in turn, severely constrained the capacity of the price level to vary. "The normal expectation that the value of output will be more stable in terms of money than in terms of any other commodity, depends of course, not on wages being arranged in terms of money, but on wages being relatively *sticky* in terms of money" (Keynes 1936, p. 237, italics in original). If wages were sticky, not in nominal but in real terms, the consequences of that "could only be to cause a violent oscillation of money-prices. For every small fluctuation in the propensity to consume and the inducement to invest would cause money-prices to rush violently between zero and infinity" (Keynes 1936, p. 239).

For Keynes, reasonable price-level stability was, as we have already seen, a necessary condition for a monetary economy to have any chance of functioning in the first place, and so, therefore, was money-wage stickiness. Reasonable price-level stability, however, so desirable when it came to facilitating business calculations in a market economy, created a serious problem in another respect, for it ensured that money, a store of value whose carrying cost was extremely low, would also be highly liquid. Hence, according to Keynes, who once more offered no evidence to support a key empirical postulate, the implicit own rate of return on holding money would fall only slowly, if at all, as its quantity increased. The rate of interest, therefore, being

---

difficult to accept the verdict of commentators such as Hansen (1954) and Patinkin (1976a) that its content was essentially irrelevant to the overall argument of a book which, according to its own title, was concerned with the roles of precisely those two factors in determining the level of employment. On the contrary, as Lawlor (1994) and Rogers (1994) have argued, it is possible to read Chapter 17 as being fundamental to Keynes's effort to explain chronic unemployment. Rogers has placed more emphasis than Lawlor on the links between the ideas that Chapter 17 sets out and a reading of the *General Theory* that emphasizes the place of long-run unemployment in its message.

the price required for parting with the liquidity provided by money, would, *"in certain circumstances such as will often occur*, . . . be insensitive . . . even to a substantial increase in the quantity of money in proportion to other forms of wealth'' (Keynes 1936, p. 233, italics added).

Because their carrying costs were higher, and also because, in the case of items of capital equipment of various sorts, they were subject to diminishing marginal productivity, the own rates of return on other assets would systematically fall as their quantity increased. It followed that ''beyond a certain point money's yield from liquidity does not fall in response to an increase in its quantity to anything approaching the extent to which the yield from other types of assets falls when their quantity is comparably increased'' (Keynes 1936, p. 233). Consequently, the higher an economy's already accumulated stock of capital, the more likely it would be that the prevailing value of the marginal efficiency of capital would be sufficiently low as to induce a rate of investment smaller than needed to absorb the volume of saving forthcoming at its full-employment level of output. Crucially, the floor placed on the rate of interest by money's liquidity premium would prevent that variable from falling in order to remedy that state of affairs.[19] Nor, in Keynes's view, was that merely a theoretical possibility:

> The post-war experiences of Great Britain and the United States are, indeed, actual examples of how an accumulation of wealth, so large that its marginal efficiency has fallen more rapidly than the rate of interest can fall in the face of the prevailing institutional and psychological factors, can interfere, in conditions mainly of *laissez-faire*, with a reasonable level of employment and with the standard of life which the technical conditions of production are capable of furnishing. (Keynes 1936, p. 219, italics in original)

A Link with Underconsumptionism

In arguing thus that a monetary economy had a chronic tendency to operate below its productive potential, Keynes placed himself in the company of such contemporary underconsumptionists as Hobson, Foster and Catchings, and Paul Douglas, whose views we have discussed earlier. They were self-conscious exponents of a point of view that had roots in the dissent of Malthus, Lauderdale, and Sismondi, among others, from Ricardian orthodoxy; and as Steven Kates (1994) has pointed out, Keynes was familiar with

---

[19] Allan Meltzer (1988), like many post-Keynesians, such as Victoria Chick (1983), regarded that particular proposition as constituting the *General Theory*'s main message, but unlike the post-Keynesians, he doubted its empirical validity. As should be clear from this chapter, I do not see why a book cannot be intended to convey more than a single message, and so I have no difficulty in agreeing with Meltzer about the importance of that matter, and disagreeing with him in downgrading the significance which Patinkin attached to the discussion of money-wage behaviour in Chapter 19.

Malthus's work and may well have been directly influenced by it.[20] Certainly, in explicitly repudiating the doctrine that "supply creates its own demand" which the classical economists had taught "from the time of Say and Ricardo" (Keynes 1936, p. 18), Keynes signalled a relationship between his own work and that dissenting tradition, and though he did not mention his American contemporaries, he did single out Hobson for several pages of praise (not altogether uncritical), drawing attention in particular to the "significant and well-founded . . . criticisms and intuitions" (Keynes 1936, p. 366) that marked his work with A. F. Mummery (Mummery and Hobson 1889).[21] Even Major C. H. Douglas, the pioneer of "social credit," was granted a lowly rank:

> – a private, perhaps, but not a major in the brave army of heretics – with Mandeville, Malthus, Gesell and Hobson, who, following their intuitions, have preferred to see the truth obscurely and imperfectly rather than to maintain error, reached indeed with clearness and consistency and by easy logic, but on hypotheses inappropriate to the facts. (Keynes 1936, p. 371)

Keynes thus believed that traditional underconsumptionist doctrine was logically flawed, but he nevertheless agreed that "practically I only differ from these schools of thought in thinking that they may lay a little too much emphasis on increased consumption at a time when there is still much social advantage to be obtained from increased investment" (Keynes 1936, p. 325). He conceded that

> in so far as millionaires find their satisfaction in building mighty mansions to contain their bodies when alive and pyramids to shelter them after death, or, repenting of their sins, erect cathedrals and endow monasteries or foreign missions, the day when the abundance of capital will interfere with abundance of output may be postponed. "To dig holes in the ground," paid for out of savings, will increase, not only employment, but the real national dividend of useful goods and services. (Keynes 1936, p. 220)

He went on to note, however, that "it is not reasonable . . . that a sensible community should be content to remain dependent on such fortuitous and

---

[20] Nevertheless, it should be noted that the received view is that Keynes, after having worked out his own ideas, noticed enough similarity between them and the ideas of Malthus to enlist Malthus among his predecessors. Allin Cottrell (1997) has made a powerful case that Malthus's analysis, which attempted to establish the possibility of general overproduction in what amounted to a barter economy, was analytically incoherent and that Keynes read more into it than was really there. Hence, Cottrell has disagreed with what he has termed the "revisionist approach" to that question taken by Kates (1994). Note that Clower and Howitt (1998, p. 7) have argued that "a post-Keynes reader of Mummery and Hobson cannot help but note so many similarities with the *General Theory* as to suspect Keynes learned more from them than he acknowledged."

[21] Though Keynes did not cite Foster and Catchings in the *General Theory*, he did mention them in the *Treatise*, and, as we have seen, their work had also attracted the careful, albeit critical, scrutiny of Evan Durbin (1933).

often wasteful mitigations when once we understand the influences upon which effective demand depends'' (Keynes 1936, p. 220).

Ultimately, because ''I am myself impressed by the great social advantages of increasing the stock of capital until it ceases to be scarce'' (Keynes 1936, p. 325), Keynes opted for state control over the level and perhaps also the composition of investment rather than the stimulation of consumption as the preferred remedy for stagnation. It would, he thought, be feasible by such means to ''bring down the marginal efficiency of capital in equilibrium approximately to zero within a single generation'' (Keynes 1936, p. 220), a result to which Keynes looked forward because it would also be ''the most sensible way of gradually getting rid of many of the objectionable features of capitalism'' (Keynes 1936, p. 221), namely, those stemming from the fact that accumulated wealth yielded an income to its owners. The best way of ensuring full employment was therefore also the best way of ensuring the disappearance – ''euthanasia'' was the term Keynes used – of the *rentier*, both of those being goals which he strongly endorsed.

Thus, to relate matters once more to the inter-war debates about chronic unemployment, having rejected money-wage cuts, and indeed expansionary monetary policy too, as solutions to a problem whose causes he believed to lie in the very nature of a market economy, Keynes committed himself to a degree of permanent state involvement in the economy which, though far from carefully specified, nevertheless seems to have gone somewhat beyond the ''temperate faith in Public Works'' that Hicks (1937, repr. 1982, p. 109) would attribute to him.[22]

The Price Level and the Cycle

Though he was mainly concerned with expounding a theory of employment, not a theory of the price level or the cycle, Keynes discussed, albeit briefly, the relationship of his new theory to the quantity theory of money, which

---

[22] Meltzer (1981) and Patinkin (1983) have had an exchange over the extent to which Keynes wished to subject the composition as well as the overall level of investment expenditure to government control. On page 164 of the *General Theory,* Keynes remarked that ''I expect to see the State, which is in a position to calculate the marginal efficiency of capital goods on long views and on the basis of the general social advantage, taking an ever greater responsibility for organising investment; since it seems likely that the fluctuations in the market estimation of the marginal efficiency of different types of capital . . . will be too great to be offset by any practicable changes in the rate of interest.'' That passage seems to me to support Meltzer in their debate, though it is the only one in the *General Theory* which refers to the structure as well as the level of investment in that way, a fact that gives weight to Patinkin's contention that, overall, Keynes was not in favour of state planning of the overall level and structure of investment expenditures. That is also the view of Bateman (1994), who argued that Keynes wished to use public-investment expenditure as a tool of policy in part directed at stabilizing the expectations that underlay private-sector investment.

had, after all, played an important part in his own earlier work, as well as its relationship to explanations of cyclical phenomena. As we shall now see, there was some novelty to his treatment of the first topic, and virtually none in his discussion of the second.

The Quantity Theory and Effective Demand

Keynes characterized the quantity theory as oversimplified, even from a purely analytic point of view:

> Thus if there is perfectly elastic supply [of output with respect to the price level] so long as there is unemployment, and perfectly inelastic supply so soon as full employment is reached, and if effective demand changes in the same proportion as the quantity of money, the quantity theory of money can be enunciated as follows: "So long as there is unemployment, *employment* will change in the same proportion as the quantity of money; and when there is full employment, *prices* will change in the same proportion as the quantity of money."
>
> Having, however, satisfied tradition by introducing a sufficient number of simplifying assumptions to enable us to enunciate a quantity theory of money, let us now consider the possible complications which will in fact influence events. (Keynes 1936, pp. 295–296, italics in original)[23]

In his system, the price level had to take whatever value was needed to equate the real wage to the marginal product of labour, given the level of money wages, and the marginal product of labour would vary systematically with the level of employment. Hence, in general, "the effect of changes in the quantity of money on the price-level can be considered as being compounded of the effect on the wage-unit and the effect on employment" (Keynes 1936, p. 295).

Keynes believed the interactions lying behind that simple statement to be extremely complex, however.[24] To begin with, the chain of causation linking money to effective demand involved the influence of money on the rate of interest and the influence of the rate of interest on investment and then the multiplier. But in addition to the secondary effect of income on the demand for money, and thence back to interest rates, the influence of current monetary policy on expectations about its future stance, not to mention distributional effects on the magnitude of the multiplier, also had to be taken into account, and those qualifications made it unlikely that effective demand would change in proportion to the quantity of money. The causative mechanism linking

---

[23] The simplifications that Keynes made were, of course, exactly those which Milton Friedman (1974) made in setting out his monetary framework.

[24] It was, indeed, in that context that Keynes's famous disquisition on the pitfalls of mathematical reasoning in economics took place. In his view, the problems under discussion were too complex to permit useful mathematical analysis.

effective demand to the price level was similarly complex; it involved the tendency of wages to rise before full employment was reached, the appearance of bottlenecks in particular markets, changes in relative input prices, the appearance of diminishing returns to specific inputs, and so forth. "Thus instead of constant prices in conditions of unemployment, and of prices rising in proportion to the quantity of money in conditions of full employment, we have in fact a condition of prices rising gradually as employment increases" (Keynes 1936, p. 296).

Keynes did recognize a limiting case of "true inflation" that would set in when it was no longer possible for output to be increased, but in general, as far as "short-period" analysis was concerned, he was unwilling to commit himself to any proposition more specific than that, to the extent that a change in the quantity of money did indeed influence effective demand, that would also lead to a change in the price level, of the same sign, but of unspecified magnitude. Effects there would, however, be asymmetric, with increases in the money supply being absorbed relatively more by price changes, and cuts relatively more by employment changes, by reason of "the assumption that the factors of production, and in particular the workers, are disposed to resist a reduction in their money-rewards, and that there is no corresponding motive to resist an increase. This assumption is, however, obviously well founded in the facts" (Keynes 1936, p. 303). Which facts he had in mind, however, he did not say.

The Secular Behaviour of Prices

Those complicated and asymmetric short-run mechanisms might nevertheless produce a rough-and-ready long-run correspondence between the behaviour of money and prices under particular historical circumstances. Keynes postulated the existence of some rather stable upper limit to the "proportion of the national income [that] people will . . . readily keep in the shape of idle balances . . . provided the rate of interest exceeds a certain psychological minimum" (Keynes 1936, p. 306, italics added), and he suggested that that probably had contributed to the secular stability displayed by the price level in the century preceding World War I. Over that time, he asserted, yet again without citing any supporting evidence, the economy had usually operated "substantially below full employment, but not so intolerably below it as to provoke revolutionary changes" (Keynes 1936, p. 308).

Consistent with everything that had gone before in the *General Theory*, however, Keynes was extremely doubtful that any of that was relevant to contemporary circumstances:

> But the most stable, and the least easily shifted, element in our contemporary economy has been hitherto, and may prove to be in future, the minimum rate of interest acceptable to the generality of wealth-owners. If a

> tolerable level of employment requires a rate of interest much below the average rates which ruled in the nineteenth century, it is most doubtful whether it can be achieved merely by manipulating the quantity of money. (Keynes 1936, p. 309)

Hence, he was ultimately agnostic about the nature of the relationship that would rule in future between the quantity of money and the price level, even in the long run, and it is difficult to avoid the conclusion that he did not regard the question as being of any great practical interest:

> ... the long run relationship between the national income and the quantity of money will depend on liquidity-preferences. And the long-run stability or instability of prices will depend on the strength on the upward trend of the wage-unit (or, more precisely, of the cost-unit) compared with the rate of increase in the efficiency of the productive system. (Keynes 1936, p. 309)

That, the closing statement of the closing chapter of the main body of the *General Theory*, read in the light of Keynes's evident belief in something close to absolute liquidity preference, can only be taken to imply that whatever might have been true in the past, the quantity theory of money had by 1936 become empirically irrelevant. As a corollary, it would also seem that, though Keynes thought the fact that money wages were largely institutionally and historically determined to be essentially irrelevant to the explanation of unemployment, he also thought that same fact to be crucial to the determination of the price level. [25]

The Cycle

All of that represented a very big step away from the position that Keynes had taken in the *Treatise on Money*, where price-level fluctuations, driven by mechanisms that we might characterize as a Wicksellian variation on the quantity theory of money, had been presented as the essential feature of the cycle. Chapter 22 of the *General Theory*, "Notes on the Trade Cycle," should be read, therefore, as an attempt to present a new (for Keynes) view of the cycle that would be consistent with the vision of the *General Theory*. As he put it,

> since we claim to have shown in the preceding chapters what determines the volume of employment at any time, it follows, if we are right, that our

---

[25] In *How to Pay for the War* (1940), however, Keynes would offer a monetary explanation for price-level behaviour, complete with an analysis of forced saving that harked back to the *Tract* and to Robertson's *Banking Policy and the Price Level*. He was, however, aware in that work that he was dealing with a fully employed economy, and it is clear that when discussing wage and price behaviour in the *General Theory* he took a state of chronic unemployment for granted. Thus, the foregoing passage should not be taken to imply that Keynes is to be held responsible for the post-war popularity of sociological "cost-push" theories of inflation against a background of high employment.

theory must be capable of explaining the phenomena of the trade cycle. (Keynes 1936, p. 313)

The explanation that followed, though not quite identical with that of Pigou and Lavington (neither of whom Keynes cited in that context), was close enough to it to support the conclusion that the economics of the *General Theory* represented something of a reversion on Keynes's part to the mainstream of the Cambridge tradition relative to the rather "monetarist" (as we might now put it) position that he had occupied in the 1920s.[26]

The centrepiece of the explanation in question was the proposition that

> the trade cycle is best regarded . . . as being occasioned by a cyclical change in the marginal efficiency of capital, though complicated and often aggravated by associated changes in the other significant short-period variables of the economic system. (Keynes 1936, p. 313)

And the marginal efficiency of capital was in turn very much the product of expectations, whose basis in "fundamentals" was extremely tenuous. Rather, it was "determined . . . by the uncontrollable and disobedient psychology of the business world" (Keynes 1936, p. 317), and variations in it were therefore highly susceptible to waves of systematic and cumulative optimism and pessimism. To put the matter in Keynes's own words,

> . . . it is an essential characteristic of the boom that investments which will in fact yield, say, 2 per cent in conditions of full employment are made in the expectation of a yield of, say, 6 per cent, and are valued accordingly. When the disillusion comes, this expectation is replaced by a contrary "error of pessimism," with the result that the investments, which would in fact yield 2 per cent in conditions of full employment, are expected to yield less than nothing; and the resulting collapse of new investment then leads to a state of unemployment in which the investments . . . in fact yield less than nothing. (Keynes 1936, pp. 321–322)

That analysis not only bears a strong resemblance to that of Pigou and Lavington, but, as the reader will note, even adopts their vocabulary.

Keynes's treatment of the upper turning-point was also essentially the same as theirs:

> . . . we have been accustomed in explaining the "crisis" to lay stress on the rising tendency of the rate of interest under the influence of the increased demand for money both for trade and speculative purposes. At times this factor may certainly play an aggravating and, occasionally perhaps, an initiating part. But I suggest that a more typical, and often the predominant, explanation of the crisis is, not primarily a rise in the rate of interest, but a sudden collapse in the marginal efficiency of capital. (Keynes 1936, p. 315)

---

[26] Thus, Haberler (1937, p. 134) classified the Keynes of the *General Theory*, along with Pigou and Lavington, as holding a "psychological" theory of the cycle.

If anything, Keynes's discussion there was inferior to Lavington's, for he never made it clear what factors might cause such a sudden collapse; whereas Lavington had explained it, as we saw earlier, in terms of the long gestation period for investment projects, which meant that when new capital equipment finally came into operation, the returns actually realized would be likely to fall short of expectations.[27]

Counter-cyclical Policy

In both the *Tract* and the *Treatise*, Keynes had been optimistic about the power of monetary policy to generate expansion in a depressed economy, far more so than most of his contemporaries, not least, once more, Pigou and Lavington. On that question, too, in 1936 he reverted to what had been the conventional Cambridge view of the 1920s. He did introduce a new element in noting that "the dismay and uncertainty as to the future which accompanies [*sic*] a collapse in the marginal efficiency of capital naturally precipitates [*sic*] a sharp increase in liquidity-preference – and hence a rise in the rate of interest" (Keynes 1936, p. 316), and that increase in the interest rate "may seriously aggravate the decline in investment" (Keynes 1936, p. 316); but that was not, in Keynes's opinion, the essential factor rendering "the slump so intractable" (Keynes 1936, p. 316) once it had begun. Rather, as Pigou and Lavington had argued, it was depressed expectations, and what was required was

> the return of confidence, to speak in ordinary language, which is so insusceptible to control in an economy of individualistic capitalism. This is the aspect of the slump which bankers and business men have been right in emphasising, and which the economists who have put their faith in a "purely monetary" remedy have underestimated. (Keynes 1936, p. 317)

As we have seen, not all economists had put their faith in a "purely monetary remedy" for the cycle before the publication of the *General Theory*, nor had it been only "bankers and business men" who had emphasized the importance of "confidence." Keynes's own adoption of that position was, however, as Bateman (1994) has noted, of relatively recent origin in 1936.

Similar though the positive substance of Keynes's sketch of cycle theory was to that of some of his Cambridge contemporaries, not to mention his scepticism regarding the expansionary powers of orthodox monetary measures in a slump, his policy conclusions were radically different from theirs.

---

[27] Lavington's analysis was related to the accelerator mechanism, of course, which would soon be brought into the Keynesian mainstream by Samuelson (1939a, b). Note that Samuelson in turn, under the guidance of Alvin Hansen, drew some inspiration from the work of the Stockholm School, particularly Lundberg (1937).

It was, as we have seen, an almost universally held view before 1936 that the best contribution to counter-cyclical policy that the monetary authorities could make was to prevent the boom from getting out of hand in the first place. Keynes would have none of that, even though he agreed that "there is, indeed, force in the argument that a high rate of interest is much more effective against a boom than a low rate of interest against a slump" (Keynes 1936, p. 320). A practice of using monetary policy to control a boom could, however, be justified only by resort to an assumption, which Keynes attributed to Robertson (without specific citation), "that full employment is an impracticable ideal and that the best we can hope for is a level of employment much more stable than at present and averaging, perhaps, a little higher" (Keynes 1936, p. 327).[28] But, he added, "such an outlook seems to me to be dangerously and unnecessarily defeatist. It recommends, or at least assumes, for permanent acceptance too much that is defective in our existing economic scheme" (Keynes 1936, p. 327).

For Keynes, therefore,

> the remedy for the boom is not a higher rate of interest but a lower rate of interest! For that may enable the so-called boom to last. The right remedy for the trade cycle is not to be found in abolishing booms and thus keeping us permanently in a semi-slump; but in abolishing slumps and thus keeping us in a permanently quasi-boom. (Keynes 1936, p. 322)

He discussed the American boom of the later 1920s in the light of that observation, concluding that, towards its end,

> the prospective yield of further additions [to the capital stock] was, coolly considered, falling rapidly . . . so that the boom could not have continued on a sound basis except with a very low long-term rate of interest. . . . In fact, the rate of interest was high enough to deter new investment except in those particular directions which were under the influence of speculative excitement and, therefore, in special danger of being over-exploited. . . . Thus an increase in the rate of interest, as a remedy for the state of affairs arising out of a prolonged period of abnormally heavy new investment, belongs to the species of remedy which cures the disease by killing the patient. (Keynes 1936, p. 323)

At first sight, that conclusion about the role of the interest rate in counter-cyclical policy would appear to have been merely carelessly inflationist, but it was in fact more radical than that.[29] It was Keynes's firmly held and frequently repeated view that the marginal efficiency of capital was extremely

---

[28] The reference probably was to Robertson's 1936 Harvard lecture, now best known under its later title "The Snake and the Worm" (1936b).

[29] That conclusion was, of course, at complete odds with the treatment of counter-cyclical monetary policy in the *Treatise*, in which Keynes had been only a reluctant advocate of counter-cyclical public-works expenditure.

unstable in a market economy and that the powers of monetary policy to deal with the consequences were limited. Only three pages prior to the passage just cited he had observed that

> with markets organised and influenced as they are at present, the market estimation of the marginal efficiency of capital may suffer such enormously wide fluctuations that it cannot be sufficiently offset by corresponding fluctuations in the rate of interest. . . . In conditions of *laissez-faire* the avoidance of wide fluctuations in employment may, therefore, prove impossible without a far-reaching change in the psychology of investment markets such as there is no reason to expect. I conclude that the duty of ordering the current volume of investment cannot safely be left in private hands. (Keynes 1936, p. 320)

Keynes's views about counter-cyclical monetary policy should, therefore, be read as complementing his equally radical, albeit, as Bateman (1994) has stressed, far from fully worked out, views about the desirability of using public-sector investment to influence private-sector expectations in such a way as fundamentally to change in future the cyclical pattern of the overall volume of investment in the economy.

Concluding Comments

The final chapter of the *General Theory* deals with the "Social Philosophy" towards which the book's theoretical core might lead and largely reiterates themes already explored earlier. It begins with the observation that "the outstanding faults of the economic society in which we live are its failure to provide for full employment and its arbitrary and inequitable distribution of wealth and incomes" (Keynes 1936, p. 372) and notes that the theory presented in earlier pages bears on both of those. Keynes suggested that the task of driving down the marginal efficiency of capital to a very low level, if undertaken by a state charged with control over the volume of investment, could be fairly easily accomplished and that

> though this state of affairs would be quite compatible with some measure of individualism, yet it would mean the euthanasia of the rentier, and, consequently, the euthanasia of the cumulative oppressive power of the capitalist to exploit the scarcity-value of capital. (Keynes 1936, pp. 375–376)

The exact balance between consumption and investment that would rule, once that state of affairs was reached, could not be fixed *a priori*, because

> only experience can show how far the common will, embodied in the policy of the State, ought to be directed to increasing and supplementing the inducement to invest; and how far it is safe to stimulate the average propensity to consume, without forgoing our aim of depriving capital of its scarcity-value within one or two generations. (Keynes 1936, p. 377)

But, granted that latter aim,

> in some other respects the foregoing theory is moderately conservative in its implications. For whilst it indicates the vital importance of establishing certain central controls in matters which are now left in the main to individual initiative, there are wide fields of activity which are unaffected. (Keynes 1936, pp. 377–378)

The state would use the taxation system and (unspecified) "other ways" to influence the propensity to consume and would set the rate of interest too; but, since it would be unlikely that the rate of interest could be set low enough to generate a full-employment level of investment, "I conceive . . . that a somewhat comprehensive socialisation of investment will prove the only means of securing an approximation to full employment" (Keynes 1936, p. 378).

Beyond that, however, because Keynes saw "no reason to suppose that the existing system seriously misemploys the factors of production which are in use" (Keynes 1936, p. 379), he concluded that decisions about the composition of consumption certainly could safely be left to market mechanisms, and perhaps also decisions about the composition of investment (as elsewhere, he left undiscussed the problem of how the overall level of investment could be controlled without state interference in its composition too). Though all of that

> would seem to a nineteenth-century publicist or to a contemporary American financier to be a terrific encroachment on individualism, I defend it . . . both as the only practicable means of avoiding the destruction of existing economic forms in their entirety and as the condition of the successful functioning of individual initiative. (Keynes 1936, p. 380)

One should not forget how attractive totalitarianism of one sort or another was in the mid-1930s, nor underestimate the degree to which, in the last resort, Keynes believed that his *General Theory* provided an intellectual underpinning for a socio-economic framework that would preserve the principal virtues of a liberal order, while eliminating those of its features which threatened to bring about its complete demise:

> The authoritarian state systems of to-day seem to solve the problem of unemployment at the expense of efficiency and of freedom. It is certain that the world will not much longer tolerate the unemployment which, apart from brief intervals of excitement, is associated – and in my opinion, inevitably associated – with present-day capitalistic individualism. But it may be possible by a right analysis of the problem to cure the disease whilst preserving efficiency and freedom. (Keynes 1936, p. 381)

All of that was a far cry from IS-LM. And yet the components of that model are indeed all to be found in the *General Theory*. A consumption function linking real consumer expenditure to real income, an inverse relationship between real investment and the rate of interest, and a demand-for-money equation with real income and the rate of interest as its arguments are all discussed at various points, as are their interactions when the nominal quantity of money is held constant and money wages and prices are allowed to vary.[30] As we shall see in the next two chapters, even some of Keynes's "classical" reviewers recognized some novelty in those aspects of the book, while they took issue with its broader themes. As we shall also see, his younger readers emphasized that material in particular, though there was some disagreement among them regarding just how new the analytic framework was.

---

[30] It is nevertheless interesting to note that in Chapter 18 of the book, which bears the title "The General Theory Restated," Keynes pointed out that an increase (decrease) in income brought about by an increase (decrease) in investment would "raise (lower) the schedule of liquidity preference" (Keynes 1936, p. 248). He did not, however, go on explicitly to derive the consequences of that for the rate of interest and the ultimate level of investment, as one would expect an exponent of IS-LM analysis to do. I am grateful to Michael Parkin for drawing my attention to that striking omission. The "independent variables" of Keynes's version of his system were, at the outset of that chapter, said to be "in the first instance, the propensity to consume, the schedule of the marginal efficiency of capital and *the rate of interest*" (Keynes 1936, p. 245, italics added).

CHAPTER 11

The Classics and Mr. Keynes

Initial Reactions

There was no intellectual vacuum in monetary economics when the *General Theory* was published. There existed no monolithic and atrophied orthodoxy, detached from economic reality and therefore ripe for overthrow. Earlier chapters of this book have provided ample evidence that there was no substance whatsoever to those old myths about the nature of macroeconomics before 1936. Rather, the *General Theory* must be seen as a contribution to a vital, diverse, and changing body of literature dealing with what we nowadays call macroeconomics. That, indeed, is how it was received upon publication: The book was reviewed and debated not just as any other book would have been, for its author's professional standing guaranteed that it would attract unusually widespread attention, but rather as a work to be read and understood in the context of the contemporary state of knowledge. Initial reactions to the *General Theory* were decidedly mixed. Among the already well-established economists, some, notably Pigou (1936) and Frank Knight (1937), were clearly irritated, even angered, by the book and hostile to it; whereas others, such as Dennis Robertson (1936a), Jacob Viner (1936), Ralph Hawtrey (1937), Alvin Hansen (1936), and Bertil Ohlin (1937), took a more constructive, albeit critical, attitude.

Nevertheless, certain themes recurred in those initial reactions which the *General Theory* provoked. That was particularly the case among those commentators who had already made substantial contributions to the macroeconomic literature before 1936, and to whom, therefore, the label "classic" (in Keynes's or Hicks's sense of the word) might reasonably, albeit loosely, be attached. Those themes included the following: first, that Keynes's claims on his own behalf to have begun a revolution in economic theory were hardly to be taken seriously; second, that his claims to have provided, in the shape of liquidity-preference theory, a "new" theory of the rate of interest were very much overblown; and third, that in expressing his ideas in terms of static analysis, he had taken a retrogressive step as far as the development of economic theory was concerned. The overall verdict was that Keynes had, at best, clarified one or two important questions, at the cost of leaving (or even rendering) others obscure. We shall discuss those criticisms here and show that in the face of them, Keynes remained unrepentant.

The Theory of Employment

No early reviewer was more hostile to the *General Theory* than Pigou. His anger is evident in the opening passage of his review.[1]

> When, in 1919, he wrote *The Economic Consequences of the Peace*, Mr. Keynes did a good day's work for the world, in helping it back towards sanity. But he did a bad day's work for himself as an economist. For he discovered then, and his sub-conscious mind has not been able to forget since, that the best way to win attention for one's own ideas is to present them in a matrix of sarcastic comment upon other people. (Pigou 1936, p. 115)

In Pigou's view, Keynes's treatment of the classical theory of employment, not least as set out in Pigou's own 1933 book on the topic, was a "macédoine of misrepresentations" (Pigou 1936, p. 119). Hawtrey (1937) also took Keynes to task, albeit more courteously, for his treatment of classical analysis of the labour market, Pigou's in particular, arguing that the treatment in question betrayed "a complete misconception of Professor Pigou's assumptions" (Hawtrey 1937, p. 169). He drew particular attention to Pigou's assumption (1933, p. 74), as discussed earlier in Chapter 6, that the long-run supply of labour was essentially inelastic with respect to the real wage, and hence to Keynes's inaccurate attribution of an upward-sloping supply-of-labour function to the classical theory that he had attacked. Hawtrey concluded that "on this point therefore Mr. Keynes's divergence from the classical school is due to a sheer misunderstanding" (Hawtrey 1937, p. 170).[2]

---

[1] The qualifier "early" is important, for Arthur Marget (1938–41) displayed more hostility than Pigou. Just as Volume I of Marget's *Theory of Prices* is an extended and hostile critique of the *Treatise on Money*, so his Volume II is in large part an attack on the *General Theory*. Its tone can be gauged from the following: "... the unprecedented success of Mr. Keynes in converting professional economists to what he is proud to regard as his heresy has been to create an example of the 'noxious influence of authority' compared with which the 'noxious influence' attributed by Jevons to the authority of Mill, and by later writers to the authority of Marshall, is as nothing" (Marget 1938–41, vol. II, p. xi). Marget's critique of the book was, however, largely beside the point, because he treated it as an attempt to contribute to the theory of the price level, rather than output and employment. Thus "the 'Multiplier', indeed, is the only type of analytical device brought into recent discussion by the Keynesian influence with which, in the present work, I have not attempted to deal in detail" (Marget 1938–41, vol. II, pp. xvii–xviii).

[2] Hawtrey might have done better to talk of Keynes's divergence from Pigou, for the idea of a supply-of-labour function that derived from agents' actions of equating the marginal disutility of work to the real wage was, of course, a staple of economics after the so-called marginal revolution. Indeed, the analysis in question had its origins in Jevons's contribution (1871) to that revolution. Pigou's vertical supply curve, which amounted to treating the size of the labour force as a given, was a novel feature of his analysis and certainly had nothing explicitly to do with the utility-maximization calculus.

A Missed Point

Frank Knight was less generous than Hawtrey. For Knight, as for Pigou, Keynes's misrepresentation of the classics was wilful, not merely a matter of his having misunderstood specific elements in the analysis of those he was attacking:

> In this chapter [entitled "The Postulates of Classical Economics"] and throughout the book, his references under this phrase are, in general, the sort of caricatures which are typically set up as straw men for purposes of attack in controversial writing. . . . In particular, it has been assumed [among theorists] that the theorist must consider a society free from the complications of speculation and of monetary changes, and hence from cyclical unemployment, before taking up these phenomena. In the interest of clarity as to the underlying meaning, the reader of Mr. Keynes's book would do well to keep in mind that references to "the classical economics" are to be interpreted as relating to economic analysis *at the stage* at which uncertainty and monetary disturbances are assumed absent. (Knight 1937, p. 101, italics in original)

By implication, Keynes had failed to give appropriate recognition to the significant contributions that had already been made to coping with those complications. "What Mr. Keynes ostensibly does . . . is to effect a revolution in general economic theory" (Knight 1937, p. 100), but for Knight, a self-styled "classic," the value of Keynes's work

> is . . . to be sought in the opposite direction from that of its pretensions, as just indicated; i.e. the treatment suggests modifications of conventional equilibrium analysis to account for temporary, possibly more or less chronic, disequilibrium conditions or, in other words, makes indirect contributions to the theory of business fluctuations. (Knight 1937, p. 100)

But, as Knight repeatedly stressed, viewed in that context, and against the background of what had already been achieved, the analysis in question could hardly be considered revolutionary. Much of what Keynes had to say, far from differing from anything that had gone before, was, in Knight's view, essentially the same, albeit dressed up in a new and often confusing vocabulary.[3]

In light of the material presented in the earlier chapters of this book, it is impossible to dismiss out of hand the general thrust of those criticisms; but it is nevertheless the case that both Pigou and Knight missed an all-important point that Keynes was, beyond a shadow of a doubt, trying to make, namely,

---

[3] That accusation of dressing up old ideas in new vocabulary found its way into Harry Johnson's discussion (1971) of Keynes and, ironically, given its origins in a commentary by a leading Chicago economist, into his discussion of Friedman too.

that the existence of money-wage flexibility may not be sufficient to guarantee that an economy, once away from full employment, will return to it. Hawtrey, on the other hand, did recognize what Keynes was getting at there. Though he thought that much of Keynes's critique of classical labour-market theory rested on "sheer misunderstanding," he also recognized that "there is a difference of more substance when he challenges 'the assumption that the general level of real wages depends on the money-wage bargains between the employers and the workers' " (Hawtrey 1937, p. 170).

Pigou (1936) demonstrably did not fully understand what Keynes was getting at, describing his analysis as follows:

> . . . he does, indeed, deny that a reduction in money wage rates can bring about a reduction in real wage rates, and so in unemployment, in the way in which he supposes other people to believe that it can do these things. But he does not, I think, deny that in *some* way, by a process of repercussion, it can in fact do them. (Pigou 1936, pp. 127–128, italics in original)

Pigou thus erroneously attributed to Keynes a belief that money wages affected employment through a chain of events in which the real wage played a critical causative role, and Knight missed Keynes's point by an even wider margin, simply attributing to him the assumption "that wages and prices cannot fall (but are free to rise)" (Knight 1937, p. 121; see also p. 106) and arguing that Keynes's results depended on that assumption.

Understanding the Issue

Hawtrey did understand the argument on which Keynes's conclusion as to the likely ineffectiveness of money-wage cuts rested, but he doubted its validity. He first quoted Keynes's proposition that what mattered there was not any direct effect of falling money wages on real wages, but "of falling wage and price level on the demand for money." Then he went on to paraphrase Keynes's conclusion about the essential similarity between falling money wages and a rising nominal money supply, and he agreed that that was the right way to analyse the matter. It is not surprising, of course, that Hawtrey should have grasped the logic of Keynes's arguments on that point so clearly, because analysis of the very same causative links had, as we saw in Chapter 5, been turning up in his own writings, expressed with increasing clarity, since 1913.

Hawtrey made it quite plain, however, that he was unconvinced by Keynes's arguments about why money-wage cuts working through those channels would not induce full employment. He accepted Keynes's views on the superiority of monetary expansion over money-wage cuts as a matter of practical policy, but noted that

... that is a totally different thing from the thesis with which Mr. Keynes started that it may be *impossible* to reduce real wages by reducing money-wages. If there is no case in which full employment cannot be attained through a reduction of wages, then the distinction between voluntary and involuntary unemployment falls to the ground. (Hawtrey 1937, p. 225, italics in original)

For Pigou, enlightenment about just what was at stake in Keynes's theoretical arguments about money-wage flexibility came a little later. In a 1937 contribution to the *Economic Journal* he returned to the theme that Keynes's analysis of money-wage cuts differed little from his own, inasmuch as it ultimately relied on effects that ran through the real wage and influenced employment by that route.[4] That paper (Pigou 1937) drew a brief reply from Keynes (1937c), a reply that left the distinct impression that its author was reluctant to become engaged in debate with Pigou, and it elicited a more extensive comment from Nicholas Kaldor (1937), who deployed Hicks's IS-LM diagram to demonstrate that Keynes's analysis of money-wage cuts relied on the consequences of a rightward shift of the LM curve for effective demand, and not on their influence on the real wage.[5] Pigou (1938), acknowledging guidance from David Champernowne, not only conceded the novelty of that reasoning but went so far as to note that Keynes's mechanism could work to increase employment, even if prices and money wages moved in proportion to one another so that real wages remained constant.

The Rate of Interest

The foregoing exchange between Pigou and Kaldor makes it plain that at least one important "Classic" had something to learn from Keynes about the significance of wage–price flexibility. But Keynes, too, sometimes gave the impression of not having fully grasped the logic of his own system. He often asserted, for example, that it showed saving and investment to be irrelevant to the determination of the rate of interest. A number of commentators took Keynes to task for his sometimes extreme assertions on that matter. Knight

---

[4] As noted in Chapter 7, Pigou actually got that point right in at least one place in his *Theory of Unemployment* (1993), without apparently grasping the significance of his own insight. Robert Leeson (1996) has made a strong case that a careful reading of Pigou's work will show that he had at one time or another anticipated all the important elements of the *General Theory*. As will be apparent to the reader, I believe that there is something to be said for that point of view. However, such a reading will have to be selective. In light of his exchange with Kaldor, it would be difficult to defend the case that Pigou had nothing to learn from the *General Theory*.

[5] In light of Kaldor's later status as a leading figure among those who downgraded the IS-LM framework as an appropriate framework for interpretation of Keynes's economic thought, it is somewhat ironic to find him an early exponent of that very framework as a means of defending Keynes against a critic.

suggested that ''the most difficult part of the whole construction to take seriously'' was Keynes's proposition that

> 'the rate of interest is *not* the price which brings into equilibrium the demand for resources to invest with the readiness to abstain from present consumption. It is *the ''price'' which equilibrates the desire to hold wealth in the form of cash with the available quantity of cash.*' (Keynes 1936, as quoted by Knight 1937, p. 112, Knight's italics)

That was because

> it is self-evident that at any time (and at the margin) the rate of interest equates *both* the desirability of holding cash with the desirability of holding non-monetary wealth *and* the desirability of consuming with that of lending and so with both the other two desirabilities. (Knight 1937, pp. 112–113, italics in original)

Other critics made essentially the same point, albeit less directly, but attributed a little more novelty, and even usefulness, to Keynes's treatment of those issues than Knight was inclined to grant. Robertson, for example, devoted a substantial portion of his *Quarterly Journal of Economics* review of the *General Theory* to discussing Keynes on the rate of interest. He showed that in terms of Keynes's own analysis, shifts of the saving or investment schedule, to the extent that they affected income, would also affect the volume of transactions and hence the overall demand for money. By that route, they would help determine the rate of interest.[6] Only if ''the liquidity schedule proper is perfectly elastic'' or if ''the monetary authority not only possesses but is constantly exercising complete power to hold the rate of interest down'' (Robertson 1936a, p. 183) would that not be so. On Robertson's reading, Keynes himself took neither of those possibilities seriously, and so, referring to Hicks (1936) as expressing a similar view, he concluded as follows:

> Ultimately, therefore, it is not as a refutation of a common-sense account of events in terms of supply and demand for loanable funds, but as an alternative version of it, that Mr. Keynes's account as finally developed must be regarded. (Robertson, 1936a, p. 183)

Jacob Viner, writing in the same issue of the *Quarterly Journal of Economics*, made exactly the same point and cited Robertson's arguments in support of his own conclusion that

---

[6] It should be recalled that in his own summary of ''the General Theory'' in Chapter 18 of that book, Keynes was silent on just that point (see Chapter 10, footnote 30, herein). It was partly on the strength of that line of criticism that Presley (1978) argued that what eventually came to be taught as Keynesian economics may have owed as much to Robertson as to Keynes himself. But Presley also stressed the importance of Robertson's collaboration with Keynes, in the 1920s, to the development of Keynes's ideas. See Presley (1989) for a succinct account of their working relationship.

> demand for cash for transaction purposes is, dollar for dollar, of equal
> influence on the rate of interest as demand for cash for hoarding purposes.
> The demand for capital and the propensity to save . . . are thus restored –
> tho, [*sic*] I admit, in somewhat modified and improved fashion – to their
> traditional rôles [*sic*] as determinants of the rate of interest. (Viner 1936,
> pp. 158–159)

In sum, the majority of Keynes's "classical" critics, namely, Hawtrey,
Viner, and Robertson (as well as Pigou after 1938), all endorsed Keynes's
claims to have clarified certain theoretical questions in a useful way. They
also thought, however, that his claims of revolutionary importance for his
insights stemmed largely from two sources: first, a tendency, which we have
already discussed, to misrepresent to his own advantage the ideas of his
predecessors; and second, an equally pronounced tendency to exaggerate the
empirical relevance of certain theoretical possibilities to which his analysis
drew attention. The key matter of contention there was the sensitivity of the
demand for money to the rate of interest.

Liquidity-Preference Theory

Viner and Hawtrey recognized a central role for a shallowly sloping demand-
for-money function in creating some of Keynes's most novel results, and
both expressed considerable scepticism about the contemporary empirical
relevance of the reasons Keynes had advanced, mainly in Chapter 17 of the
General Theory, for expecting that to be a persistent phenomenon. In 1939
Robertson would also take up that theme in lectures which built upon his
1936 review; see Robertson (1940). Hawtrey was unequivocal on the matter:

> I do not think Mr. Keynes's claims to have superseded the postulates of the
> classical theory of interest can be sustained. The capacity of idle balances
> to be the decisive factor in determining the rate of interest depends on their
> magnitude. If they are small relatively to the total of cash balances (as
> appears hitherto to have been the case . . .), they do not materially modify
> the sequence of events shaped in accordance with the classical theory.
> (Hawtrey 1937, p. 6)

Viner's view was similar. The issue was not that Keynes had overrated the
strength of the community's preference for liquidity, though Viner thought
that in all likelihood he had; rather, it was that Keynes seemed to be assuming
"that liquidity-preferences can be satisfied solely by the holding of non-
investment assets" (Viner 1936, p. 154) and that he underestimated the capacity of the supply of such liquid assets to expand in response to any
increase in the demand for them. As Viner pointed out,

> the satisfaction of liquidity preference on the one hand and of investment
> on the other, are opposite phenomena only if the range of assets which can

> satisfy investment demand corresponds with the range of assets which can
> satisfy liquidity-preferences, so that it shall be impossible to satisfy both by
> the same transaction. (Viner 1936, p. 155)

Viner noted that Keynes had not systematically examined the question of just
what should be treated as "money" for purposes of giving empirical content
to liquidity-preference theory, but he drew attention to one passage in the
General Theory (1936, p. 167, fn. 1) in which Keynes had said that " 'as a
rule, I shall . . . assume that money is co-extensive with bank deposits' "
(Keynes 1936, as quoted by Viner 1936, p. 155). In Viner's view, the range
of assets available to satisfy liquidity preference was in fact much broader
than that, so that the dichotomy between satisfying liquidity preference *or*
investment demand was far from sharp:[7]

> . . . the conversion of newly-acquired cash into any other form of asset either
> involves investment directly or transfers the decision as between hoarding
> and investment to a banker or other intermediary between the original saver
> and the ultimate borrower for investment. If the banker permits his invest-
> ments to remain constant while his cash reserves are increasing, or if he
> maintains the same cash reserves for idle as for active demand deposits, or
> for time deposits as for demand deposits, or for deposits as for banknotes in
> circulation, then the propensity to hoard which manifests itself in the main-
> tenance of idle bank deposits does operate to check investment, but only
> with the connivance and support of the banking mechanism. (Viner 1936,
> pp. 155–156)

To a further possible objection, namely, that even if agents did indeed
satisfy liquidity preferences by acquiring not just money but other short-term
debts as well, that would still inhibit long-term investment, Viner responded
by pointing out that

> the relation between the period of investment intended by the saver and that
> intended, or in fact resulting, by the borrowing entrepreneur . . . approaches
> to free variability at the discretion of the borrower. Every money market
> has an elaborate machinery for transmuting short-term loans into long-term
> investments and long-term loans into short-term investments, to suit the
> convenience of original lenders and ultimate borrowers. (Viner 1936,
> p. 156)

Though he did not deny the theoretical relevance of liquidity preference in
general for the demand for money in particular, Viner further noted that

---

[7] Victoria Chick (1992, ch. 12), echoing a theme much discussed by John Hicks (e.g., 1967),
has argued that the evolution of banking institutions over time requires a parallel evolution of
monetary theory if it is to retain its relevance. In light of her admiration for Keynes's
sensitivity to that issue, and that sensitivity certainly was much on display in the *Treatise*, it is
ironic to find two of his leading "classical" critics (Hawtrey being the other, as discussed
later) taking him to task for neglecting a particular example of that point in the *General
Theory*.

> what we do know about the holders of cash balances in the United States
> points strongly to the importance of the transactions-motive for liquidity
> and to the relative insignificance in ordinary times of hoarding. (Viner 1936,
> p. 159)[8]

Hence his conclusion that

> in what seems to me the most vulnerable part of his analysis, his explanation
> of the determination of the rate of interest, Keynes assigns to the desire for
> cash for hoarding purposes a grossly exaggerated importance. (Viner 1936,
> p. 157)

Hawtrey's previously mentioned scepticism about the practical relevance of
liquidity preference as a long-run phenomenon had a basis similar to that of
Viner's scepticism. Like Viner, he noted that capital markets offered an array
of securities of various terms to savers, so that there was available to satisfy
that desire a range of assets much wider than those usually called "money":

> It is not liquidity, but the absence of any appreciable risk of capital loss,
> that requires not only time deposits but all forms of short-term investment
> to be classified with cash for the purposes of the speculative motive.
>   Whatever the applicability of Mr. Keynes's theory of liquidity preference
> to the long-term rate of interest may be, it cannot offer any explanation at
> all of the short-term rate . . . because liquidity preference so far as directed
> to the speculative motive does not distinguish between short-term invest-
> ments and cash.
>   There is of course a relation between the long-term and short-term rates.
> . . . Though . . . the average short-term rate is prevented from diverging too
> far from the long-term rate [by the banks and other short-term lenders],
> there may be very wide fluctuations about that average. Those fluctuations
> are not directly related to the variations in idle balances which, according to
> Mr. Keynes's theory, determine the long-term rate; they have to be ac-
> counted for on quite different lines. (Hawtrey 1937, pp. 198–199)

The Interest-Rate Floor

Hawtrey was also sceptical about the existence of a "conventional" value
for the long-term rate of interest sticky enough over time to give rise to a
persistent, large-scale, and highly interest-elastic demand for idle balances.
That postulate, however, was crucial to Keynes's concerns about the feasibility of driving the rate down to a level which would induce a full-employment
rate of investment expenditure. In Hawtrey's view, if the marginal efficiency
of capital fell over time, then so would the long-term interest rate. There was
no conventional and downwardly rigid value for that variable, determined

---

[8] Viner gave no citation for the source of "what we do know about the holders of cash
balances," but the empirical work of Lauchlin Currie (1934b), who by 1936 was Viner's close
associate, would certainly support his judgement.

independently of the marginal efficiency of capital, whose effect would be to produce a state of chronic underinvestment. Noting Keynes's own view that during the nineteenth century, "rates of interest were modest enough to encourage a rate of investment consistent with an average of employment that was not intolerably low" (Keynes 1936, as quoted by Hawtrey 1937, p. 210), he went on to ask the following:

> What has happened since the War? The gilt-edged rate in Great Britain reached 6 per cent. in 1920. In the succeeding years it fell rapidly, and remained about 4½ per cent. (with some fluctuations) till 1932. . . . Mr. Keynes says that investors have since become accustomed to the successively lower rates, which have now reached 3 per cent. It seems to follow that in Great Britain at any rate idle balances have not hitherto been very important. (Hawtrey 1937, p. 210)

Hawtrey adduced other, more direct, evidence to support the conclusion that liquidity preference was an empirically unimportant phenomenon:

> A mortgage which can be called up on six months' notice at any time is safeguarded against capital depreciation, and would serve just as well as a time deposit to satisfy the speculative motive. Yet mortgages, even when amply secured, yield as high a rate of interest as securities with no such safeguard. The inference would seem to be that people are not willing to pay anything appreciable for the safeguard, and that their liquidity preference is a negligible factor. (Hawtrey 1937, p. 216)

In short, Hawtrey, like Viner, recognized the theoretical novelty of Keynes's attempt to refocus analysis of the determination of the rate of interest primarily on the interaction between the supply of and demand for money; but he argued that the phenomena to which Keynes had drawn attention were usually empirically unimportant.

"Usually" is not quite the same as "always," however. Hawtrey, again like Viner, conceded the possibility of what Robertson (1940, pp. 183, 185) would term a "liquidity trap" occurring as a temporary phenomenon in certain circumstances: the banking system might let reserves build up for a while, thereby temporarily inhibiting the transformation of saving into investment. Hawtrey's concession on that point, however, was not surprising in light of his already well-developed views on the possibility of a "credit deadlock" disrupting the normal operations of the monetary system under depression conditions.[9] If, in such circumstances, traders accumulated cash and repaid bank advances in sufficient amounts, Hawtrey argued that the

---

[9] Note that the "credit-deadlock" idea amounted to an application of something very like the liquidity-trap hypothesis not to the public's demand for money but to the banking system's demand for reserves. In 1937, however, the notion of a stable demand for reserves as a function of the rate of interest had not yet been broached or investigated. That came later, with the work of A. J. Brown (1938) and Richard Goodwin (1941).

banks in their turn would initially be induced to buy securities. But if that happened on a sufficiently large scale, then the price of those securities might be driven

> to a level which seems to intending investors to be artificial. The "speculative motive" then operates, and money is withheld from investment.... Under such conditions the banks themselves may be deterred by the high prices of securities and acquiesce in a contraction of their earning assets. But this state of things is not a cause but a consequence of a depression, though it may intensify a depression once started. When it occurs, it is not to be regarded as supplying a demonstration of the existence of idle balances under other conditions. (Hawtrey 1937, p. 220)

Robertson (1940, pp. 183ff.) took a similar view summing up the whole matter as follows. He posed the question "... how far is the existence of the liquidity trap for thrift likely to hamper the banking system in ... bringing the fruits of thrift to birth?" (Robertson 1940, p. 183), to which his answer was that

> so far as the desire for liquidity is due to the "speculative" motive, i.e., the belief that the rate of interest will rise, it does not seem reasonable to expect it to be proof against a prolonged fall due to a successful accumulation of capital wealth; while so far as it is due to uncertainty in a broader sense, there are reasons for supposing the curve representing it to be much more inelastic in the long run than the short. (Robertson 1940, p. 184)

Statics and Dynamics

Some of Keynes's "classical" contemporaries thus acknowledged that he had made a contribution to clarifying the analytic inter-relationships among saving, investment, and portfolio allocation decisions, but disagreed with his specific judgements about the relative importance to be accorded to each of those particular phenomena for the overall outcome of that interaction. However, some of those critics went further. They questioned the simple form of the consumption function upon which Keynes's version of the multiplier relied, and, more fundamentally, they expressed grave reservations about his static formulation of that relationship.

The Consumption Function

Viner characterized Keynes's fundamental psychological law, that there existed a marginal propensity to consume out of current income of less than unity, as "altogether reasonable" (Viner 1936, p. 166), but, even so, he did not also accept Keynes's view that other variables were essentially irrelevant to the determination of consumption. He believed that that component of expenditure was also likely to depend upon ". . . the amount of accumulated resources measured in wage units held by the individual'' (Viner 1936, p. 165), and he argued that in rich countries, that ''should operate to level out the rate of consumption in the face of fluctuations in income, and therefore to check both the downward and the upward phases of the cycle'' (Viner 1936, pp. 164–165). Viner further suggested that ''at least over short periods'' (p. 164) the response of consumption expenditure to changes in real income might vary depending upon whether the latter were induced by price-level changes or money-wage changes. Those points were soon to become the basis of what we nowadays call the *Pigou effect*, the effect of a falling price level on consumption expenditure which renders the slope of the LM curve irrelevant as far as assessing the consequences for income and employment of wage and price flexibility.[10]

The first of those points also perhaps carried with it a pre-echo of what was eventually to become the permanent-income hypothesis of consumption, but Viner was neither the only commentator to hint at that matter nor the one to develop it at greatest length in 1936. Alvin Hansen (1936), for example, explicitly brought expected income into his discussion of Keynes's consumption function, remarking that

> it is . . . difficult to be sure precisely how Keynes would measure quantitatively the propensity to consume. Is it the ratio of anticipated consumption to anticipated income, or is it the ratio of planned consumption of the current period to the realized income of the preceding period? If it is the former, then, indeed, the propensity to consume might remain very nearly constant, regardless of fluctuations in optimism and pessimism. . . . If, however, it is the latter, then the propensity to consume would fluctuate violently with waves of pessimism and optimism. (Hansen 1936, pp. 675–676)

In a footnote to that passage, he also canvassed the relevance of ''anticipated increases in the market values of capital assets'' (Hansen 1936, p. 675, fn. 16) to the consumption decision.

It is perhaps significant that Hansen (1936, p. 667, fn. 1) expressed his appreciation for discussions with Dr. Tord Palander of the University of Stockholm. John Hicks (1936) drew attention to the important role played by expectations in Keynes's analysis and noted the strong affinity of that aspect of his work to that of contemporary Swedish economists. Most important of

---

[10] That argument implied that from a theoretical point of view, a market economy in which at least some of agents' net wealth was denominated in units of nominal money was self-stabilizing. Its most elaborate statement probably was that by Patinkin (1948), but it had been set out earlier by Pigou (1943), hence its eponymous label. According to Patinkin (1948, p. 258, fn. 4), the first full statement of it seems to have appeared in the 1941 edition of Haberler's *Prosperity and Depression* (1937, 3rd ed. 1941, pp. 242, 389, 403, 491–503). It should be noted, however, that the relevant passage, from page 403 of the 1941 edition, also appeared in the first edition (1937, pp. 298–299).

all, Bertil Ohlin, in his two-part *Economic Journal* article on the "Stockholm Theory of Savings and Investment" (1937), broached exactly the same matter, but perhaps with even greater clarity than Hansen, and went on to criticize Keynes for not carrying the analysis of expectations far enough in his treatment of consumption:

> On what does this sum total of planned consumption depend? First of all on the consumer's income expectations. Not his expected income during the first coming period only, but on what he expects to earn over a long period in the future. If a man gets a temporary, well-paid job which gives him a much higher salary than he is used to and more than he can expect to earn later on, his standard of consumption will obviously be much affected by consideration of this latter fact.
>
> As a parenthesis let me observe that Keynes's analysis on this point seems a little superficial. (Ohlin 1937, p. 62)

Evidently Ohlin regarded the definiteness introduced into the consumption–income relationship, and therefore into the multiplier too, by treating expected income as essentially equal to its currently realized value, artificial and potentially misleading.

The Static Multiplier

Closely related to that point, Keynes's insistence that "the logical theory of the multiplier . . . holds good continuously, without time lag, at all moments of time" (Keynes 1936, p. 122), as quoted here in Chapter 10 and also quoted by Knight (1937, p. 110), also came in for a good deal of criticism. Given that saving and investment were, in Keynes's 1936 terminology, equal to one another by definition, then that "logical theory" did indeed have to hold continuously, though that also required that the marginal propensity to consume had to be defined simply as the ratio of the change in consumption to the change in income observed at any particular moment. Such a "logical theory" was not, however, merely "a drastic simplification of an argument developed by Mr. R. F. Kahn," as Knight (1937, p. 110) termed it. Rather, it was a tautology, devoid of any behavioural significance whatsoever, and not the theory of income determination that Keynes intended it to be.[11] That, at least, was Hawtrey's view:

---

[11] As late as 1969, Roy Harrod was stating the multiplier theorem in tautological terms: "$Y = 1/s \ldots s$ is the fraction of income saved" (1969, p. 167). Marget, who did not pay close attention to the role of the multiplier in Keynes's analysis, was nevertheless critical of the "mechanical" nature of Keynes's treatment of the relationship, particularly coming from someone who was not averse to disparaging the "mechanical" nature of the quantity theory of money (Marget 1938–41, vol. II, pp. 476–77). Marget's criticism could certainly be applied to Harrod.

> Identity so established does not prove anything. The idea that a tendency
> for saving and investment to become different has to be counteracted by an
> expansion or contraction of the total of incomes is an absurdity; such a
> tendency cannot strain the economic system; it can only strain Mr. Keynes's
> vocabulary. (Hawtrey 1937, p. 176)

The first step in Hawtrey's solution to that terminological impasse was to
distinguish between what he called " 'designed' or 'active' investment'' on
the one hand and " 'undesigned' or 'passive' investment'' on the other
(Hawtrey 1937, pp. 176–177). The second was to think of the inducement to
invest operating only upon the active component of the aggregate (which
could obviously differ from saving). The third was to recognize that ''passive'' investment involved the unintended accumulation or decumulation of
stocks of goods, which would act ''to preserve the identity of saving and
investment'' (Hawtrey 1937, p. 179).[12] The final step was to note that

> the adjustment of income by which saving and active investment are made
> equal *takes time*. . . . The recognition of transitional periods when such pro-
> cesses of adjustment are at work is the characteristic of a dynamic theory.
> And perhaps Mr. Keynes's theory resembles the classical theory in being
> static. (Hawtrey 1937, p. 180, italics in original)[13]

Ohlin found Keynes's treatment of the multiplier ''old fashioned,'' because, unlike most recent economic theory, not least that of the Stockholm
School, it attempted to work in terms of what he called ''orthodox equilibrium constructions'' (Ohlin 1937, pp. 235–236); and he thought that it failed
to come to grips with any problem of substance because it did not distinguish
clearly between planned and realized magnitudes of variables:

> . . . either Keynes's reasoning is *ex-post*, and then it explains nothing, or it
> is *ex-ante*, and then it is entirely wrong. There is no reason why the planned
> investment plus the planned consumption should be equal to the expected
> total income for society as a whole. (Ohlin 1937, p. 237)

Not surprisingly, Ohlin insisted that the issue required an explicitly dynamic
analysis in which such *ex ante* inequalities would cause realized investment,
saving, and income to differ *ex post* from what had been expected, with
expectations and plans being revised as a result, in an ongoing process (Ohlin
1937, pp. 63–64, 235–237).

---

[12] It should be recalled that around 1930, Hawtrey himself had worked out a version of the
multiplier in the course of correspondence with Keynes, but had failed to incorporate it into
the heart of his own analysis. See Chapter 7, footnotes 21 and 23.

[13] The classical theory to which Hawtrey was referring, it should be said, was the classical
theory of interest, as described by Keynes (1936, p. 175, as quoted by Hawtrey 1937, p. 164),
in which the latter variable was determined by the intersection of supply and demand curves
for ''investible resources.'' He was not referring to any of the pre-1936 theories of cyclical
fluctuations that form the subject matter of this book.

The Accelerator

Ohlin was also critical of Keynes's treatment of investment as essentially exogenous in the analysis of the multiplier. He suggested that Keynes's neglect of "the reaction of a certain change in the volume of output and in the general business situation on profit expectations and the willingness to invest (the marginal efficiency of capital)" was "the chief reason why the multiplier theory can tell us but little about the effects of a certain increase in investment" (Ohlin 1937, p. 240). He cited Erik Lundberg in support of that contention:

> "Since the business cycles are mainly characterised *by variations* in this relation – between the value of new investments and consumption expenditures . . . *the theory must explain the changes in the multiplier* instead of assuming that the latter is given." (Lundberg 1937, p. 37, as quoted by Ohlin 1937, p. 240, fn. 1, Lundberg's italics)

Now Ohlin explicitly acknowledged the influence of Robertson on the Stockholm School's methods of dynamic analysis (Ohlin 1937, p. 55), and it is not surprising to find that Robertson, too, regarded Keynes's static treatment of the multiplier as a retrograde step, not least in the way it obscured questions having to do with the monetary element in the expansion process: ". . . if . . . we are prepared to forget about the period of transition, we can declare the problem of the finance of the process of investment to be self-solving" (Robertson 1936a, p. 172). Robertson preferred his own explicitly dynamic approach, as developed in an *Economica* article (1933), to analyse the multiplier, as indeed did Hansen (1936, pp. 674–675). That approach defined the period of analysis, what the Stockholm School would have termed the "unit period," as that in which "each unit of money enters once into income" (Robertson 1936a, p. 172), and it made current consumption a function of lagged income. It thus drew attention to the need for money creation (and/or dishoarding, as Hansen was careful to point out) equal to the excess of current investment over saving out of the previous period's income, if the multiplier were to work itself out fully; and it also made it clear that public-works expenditures had to be ongoing if their effect on income was to be anything but temporary.

Robertson's specific dynamic method of analysing the multiplier process, which he had first set out in 1933, thus gave him a means of highlighting issues that Keynes's static analysis obscured. Its direct empirical relevance was questionable, however, as Robertson himself realized:

> . . . the instructiveness of the story told . . . depends very largely on the strength of our reasons for supposing that, in the absence of continued activity by the [investing] Authority, all the induced savings of the public would have become abortive, instead of finding a vent in real investment

> either directly or through the machinery of a normally functioning stock
> exchange. (Robertson 1936a, p. 174)

And such a story, he thought, was "too pessimistic" (Robertson 1936a,
p. 174). Like Ohlin and Lundberg, he recognized that there would in fact be
important feedback from consumption to private investment while the multiplier process was working itself out:

> For the enhanced expenditure on consumption goods will normally afford a
> stimulus to increased investment, as well as the increased investment pro-
> viding the wherewithal for increased consumption. Dogs wag tails as well
> as tails dogs. (Robertson 1936a, p. 174)

Robertson then proceeded to describe, albeit informally, the operations of the
accelerator mechanism and its interaction with the multiplier in an expanding
economy.

Secular Stagnation

There was much more to the *General Theory* than a rather general analytic
framework. As we have seen, the book also used that framework as a means
of expounding Keynes's pessimistic views about the future of the market
economy. Keynes had made much of the prospects for long-term stagnation,
which in his view could be overcome by income redistribution and the
"socialization of investment." He believed that without such intervention,
stagnation would be the consequence of a highly interest-sensitive demand
for money as a store of value. That, in turn, was not just a temporary
phenomenon, perhaps to be encountered at certain phases of the cycle, but a
permanent and increasingly important characteristic of a modern capitalist
economy, whose other key feature was a low and declining marginal efficiency of capital. It is hardly surprising, therefore, that those of Keynes's
critics who thought that he had overemphasized the importance of liquidity
preference as an influence on the demand for money also found it difficult to
take his long-term prognostications seriously.

We have already discussed Hawtrey's belief that in the long run the
marginal efficiency of capital would dominate the determination of the long-
term rate of interest and that liquidity preference would not act as a permanent
obstacle to achieving a level of investment compatible with a satisfactory
level of employment. Robertson's opinion was similar, as the following
dismissive comments make clear:

> As regards future trends in the West, the whole matter is, as Professor Pigou
> has said, highly speculative. I could wish that Mr. Keynes had found it
> possible to say his say about it without, as I think, cumbering our judge-
> ments with an apparatus which accords to Liquidity a unique position in the

theory of interest to which, even in the short run, it is not, I have attempted to argue, entitled. (Robertson 1936a, p. 191)

Robertson presumably was referring to Pigou's *Economica* review (1936) of the *General Theory*, where the role accorded by Keynes to liquidity preference in generating long-term stagnation was explicitly questioned. In that review, Pigou conceded the possibility that in a temporarily depressed economy, a significant amount of wealth might be held in liquid form in anticipation of "a brighter future." But if depression was chronic, so that there was no prospect of revival, then

> even if the prospective return were low, so long as it did not fall to nothing, it would pay a rich man to invest . . . rather than convert more and more income into completely sterile hoards. (Pigou 1936, pp. 129–130)

He treated Keynes's argument that falling money wages might reduce the marginal efficiency of capital, through their effect on expectations, in a similar way.[14] On a cyclical downswing, such expectations might cause investment to be delayed, but in a stagnant economy, because,

> *ex hypothesi*, no investment would be taking place, actual wage reductions could not, by creating expectation of future ones, hold investment up, and so would be more effective than they would be in ordinary slumps. This whole matter is highly speculative, but I should not myself pay a high premium to insure against Mr. Keynes's day of judgement! (Pigou 1936, p. 130)

Knight was equally dismissive of Keynes's views on the possibilities of secular stagnation. He quoted a passage from page 236 of the *General Theory* and commented as follows:

> This, if I understand it at all, is . . . Mr. Keynes's way of saying that if new capital wealth is to be produced, its anticipated yield, including appreciation, must exceed interest on the money expended in production. Possibly this is a revelation in economic insight. (Knight 1937, p. 116)

He went on to describe Keynes's call for the socialization of investment to deal with stagnation as "more like the language of the soap-box reformer than that of an economist writing a theoretical tome for economists" (Knight 1937, p. 119).[15] His colleague Henry Simons, in a brief review aimed at a lay readership, was similarly scornful:

---

[14] Here it is worth recalling that the economists of the 1930s lacked any theory of how expectations might be formed and therefore always had large latitude for disagreeing with one another on the basis of different ad hoc postulates about that matter.

[15] Knight was invariably puritanical about the use of economic analysis to defend political positions. His criticism of Keynes was along lines similar to those he followed, albeit in private, in criticizing his colleague Paul Douglas. On the latter matter, see Stigler (1988, ch. 12). Nevertheless, his animosity to Keynes seems to have been durable. In 1940 he seems to have played a role in preventing Keynes's nomination as a candidate for an honorary doctor-

> Not content to point out the shortcomings of traditional views, Mr. Keynes
> proceeds to espouse the cause of an army of cranks and heretics simply on
> the grounds that their schemes or ideas would incidentally have involved or
> suggested mitigation of the deflationary tendencies in the economy. (Simons
> 1936b, p. 1017)

Alvin Hansen, too, resorted to sarcasm. He noted, as had Simons, the
relationship of Keynes's new work to the underconsumptionist tradition, and
he contrasted Keynes's new-found enthusiasm for J. A. Hobson with the
hostility he had displayed in a 1913 review of one of Hobson's books:

> In this review Mr. Keynes says: "One comes to a new book by Mr. Hobson
> with mixed feelings, in hope of stimulating ideas and of some fruitful
> criticisms of orthodoxy from an independent and individual standpoint, but
> expectant also of much sophistry, misunderstanding, and perverse thought.
> . . . The book is . . . made much worse than a really stupid book could be,
> by exactly those characteristics of cleverness and intermittent reasonable-
> ness which have borne good fruit in the past." This characterisation by Mr.
> Keynes himself is not altogether inapplicable, some will perhaps say, to his
> own book. (Hansen 1936, p. 667, fn. 3)

Hansen was, of course, very soon to become a leading exponent of the
secular-stagnation hypothesis (Hansen 1939). In 1936, however, perhaps still
under the influence of Schumpeter, whose own review of the *General Theory*
(Schumpeter 1936) had concentrated almost exclusively on Keynes's neglect
of the role of technical progress in maintaining the marginal efficiency of
capital, he still looked to that phenomenon as a source of continued investment opportunities:

> In brief, it is not improbable that the continued workability of the system of
> private enterprise will be made possible, not by changes in prevailing eco-
> nomic institutions (such as those advocated by Keynes), but rather by the
> work of the inventor and the engineer. (Hansen 1936, p. 683)

He noted that Keynes's proposals "are currently popular and . . . likely to be
tried on an expanding scale" (Hansen 1936, p. 683). They were, as Keynes
himself had pointed out, "a reversion to the economic doctrines of mercantilism" (p. 683), but, Hansen conceded, "the enigma of unemployment and
business depression has already impelled modern capitalistic economies far
towards the reconstruction of the mercantilistic world" (p. 684). All in all,
Hansen's judgement of the *General Theory* was much like those of other
"classic" reviewers. He found certain virtues in the book – "Keynes's
interest theory contains promising suggestions . . . the brilliant chapter on

---

ate from The University of Chicago as part of its fiftieth-anniversary celebrations. See
Patinkin (1979, pp. 300–301).

long term expectation" – but all in all it was "not a landmark in the sense that it lays a foundation for a 'new economics'."[16] It was "more a symptom of economic trends than a foundation stone upon which a science can be built" (Hansen 1936, p. 686).

Keynes's Responses

Keynes's most extensive contributions to the discussion that his book provoked appeared in the February 1937 issue of the *Quarterly Journal of Economics* and the June 1937 issue of the *Economic Journal*. He used those articles not just to reply to specific criticisms, but also, particularly in the case of the first of them, to restate what he believed to be the central message of his book.

With one exception, Keynes's disagreements with Robertson were about the provenance of ideas rather than their substance. He expressed surprise that Robertson "should think that those who make sport with the velocity of the circulation of money have much in common with the theory of the multiplier" (Keynes 1937a, p. 210) and denied the usefulness of Robertson's demonstration that if the latter relationship were treated dynamically, it would be difficult to avoid questions about the sources of the cash needed to finance growing expenditures; but otherwise he accepted Robertson's comments. He suggested that "my differences, such as they are, from Mr. Robertson chiefly arise out of my conviction that both he and I differ more fundamentally from our predecessors than his piety will allow" (Keynes 1937a, p. 210).[17] In particular, he insisted that the feedback running from output through the transactions demand for money to the rate of interest, which Robertson had analysed at length, was,

> essentially, a part of the liquidity theory of the rate of interest, and not of the "orthodox" theory. Where he states . . . that my theory must be regarded "not as a refutation of a common-sense account of events in terms of supply and demand for loanable funds, but as an alternative version of it," I must ask, before agreeing, for at least one reference to where this common-sense account is to be found. (Keynes 1937a, p. 210)

And Keynes repeated essentially the same point in the second article (1937b, p. 244).

---

[16] It is amusing to note that Hansen excised that judgement from all subsequently reprinted versions of that review.

[17] Keynes's general tone in his 1937 papers was combative, but he was conciliatory towards Robertson. It is well known that the relationship between the two was under great strain at that time, and Keynes's gentleness towards Robertson was symptomatic of his tendency to minimize points of difference between them, as noted by Moggridge (1992, p. 601). See also Presley (1989, pp. 41ff.) on their difficult working relationship after 1931.

The Demand for Money and the Rate of Interest

Now Robertson surely would have had no trouble in finding references in earlier literature to the possibility that the interaction of the supply of and demand for money might impinge upon the market for loanable funds, but Keynes still insisted that ''the theory of the rate of interest which prevailed before (let us say) 1914 regarded it as the factor which ensured equality between saving and investment. It was never suggested that saving and investment could be unequal'' (Keynes 1937b, pp. 248–249). Keynes thus chose to ignore the analysis of Mill and Marshall, among others, of the way in which the credit-market activities of banks could drive the rate of interest away from what they both called its ''natural'' value, which they did indeed think of as being determined by saving and investment. He did so, apparently, because he did not regard such analysis as an ''alternative version'' of his own. His refusal (Keynes 1937b) to accept the validity of Ohlin's use (1937) of essentially that analysis to criticize his liquidity-preference theory of the rate of interest made that clear.

It was a central contention of Keynes (1937b) that the interaction of the demand for money as a store of value with the supply of money dominated the determination of the rate of interest, not merely from time to time in conditions of deep depression, but as a long-run phenomenon. In the *Economic Journal* article (1937b), as he had in his summary of his ''General Theory'' (1936, ch. 18), Keynes treated feedbacks from saving and investment decisions, running through their effects on the transactions demand for money, as minor theoretical complications with no empirical significance. That theme also played a prominent role in his *Quarterly Journal of Economics* article (1937a), particularly in those sections of it in which he responded to Viner. There Keynes suggested that in criticizing his views on the significance of the speculative demand for money as an influence on the rate of interest, Viner had confused arguments about ''the quantity of money actually hoarded'' with those concerning ''the rate of interest as being the inducement *not* to hoard'' (Keynes 1937a, p. 210, italics in original). The point which Viner had allegedly missed was that

> when, as happens in a crisis, liquidity-preferences are sharply raised, this shows itself not so much in increased hoards – for there is little, if any, more cash which is hoardable than there was before – as in a sharp rise in the rate of interest. . . . Nor is my argument affected by the admitted fact that different types of assets satisfy the desire for liquidity in different degrees. The mischief is done when the rate of interest corresponding to the degree of liquidity of a given asset leads to a market-capitalization of that asset which is less than its cost of production. (Keynes 1937a, p. 211)

That response to Viner's criticisms was surely unsatisfactory, for Keynes had shifted to an argument about the role of liquidity preference not in the long run, but in conditions of financial crisis. Moreover, it is difficult to find traces of the confusion which Keynes attributed to him in Viner's review, for the whole point of Viner's comment on the capacity of assets other than money to satisfy liquidity preference (as of Hawtrey's similar 1937 comment) was that any increase in liquidity preference would *bid up* the market capitalization of the assets in question and *increase* the likelihood that goods whose production could be financed by issuing them would indeed be produced. Viner's point (and Hawtrey's too) was not that shifts in liquidity preference could not occur and could not cause short-run trouble; rather, it was that Keynes had exaggerated the long-run aspects of his analysis and had ignored the capacity of the capital market and financial intermediaries to supply assets, other than money balances, which could simultaneously satisfy liquidity preferences while providing finance for investment expenditure. Hence he had exaggerated the capacity of liquidity preference to disrupt the co-ordination of saving and investment decisions by interest-rate movements, except perhaps temporarily at times of crisis.[18]

The Restatement of the General Theory

The bulk of Keynes's *Quarterly Journal* article was devoted to re-expressing what he believed to be the "simple fundamental ideas which underlie my theory" (Keynes 1937a, p. 211). Clearly, one of those ideas was that as an empirically relevant approximation, the supply of and demand for money determined the rate of interest. Another was that

> Edgeworth and Professor Pigou and other later and contemporary writers ... like their predecessors were still dealing with a system in which the amount of factors employed was given and ... facts and expectations were assumed to be given in a definite and calculable form; and risks, of which, tho admitted, not much notice was taken, were supposed to be capable of an exact actuarial computation. The calculus of probability, tho mention of it was kept in the background, was supposed to be capable of reducing uncertainty to the same calculable status as that of certainty itself. (Keynes 1937a, pp. 212–213)

Keynes contrasted that view with his own position, namely, that "the fact that our knowledge of the future is fluctuating, vague and uncertain, renders

---

[18] It is worth noting that exactly the same debate as took place between Keynes and Viner on that matter also arose in the course of the exchange between Kahn and Haberler in the wake of Kahn's critical review (1937) of *Prosperity and Depression*. As in the exchange between Keynes and Viner, I believe that, in what amounted to a dialogue of the deaf, Haberler's criticisms of Keynes's analysis were more convincing than the defence of it mounted by Kahn. See Haberler (1938) and Kahn (1937, 1938).

Wealth a peculiarly unsuitable subject for the methods of the classical economic theory" (Keynes 1937a, p. 213). Fundamental uncertainty, as we would now call it, caused agents, first, to rely heavily on the present as a guide to the future and, second, to believe that current opinion based on such information was correct "unless and until something new and relevant comes into the picture" (Keynes 1937a, p. 214), so that, third,

> we endeavor to conform with the behavior of the majority or the average. The psychology of a society of individuals each of whom is endeavoring to copy the others leads to what we may strictly term a *conventional* judgement. (Keynes 1937a, p. 214, italics in original)

Such a judgement, in turn, "is subject to sudden and violent changes" (Keynes 1937a, pp. 214–215), creating a world in which

> all these pretty, polite techniques, made for a well-panelled Board Room and a nicely regulated market, are liable to collapse. At all times the vague panic fears and equally vague and unreasoned hopes are not really lulled, and lie but a little way below the surface. (Keynes 1937a, p. 215)

Classical economics itself was indeed "one of these pretty, polite techniques which tries to deal with the present by abstracting from the fact that we know very little about the future" (Keynes 1937a, p. 215), not least its treatment of money, which, according to Keynes, dealt with a "money of account" which "facilitates exchanges," in which role money "is devoid of significance or real influence" as "a store of wealth" (Keynes 1937a, p. 215). All of that was a preliminary to Keynes's reassertion that money's store-of-value role was crucial in an uncertain world and that "the possession of actual money lulls our disquietude; and the premium which we require to make us part with money is the measure of the degree of our disquietude." From that it was said to follow that "changes in the propensity to hoard, or in the state of liquidity preference as I have called it, primarily affect, not prices, but the rate of interest" (Keynes 1937a, p. 216).[19]

Keynes's response to suggestions that liquidity preference, to the extent that it was important, could be satisfied by holding assets other than money was thus to ignore them almost completely; and he dismissed the possibility that he was, in any event, exaggerating the importance of the phenomenon, asserting that "if . . . our knowledge of the future was calculable and not subject to sudden changes, it might be justifiable to assume that the liquidity-preference curve was both stable and very inelastic" (Keynes 1937a,

---

[19] Note that the problem in the monetary mechanism to which Keynes was pointing involved the effects of shifts in the demand-for-money function on the rate of interest, rather than the inability of changes in the supply of money to change that variable. Thus his argument surely appertained to short-run cyclical problems rather than to any long-run fault in the system. Here one can still detect the shadow of the American experience in 1932.

pp. 218–219). But since such knowledge was incalculable, and since fundamental uncertainty also underlay opinions about the marginal efficiency of
capital,

> it is not surprising that the volume of investment . . . should fluctuate widely
> from time to time. For it depends on two sets of judgements about the
> future, neither of which rests on an adequate or secure foundation – on the
> propensity to hoard and on opinions of the future yield of capital assets.
> (Keynes 1937a, p. 218)

From that conclusion, Keynes proceeded to his "next difference with the
traditional theory . . . its apparent conviction that there is no necessity to work
out a theory of the demand and supply for *output as a whole*" (Keynes
1937a, p. 219, italics in original). In contrast, his new theory dealt with
"effective demand." As we have already seen, Keynes's claims to originality
in focusing on that aggregate per se were quite unsustainable in the face of
Hawtrey's repeated use of just that phrase to characterize just that concept.[20]
Rather, his contribution was to carry such analysis further in dividing up the
demand for output as a whole between "investment-expenditure" and
"consumption-expenditure," in analysing their determinants separately, as
well as their interaction through the multiplier, and, crucially, in bringing the
concept of effective demand into the analysis of questions concerning the
inter-temporal allocative mechanism.

In the *Quarterly Journal* article, Keynes reiterated his conviction that the
"prevailing psychological law . . . that when aggregate income increases,
consumption-expenditure will also increase but to a somewhat lesser extent"
(Keynes 1937a, p. 219) was "absolutely fundamental to the theory of effective demand as set forth in my book. But few critics or commentators so far
have paid particular attention to it" (Keynes 1937a, p. 220). It was fundamental because it implied that "the amount of consumption-goods which it
will pay entrepreneurs to produce depends on the amount of investment-
goods which they are producing" (Keynes 1937a, p. 220). Keynes was thus
unrepentant about treating the multiplier (which he illustrated with a numerical example in which the marginal and average propensities to consume were
assumed to be equal to nine-tenths) as a static relationship, holding at every
moment. Furthermore, he gave only passing acknowledgement to the possibility of influences running from consumption to investment, with no hint
that something beyond static analysis might be needed to investigate their
significance:

> The formula is not, of course, quite so simple as in this illustration. . . . But
> there is always a formula, more or less of this kind, relating the output of

---

[20] On the relationship between Hawtrey's and Keynes's ideas on effective demand, see Chapter
10, footnote 4.

consumption-goods which it pays to produce to the output of investment-goods; and I have given attention to it in my book under the name of the *Multiplier*. The fact that an increase in consumption is apt in itself to stimulate this further investment merely fortifies the argument" (Keynes 1937a, pp. 220–221, italics in original)

Thus, there again, in restating his theory, Keynes largely ignored his critics. Though he conceded that the policy recommendations of the *General Theory* were "not worked out completely [and] not meant to be definitive" (Keynes 1937a, p. 221), it was a different matter when it came to his "theory of why output and employment are so liable to fluctuation."[21] He summarized that theory as follows:

> . . . aggregate output depends on the propensity to hoard, on the policy of the monetary authority as it affects the quantity of money, on the state of confidence concerning the prospective yield of capital-assets, on the propensity to spend and on the social factors which influence the level of the money-wage. But of these several factors it is those which determine the rate of investment which are most unreliable, since it is they which are influenced by our views of the future about which we know so little. (Keynes 1937a, p. 221)

The Critique of Traditional Theory

All of that, Keynes claimed, differed significantly from "traditional theory," and, he averred, "my main reasons for departing from traditional theory . . . are of a highly general character and are meant to be definitive" (Keynes 1937a, p. 222). In light of that characterization, those reasons are worth quoting at some length:

> (1) The orthodox theory assumes that we have a knowledge of the future of a kind quite different from that which we actually possess . . . The result has been a mistaken theory of the rate of interest . . . [with] the marginal efficiency of capital . . . setting the pace. But the marginal efficiency of capital depends on the price of capital-assets; and since this price determines the rate of new investment, it is consistent in equilibrium with only one given level of money-income . . . In a system in which the level of money-income is capable of fluctuating, the orthodox theory is one equation short of what is required to give a solution . . . Undoubtedly the reason why the orthodox system has failed to discover this discrepancy is because it has always tacitly assumed that income *is* given, namely, at the level corresponding to the employment of all available resources. . . .
> (2) The orthodox theory would by now have discovered the above defect,

---

[21] Hence the scope that existed for disagreement about just how much state involvement in the determination of the level and composition of investment Keynes was willing to countenance. On that matter, see Chapter 10, footnote 22.

if it had not ignored the need for a theory of the supply and demand of
output as a whole. I doubt if many modern economists really accept Say's
Law that supply creates its own demand. But they have not been aware that
they were tacitly assuming it. Thus the psychological law underlying the
Multiplier has escaped notice. (Keynes 1937a, pp. 222–223, italics in original)

Conclusion

In the Preface to the *General Theory*, Keynes speculated that "those, who
are strongly wedded to what I shall call 'the classical theory', will fluctuate,
I expect, between a belief that I am quite wrong and a belief that I am saying
nothing new" (Keynes 1936, p. xxi). But with the exception of Frank Knight,
who explicitly admitted to confirming that prediction (Knight 1937, p. 122,
fn. 22), and perhaps also the exception of Pigou before his 1937–38 exchange
with Kaldor, Keynes was quite evidently mistaken. That he had produced a
novel way of looking at the interactions among saving, investment, and
money in the determination of the rate of interest was recognized, as was the
fact that that insight also clarified the channels whereby money-wage cuts
could affect income and employment.[22] Closely related to those matters, it
was also conceded that there was some novelty to the theory of liquidity
preference. Keynes's treatment of the theory in question was criticized because the commentators who did so, Hawtrey and Viner in particular, thought
that he had exaggerated its empirical importance, not that he had committed
any analytic error in that context. On the matter of the multiplier, the main
complaints were that Keynes had overemphasized the substantive significance
of his definitions of saving and investment, that he had failed to distinguish
between planned and realized magnitudes, and that he had failed to appreciate
the essentially dynamic (not to mention two-way) nature of the interaction
between consumer expenditure and investment.

In short, the reception accorded the *General Theory* by Keynes's "classical" contemporaries was just as one would have expected for an important
addition to an already thriving literature, coming from an already distinguished contributor. The book was widely and constructively debated, and if
its claims to revolutionary status were not taken seriously, what was genu-
inely novel in it was both widely recognized and extensively discussed.

Keynes (1937a,b), however, continued to claim that his contribution was
of more fundamental significance. He insisted that his account of "Classical
Economics" was in fact an accurate characterization of what had preceded

---

[22] Thus the classical critics, particularly Hawtrey and Viner, may be said to have found in the
General Theory something very like the mechanisms encapsulated in the IS-LM model, to
have judged that analysis novel, but to have failed to find it of revolutionary significance.

his work, and he insisted on the overriding importance of his theory of liquidity preference as underpinning a new and revolutionary theory of the determination of the interest rate which was appropriate to a world in which decision making in conditions of fundamental uncertainty was of the essence. There is no need to pass judgement on those claims, but it should be noted that neither of them seems to have more than a passing connection with the IS-LM diagram; nor, incidentally, does that diagram have much relevance to at least one basic problem with the *General Theory*, in the eyes of his classical critics, namely, that the static nature of the theory of income determination, upon which Keynes insisted, obscured a number of crucial issues. How the IS-LM diagram and, more generally, the theoretical framework which it represented found their way to the centre of the story is the subject of the following chapter.

CHAPTER 12

IS-LM

IS-LM in Post–World War II Macroeconomics

It was noted in the opening chapter of this book that the IS-LM diagram and the model it portrayed were, from the early 1950s until the mid-1970s, the *sine qua non* of macroeconomics. The IS-LM model had, by then, come to be regarded as the principal contribution of the "Keynesian revolution," which had been launched by the publication of the *General Theory* and had overwhelmed a previously dominant "classical" orthodoxy. There is no need at this stage to labour the obvious points that the classical orthodoxy which appeared in that myth was at best a caricature of a subset of the rich and complex literature that existed before 1936 and that the *General Theory* itself incorporated, albeit selectively, a significant number of insights to be found in that literature. All of that should be clear enough from the preceding chapters, as it should be that at least some of that earlier literature's creators, far from being uncomprehendingly hostile, found new and interesting things in the *General Theory*.

Nevertheless, the impression of continuity in the development of macroeconomics which one might get from the very selective survey of reactions to the *General Theory* presented in the foregoing chapter would be misleadingly incomplete. A break did occur around 1936, and it did centre on the *General Theory*. The break in question, however, arose not directly from that book itself, but from the IS-LM model, which a number of younger commentators found in it and used to expound not just what they took to be its main message, but that of an earlier classical tradition too. It is to those developments that we now turn.

IS-LM and the *General Theory*

The IS-LM figure is sometimes referred to as the Hicks-Hansen diagram, and, for once in the history of economic thought, the designation in question, even in its violation of alphabetical ordering of the names, is appropriate enough. John Hicks (1937 repr. 1982) did draw a version of the diagram first, but in interest-rate–*money-income* space, whereas the interest-rate–*real-income* version that found its way into the textbooks was Alvin Hansen's formulation (1954).[1] The labels attached to the curves were Hansen's too, for Hicks's original mnemonics had been IS and LL. Note that I refer to the *diagram* at this point. As Warren Young (1987) has shown, Hicks created a geometric formulation of a model which a number of readers of the *General Theory* had developed in algebraic or verbal terms. That formulation seems to have evolved in the course of his interactions with at least two of the latter, James Meade and, in particular, Roy Harrod, prior to the September 1936 Oxford conference of the Econometric Society at which all three presented versions of what was, at heart, the same simultaneous-equations model. As Young has shown, the basic model was Harrod's, the notation Meade's, but the geometry was Hicks's; and it was that geometry which gave him and, a little later, Hansen so wide an audience for their exposition of the model in question.

Hicks's diagram appeared in an article entitled "Mr. Keynes and the Classics: A Suggested Interpretation," with Hansen's version of it presented in a book entitled *A Guide to Keynes*. Those titles were revealing. There was a tentative tone to Hicks's attempt to expound Keynes in IS-LM terms – his was a *suggested* interpretation – but in 1954 Hansen presented the framework as, to use Young's words, "the only possible way of interpreting and representing Keynes's *General Theory*" (Young 1987, p. 121), in effect completing what Young has called "the IS-LMization" of that book.[2] Young (1987)

---

[1] According to Warren Young (1987, p. 6), it was Oscar Lange (1938), Mabel Timlin (1942), and Franco Modigliani (1944) who gave us the real-income formulation of the system which Hansen was to popularize, and though nothing in the current exposition hangs on the issue, that formulation was surely an improvement. In particular, any attempt to go behind the IS curve to Keynes's consumption function, with its marginal propensity to consume lower than the average propensity, ran into trouble if the relationship was not expressed in real terms; Modigliani (1944), indeed, fell into just such a trap. Though it is beyond the scope of this book to discuss the matter, it should be noted that as the IS-LM model found its way into a dominant position in the textbooks, it was subjected to considerable simplification, as Ingo Barens and Volker Caspari (1997) have shown.

[2] It should be apparent from what has been said earlier, particularly in Chapter 10, that, in my view, there was a great deal that was important in the *General Theory* that did not find its way into the IS-LM model, even in its specifically "Keynesian" formulations (i.e., a shallow or horizontal LM curve). For a recent, powerfully argued version of the alternative viewpoint, see Patinkin (1990). It is also the case that Keynes himself gave something of an imprimatur to IS-LM in a letter to Hicks, commenting on a draft of "Mr. Keynes and the Classics." Hicks would later remark, with respect to that letter of March 31, 1937, as follows: "I think I may conclude from this letter (as I have always done) that Keynes accepted the SILL [*sic*] diagram as a fair statement of his position – of the nucleus, that is, of his position" (Hicks 1973, p. 10). However, as Skidelsky (1992, p. 614) has noted, the letter in question was written six months after Keynes received Hicks's paper, and such qualifications as he offered to his opening accolade, "I found it very interesting and really have next to nothing to say by way of criticism," were, in Skidelsky's words, "quibbles, as though Keynes was not very interested." If we contrast that letter with what Keynes said in important journals (1937a,b) about what he believed the essence of his contribution to be, it is difficult to accept Hicks's reading of the letter at face value. See also footnote 5 in this chapter.

has already dealt with the story of how the later dominance of the diagram and the model it summarized came about, and that development is, in any event, beyond the scope of this chapter, which is mainly concerned with the nature of the IS-LM model itself and the uses to which its creators put it.

IS-LM as the Central Message

The equations whose geometric analogue was the IS-LM diagram made their first public appearance in the June 1936 issue of the *Economic Record* in a review of the *General Theory* by Brian Reddaway, where their role in encapsulating what Reddaway took to be the central message of the *General Theory* was just as well defined as it was to be in Hansen's much later exposition of the matter. If Hansen "completed the IS-LMization of Keynes," as Young put it, then it was surely Reddaway who initiated the process.

In Reddaway's view, the purpose of the *General Theory* was to attack "one of the fundamental assumptions which has underlain orthodox theory since the days of Ricardo . . . the doctrine which used to be expressed categorically in the phrase 'Supply creates its own demand' " (Reddaway 1936, p. 32) and "to substitute a monetary theory of production according to which unemployment may be due, not to labour's refusal to accept a lower reward, but to a deficiency of 'effective demand' " (Reddaway 1936, p. 32). Effective demand, in turn, was the sum of consumption expenditure and investment, with the latter being the driving force, and its level was determined as the outcome of a system of four equations and four unknowns which Reddaway (1936, p. 37), using what is nowadays almost standard notation, expressed as follows:

$$S = f(Y) \tag{12.1}$$
$$I = g(r) \tag{12.2}$$
$$I = S \tag{12.3}$$
$$M = L(Y) + L(r) \tag{12.4}$$

Quite evidently, the first three of these equations reduce to an IS curve, and the fourth, with M given, defines an LM curve. As to Keynes's own failure to set out his analysis in those terms, Reddaway remarked that

> Mr. Keynes, quite rightly in my opinion, deprecates the spurious air of exactness introduced by too much mathematics. But in his endeavour to describe the system without this sort of shorthand he has tended to obscure the fact that the determination is mutual. (Reddaway 1936, p. 37)

What is interesting here is that Reddaway regarded the IS-LM system as being, in and of itself, a formal representation of the main contribution of the *General Theory*, one to whose elucidation it was worth devoting virtually the whole of his review. So, too, did James Meade, as the very title of his *Review of Economic Studies* commentary on the *General Theory*, namely, "A Simplified Model of Mr. Keynes' System" (1937), made clear enough. The opening sentences of that paper further confirmed such a reading of it:

> The object of this article is to construct a simple model of the economic system discussed in Mr. Keynes' 'The General Theory of Employment, Interest and Money' in order to illustrate:
> (i) the conditions necessary for equilibrium;
> (ii) the conditions necessary for stability of equilibrium; and
> (iii) the effect on employment of changes in certain variables.
>
> (Meade 1937, p. 129)

To be sure, Meade's was an eight-equation model, rather than a four-equation model. It included supply curves for capital and consumption goods and determined the division of national income between wages and profits. It also treated expected profits, and hence the marginal efficiency of capital, as endogenous variables, linked to current profits by a simple elasticity parameter, rather than as driven by exogenous animal spirits. But its demand side was, nevertheless, essentially an IS-LM framework through which the overall volume of employment was determined as a function of the marginal propensity to save, the quantity of money, and the money-wage rate, with the relative impacts of changes in the latter two variables depending upon the effects of money-wage cuts and hence price-level cuts on future profit expectations. Money-wage cuts did not work through any direct effect on the real wage and thence to the demand for labour.

In 1937, Joan Robinson also provided "a simplified account of the main principles of the Theory of Employment for students who find that they require some help in assimilating Mr. Keynes' *General Theory of Employment, Interest and Money*, and the literature which is growing around it" (Robinson 1937, p. v). It is particularly noteworthy, in light of her later scorn for the system, as mentioned in Chapter 1, that her 1937 account was also cast in essentially IS-LM terms.[3] Saving, investment, and the multiplier were discussed first. Then, with the IS side of the model thus developed, the theory of liquidity preference was introduced, and the influence of the banking system over the rate of interest was analysed as a preliminary to explaining why

> in normal times full employment can never be attained. When unemployment has fallen very low, a rapid rise in money wages sets in, the demand

---

[3] It is also worth noting that the first edition of that book remained continuously in print until being replaced with a second edition in 1969 which differed from the first only in containing a new Introduction by Mrs. Robinson that made it clear that some of its arguments were by then, in her view, of more historical than contemporary interest. But even then she did not repudiate its overall logical structure.

for money in the active circulation increases, the rate of interest is driven up, investment falls off, and unemployment increases again. (Robinson 1937, p. 62)

The IS-LM framework (although informal and dynamic) underlying that analysis was readily apparent. It is also interesting to note that Mrs. Robinson, in explaining why an economy in which the inducements to investment were chronically weak would tend to generate unemployment, paid particular attention to the monetary authorities' fear of inflation and, in an open-economy setting, of repercussions for the exchange rate. She did not stress the role of a floor to the rate of interest, stemming from the fundamental properties of a monetary economy, in rendering such an economy prone to continual depression.[4]

IS-LM as a Means of Expounding Competing Messages

Even so, not all pioneers of IS-LM analysis ignored Keynes's pronouncements about the inherent limitations imposed by the very nature of money on the economy's ability to generate full employment. Rather than presenting IS-LM, in and of itself, as an adequate representation of the substantive content of the *General Theory*, some of them therefore treated the system as a means both for developing that more specific result and for contrasting it with a less pessimistic alternative. Among the early exponents of IS-LM, that is to say, there was complete agreement that Keynes was discussing a system in which, to use Roy Harrod's words,

> if the schedules expressing the marginal productivity of capital, the propensity to consume, and the liquidity preference are known and the total quantity of money in the system is known also, the amount of investment, the level of income and the rate of interest may readily be determined. (Harrod 1937, p. 79)

There were also, however, differences of opinion, though no active debate, as to whether or not such a system represented a new contribution in and of itself.

Evidently Reddaway, Meade, and Joan Robinson found considerable novelty in the system per se, but Harrod, for one, did not. He asserted, on the contrary, that in setting out such a framework, "Mr. Keynes has not affected

---

[4] The relatively conservative nature of Robinson's reading of Keynes was nowhere more evident than in her careful discussion of the implications of his analysis for the desirability of thrift: "An increase in thriftiness does not by itself cause an increase in capital accumulation to take place. . . . But when . . . the rate of investment is pressing against the limit set by available resources, and all the workers are fully employed, . . . an increase in consumption . . . instead of setting idle resources to work, can only be made at the expense of investment" (Robinson 1937, pp. 47–48). Such considerations, she said, "warn us against too extreme a reaction from the traditional view of thriftiness as the first of the economic virtues" (p. 49). Her discussion of those issues drew a barbed compliment from Dennis Robertson (1939, p. 169).

a revolution in fundamental economic theory'' (Harrod 1937, p. 85). What Harrod did believe was that in Keynes's exposition, ''old pieces in the traditional theory reappear, but sometimes in new places'' (Harrod 1937, p. 85), so that while ''Mr. Keynes' conclusions need not be deemed to make a vast difference to the general theory, . . . they do make a vast difference to a number of short-cut conclusions of leading importance'' (Harrod 1937, p. 75). In saying that, Harrod was evidently in essential agreement with such critics as Hawtrey, Robertson, and Viner. Where he differed from them was in the significance he attached to the short-cuts. Even Keynes's most sympathetic classical critics had found those to be empirically unsupported and therefore misleading, but it was Harrod's judgement that ''Mr. Keynes' views constitute a genuine revolution in many fields'' (Harrod 1937, p. 85).

Hicks (1937) used his geometric version of IS-LM to present Keynes's contribution in exactly the same light as Harrod. He used it not only to expound Keynes's particular ''short-cuts,'' but alternatives too, which he attributed to the ''Classics.'' Hicks described the IS-LM model's role as follows: ''In order to elucidate the relation between Mr. Keynes and the 'Classics,' we have invented a little apparatus'' (1937, repr. 1982, p. 111). His versions of both classical theory and what he called ''Mr. Keynes' *special theory*'' (Hicks 1937, repr. 1982, p. 107, italics in original) were presented in algebraic and verbal terms before the IS-LM diagram (IS-LL, in Hicks's notation) was presented, though the two theories were subsequently discussed with reference to that diagram. And as far as gaining the attention of a generation of subsequent readers for his own exposition was concerned, that diagrammatic representation was crucial.

The classical theory and, by implication, Keynes's ''special'' and ''general'' theories, too, were said by Hicks to be concerned with the relationship between ''money wages and employment'' (Hicks 1937, repr. 1982, p. 102), though there was only a brief discussion of that relationship in his subsequent exposition.[5] Hicks made it clear to the reader that the version of ''classical'' economics presented was his own, rather than the formulation of that doctrine at which Keynes had aimed his ''Dunciad,'' which Hicks himself clearly regarded as something of a caricature:[6]

---

[5] Meade (1937) had, of course, paid a great deal more attention to that question, showing in particular that in his model, the extent to which monetary expansion and money-wage cuts were equivalent policies would depend on the influence of the latter on profit expectations. In so doing, he gave Keynes's arguments about that question, as expressed in Chapter 19 of the *General Theory*, their due – something which Hicks failed to do. Here, perhaps, is another reason for doubting the importance of Keynes's own accolade to Hicks's paper (see footnote 2, this chapter).

[6] Note, however, that Hicks pinned some of the blame on Keynes for having based his account of the ''classical'' theory on Pigou (1933). In light of his failure to remark upon the demon-

... it is ... clear that many readers [of the *General Theory*] ... even if they are convinced by Mr Keynes's arguments and humbly acknowledge themselves to have been "classical economists" in the past, ... find it hard to remember that they believed in their unregenerate days the things Mr Keynes says they believed. ...

One of the main reasons for this situation is undoubtedly to be found in the fact that Mr Keynes takes as typical of "Classical economics" the later writings of Professor Pigou, particularly *The Theory of Unemployment* ...

In these circumstances, it seems worth while to try to construct a typical "classical" theory, built on an earlier and cruder model than Professor Pigou's. (Hicks 1937, repr. 1982, pp. 101–102)

Even so, Hicks made no claim that the typical theory in question could in fact be found, in the form he gave it, in that earlier literature. On the contrary, he was quite explicit that "since our purpose is comparison, I shall try to set out my typical classical theory in a form similar to that in which Mr Keynes sets out his own theory" (Hicks 1937, repr. 1982, pp. 102–103). As we shall now see, Hicks's version of classical economics was, in light of the material presented earlier in this book, every bit as much a caricature as was Keynes's version.

The Classical Version of IS-LM

The model used by Hicks to expound his version of classical economics was an explicitly short-run structure in which capital stocks were held constant, and it had two features not usually found in later textbook accounts of "classical economics," but both of which were found in Meade's aforementioned account of the *General Theory*. First, instead of attributing a belief in wage flexibility to the "Classics," Hicks assumed that "the rate of money wages per head, can be taken as given" (Hicks 1937, repr. 1982, p. 103). That money-wage rigidity assumption did violence to pre-1936 trade-cycle theory, particularly but by no means uniquely British theory, only to the extent that it simplified the usual wage-*stickiness* assumption. In any event, its use was defensible in the light of Keynes having also employed it, also purely for purposes of simplification, in his own analysis. Second, Hicks distinguished between the production functions, and therefore the supply curves, for the consumption-goods and investment-goods industries. That division of production into two sectors played an unessential complicating role in his exposition.

---

strable unfairness of Keynes's treatment of it, as discussed in Chapter 11, one wonders how carefully Hicks had actually read Pigou's book.

The Role of the Cambridge Equation

The key feature of Hicks's "Classical" model was the "Cambridge Quantity equation," which he wrote

$$M = kI \tag{12.5}$$

where M was "the *given* quantity of [nominal] money" (Hicks 1937, repr. 1982, p. 103, italics in original), and I was aggregate nominal income. Its deployment in that form ensured that the quantity of money would completely determine nominal income, and therefore, given money wages, real income too.[7] The level of employment could in turn be solved for by working back through the short-run supply functions for the economy's two sectors, and thus it depended upon the division of production

> between investment and consumption-goods trades. (If . . . the elasticities of supply were the same in each . . . then a shifting of demand between them would produce compensating movements in Nx and Ny, and consequently no change in total employment.) (Hicks 1937, repr. 1982, p. 104)

Investment (I_x) depended upon the rate of interest (i): "This is what becomes the marginal-efficiency-of-capital schedule in Mr Keynes' work" (Hicks 1937, pp. 103–104).

$$I_x = C(i) \tag{12.6}$$

Saving depended upon both income and the rate of interest, so that the preceding pair of equations, along with the saving-equals-investment equilibrium condition,

$$I_x = S(i, I) \tag{12.7}$$

would determine the rate of interest as well as the division of output between consumption and investment, and hence, indirectly, employment too.

In that model, a rise in money wages would diminish employment and increase real wages, because "an unchanged money income cannot continue to buy an unchanged quantity of goods at a higher price-level; and unless the price-level rises, the prices of goods will not cover their marginal costs" (Hicks 1937, repr. 1982, p. 105). Thus, it was through its influence on what we would now call aggregate demand that a rise in money wages had its

---

[7] It is interesting to note that in his 1937 letter to Hicks (see footnote 2), Keynes did not accept Hicks's version of classical economics. "The inconsistency creeps in . . . as soon as it comes to be generally agreed that the increase in the quantity of money is capable of increasing employment. A strictly brought up classical economist would not, I should say, admit that" (Keynes to Hicks, March 31, 1937, as quoted by Hicks 1973, p. 9).

effect, rather than through any direct effect on real wages, and thence on the demand for labour. Hicks did not draw that distinction clearly, remarking only that

> since a change in money wages is always accompanied by a change in real wages in the same direction . . . no harm will be done, and some advantage will perhaps be secured, if one prefers to work in terms of real wages. Naturally most "classical economists" have taken this line. (Hicks 1937, repr. 1982, p. 105, passage originally in parentheses)[8]

Though a geometric version of it was not explicitly presented by Hicks, that "classical" model clearly was a vertical-LM-curve IS-LM system, although the IS-LM curves would be drawn in interest-rate–money-income space, rather than in interest-rate–real-income space. According to Hicks,

> historically, this theory descends from Ricardo, though it is not actually Ricardian; it is probably more or less the theory that was held by Marshall. But with Marshall it was already beginning to be qualified in important ways; his successors have qualified it still further. What Mr Keynes has done is to lay enormous emphasis on the qualifications, so that they almost blot out the original theory. (Hicks 1937, repr. 1982, p. 105)

Hicks's attributions of that model to a Ricardian tradition, and to Marshall, were completely undocumented, not to say spurious. If one were to look for something resembling it in the pre–*General Theory* literature, one would be most likely to find it not in their work, but rather, as we have seen earlier, in Hawtrey's writings from the mid-1920s onward. A vertical LM curve would capture one essential feature of his analysis, even though the fact that Hawtrey invariably thought in terms of a dynamic system, with endogenous money, would mean that the resemblance would be anything but perfect.[9]

Lange and Lerner on the "Classical" Variant

Hicks was not alone in offering his readers a caricature of classical economics along the foregoing lines; two other contemporary commentators on the *General Theory* also formulated such classical frameworks to which Keynes's

---

[8] There is, of course, a limiting case of a fixed-proportions technology in which a change in money wages leaves real wages unchanged, but still results in a change in employment generated by effective demand. Pigou himself acknowledged that in his 1938 response to Kaldor.

[9] It will be recalled that Marshall's analysis of the consequences of money-wage stickiness had nothing to do with its consequences for prices and therefore for what Hawtrey would later call "effective demand." On the contrary, it was to the influence of price flexibility interacting with wage stickiness on the real wage that he looked to explain cyclical unemployment. The reader will recall that the mechanisms which Hawtrey came to emphasize in the 1920s also played a key role in the arguments of Keynes's "Economic Consequences of Mr. Churchill" (1925). See Chapter 7.

contribution could be compared, namely, Oscar Lange (1938) and Abba Lerner (1936).

Lange explicitly acknowledged Hicks's (1937) paper, so his formulation of what he called the "classical theory of interest" was in no sense an independent one. But the fact remains that he, too, noted that inclusion of the Cambridge equation in what was essentially an IS-LM framework produced a model in which the quantity of money determined the level of income, and in which,

> total income being given, the rate of interest is determined exclusively . . . by the propensity to consume, by the marginal efficiency of investment . . . and by the condition that investment is equal to the excess of income over expenditure on consumption (i.e. saving). (Lange 1938, p. 178)

Abba Lerner (1936) also took up the role of the quantity theory of money, albeit in (income) velocity form, as a means of validating analysis in which the rate of interest successfully equilibrated independently taken saving and investment decisions. Lerner noted that Keynes himself "usually refuses to have anything to do with such simple 'quantity equations' " (Lerner 1936, p. 67), but he nevertheless suggested that some versions of that "classical" proposition involved "assuming MV . . . as unchanging." That assumption was, Lerner claimed, "frequently very tacit," but "really means that unless something special from outside – 'hoarding' – intervenes, we may expect MV to remain constant and that any decision to save will somehow result in somebody investing an equal amount" (Lerner 1936, p. 67). Thus he conceded that equilibrium at less than full employment was quite possible, even in the absence of a failure on the part of the rate of interest to co-ordinate saving and investment decisions; and he recognized what earlier writers had sometimes called "hoarding" as a factor capable of disrupting the intertemporal co-ordination mechanism. Although Lerner was clearly sympathetic to Keynes's refusal to countenance that line of argument, he pointed out to his readers that the conclusions to which it led were not far removed from those which Keynes derived from his analysis of shifts in liquidity preference. As he put it, "Dr. Haberler . . . concentrates on this line of attack, which is only a more orthodox (and more complicated) route that leads to the same conclusions as obtained by Keynes" (Lerner 1936, p. 67).[10]

It is apparent, then, that some commentators who used the IS-LM model

---

[10] Lerner's reference to Haberler's analysis of those issues (as developed in *Prosperity and Depression*), in an article which came with an endorsement from Keynes (Lerner 1936, p. 55), is interesting in light of the exchange which Haberler (1938) had with Richard Kahn (1937, 1938) in the *Economic Journal*. Kahn was quite unwilling to see any resemblance between Haberler's discussion of "hoarding" as involving a fall in velocity and Keynes's analysis of the effects of a change in liquidity preference. Keynes, too, was at cross purposes with Viner over that issue in 1937, as we saw in Chapter 11.

to elucidate the *General Theory* understood that the framework was also capable of accommodating a rather Hawtreyesque, albeit static, special case in which the quantity of money was the principal direct determinant of the level of aggregate demand, as well as extensions of that analysis to allow for changes in velocity.

The Interest Sensitivity of the Demand for Money

Hicks was aware of the fact that Marshall and his successors – he did not mention Hawtrey explicitly in that context – were concerned with "the analysis of industrial fluctuations" (Hicks 1937, repr. 1982, p. 150). He understood that such fluctuations could be accommodated in his classical model only by variations in M and/or k, and he also knew well enough that the rate of interest played a prominent role in pre–*General Theory* treatments of both possibilities. Thus, Marshall (and indeed every classical economist since Henry Thornton, though in 1937 Hicks seems to have been unaware of that) thought of changes in the quantity of money as coming about through the lending activities of the banking system, and, therefore, as involving variations in the rate of interest while they were taking place. More pertinently, Lavington, and Pigou too, on Hicks's reading (see 1937, repr. 1982, p. 106, fn. 3), had argued that

> "the quantity of resources which (an individual) holds in the form of money will be such that the unit of money which is just and only just worth while holding in this form yields him a return of convenience and security equal to the yield of satisfaction derived from the marginal unit spent on consumables, and equal also to the net rate of interest." (Lavington 1921, p. 30, as quoted by Hicks 1937, repr. 1982, p. 106)[11]

Keynes's "Special Theory"

According to Hicks, it was precisely that latter qualification of "Classical economics," the dependence of the demand for money on the rate of interest, labelled by Keynes "Liquidity Preference," that differentiated Keynes's theory from the classical construct. Hicks's version of "Mr Keynes's *special theory*" (Hicks 1937, repr. 1982, p. 107, italics in original) differed from his classical model in two ways: first, it dropped the rate of interest from the

---

[11] Hicks first had his attention drawn to Lavington's contribution in connection with "A Suggestion for Simplifying the Theory of Money" (Hicks 1935). Paul Mizen and John Presley (1995) have shown that Robertson, in commenting on a draft of "Mr. Keynes and the Classics," went to great pains to draw Hicks's attention to the role that the rate of interest had played in earlier Cambridge analysis of the demand for money, that of Lavington above all, but of Marshall and Pigou also.

saving function, and, second, it *replaced* money income with the rate of interest in the demand-for-money function, to give

$$I_x = C(i) = S(I) \tag{12.8}$$

$$M = L(i) \tag{12.9}$$

The first of those modifications was inessential, since, taken in conjunction with the Cambridge equation, it still produced a system in which

> it is impossible to increase investment without increasing the willingness to save or the quantity of money . . . identical with that which, a few years ago, used to be called the "Treasury View." *But Liquidity Preference transports us from the "Treasury View" to the "General Theory of Employment."* (Hicks 1937, repr. 1982, p. 107, fn. 4, italics added)[12]

By that last remark Hicks meant that with the demand for money depending upon the rate of interest alone, "this system of equations . . . yields the startling conclusion, that an increase in the inducement to invest, or in the propensity to consume, will not tend to raise the rate of interest, but only to increase employment" (Hicks 1937, repr. 1982, p. 107).

It is worth noting that that version of the IS-LM system was also canvassed by Lange (1938, p. 178), but, again presumably following Hicks, he found it unsatisfactory as an account of Keynes's overall argument. Hicks himself qualified its relevance in that regard as follows: ". . . in spite of the fact that quite a large part of the argument runs in terms of . . . this system alone, *it is not the General Theory* . . . The General Theory is something appreciably more orthodox" (Hicks 1937, repr. 1982, p. 107, italics in original). Specifically, Hicks argued that to capture the main thrust of Keynes's argument, money income had to go back into the demand-for-money function alongside the rate of interest,

$$M = L(I, i) \tag{12.10}$$

and "with this revision, Mr Keynes takes a big step back to Marshallian orthodoxy" (Hicks 1937, repr. 1982, p. 108).

Hicks on Keynes's "General Theory"

It was at that crucial stage in the argument that the famous diagram was first deployed by Hicks, with a downward-sloping curve labelled IS intersecting an *always upward-sloping* curve labelled LL (rather than LM), determining

---

[12] Even when referring to the Treasury view, Hicks made no explicit reference to Hawtrey.

simultaneously the rate of interest and money income, and therefore, by implication, the level of employment too. The diagram in question was, of course, an exact geometric analogue to the four-equation system which Reddaway (1936) had presented as the major contribution of the *General Theory* itself, as well as the model Harrod (1937) had constructed to elucidate its ideas and a simplified variant of the model which James Meade (1937) had also extracted from that book. The diagram was also essentially the same as that later drawn by Hansen (1954, p. 146, fig. 16), which was thereafter transmitted to economists at large as *the* correct geometric interpretation of the *General Theory*.

In Hicks's exposition, however, that specific diagram was only the beginning of the matter, because the version of the IS-LM system relevant to the task of expounding the essentials of Keynes's arguments was not, in his view, one with an always positively sloped LM (LL) curve. He ended the section of his paper in which the diagram appeared by suggesting that Keynes had made a contribution in framing an explanation of unemployment in terms of general-equilibrium analysis, and he argued that

> Mr Keynes' innovation is closely parallel . . . to the innovation of the marginalists. The quantity theory tries to determine income without interest, just as the labour theory of value tried to determine price without output; each has to give place to a theory recognising a higher degree of interdependence. (Hicks 1937, repr. 1982, p. 109)

He began his next section, however, with the following question: "But if this is the real 'General Theory', how does Mr Keynes come to make his remarks about an increase in the inducement to invest not raising the rate of interest?" (Hicks 1937, repr. 1982, p. 109). Hicks's answer was a somewhat qualified version of that given a little later by Lange: namely, that that result could be obtained either when the demand for money depended solely upon the rate of interest or "when the interest-elasticity of the demand for liquidity is infinite." And "since Mr. Keynes recognises *expressis verbis* the dependence of the demand for liquidity on total income it is obviously the last case he must have in mind" (Lange 1938, p. 178).[13]

Hicks put the matter a little less starkly, but nevertheless focused on the interest elasticity of liquidity preference. He noted that his question "brings

---

[13] It is interesting to note that Lange (1938, pp. 178–179) argued that "it is a feature of great historical interest that the essentials of this general theory [of the rate of interest, i.e., the IS-LM model] are contained already in the work of Walras." But the textual evidence which he adduced to support that proposition was in better accord with the more modest claim he made on Walras's behalf immediately after presenting that evidence, namely, that "whatever the shortcomings of his presentation, the liquidity preference function has been indicated clearly by Walras" (p. 179). Closely related arguments in support of paying more attention to Walras's contributions to the theory of the demand for money had already been made by Arthur Marget (1931), but Lange did not refer to that work.

us to what, from many points of view, is *the most important thing* in Mr Keynes' book'' (Hicks 1937, repr. 1982, p. 109, italics added), namely, that "it is . . . possible to say something about the shape of the [LM] curve. It will probably tend to be nearly horizontal on the left, and nearly vertical on the right'' (Hicks 1937, repr. 1982, p. 109). If, therefore, the economy's inducement to invest or propensity to consume was strong, then the IS curve would intersect LM where it was

> decidedly upward sloping, and the classical theory will be a good approximation, needing no more than the qualification which it has in fact received at the hands of the later Marshallians. An increase in the inducement to invest will raise the rate of interest, as in the classical theory, but it will also have some subsidiary effect in raising income, and therefore employment as well. (Mr Keynes in 1936 is not the first Cambridge economist to have a temperate faith in Public Works.) (Hicks 1937, repr. 1982, p. 109)

But if equilibrium "lies to the left of the [LM] curve, then the *special* form of Mr Keynes's theory becomes valid . . . We are completely out of touch with the classical world'' (Hicks 1937, repr. 1982, pp. 109–110, italics in original).

For Hicks, therefore, the existence of a minimum to the rate of interest, imposed by liquidity preference, was of "central importance." When the economy was depressed, it prevented interest-rate variations from intruding upon the effects of increases in investment on income and employment; and in "this doldrum to the left of the diagram" (Hicks 1937, repr. 1982, p. 111) it made it impossible to increase employment by increasing the quantity of money:

> . . . if IS lies to the left . . . merely monetary means will not force down the rate of interest any further.
> So the General Theory of Employment is the Economics of Depression. (Hicks 1937, repr. 1982, p. 111)

And, we may add, its properties were captured not by the IS-LM diagram nor by an algebraic expression thereof, in general, but by a very special formulation of that apparatus, one whose empirical basis in a highly interest-sensitive demand for money, except as a temporary phenomenon in a situation of financial crisis, had been explicitly questioned by Hawtrey and Viner.

Hicks's Extensions of the Basic Model

Not only did Hicks's paper "elucidate the relation between Mr Keynes and the 'Classics' " (Hicks 1937, repr. 1982, p. 111); it also gave the "little apparatus" developed for that first purpose "a little run on its own" (Hicks 1937, repr. 1982, p. 111), expanding it in two ways to produce what its author called "The Generalized General Theory" (Hicks 1937, repr. 1982, p. 112). First, for the sake of mathematical elegance, income was added as an argument to the IS curve, rendering the curve more shallowly sloped, and indeed perhaps upward-sloping, thus making the model potentially dynamically unstable. Hicks did not follow that line of reasoning very far, and there is no need for us to comment on it further here, except to note explicitly that to add the *level* of income to the investment function was not to introduce an accelerator relationship into the system. That would have required that the *rate of change* of income be included.

Endogenous Money in IS-LM

Hicks's second modification of the model is worthy of more attention, however:

> ... we can ... generalise our LL curve a little. Instead of assuming, as before, that the supply of money is given, we can assume that there is a given monetary system – that up to a point, but only up to a point, monetary authorities will prefer to create new money rather than allow interest rates to rise. (Hicks 1937, repr. 1982, p. 113)

There he had an idea which, like the IS-LM model itself, passed into the mainstream of post-war macroeconomics, namely, that rather than fix the quantity of money and have the rate of interest an endogenous variable, the authorities could instead peg the interest rate and allow the quantity of money to adjust so as to maintain equilibrium between the supply of and demand for money at whatever level of income was compatible with the rate of interest in question on the IS curve.

The idea itself was much older than Hicks's discussion of it, and indeed was pervasive in much of the cycle theory, not least that stemming from Wicksell, that preceded the *General Theory,* as Hicks himself partially recognized at the time:[14]

> When generalised in this way, Mr Keynes's theory begins to look very like Wicksell's. ... There is indeed one special case where it fits Wicksell's construction absolutely. If there is "full employment" in the sense that any rise in Income immediately calls forth a rise in money wage rates; then it is *possible* ... that IS is horizontal [in money-income–interest-rate space] ... [and] if IS is horizontal ... the investment [interest] rate becomes Wick-

---

[14] Hicks was, of course, familiar with the work of the Stockholm School, a fact to which Lerner alluded (1936, p. 69). He had, for example, reviewed the German version of Myrdal's *Monetary Equilibrium* for *Economica* (Hicks 1934b). Furthermore, the English translation of Lindahl's writings which appeared in 1939, which provided the basis for my discussion of Lindahl's work in Chapter 3, was produced under the editorship of Ursula Hicks and was already under way in 1937.

sell's *natural rate,* for in this case it may be thought of as determined by real causes; if there is a perfectly elastic monetary system, and the money rate is fixed below the natural rate, there is cumulative inflation; cumulative deflation if it is fixed above. (Hicks 1937, repr. 1982, p. 114, italics in original)

In making that link with Wicksell, and indeed with more modern Swedish economics too – for a footnote to that passage cited the German version of Myrdal's *Monetary Equilibrium* (Hicks 1937, repr. 1982, p. 114, fn. 10) – Hicks was pushing his "little apparatus" into service to elucidate aspects of yet another body of theory, one related to, but nevertheless separate from, that of either Mr. Keynes or the (Marshallian) "classics." But he was also pushing it as far as it would comfortably go. The next step in the analysis was, as I have already noted, to go beyond the horizontal Wicksellian "full-employment" IS curve to one that might slope upwards, and the essentially static nature of the IS-LM model was, as Hicks himself was well aware, incapable of coping with the problems of dynamic stability that such an extension implied.

IS-LM had, after all, been created in order, among other things, to elucidate the *General Theory,* which was, in Hicks's words, "a useful book; but it is neither the beginning nor the end of Dynamic Economics" (Hicks 1937, repr. 1982, p. 115).[15]

A Summing Up

Now the reactions to the *General Theory* discussed in this chapter had an altogether more "modern" tone than did those dealt with in the preceding chapter, but the two groups of papers were written at the same time. More than anything else, what distinguished their authors from one another were their ages and the extents to which they had been directly concerned in the creation of the business-cycle literature of the 1920s and early 1930s. One common thread ran through the opinions of even the more sympathetic of Keynes's older critics (Hansen, Hawtrey, Ohlin, Robertson, and Viner), namely, that the *General Theory*'s essentially static analysis obscured important problems. The younger commentators, on the other hand, exploited that

---

[15] One wonders if the appearance of the phrase "Dynamic Economics" was an oblique reference to Harrod, to whose 1937 paper Hicks had had access before preparing his own. Daniele Besomi (1996) has argued that one reason why Harrod regarded the *General Theory* as having made no revolutionary breakthrough in economic theory per se was the static nature of its analysis, which stood in stark contrast to his own efforts to combine the multiplier and accelerator into a dynamic theory of the cycle and growth. Harrod's discussion (1936) of those matters will be dealt with briefly in Chapter 13. It is interesting to note that that final sentence was excluded from the version of that paper reprinted in Hicks's *Critical Essays in Monetary Theory* (1967).

very feature of the work. It was precisely that property which enabled them to summarize whatever substantive message they took from Keynes's book in a simple system of simultaneous equations whose properties were only marginally more difficult to analyse than those of a standard partial-equilibrium supply-and-demand apparatus.

The Analytic Message of IS-LM

To be sure, the messages which they took from the book and transmitted to future generations of economists, with the aid of the IS-LM model, were somewhat bowdlerized in the process, and not altogether unique to Keynes. They all agreed that employment depended upon output and that, to use Joan Robinson's words, "the output of goods and services that will be produced depends upon the demand for them. 'Demand' implies money expenditure, not desire or need" (Robinson 1937, p. 2). They also found it useful to divide private-sector expenditure between consumption and investment and to treat the former as depending on output, and the latter on the rate of interest. None of those propositions, summarized in the first three of Reddaway's four equations (1936), originated in the *General Theory*, nor did the idea expressed in the fourth of those equations, namely, that the demand for money depended upon the rate of interest and the level of income. But all of those ideas did appear in the *General Theory*, and Keynes's analysis there of their interactions did not have exact precedents. That analysis was neither clear nor always consistent, as we saw in Chapter 10, but once the equations were written down as an algebraic system and were translated into the diagrammatic form, many obscurities and ambiguities vanished. To have effected that clarification was surely the major contribution of the work we have discussed in this chapter.[16]

The Policy Message

The IS-LM model's properties turned out to be highly dependent upon the precise configuration of the equations that made it up, notably that of the demand-for-money function. At one limit, it could be made to yield "the Treasury view" of the workings of the macroeconomy, in general, and of the ineffectiveness of public-works expenditures, in particular. At the other limit, it generated the precisely contrary policy position. Not only was the

[16] For example, the convoluted debate between Robertson and Keynes as to whether liquidity preference provided a new theory of the rate of interest or merely modified the old one, of which we saw a little in Chapter 11, becomes difficult to take seriously once one has the help of this model to consider the issue.

system simple, therefore, but also it was an apparently ideal framework for formulating questions about important policy decisions. Between those limiting cases, where a number of the model's early exponents believed Keynes's own message to lie, moreover, its more qualified implications about the powers of monetary and fiscal policy were already widely held. Abba Lerner commented on just that point as follows:

> Keynes' conclusion that the amount of employment has to be governed by operating on the amount of consumption and investment, *via* the rate of interest or otherwise, may seem at first sight to be a very small mouse to emerge from the labour of mountains. Everybody has known that cheaper money is good for business, and so is any increase in net investment or expenditure. But except for occasional lapses from scientific purity to momentary commonsense, the pundits of economic science have been declaring that people should practice more thrift. There has been a weakening of this attitude recently – I am not clear to what extent this is due to the cyclical fluctuation in the attitude of economists and how much to the influence of Keynes' ideas and some parallel development by J. R. Hicks and the Swedish writers. But we must not forget that it is not so very long ago that we had Professor Robbins and Mr. Keynes on the wireless respectively advising the world to save more and to spend more. (Lerner 1936, pp. 68–69)

The fact that Robbins was the only "pundit of economic science" actually named there was surely significant. It reminds us that demand expansion was not everyone's remedy for the depression. It also, and crucially, reminds us that that alternative viewpoint did have a theoretical basis in Austrian cycle theory, which before the arrival of IS-LM was better developed and more coherent than anything available to its opponents.[17] But IS-LM was coherent and easily taught and grasped, and it also provided a logical basis for policy conclusions that already had widespread support. It was surely those properties, rather than the more debatable claim that it embodied the crucial contribution of *The General Theory of Employment, Interest and Money*, that earned it a central place in the subsequent development of economics.

---

[17] It should be recalled that though Lerner had been exposed to Austrian analysis at the London School of Economics and to Keynes's thinking through his contacts with Cambridge, he was nevertheless a very junior faculty member in 1936, and there is no reason to believe that he was particularly well read in the literature of the 1920s as a whole, where the case for public works was, as we have seen, something of a commonplace, though it lacked a coherent theoretical base.

Conclusion

CHAPTER 13

Selective Synthesis

IS-LM, Economic Policy, and Economic Theory

The most striking characteristic of the inter-war literature dealing with money, the cycle, and employment was its diversity. Even now, with the benefit of more than half a century of hindsight, its overall shape is difficult to grasp, and the difficulties faced by those who sought to master its complexities in the 1930s can only be imagined. Nor, it is worth stressing, were those difficulties purely intellectual. The inter-war depression, which had begun in Europe long before 1929, had appalling social and political consequences. While it was in progress, those involved in the effort to understand it and to devise measures to cope with it faced not just challenging academic puzzles, but problems on whose solutions the future path of the socio-political order seemed to depend.

Economists, with their attachment to deductive theorizing, often are inclined to believe that, as a matter of logic, theoretical understanding of a problem should precede the design of a policy to cope with it. Science, however, often seems to work backwards, from coping with practical problems towards a deeper understanding of why some methods of coping work better than others. So it seems to have been in the case of the inter-war depression. The activist economic policies that were popularly associated with the ''Keynesian revolution'' had been widely proposed and supported long before 1936. Schemes involving cheap and/or abundant money and, where that was deemed insufficient, public-works expenditures, fiscal deficits, and so on, were commonplace in the inter-war literature. So, too, however, were arguments for wage cuts, or simply waiting until things righted themselves, and in light of the literature of the time, those were at least as well grounded in economic analysis as were the activist alternatives. Even so, it is difficult to argue that economic theory played a major role in delaying the implementation of activist remedies. Once attempts to restore the gold standard were abandoned in the early 1930s, policy-makers did not have to await the publication of the *General Theory* or ''Mr. Keynes and the Classics'' to take action. The relevant policy debate had largely been won long before Keynes's book appeared, and before a younger generation of economists extracted the IS-LM model from it.[1]

The IS-LM model was nevertheless important from a policy standpoint. Before its arrival, there was an improvisatory element to policy proposals, particularly those for public-works expenditures. It provided, even if *ex post*, a straightforward theoretical justification for supporting already popular measures and rejecting unpopular ones. That model, in its fixed-price-level form, had the economy's equilibrium levels of income and employment determined by the intersection of IS and LM, and it implied that if no policy measures were taken, the equilibrium would persist unless some exogenous factor shifted one of the curves. IS-LM thus reduced the policy passivity advocated by the Austrians and other pessimists to a matter of leaving recovery to chance, that is, to no policy at all. The model also implied that an economy could be expanded by shifting the LM curve to the right, which in turn could be accomplished either by monetary expansion or by across-the-board money-wage cuts. The latter measures, inevitably unpopular and politically difficult to implement, were therefore shown to be, at best, superfluous. Further implications were that under well-defined conditions, monetary policy would have little or no effect, but that the economy could be expanded by increasing government expenditure and/or by cutting taxes, and those latter measures would be at their most effective under the very circumstances which rendered monetary policy unreliable. The behaviour of the United States economy in the early 1930s, particularly in 1932, was, furthermore, widely believed to have confirmed the practical relevance of the circumstances in question. Small wonder, then, that the IS-LM model attracted attention. It enabled economic analysis to catch up with political reality, by apparently showing that already unpopular economic-policy proposals were either misguided or ineffective and that already popular measures were, after all, scientifically appropriate.

That congruence between a new economic model and an already existing attitude to policy was, however, neither a coincidence nor the outcome of some stroke of professional opportunism on the part of the creators of IS-LM. Rather, it arose from the fact that IS-LM itself represented a synthesis,

---

[1] I am deeply indebted to Peter Howitt for discussions of the issues raised here concerning the way in which scientific advances move from the pragmatic and specific towards the theoretically general. The debate about stabilization policy began long before the 1920s. As shown earlier (Laidler 1991), the case for deploying monetary policy as a counter-cyclical device began to be developed in the last quarter of the nineteenth century, and the potential for conflict with the rules of the gold standard was understood then too, by such people as Marshall and Fisher. What happened in the 1920s was that such matters became grist for practical politics in a way that they had not been before World War I, and the argument for public-works expenditures became a more prominent part of the debate, with theoretical explications of their pros and cons becoming more focused.

albeit a very selective synthesis, of theoretical ideas which long antedated its appearance and which had underpinned the policy attitude in question. The model was, nevertheless, logically self-contained; it could be, and soon was, taught independently of the literature in which it had its roots. IS-LM thus seemed to embody a revolution in economics, in the sense that an old order had been swept away and replaced with something brand-new. But the revolution associated with IS-LM was in fact synthetic in two interrelated senses. It was *ersatz*, precisely because, far from sweeping aside what had gone before, it had been created from components of that earlier economics.

The Wicksell Connection and the Quantity Theory

No matters were more discussed in the literature of the 1920s and early 1930s than the role of market mechanisms in co-ordinating saving and investment decisions, and the consequences of their failure to do so, what Axel Leijonhufvud (1981) called the *Wicksell connection*. As we saw in Part I of this book, Wicksell had shown how the activities of the banking system could establish and maintain a value for the rate of interest at which the intertemporal allocative plans of savers and investors would be mutually inconsistent, and he had also conceived of a particular configuration of a monetary system, namely, his pure credit economy, in which there seemed to be no automatic mechanism capable of restoring equilibrium.[2] And we have also seen that Wicksell's work on those matters prompted others, notably the Austrians and the Stockholm School, to replace the quantity-theory link between the stock of money and the price level with that between rate of interest and saving and investment as the central relationship around which monetary theory might develop.

In the vocabulary of its proponents, the phrase "quantity theory" referred, strictly speaking, to a theory of the price level. In Chapter 4, however, we saw that, particularly in Marshall's hands, the quantity theory had been more than that. Specifically, it had provided the starting point for theorizing about the cycle, including fluctuations in unemployment, even before Wicksell had written; and in subsequent chapters in Parts II and III we saw that the quantity theory continued to play that role in the inter-war period, even though the Wicksell connection by then had come to provide an alternative basis for cycle theory.

As the labels themselves indicate, elements of both the Wicksell connection

---

[2] The reader is reminded that Wicksell himself treated the case of a pure credit economy as a theoretical abstraction and a building block in his full cumulative process which took account of the operations of fractional-reserve banking; see Laidler (1991, ch. 5) for a discussion. It was only in the 1920s that his successors, both Austrian and Swedish, particularly the latter, began to treat the pure credit economy as important and empirically relevant in its own right.

and the quantity theory were preserved in IS-LM analysis. The former label, "investment equals saving," echoed the Wicksell connection, and the latter, "liquidity preference equals the supply of money," the quantity theory. In Chapter 6 it was shown how, in the *Treatise*, Keynes tried to combine Wicksell's work with the Cambridge quantity theory in order to produce a definitive theory of the cycle. It was also shown that his effort failed, but it is hardly surprising that the same intellectual themes found their way into the *General Theory*, where they could be discovered by that book's younger interpreters and incorporated in their formal presentation of what they took to be its theoretical core.

IS as a Variation on Wicksell's Theme

It was nevertheless a significantly truncated variation on Wicksell's analysis that left its traces in the IS curve, not one that would have been owned by some of his followers, particularly the Austrians, whose analysis was described in Chapter 2. In the IS-LM model, regardless of the particular configuration of its component equations, income and employment were determined by aggregate demand.

Current investment activity, however, necessarily involved additions to the capital stock in one or both sectors of any economy, with consequences for their future capacity to produce output.[3] The Austrian vision of the cycle, as a manifestation of Wicksellian co-ordination failure, was one in which false *current* signals, emanating from the banking system, led to the *current* construction of capital goods, whose *future* capacity to create output would be incompatible with the *future* division of demand between consumption and further investment. A banking system which, in a fully employed economy, set or held an interest rate below its natural level would cause the capital-goods sector to overexpand at the expense of the consumption-goods sector, which thereby would be rendered incapable of meeting consumer demand when it materialized. As IS-LM became the dominant orthodoxy in macroeconomics, those considerations simply vanished from the mainstream literature.[4] The version of the Wicksell connection which survived in IS-LM

---

[3] The economy's supply side did make an appearance, in the shape of separate production functions for capital and consumption goods, in early versions of it – Harrod (1937), Meade (1937), and, following them, Hicks (1937), to give three examples – but that complication was of minor significance, affecting, at most, in Hicks's version, only the quantitative relationship between income and employment once the former had been determined by aggregate demand. It would soon disappear from standard expositions of the system. It is worth noting that the two-sector economy was a rather crude approximation to the Austrian vision in which the "roundaboutness" of production was best thought of as being continuously variable.

[4] Austrian analysis disappeared from the mainstream economics literature during the 1940s, to the extent that George Shackle (1967) was able to write a highly regarded history of the development of economic theory in the inter-war years in which Hayek's name appeared only

focused on the consequences of saving–investment co-ordination failures not for the *future structure of aggregate supply* in conditions of full employment, but rather for the *current level of aggregate demand* as a determinant of the level of employment.

As we saw in Chapters 3 and 4, that second approach to the analysis of saving and investment was, by and large, the one taken by the Stockholm School and by some of Marshall's successors in England, notably Dennis Robertson.[5] The dichotomy between supply-side and demand-side considerations was not, of course, always sharply observed by those groups. For example, both Lindahl and Robertson considered expansionary cumulative processes at full employment in which forced saving very much along Austrian lines not only occurred but could produce disequilibria between the composition of aggregate demand and supply. Unlike the Austrians, however, both also raised the possibility of endogenous equilibrating forces, such as changes in income distribution (Lindahl) or induced lacking (Robertson).

Cambridge and Stockholm analyses stood apart from that of the Austrians in putting greater emphasis on the influence of the current level of aggregate demand on output, and that characteristic was closely related to a willingness on the part of both groups to assume the existence of unemployed resources as a starting point for conceptual experiments. The Austrians may have been more rigorous theorists in insisting that if the analytic problem was to explain unemployment, one should start with a situation from which it was absent and show how it could develop; but the more relaxed attitude of the Swedes and their Cambridge contemporaries, which permitted them to start out with unemployment and then ask what factors might cause it to change, turned out to be more fruitful. In their hands, a Wicksellian analysis of price-level fluctuations, as consequences of the failure of saving and investment to be co-ordinated at their full-employment values, evolved, by fits and starts, into a story about how output and employment variations could stem from changes in effective demand that were themselves consequences of that same co-ordination failure.

The key to completing the aforementioned transformation, as Leijonhufvud (1968) and Patinkin (1976a), each in his own way, have stressed, was a systematic functional relationship between consumption expenditure and income. The capacity of spillover effects, implicit in the fact that expenditures

---

in connection with his having edited the 1933 German-language edition of Myrdal's *Monetary Equilibrium*. John Hicks's essay (1967, ch. 12) on that disappearance probably was the first step in the process of redirecting the attention of mainstream macroeconomics to that important body of literature.

[5] As we noted in Chapter 4, however, it seems likely that Robertson was subjectively original in introducing those considerations into English economics, rather than being self-consciously inspired by a knowledge of Wicksell's work. That, at least, was his own view of the matter.

by agents involved in one sector of the economy become the incomes of agents engaged in other sectors, to amplify initial shocks to demand had been recognized by Bagehot (1873) and the Marshalls (1879), among others, not to mention the underconsumptionists. But, as we noted in Chapter 7, it took a long time for any consensus to be reached concerning what forces might put a limit on the deviation-amplifying tendencies – the phrase is Leijonhufvud's (1968, p. 56) – of such spillovers. Clarification required two steps. First, it was necessary to distinguish between, on the one hand, the influence of factor incomes on the consumption expenditures of their recipients and, on the other, inter-industry spillovers stemming from the demand for intermediate inputs. Then it was necessary to focus on the former and relate them to the inter-temporal co-ordination issue by way of a theory of saving behaviour. As late as 1929 Keynes had been none too clear about just what kind of spillover effects might amplify the influence of public-works expenditures, let alone about just what mechanisms might render that influence self-limiting. A clear formulation of the matter eluded the Stockholm School too.[6]

As we saw in Chapter 7, the first analysis that dealt satisfactorily with both issues was Richard Kahn's treatment (1931) of the employment multiplier. That focused on income–consumption interactions and suggested that their self-limiting nature arose principally from the leakage of expenditures into imports, along with "savings of the dole," though savings out of profit income also played a supporting role in his story. Jens Warming (1932) then showed clearly that a fractional marginal propensity to consume was enough to do the trick by itself. Thereafter, in what I have argued in Chapter 10 was a crucial theoretical step in its own right, it was left to Keynes to show that that solution implied that income and employment movements should themselves be thought of as the principal factors co-ordinating choices about the inter-temporal allocation of resources.

Now Mises (1924, tr. 1934), in particular, had emphasized that Wicksell's model of the pure credit economy lacked any automatic mechanism to restore equilibrium between saving and investment once that equilibrium had been disturbed. It is worth remarking that those aspects of Keynes's analysis from which the IS curve derived similarly lacked any endogenous mechanism to restore full employment after a shock.[7] Even so, we must not push any

---

[6] See Chapter 7, footnote 18, on the confusion about those matters displayed by Keynes and Henderson in *Can Lloyd George Do It?* On the Stockholm School, I follow Patinkin (1982) rather than, for example, Hans Brems (1978). The matter is, nevertheless, controversial. See Chapter 3, "Equilibrating Tendencies," for further discussion.

[7] As Leijonhufvud (1981) has noted, in that analysis a fall in the marginal efficiency of capital would require a fall in the rate of interest to offset it, but if income were to contract, the excess supply of saving needed to signal that would not materialize. Instead, unemployment would put downward pressure on wages, both nominal and real, but wage adjustments would be beside the point, because the problem would lie not in the labour market, but in the capital

parallel with Mises's reading of Wicksell too hard. The expectations lying behind the marginal efficiency of capital in Keynes's analysis of investment were, as pointed out in Chapter 10, dominated by the current state of "animal spirits," and he treated savings behaviour as determined by a "fundamental psychological law." Neither was treated as the outcome of utility-maximizing behaviour. The inter-temporal co-ordination failure Keynes envisaged, which found its way into IS-LM, thus bore little resemblance to anything contemplated by the Austrians. A level of investment that would fill the gap between consumption and income at full employment was desirable in Keynes's (and IS-LM) analysis because it would create full employment, not because it would have any significance as an allocatively efficient outcome.

In short, though the IS curve was a faithful, albeit partial, summary of what Keynes had to say about inter-temporal allocative matters, and though its connection with Wicksell was genuine, the connection in question was far from direct or complete. Many more economists than Wicksell and Keynes, or indeed the creators of IS-LM, had a hand in formulating the message conveyed by that piece of analysis. In particular, some of its key ingredients derived from earlier Cambridge work, with its scepticism about the relevance of rational maximizing behaviour for investment decisions, rather than from the more confident, not to say rigorously formulated, Walrasian and Austrian traditions, within which Wicksell's own contributions were properly located.[8]

LM and the Quantity Theory

The IS curve was not the whole model, however; and when the LM curve, which represented the system's link to the quantity-theory tradition, was brought into the picture, it began to look even less Wicksellian. I have noted that the phrase *quantity theory of money* usually referred to a theory involving a unidirectional causative relationship between the quantity of money, somehow defined, and the general price level. Other things equal, the relationship in question was one of strict proportionality. As I have also noted, however, the quantity theory was a starting point for much cycle analysis, and neither

---

market. Here I am describing the properties of what Leijonhufvud called the "Z model," a hybrid constructed of components selected by him from the *Treatise* and the *General Theory*, which never appeared in quite so clear-cut a form in the literature of the 1930s, but which is nevertheless very useful for illustrating clearly the issues that were at stake in that literature.

[8] The origins of that rather casual (by the standards of the 1990s, shockingly so) attitude to maximizing behaviour are surely to be traced to Marshall's partial-equilibrium approach to microeconomics, combined with his caution about not attributing to agents within his models a degree of foresight and capacity for making nicely calculated decisions which one would be unlikely to encounter in their real-world counterparts. Thus, it was not that Keynes was in any sense an economic theorist inferior to those who followed Walras, but only that his theorizing followed a very different set of methodological precepts.

Fisher nor the Cambridge economists applied such a straightforward formulation of it in that setting. Rather, they recognized the endogeneity of bank deposits, and hence of money (if they were defined as such) or of velocity (if they were not). Hawtrey and Fisher, in particular, made the interactions between an endogenous supply of money and the demand for it the centre-piece of purely monetary explanations of the cycle. A large number of others, both in Britain and in the United States, accorded that same interaction an important place in more eclectic treatments of the topic.[9]

Though there was much variety among the aforementioned approaches to the role of money in the cycle, certain common features stood out. First, all of them stressed the banking system as an important source of business loans and regarded the spread between the profit rate expected by borrowers and the rate of interest offered to them by that system as being a crucial determinant of the volume of lending. That spread, at first sight, looks like an alternative formulation of Wicksell's idea of a discrepancy between the natural and market rates of interest; and Wicksell's work and the work we are discussing here undoubtedly had a common origin in the treatment of that topic by Henry Thornton in his *Paper Credit* (1802).[10]

Three factors, however, differentiate the Fisher-Hawtrey extension of the quantity theory, by way of what we may term a *two-interest-rate model* of the interaction of the banks and the rest of the economy, from Wicksell's treatment of the same issue. First, the rate of profit expected from projects financed by bank lending, which appeared in the Fisher-Hawtrey analysis, was a less well defined concept than the marginal product of capital per unit of capital ruling in the economy, or the rate of interest at which full-employment saving and investment might in the aggregate be equated to one another. Second, Wicksellian analysis saw the direct influence of the interest-rate spread on the demand for investment goods as crucial, with associated credit creation playing a passively permissive role in the expansion or contraction thereby engendered. Quantity-theory-based models, on the other

---

[9] Thus, endogenously driven variations in the money supply, which nevertheless had subsequent causal significance for real income and prices, played an important role in the cycle theories of Lavington, Pigou, and Robertson, described in Chapter 4, and in the analyses of Mitchell, Hansen, Douglas and Director, and a number of other Chicago economists discussed in Chapters 8 and 9. None of those, however, offered so monocausal an analysis as did Hawtrey or Fisher or, in the early 1930s, Currie.

[10] That is why, as was noted in Chapter 1, the place of that particular book in the history of economic thought is so difficult to pin down, for two bodies of analysis have descended from it, and they are not the same. Thomas Humphrey (1990, repr. 1993) provided a useful account of the development, during the nineteenth century, of cumulative-process models along lines laid down by Thornton. However, relative to the perspective taken in this book, he paid less attention to the influence of Austrian capital theory on Wicksell, and hence perhaps understated the extent to which Wicksell's analysis departed from what might loosely be called a quantity-theory approach to those matters.

hand, focused on the interaction between credit (and therefore bank money) creation and the time path of the demand for money. They emphasized the effects, on the demand for goods, of both the level and the rate of change of the resulting excess supply of money, rather than any direct influence flowing from interest rates. Third, it is a matter of fact, though inessential here, that quantity-theory work paid more attention to the influence of inflation expectations on the interest rates involved.[11]

As we have seen, particularly in Chapters 4, 5, 8, and 9, most extensions of the quantity theory along such lines had monetary expansion affecting output because it raised the price level relative to money wages. The Marshalls had treated the matter in that way as early as 1879, and in the 1920s and 1930s the same mechanism was deployed by, among others, Keynes, Pigou, and a large number of American exponents of monetary expansion as a cure for the depression. That analysis was not quite coherent, however, because it neglected potential feedbacks, running through factor incomes from output changes to aggregate demand. As we have seen, Hawtrey in particular, not to mention his sometime teaching assistant Lauchlin Currie, took a different track. They argued that, to use Hawtrey's own vocabulary, disturbances to the unspent margin would influence effective demand, and hence output, precisely to the extent that money-wage stickiness delayed changes in the general price level. It was that Hawtreyan variation on the quantity-theory connection that came to be embedded in the LM curve.

The LM side of the IS-LM model nevertheless complicated what Hawtrey had to say about such matters in one important way, but simplified it in two others. First, it made the demand for money interest-sensitive; second, it reduced the transmission mechanism of money-supply changes to interest-rate effects that involved movements along the IS curve, eliminating the traditional cash-balance mechanics that might better have been captured by shifts of that curve; and third, as was noted in Chapter 12, the IS-LM model was quite unable to accommodate Hawtrey's notions about the cyclical endogeneity of the quantity of bank money. Within that model's comparative static framework it was logically possible to display the consequences of a difference between the rate of interest at which investment would fill the gap between full-employment output and full-employment consumption – the analogue to Wicksell's natural rate – and the market rate of interest; but it was not possible to accommodate a difference between the current profit

---

[11] Wicksell was nevertheless aware of the potential for inflation expectations to affect nominal interest rates, and he was certainly familiar with Fisher's work on those issues. That he nevertheless paid relatively little attention to those matters seems to me to have been the result of the particular time structure of events embedded in the pure-credit-economy model (1898, ch. 9), from whose properties he then overgeneralized. For a detailed discussion, see Laidler (1991, pp. 139ff.).

expectations of borrowers and that same market rate of interest, and hence a changing money supply.[12] The model's static nature dictated instead that the long-outmoded assumption of a quantity of money exogenously given to the system be reinstated. As a result, the model could get no closer to Hawtrey than a simple caricature in which, with a vertical LM curve, income was determined solely by a given quantity of money and, as a corollary, the "Treasury view" of fiscal policy held true.

IS-LM and the Explanation of Chronic Unemployment

Beyond doubt, the fact that IS-LM was a comparative static system directly reflected the influence of Keynes's *General Theory* on the evolution of macroeconomics, but lying in the background was an earlier influence, namely, the essentially Marshallian literature, discussed in Chapter 7, that analysed the causes of unemployment in terms of the comparative statics of the supply of and demand for labour. One message of the *General Theory* was that money-wage cuts were equivalent to money-supply increases and would help to reduce unemployment only to the extent that they lowered the rate of interest. Comparative statics provided Keynes, not to mention the exponents of IS-LM, tools adequate to demonstrate that result and to show that the outcome depended on the interest sensitivity of the demand for money or, in terms of IS-LM, on the slope of the LM curve, as Hicks (1937), with his discussion of the classical and Keynesian ranges of that relationship, explicitly pointed out.

It was shown in Chapter 4 that long before Keynes created a theory of employment in which a high interest sensitivity of the demand for money played so crucial a role, Lavington had argued that a systematic interest-rate–demand-for-money relationship was implicit in the desire of asset-holders to keep their options open in an uncertain environment.[13] That was the idea that Keynes named *liquidity preference*, and no critic of the *General Theory* argued against its theoretical significance. As we saw in Chapter 11, however, Hawtrey and Viner, in particular, suggested that Keynes had exaggerated its empirical importance. Both of them noted that there was a wide array of assets other than money available to satisfy liquidity preference, and they

---

[12] Keynes himself denied that Wicksell's concept of the natural interest rate had any relevance to the analysis of the *General Theory* (1936, pp. 242–244). However, he did concede that there was a value for that rate which, if it was attained, would induce sufficient investment to fill the gap between income and consumption. It does not seem to me to do any violence to the concept of the natural rate of interest to identify it with that value.

[13] But more than a trace of that idea was to be found in earlier Cambridge writings too, particularly by Pigou (1917). That matter has been discussed elsewhere (Laidler 1991, pp. 60–64).

concluded that Keynes had overemphasized its capacity to disrupt the capital market's ability to harmonize saving and investment plans. Hicks, on the other hand, seems to have believed that the LM curve did indeed, as a matter of fact, approach the horizontal at low interest rates.

But the important point was analytic. With a shallow LM curve, the Wicksell connection dominated the model's behaviour, and with a steep LM curve, the quantity theory did so. Thus IS-LM turned out to nest, within one simple framework, versions of the Wicksell connection and of the quantity theory too; and it also reduced some theoretical tensions of immense complexity that had been implicit in the literature of two decades or more to a straightforward quantitative question about the parameter linking the demand for money to the rate of interest. Small wonder that that parameter would in due course become the object of a great deal of econometric attention.[14] And small wonder that as empirical evidence against the "liquidity-trap" hypothesis built up, attention also turned to questions concerning the nature and extent of wage–price flexibility, in the guise of debates about the Phillips curve.

If IS-LM seems nowadays to be simple, mechanical, even intellectually trivial, or appropriately described by any of the other terms of disparagement heaped upon it by exponents of the body of theory (misnamed new-classical) that eventually replaced it, that is precisely because it was the carefully refined product of two decades or so of efforts to achieve analytic clarity about certain important questions. It was stressed in Chapter 1 that the main purpose of any formal economic model is to reduce the outcome of creative thought to a series of well-specified assumptions and mechanical deductions that can render the product of that thought accessible to anyone able and willing to master the model's logic. That an explanation of chronic unemployment, and the choices of policies to combat it, could be reduced to a matter of four equations capable of being displayed in a two-dimensional diagram was something akin to an intellectual miracle. The fact that, once the model had emerged, mastering its properties did not present much of an intellectual challenge was a major point in its favour, not something to be held against it.

Expectations, Uncertainty, and IS-LM

The synthesis represented by IS-LM was selective. The fact that its creation by Reddaway, Harrod, Meade, Hicks, and others would have been unimagin-

---

[14] It is of some interest to note that the first attempt to estimate the relationship between the demand for money and the rate of interest, by A. J. Brown (1939), dated from before World War II. However, it was not until Friedman's paper (1959), which seemed to find no such relationship, that the matter became controversial.

able without the *General Theory* and the fact that the model in due course became the very core of what was taught as macroeconomics do not between them imply that it also encapsulated the central message which Keynes intended to convey in that book. That "a monetary economy . . . is essentially one in which changing views about the future are capable of influencing the quantity of employment and not merely its direction" (Keynes 1936, p. xxii) is not the first idea to come to mind when one contemplates the Hicks-Hansen diagram, but that was Keynes's own way of summarizing the *General Theory*'s theme. IS-LM was logically compatible with that theme, perhaps, but that was about all.

The "changing views about the future" to which Keynes referred were those underlying the marginal efficiency of capital and could be thought of as factors that would shift the IS curve. In terms of the system's logic, they were thus on a par with, for example, shifts in the average propensity to consume or changes in fiscal policy. Arguments that a market economy was incapable of dealing unaided with fundamental uncertainty and that orthodox economic theory was itself "one of these pretty, polite techniques which tries to deal with the present by abstracting from the fact that we know very little about the future" (Keynes 1937a, p. 215) were not of a kind readily to be conveyed by four equations in four unknowns that purported to describe current behaviour.[15]

And yet *part* of Keynes's message concerning changing views about the future was indeed implicit in the IS-LM model, for, *given* a change in those views, whatever its source, the model did display the mechanics whereby changes in real income, and therefore in the level of employment, would then be brought about. Furthermore, not just Keynes, but, as we have seen, all of his contemporaries, faced enormous difficulties in dealing with forward-looking behaviour. The idea that expectations were of the first order of importance for current behaviour was close to commonplace in the early 1930s, but no one knew how to cope analytically with the point. To postulate the importance of error, or of conventional judgements that were subject to change, in the context of an explicitly dynamic approach to macroeconomic analysis was to render the outcome of the analysis dependent upon guesses about how those errors or judgements actually evolved over time. Seen in that light, as Hicks stressed in his *Economic Journal* review (1936) of the *General Theory*, static analysis, which treated short-term expectations as given by the realized values of variables, and long-term expectations as exogenous, was a step forward. It allowed those problems amenable to inves-

---

[15] Once again, the essentially Marshallian roots of Keynes's reluctance to push the analysis of maximizing behaviour too far should be noted (cf. footnote 9).

tigation with the existing analytic tools to be distinguished from those that were not, so that researchers could concentrate on the former.

Dynamic Analysis and IS-LM

Even so, explicitly dynamic analysis hardly vanished from macroeconomics after 1936. We have seen that the accelerator played an important part in discussions of the cycle in the 1920s and 1930s, particularly in the United States, and in Chapter 11 we noted that its absence from the *General Theory* disturbed a number of the book's early critics. We have also seen that Erik Lundberg (1937) had quickly recognized the possibilities of combining the dynamics of the multiplier process with that relationship. He was not the only one. Roy Harrod's *The Trade Cycle* (1936) had the same analytic starting point, although that book's theoretical ambitions extended well beyond anything contemplated by Lundberg.[16] Its intention was nothing less than to shift the focus of economic analysis away from static equilibrium concepts, which Harrod found completely inadequate for analysing any system in which the rates of saving and investment were positive. As he stressed, "if any net saving is occurring, the quantity of capital and the income-earning capacity of the community must be growing, and the factor of growth does not appear among the static assumptions" (Harrod 1936, p. viii).

Multiplier–Accelerator Interaction

In Harrod's view, to postulate that investment was linked to income through the multiplier, without also recognizing that the two magnitudes were linked by the capital–output ratio, and hence the accelerator, was to miss an all-important point, namely, that equilibrium in the presence of positive saving had to be represented not by a certain level of income, but by a growth path along which the constraints implicit in those two relationships would be continuously satisfied. As a corollary, the cycle was to be explained as a symptom of the disequilibrium that resulted when they were not. Now Harrod (1936) offered a purely verbal analysis of multiplier–accelerator interaction, and he was no more successful than Lundberg in generating clear-cut and analytically manageable results. Indeed, Jan Tinbergen (1937) extracted a first-order differential equation from Harrod's verbal argument and concluded that his analysis was incapable of yielding cyclical behaviour; instead, Tinbergen claimed, any disturbance to the system Harrod had described would

---

[16] On that matter, as indeed much else appertaining to Harrod's contributions to economic theory in the 1930s, see Daniele Besomi (1996).

produce monotonically explosive movements away from the equilibrium time path.

This is not the place for an elaborate discussion of the subsequent development of that line of analysis. Suffice it to note, first, that Paul Samuelson (1939a,b), writing under the acknowledged influence of Alvin Hansen, and giving appropriate recognition to the efforts of Lundberg and Tinbergen, was soon to develop a second-order difference-equation formulation of multiplier–accelerator interaction which was both complex enough to yield cyclical behaviour as a possible outcome and simple enough to be analytically tractable; second, that Samuelson's analysis in due course became the prototype for a large family of such models of the cycle; and third, that that family of models provided a standard approach to the business cycle that, in more advanced courses, came to be taught as a natural dynamic extension of IS-LM analysis.[17]

Now Keynes himself had nothing, or next to nothing, to do with that particular development. He did not originate the multiplier, and it was that relationship's static-equilibrium limit, rather than its out-of-equilibrium dynamics, that he stressed in the *General Theory*. Nor did he even utilize the accelerator; his explanation for fluctuations in investment stressed variations in "animal spirits," or "error" as his older Cambridge colleagues had called the phenomenon. Multiplier–accelerator models did, however, rely on the notion that output was determined by a level of aggregate demand equal to the sum of consumption and investment, and it was just that feature that enabled them to be linked to IS-LM and hence to be assimilated into what came to be called "Keynesian" economics. In order to accomplish that link, however, the role played by money, and hence the LM curve, in their workings had to be accounted for, or, more often than not, assumed away (for reasons of technical difficulty, one suspects).[18] The almost universally adopted trick was to make whatever assumptions were required to render the LM curve horizontal, thus cutting out any feedback from the monetary system that might disturb the smooth progress of whatever linear-difference-equation dynamics were to be analysed.

---

[17] Pearce and Hoover (1995, pp. 193ff.) have noted the tenuous nature of the relationship between Samuelson's multiplier–accelerator model and Keynes's economics, and they have also noted Samuelson's acknowledgement of Hansen's guidance. In turn, Hansen's acquaintance with the Swedish literature was noted in Chapter 11.

[18] It is interesting to note, for example, that none of the mathematical appendices which Hicks (1950) provided for his readers dealt with the material on "the Monetary Factor" introduced in Chapters 11 and 12 of that book, in which he tried to relate multiplier–accelerator interaction to IS-LM (SI-LL in that instance) analysis. The analysis in question was quite informal; though a critique is beyond the scope of this book, perhaps I should record that it does not seem to me to be very helpful either.

Endogenous Money

As we have seen in earlier chapters, the literature of the inter-war years offered a number of ways of rendering the quantity of money irrelevant. The highly interest-elastic range of the liquidity-preference function to be found in the *General Theory* was just one of them. The cruder belief that if the supply of money did not vary to accommodate changes in money income, then velocity would, a belief we encountered in the writings of such American anti-quantity theorists as Benjamin Anderson, was another; and far from dying out, that approach gained a new lease on life in post-war Cambridge economics, as the evidence of Kahn and Kaldor to the Radcliffe Committee bears witness.[19] And if neither of those was found satisfactory, then there was always available the assumption about monetary mechanisms that had underlain Richard Kahn's analysis of the dynamics of the multiplier, as well as a host of other analyses of cyclical upswings, namely, that "the intelligent co-operation of the banking system is being taken for granted."

Harrod dealt with the explanation of cyclical variations in terms of multiplier–accelerator interaction, "the most essential part of my theory" (Harrod 1936, p. 110), before he took up the topics of money and interest. In dealing with the latter, he set the tone for virtually all discussions of those topics for the next two decades; for if the cycle was indeed dominated by real forces, it had to be the case, first, that movements of the interest rate would be severely circumscribed and, second, that either the quantity of money or its velocity of circulation, or some combination of the two, would respond endogenously to any systematic fluctuations in income. As Harrod, who discussed all three of the aforementioned ways of reaching the conclusion, put it, "those forces which have been enumerated [i.e., the multiplier and the accelerator] govern the volume of output and the level of prices; these in turn cause . . . (MV) to be what it is" (Harrod 1936, p. 126).

It will be recalled from Chapter 12 that Hicks made a similar adjustment to his version of the IS-LM model when, having finished using it to expound the views he attributed to Mr. Keynes and the Classics, he came to give it "a little run on its own" and applied it to certain issues in dynamics (which did not include multiplier–accelerator interaction, however). Specifically, Hicks

---

[19] I do not, however, mean to suggest that there was any direct influence running from such American economists as Anderson or Willis to post–World War II Cambridge monetary theorists. Their insistence that the quantity of money and/or its velocity were passively endogenous variables seems to have been home-grown. Elsewhere I have discussed the evidence given by Kahn and Kaldor to the Radcliffe Committee (Laidler 1989). Note that Richard Kahn's hostility to the quantity theory was, as he recounted (1984), of long standing. Nevertheless, they and the Americans undoubtedly had common intellectual ancestors in the persons of the Banking School.

considered the model's properties when, "up to a point, *but only up to a point*, monetary authorities will prefer to create new money rather than let interest rates rise" (Hicks 1937, p. 157, italics added); and it was all too easy for later writers to ignore the note of caution implicit in the italicized phrase, particularly when Hicks himself also ignored it on the very next page as a prelude to developing a Wicksellian variation on IS-LM.[20]

In short, the IS-LM framework turned out to be capable of encompassing not just stylized static versions of the views of Mr. Keynes and the Classics about how the economy might function with an exogenous quantity of money, but a third, dynamic possibility as well, in which the monetary authorities would control the rate of interest instead of the quantity of money. In that variant of the model, the quantity of money would become not just endogenous, but passively so. It would lie at the very end of a chain of causation and would have no further significance for the behaviour of the system. That third variant of IS-LM broke the system's connection to the quantity-theory tradition. To have dealt with an exogenous-interest-rate–endogenous-money system, and yet have remained in that tradition, explicit analysis along Fisherine or Hawtreyan lines would have been required. It would have been necessary to trace through the effects, on aggregate demand, of credit-market transactions between the banks and their customers and the subsequent influence on effective demand of changes in the money supply generated as by-products of those transactions. IS-LM could not encompass those effects.

When it came to the dynamics of the cycle, therefore, the quantity-theory connection preserved by the static version of the model was broken, and macroeconomics was left with a core theoretical framework in terms of which it seemed impossible systematically to discuss monetary explanations for the cycle in general and, perhaps more important, for the Great Contraction in particular. It was only in the 1960s and 1970s, with the *monetarism* of Karl Brunner and Allan Meltzer, as well as Milton Friedman and Anna Schwartz, that the connection began to be re-established. The former began to emphasize the importance of credit-market–money-market interaction within a comparative static framework; see Brunner and Meltzer (1993) for a retrospective account of their work. Friedman and Schwartz (1963) provided a new lease on life for a monetary approach to business-cycle analysis in the tradition of Hawtrey and Fisher.

---

[20] Nevertheless, Hicks (1950, ch. 11 and 12) did try to qualify his analysis of multiplier–accelerator interaction with reference to a monetary sector which exercised some independent influence over the course of the cycle, particularly at its crisis phase. As I have already noted, his attempt was not all that successful.

Microeconomic Foundations

This is not the place to present an analysis of the nature of the "Monetarist Counter-Revolution," as Harry Johnson (1971) would call it.[21] Suffice it to assert that monetarism represented an informal blend of IS-LM analysis, cycle theory in the tradition of Hawtrey and Fisher, and, in Friedman's variant, a specifically American feature of inter-war macroeconomics, namely, the systematic empiricism of the National Bureau of Economic Research, as Abraham Hirsch and Neil de Marchi (1990, ch. 2) first suggested and as J. Daniel Hammond (1996) has more recently shown in more detail. But Friedman's work on the consumption function (1957) and the demand-for-money function (1956), as well as Brunner and Meltzer's emphasis on the role of relative prices in monetary policy's transmission mechanism, brought another element into the picture, namely, the application of explicit maximizing microeconomic models.

That feature of monetarism was not unique, for the scepticism, noted earlier in this book, of Cambridge economists in general, and Keynes in particular, regarding the wisdom of taking too seriously postulates about the scope for consciously maximizing behaviour, and the capacity of markets to co-ordinate it, did not long play a prominent role in post-war macroeconomics. Economists very soon began to investigate the implications of partial-equilibrium maximizing models for the particular equations that underlay IS-LM and, given the rapid development of computer technology from the late 1950s onwards, to investigate their empirical robustness too. They also began, under the prodding of Patinkin (1957), Clower (1965), and Leijonhufvud (1968), none of whom had forgotten that IS-LM had its origins in debates about co-ordination issues, to investigate the microeconomics of the market mechanisms that might underlie the seemingly arbitrary way in which IS-LM was constructed. The possibility of interpreting that model as a fixed-price Walrasian general-equilibrium theory was in due course revealed, notably by Robert Barro and Herschel Grossman (1976, ch. 3), and the way was also opened for a more conventional formulation of the economics of "the Lau-

---

[21] As with the "Keynesian revolution," so with the "Monetarist Counter-Revolution," too, there was a good deal of myth-making involved, as Johnson noted. Beyond the material presented in Chapter 9, I have chosen not to enter here into the debate concerning the relationship between the Chicago tradition of the 1930s and Friedman's monetarism of the 1950s and 1960s. For the record, however, let me state explicitly that I do not regard the Chicago tradition of the 1930s as a fabrication, as should be plain from Chapter 9. Nevertheless, George Stigler's judgement (1988, p. 150) that the "study of monetary economics . . . had become moribund" at Chicago prior to Friedman's taking up a position there in 1946 makes it difficult to accept that the tradition in question had continued to flourish in the late 1930s and early 1940s.

sanne school'' to become the basis for understanding the economics of money, the cycle, and employment.

My use of the phrase "the Lausanne school" is deliberate. It is the same as that used by Hayek (1929, tr. 1933) to describe the economic theory, based on maximizing behaviour in competitive markets, which he believed had to be the starting point for any properly formulated theory of the cycle. It thus came about that elements of the Austrian research agenda, particularly its deductivist and methodological-individualist components, which for a while had threatened to dominate macroeconomics in the inter-war years and then had vanished almost without a trace, were revived in the 1970s. As we now know, during this second attempt, in conjunction with advances in the modelling of endogenous forward-looking expectations as the outcome of maximizing behaviour, that agenda's success as a new macroeconomic orthodoxy has been as complete as was its failure in the 1930s. How that came about, and the nature of the relationship of the new-classical economics of the 1970s and 1980s to monetarism, and indeed more generally to the macroeconomics of the 1940–70 period, are questions that I shall leave for others to investigate.

References

Aftalion, A. (1913). *Les Crises périodique du surproduction.* Paris: Marcel Riviere.
  (1927). "The Theory of Economic Cycles Based on the Capitalistic Technique of Production." *Review of Economic Statistics* 9 (October): 165–170. Reprinted 1953 in *Readings in Business Cycles and National Income,* ed. A. H. Hansen and R. V. Clemence, pp. 129–138. New York: Norton.
Anderson, B. M. (1917). *The Value of Money.* New York: Macmillan.
  (1925). "The Gold Standard versus 'A Managed Currency'." *Chase Economic Bulletin* 5, March 23.
  (1926). "Bank Money and the Supply of Capital." *Chase Economic Bulletin* 6, November 8.
  (1927). "State and Municipal Borrowing in Relation to the Business Cycle." *Proceedings of the Academy of Political Science* 12 (3) *Stabilizing Business* (July): 1.
  (1930). "The 'Free Gold' of the Federal Reserve System and the Cheap Money Policy." *Chase Economic Bulletin* 10, September 3.
  (1935). "Money and Credit in Boom, Crisis and Depression." *The Annalist* (May 3): 661–670, 688.
Angell, J. W. (1936). *The Behavior of Money.* New York: McGraw-Hill. Reprinted 1969, New York: Augustus M. Kelley.
Backhouse, R. E. (1995). *Interpreting Macroeconomics: Explorations in the History of Macroeconomic Thought.* London: Routledge.
Bagehot, W. (1873). *Lombard Street: A Description of the Money Market.* London: P. S. King & Son. Reprinted 1962, F. C. Genovese (ed.), by Richard Irwin, Homewood, IL.
Barber, W. J. (1985). *From New Era to New Deal: Herbert Hoover, the Economists and American Economic Policy, 1921–1933.* Cambridge University Press.
  (1996). *Designs Within Disorder: Franklin D. Roosevelt, the Economists, and the Shaping of American Economic Policy, 1933–1945.* Cambridge University Press.
Barens, I. (1987). "Spiethoff, Arthur August Kasper." In: *The New Palgrave: A Dictionary of Economics,* ed. J. Eatwell, M. Milgate, and P. Newman, vol. 4, pp. 438–439. London: Macmillan.
Barens, I., and Caspari, V. (1997). "Destruction by Simplification: The Sad History of Textbook Keynesian Macroeconomics." Paper presented at the 1997 ESHET annual conference, Marseille, France, February 27–March 2, 1997. Wuppertal/ Darmstadt: Bergische Universität Wuppertal, Technische Hochschule Darmstadt.
Barkai, H. (1993). "Productivity Patterns, Exchange Rates, and the Gold Standard

Restoration Debate of the 1920s." *History of Political Economy* 25 (Spring): 1–37.

Barro, R. J., and Grossman, H. (1976). *Money, Employment and Inflation.* Cambridge University Press.

Bateman, B. W. (1994). "Rethinking the Keynesian Revolution." In: *The State of Interpretation of Keynes,* ed. J. B. Davis, pp. 103–122. Dordrecht: Kluwer.

Benjamin, D., and Kochin, L. P. (1979). "Searching for an Explanation of Unemployment in Interwar Britain." *Journal of Political Economy* 87 (June): 441–478.

Besomi, D. (1996). "The Making of Harrod's Dynamics." Doctoral thesis, University of Loughborough.

Beveridge, W. (1909). *Unemployment, a Problem of Industry.* London: Longman Group.

Bickerdike, C. (1914). "A Non-monetary Cause of Fluctuations in Employment." *Economic Journal* 24 (September): 357–370.

Bigg, R. J. (1987). "Hawtrey, Ralph George." In: *The New Palgrave: A Dictionary of Economics,* ed. J. Eatwell, M. Milgate, and P. Newman, vol. 2, pp. 605–609. London: Macmillan.

Blitch, C. (1996). *Allyn Young: The Peripatetic Economist.* Houndmills, Basingstoke, Hampshire: Macmillan.

Boehm, S. (1990). "The Austrian Tradition: Schumpeter and Mises." In: *Neoclassical Economic Theory, 1870–1930,* ed. K. Hennings and W. Samuels, pp. 201–241. Dordrecht: Kluwer.

Böhm-Bawerk, E. (1884). *Kapital und Kapitalzins.* Translated 1890 as *Capital and Interest.* London: Macmillan.

Boianovsky, M. (1995). "Wicksell's Business Cycle." *European Journal of the History of Economic Thought* 2 (Autumn): 375–411.

Bonar, J. (1923). "Ricardo's Ingot Plan – a Centenary Tribute." *Economic Journal* 33 (September): 281–304.

Bordo, M. D., and Schwartz, A. J. (1979). "Clark Warburton: Pioneer Monetarist." *Journal of Monetary Economics* 5 (January): 43–66.

Brady, M. E. (1994). "A Note on the Keynes–Pigou Controversy." *History of Political Economy* 26 (Winter): 697–705.

Brems, H. (1978). "What Was New in Ohlin's 1933–34 Macroeconomics?" *History of Political Economy* 10 (Fall): 398–412.

Bridel, P. (1987). *Cambridge Monetary Thought: The Development of Saving-Investment Analysis from Marshall to Keynes.* Houndmills, Basingstoke, Hampshire: Macmillan.

Brown, A. J. (1938). "The Liquidity Preference Schedules of London Clearing Banks." *Oxford Economic Papers* 1 (October): 49–82.

(1939). "Interest, Prices, and the Demand Schedule for Idle Money." *Oxford Economic Papers* 1 (May): 46–69.

Brown, D. V., et al. (1934). *The Economics of the Recovery Program.* Cambridge, MA: Harvard University Press.

Brunner, K. (1968). "On Lauchlin Currie's Contribution to Monetary Theory." In: L. Currie, *The Supply and Control of Money in the United States,* pp. ix–

xxxv. Cambridge, MA: Harvard University Press. Reprinted 1968 by Russell & Russell, New York.

(1987). "The Sociopolitical Vision of Keynes." In: *The Legacy of Keynes*, ed. D. A. Reese, pp. 23–56. New York: Harper & Row.

Brunner, K., and Meltzer, A. H. (1993). *Money and the Economy: Issues in Monetary Analysis*. Cambridge University Press, for the Raffaele Mattioli Foundation.

Burgess, W. R. (1927a). *The Reserve Banks and the Money Market*. New York: Harper & Row. Second edition 1936 by Harper & Row, New York.

(1927b). "What the Federal Reserve System Is Doing to Promote Business Stability." *Proceedings of the Academy of Political Science* 12 (5) *Stabilizing Business* (July): 139–147.

Cain, N. (1979). "Cambridge and Its Revolution: A Perspective on the Multiplier and Effective Demand." *Economic Record 55* (June): 108–117.

Cannan, E. (1919). *The Paper Pound 1797–1821* (the bullion report of 1810). London: P. S. King & Son.

(1921a). "The Meaning of Bank Deposits." *Economica* 1 (January) 28–36.

(1921b). "The Application of the Theoretical Apparatus of Supply and Demand to Units of Currency." *Economic Journal* 31 (December): 453–461.

(1927). "Review of T. Gregory, *The First Year of the Gold Standard*." *Economic Journal* 37 (March): 81–83.

(1930). "The Problem of Unemployment." *Economic Journal* 40 (March): 45–55.

Cassel, G. (1903). *The Nature and Necessity of Interest*. London: Macmillan. Reprinted 1957 by Augustus M. Kelley, New York.

(1918). English translation (1923): *The Theory of Social Economy,* 2 vols. London: Jonathan Cape.

(1922). *Money and Foreign Exchange after 1914*. New York: Macmillan.

Chamberlin, E. (1934). "Purchasing Power." In: *The Economics of the Recovery Program*, ed. D. V. Brown et al., pp. 22–37. Cambridge, MA: Harvard University Press.

Chambers, S. P. (1934). "Fluctuations in Capital and the Demand for Money." *Review of Economic Studies* 2 (October): 38–50.

Chick, V. (1983). *Macroeconomics after Keynes*. Deddington, UK: Philip Allan.

(1992). *On Money, Method, and Keynes: Selected Essays*, ed. P. Arrestis and C. Dow. Houndmills, Basingstoke, Hampshire: Macmillan.

Clark, J. M. (1917). "Business Acceleration and the Law of Demand: A Technical Factor in Economic Cycles." *Journal of Political Economy* 25 (March): 217–235.

(1934). *Strategic Factors in Business Cycles*. New York: National Bureau of Economic Research, in cooperation with the Committee on Recent Economic Changes. Reprinted 1949 by Augustus M. Kelley, New York.

Clarke, P. (1988). *The Keynesian Revolution in the Making 1924–1936*. Oxford University Press.

Clay, H. (1928). "Unemployment and Wage Rates." *Economic Journal* 38 (March): 1–15.

Clower, R. W. (1965). "The Keynesian Counter-revolution – A Theoretical Appraisal." In: *The Theory of Interest Rates*, ed., F. H. Hahn and F. R. P. Brechling, pp. 103–125. London: Macmillan.

Clower, R., and Howitt, P. (1998). "Keynes and the Classics: An End of Century View." In: *Keynes and the Classics Reconsidered*, ed. J. Ahiakpor. Dordrecht: Kluwer.

Coddington, A. (1976). "Keynesian Economics: The Search for First Principles." *Journal of Economic Literature* 14 (December): 1258–1273.

Colander, D. C., and Landreth, H. (eds.) (1996). *The Coming of Keynesianism to America: Conversations with the Founders of Keynesian Economics*. Cheltenham, UK: Edward Elgar.

Corry, B. A. (1962). *Money, Saving and Investment in English Economics 1800–1850*. London: Macmillan.

(1992). "Involuntary Unemployment – A Historical Note." Paper 262 (mimeograph), Queen Mary and Westfield College, University of London.

Cottrell, A. (1994). "Keynes' Appendix to Chapter 19: A Reader's Guide," and "Brady on Pigou and Keynes: Comment." *History of Political Economy* 26 (Winter): 681–695, 707–711.

(1997). "Keynes, Ricardo, Malthus and Say's Law." Unpublished manuscript, Department of Economics, Wake Forest University.

Craver, E. (1986). "Patronage and the Direction of Research in Economics: The Rockefeller Foundation in Europe, 1924–1938." *Minerva* 24 (Summer–Autumn): 205–222.

Currie, L. (1931a). "Bank Assets and Banking Theory." Unpublished Ph.D. thesis, Harvard University.

(1931b). "Review of Harold Reed: *Federal Reserve Policy 1921–1930.*" *American Economic Review* 31 (March): 162–164.

(1933a). "Treatment of Credit in Contemporary Monetary Theory." *Journal of Political Economy* 41 (February): 58–79.

(1933b). "Member Bank Reserves and Bank Debits." *Quarterly Journal of Economics* 46 (February): 509–525.

(1934a). "The Failure of Monetary Policy to Prevent the Depression of 1929–32." *Journal of Political Economy* 42 (April): 145–177.

(1934b). *The Supply and Control of Money in the United States*. Cambridge, MA: Harvard University Press. Reprinted 1968, with an introduction by Karl Brunner and other additions, by Russell & Russell, New York.

(1935). "A Reply to Dr. B. M. Anderson, Jr." *Quarterly Journal of Economics* 49 (August): 694–704.

(1936). "Review of James W. Angell: *The Behaviour of Money: Exploratory Studies.*" *American Economic Review* 26 (December): 789–791.

(1978). "Comments and Observations." *History of Political Economy* 10 (Winter): 541–548.

Currie, M., and Steedman, I. (1989). "Agonising over Equilibrium: Hayek and Lindahl." *Quaderni di Storia dell'Economica Politica* 7 (1): 75–99.

Daly, H. E. (1980). "The Economic Thought of Frederick Soddy." *History of Political Economy* 12 (Winter): 469–488.

Darity, W., Jr., and Young, W. (1997). "Reply to 'Hawtrey and the Multiplier' by Robert W. Dimand." *History of Political Economy* 29 (Fall): 557–559.

Davidson, P. (1972). *Money and the Real World.* London: Macmillan.

Davis, E. G. (1980). "The Correspondence between R. G. Hawtrey and J. M. Keynes on the *Treatise*: The Genesis of Output Adjustment Models." *Canadian Journal of Economics* 13 (November): 716–724.

Davis J. R. (1971). *The New Economics and the Old Economists.* Ames: Iowa State University Press.

Del Mar, A. (1885). *The Science of Money.* London: George Bell.

Deutscher, P. (1990). *R. G. Hawtrey and the Development of Macroeconomics.* London: Macmillan.

Dimand, R. W. (1988). *The Origins of the Keynesian Revolution.* Aldershot, Hampshire: Edward Elgar.

(1993a). "The Dance of the Dollar: Irving Fisher's Monetary Theory of Economic Fluctuations." *History of Economics Review* (Summer): 161–172.

(1993b). "When Giants Walked the Earth." *History of Economics Review* (Summer): 185–189.

(1995). "Minnie Throop England on Crises and Cycles: a Neglected Early Macroeconomist." Mimeograph, Brock University, Saint Catharines, Ontario.

(1997). "Hawtrey and the Multiplier." *History of Political Economy* 29 (Fall): 549–556.

Douglas, P. H. (1927). "The Modern Technique of Mass Production and Its Relation to Wages." *Proceedings of the Academy of Political Science* 12 (3) *Stabilizing Business* (July): 17–42.

(1932). *The Coming of a New Party.* New York: McGraw-Hill.

(1933). *Collapse or Cycle?* Chicago: American Library Association.

(1935). *Controlling Depressions.* New York: Norton.

(1972). *In the Fullness of Time: The Memoirs of Paul H. Douglas.* New York: Harcourt Brace Jovanovich.

Douglas, P. H., and Director, A. (1931). *The Problem of Unemployment.* New York: Macmillan.

Durbin, E. F. M. (1933). *Purchasing Power and Trade Depression, a Critique of Underconsumption Theories.* London: Jonathan Cape.

(1935). *The Problem of Credit Policy.* New York: Wiley.

Edgeworth, F. Y. (1888). "The Mathematical Theory of Banking." *Journal of the Royal Statistical Society* 51 (March): 113–126.

Edie, L. D. (1931). *The Banks and Prosperity.* New York: Harper & Row.

Ellis, H. S. (1934). *German Monetary Theory 1905–1933.* Cambridge, MA: Harvard University Press.

Ely, R. T. (1923). *Outlines of Economics.* New York: Macmillan. (Revised edition prepared by T. S. Adams, M. Lorenz, and Allyn A. Young.)

England, M. T. (1912). "Fisher's Theory of Crises: A Criticism." *Quarterly Journal of Economics* 27 (November): 95–106.

(1913). "Economic Crises." *Journal of Political Economy* 21 (April): 345–354.

Fanno, M. (1912). *The Money Market* (part II of *Le Banche e il Mercato Monetaro*). Translated 1995 by C. P. Blamires, London: Macmillan.

Fisher, I. (1896). "Appreciation and Interest." *American Economic Association Publications, Series Three* 2: 331–442.

  (1907). *The Rate of Interest; Its Nature, Determination, and Relation to Economic Phenomena.* New York: Macmillan.

  (1911). *The Purchasing Power of Money: Its Determination and Relation to Credit, Interest and Crises.* New York: Macmillan.

  (1922). *The Making of Index Numbers.* Boston: Houghton Mifflin.

  (1923). "The Business Cycle Largely a 'Dance of the Dollar'." *Journal of the American Statistical Association* 18 (December): 1024–1028.

  (1925). "Our Unstable Dollar and the So-called Business Cycle." *Journal of the American Statistics Association* 20 (June): 179–202.

  (1928). *The Money Illusion.* New York: Adelphi Company.

  (1930a). *The Theory of Interest.* New York: Macmillan.

  (1930b). *The "Noble Experiment."* New York: Alcohol Information Committee.

  (1932). *Booms and Depressions.* New York: Adelphi Company.

  (1933). "The Debt-Deflation Theory of Great Depressions." *Econometrica* 1: 337–357.

  (1934). *Stable Money: A History of the Movement.* New York: Adelphi Company.

  (1935). *100 per cent. Money.* New York: Adelphi Company.

Flanders, M. J. (1989). *International Monetary Economics 1870–1960 – Between the Classical and the New-Classical.* Cambridge University Press.

Foster, W. T., and Catchings, W. (1923). *Money.* Boston: Houghton Mifflin.

  (1925). *Profits.* Boston: Houghton Mifflin.

  (1927). *Business Without a Buyer.* Boston: Houghton Mifflin.

  (1928). *The Road to Plenty.* Boston: Houghton Mifflin.

Foxwell, H. S. (1886). *Irregularity of Employment and Fluctuations of Prices.* Edinburgh: Co-operative Printing Co. Ltd.

Fregert, K. (1993). "Erik Lindahl's Norm for Monetary Policy." In: *Swedish Economic Thought: Explorations and Advances*, ed. L. Jonung, pp. 125–142. London: Routledge.

Friedman, M. (1956). "The Quantity Theory of Money, a Restatement." In: *Studies in the Quantity Theory of Money*, ed. M. Friedman, pp. 3–21. University of Chicago Press.

  (1957). *A Theory of the Consumption Function.* Princeton, NJ: Princeton University Press.

  (1959). "The Demand for Money, Some Theoretical and Empirical Results." *Journal of Political Economy* 67 (June):327–351.

  (1967). "The Monetary Theory and Policy of Henry Simons." *Journal of Law and Economics* 10 (October):1–13.

  (1968). "The Role of Monetary Policy." *American Economic Review* 58 (March): 1–19.

  (1974). *Milton Friedman's Monetary Framework*, ed. R. J. Gordon. University of Chicago Press.

Friedman, M., and Schwartz, A. J. (1963). *A Monetary History of the United States*

1867–1960. Princeton, NJ: Princeton University Press, for the National Bureau of Economic Research.

Gårdlund, T. (1958). *The Life of Knut Wicksell*. Translated by Nancy Adles and republished 1996, Aldershot, Hampshire: Edward Elgar.

Garvey, G. (1978). "Carl Snyder, Pioneer Economic Statistician and Monetarist." *History of Political Economy* 10 (Fall): 454–489.

Gayer, A. D. (1935a). *Monetary Policy and Economic Stabilization: A Study of the Gold Standard*. London: A. & C. Black.

(1935b). *Public Works in Prosperity and Depression*. New York: National Bureau of Economic Research.

Giffen, R. (1877). *Stock Exchange Securities*. London: George Bell.

Gilbert, J. C. (1953). "The Demand for Money: The Development of an Economic Concept." *Journal of Political Economy* 61 (April): 144–159.

Girton, L., and Roper, D. (1978). "J. Laurence Laughlin and the Quantity Theory of Money." *Journal of Political Economy* 86 (August): 599–625.

Goldenweiser, E. A. (1930). "Introduction." In: Riefler, W. W., *Money Rates and Money Markets in the United States*. New York: Harper & Row.

Goodhart, C. (1992). "Robertson and the Real Business Cycle." In: *Essays on Robertsonian Economics*, ed. J. R. Presley, pp. 8–34. London: Macmillan.

Goodwin, R. (1941). "The Supply of Bank Money in England and Wales 1920–1938." *Oxford Economic Papers* 5 (June): 2–29.

Gregory, T. E. (1928). *An Introduction to Tooke and Newmarch's A History of Prices*. London: P. S. King & Son. Reprinted 1962 by London School of Economics, series of reprints of *Scarce Works on Political Economy*, no. 16.

(1933). *Gold, Unemployment and Capitalism*. London: P. S. King & Son.

Haberler, G. von (1932). "Money and the Business Cycle." In: *Gold and Monetary Stabilization: Lectures on the Harris Foundation*, ed. Q. Wright, pp. 43–74. University of Chicago Press.

(1937). *Prosperity and Depression*. Geneva: League of Nations. Third revised edition 1941, Geneva: League of Nations. Sixth edition 1964, Cambridge, MA: Harvard University Press.

(1938). "Some Comments on Mr. Kahn's Review of *Prosperity and Depression*." *Economic Journal* 48 (June): 322–333.

Hagemann, H. (1994). "Hayek and the Kiel School: Some Reflections on the German Debate on Business Cycles in the Late 1920s and Early 1930s." In: *Money and Business Cycles: The Economics of F. A. Hayek*, vol. 1, ed. M. Colonna and H. Hagemann, pp. 101–120. Aldershot, Hampshire: Edward Elgar.

Hagemann, H., and Rühl, C. H. (1990). "Nicholas Johannsen and Keynes' 'Finance Motive'." *Journal of Institutional and Theoretical Economics* 146: 445–469.

Hahn, L. (1924a). *Geld und Kredit*. Neue Folge 1929. Tübingen: J. C. B. Mohr.

(1924b). "Zur Frage des sogenanten 'Vertrauens in die Wahrung'." *Archiv für Sozialwissenschaft und Sozialpolitik* 52 (2): 289–316.

Hammond, J. D. (1996). *Theory and Measurement – Causality Issues in Milton Friedman's Monetary Economics*. Cambridge University Press.

Hansen, A. H. (1921). *Cycles of Prosperity and Depression in the United States,*

Great Britain and Germany: A Study of Monthly Data 1902–1908. Madison: University of Wisconsin Press.

(1927). *Business-Cycle Theory: Its Development and Present Status.* Boston: Ginn.

(1932). *Economic Stabilization in an Unbalanced World.* New York: Harcourt Brace & Co.

(1936). "Mr. Keynes on Underemployment Equilibrium." *Journal of Political Economy* 44 (October): 667–686.

(1939). "Economic Progress and Declining Population Growth." *American Economic Review* 29 (March): 1–15.

(1954). *A Guide to Keynes.* New York: McGraw-Hill.

Hansen, A. H., and Tout, H. (1933). "Annual Survey of Business Cycle Theory: Investment and Saving in Business Cycle Theory." *Econometrica* 1 (April): 119–147.

Hansson, B. A. (1982). *The Stockholm School and the Development of Dynamic Method.* London: Croom Helm.

(1987). "Forced Saving." In: *The New Palgrave: A Dictionary of Economics,* ed. J. Eatwell, M. Milgate, and P. Newman, vol. 2, pp. 398–400. London: Macmillan.

(1990). "The Swedish Tradition: Wicksell and Cassel." In: *Neoclassical Economic Theory, 1870–1930,* ed. K. Hennings and W. Samuels, pp. 251–279. Dordrecht: Kluwer.

Harcourt, G. C. (1972). *Some Cambridge Controversies in the Theory of Capital.* Cambridge University Press.

Hardy, C. O. (1932). *Credit Policies of the Federal Reserve System.* Washington, DC: Brookings Institution.

Harris, S. E. (1934). "Higher Prices." In: *The Economics of the Recovery Program,* ed. D. V. Brown et al., pp. 90–138. Cambridge, MA: Harvard University Press.

Harrod, R. F. (1936). *The Trade Cycle.* Oxford: Clarendon Press. Reprinted 1961 by Augustus M. Kelley, New York.

(1937). "Mr. Keynes and Traditional Theory." *Econometrica* 5 (January): 74–86.

(1969). *Money.* London: Macmillan.

Hart, A. G. (1935). "The *'Chicago Plan'* of Banking Reform." *Review of Economic Studies* 2: 104–116. Reprinted 1952 in *Readings in Monetary Theory,* ed. F. A. Lutz and L. W. Mints, pp. 437–456. London: Allen & Unwin.

Hawtrey, R. G. (1913). *Good and Bad Trade.* London: Constable. Reprinted 1962, with a new foreword by the author, by Augustus M. Kelley, New York.

(1919). *Currency and Credit.* London: Longmans Group (2nd ed., 1923; 3rd ed., 1927).

(1925). "Public Expenditure and the Demand for Labour." *Economica* 5 (March): 38–48.

(1926). "Mr. Robertson on Banking Policy." *Economic Journal* 36 (September): 417–433.

(1927). "The Monetary Theory of the Trade Cycle and Its Statistical Test." *Quarterly Journal of Economics* 41 (May): 471–486.

(1929). "The Monetary Theory of the Trade Cycle." *Economic Journal* 39 (December): 636–642.

(1932a). *The Art of Central Banking*. London: Longman Group. Reprinted 1962 by Frank Cass, London.

(1932b). "Review of F. A. von Hayek, *Prices and Production.*" *Economica* 12 (February): 119–125.

(1937). *Capital and Employment*. London: Longman Group.

Hayek, F. A. von (1925). "Die Wahrungspolitik der vereinigten Staaten seit der Überwindung der Krise um 1920." *Zeitschrift für Volkswirtschaft und Sozialpolitik* N.S. 5: 25–63, 254–317. English translation of an extract (1984): "The Monetary Policy of the United States after the Recovery from the 1920 Crisis." In: *Money, Capital and Fluctuations – Early Essays*. University of Chicago Press.

(1928). "Das intertemporale Gleichgewichtssystem der Preise und die Bewegungen das 'Geldwertes'." *Weltwirtschaftliches Archiv* 2: 33–76. English translation (1984): "Intertemporal Price Equilibrium and Movements in the Value of Money." In: *Money, Capital and Fluctuations – Early Essays*. University of Chicago Press.

(1929). *Geldtheorie und Konjunkturtheorie*. Beitrage zur Konjunkturforschung, herausgegeben vom Österreichisches Institut für Konjunkturforschung, No. 1, Vienna. English translation (1933): *Monetary Theory and the Trade Cycle*, trans. N. Kaldor and H. Croome. London: Routledge & Kegan Paul. Reprinted 1966 by Augustus M. Kelley, New York.

(1931a). *Prices and Production*. London: Routledge (2nd rev. ed., 1935).

(1931b). "Reflections on the *Pure Theory of Money* of Mr. J. M. Keynes. Part I." *Economica* 11 (August): 270–295.

(1932a). "Reflections on the *Pure Theory of Money* of Mr. J. M. Keynes. Part II." *Economica* 12 (February): 22–44.

(1932b). "A Note on the Development of the Doctrine of 'Forced Saving'." *Quarterly Journal of Economics* 47 (November): 123–133.

(1934). "Capital and Industrial Fluctuations – A Reply to Criticism." *Econometrica* 2 (April): 152–167.

(1937). "Economics and Knowledge." *Economica, New Series* 4 (February): 33–54.

(1939). *Profits, Interest and Investment and Other Essays on the Theory of Industrial Fluctuations*. London: Routledge & Kegan Paul.

(1941). *The Pure Theory of Capital*. London: Routledge & Kegan Paul. Reprinted 1975 by University of Chicago Press.

Hennings, K., and Samuels, W. (eds.) (1990). *Neoclassical Economic Theory, 1870–1930*. Dordrecht: Kluwer.

Hepburn, J., and Anderson, B. M. (1921). "The Gold and Rediscount Policy of the Federal Reserve Banks." *Chase Economic Bulletin* 1, July 20.

Hicks, J. R. (1934a). *The Theory of Wages*. London: Macmillan.

(1934b). "Review of Myrdal's Contribution to F. A. von Hayek (ed.), *Beiträge zur Geldtheorie.*" *Economica, New Series* 1 (November): 479–483.

(1935). "A Suggestion for Simplifying the Theory of Money." *Economica, New Series* 2: 1–19. Reprinted 1982 in J. R. Hicks, *Money, Interest and Wages: Collected Essays on Economic Theory*, vol. II, pp. 46–63. Cambridge, MA: Harvard University Press.

(1936). "Mr. Keynes' Theory of Employment." *Economic Journal* 46 (June): 238–253. Reprinted 1982 in J. R. Hicks, *Money, Interest and Wages: Collected Essays on Economic Theory*, vol. II, pp. 84–93. Cambridge, MA: Harvard University Press.

(1937). "Mr. Keynes and the Classics: A Suggested Interpretation." *Econometrica* 5 (April): 147–159. Reprinted 1982 in J. R. Hicks, *Money, Interest and Wages: Collected Essays on Economic Theory*, vol. II, pp. 101–115. Cambridge, MA: Harvard University Press.

(1939). *Value and Capital*. Oxford: Clarendon Press.

(1950). *A Contribution to the Theory of the Trade Cycle*. Oxford: Clarendon Press.

(1966). "A Memoir – Dennis Holme Robertson." In: D. H. Robertson, *Essays in Money and Interest, Selected by Sir John Hicks*. London: HMSO, Fontana Library.

(1967). *Critical Essays in Monetary Theory*. Oxford University Press.

(1973). "Recollections and Documents." *Economica, New Series* 40 (February): 2–11.

(1974). *The Crisis in Keynesian Economics*. Oxford: Blackwell.

Hicks, J. R., and Allen, R. G. D. (1934). "A Reconsideration of the Theory of Value." *Economica* 1 (February, May): 52–76, 196–219.

Hill, P., and Keynes, R. (1989). *Lydia and Maynard: The Letters of John Maynard Keynes and Lydia Lopokova*. New York: Scribner.

Hirsch, A., and de Marchi, N. (1990). *Milton Friedman: Economics in Theory and Practice*. Hemel Hempstead, U.K.: Harvester-Wheatsheaf.

Hobson, J. A. (1923). *The Economics of Unemployment*. New York: Macmillan.

Hoover, H. (1923). "Foreword." In: W. C. Mitchell et al., *Business Cycles and Unemployment*, pp. v–vi. New York: McGraw-Hill.

Hopkins, R. (1931). "Evidence" (to the Macmillan Committee). In: Committee on Finance and Industry, *Minutes of Evidence Taken before the Committee on Finance and Industry*, vol. II. London: HMSO.

Howitt, P. W. (1992). "Interest Rate Control and Nonconvergence to Rational Expectations." *Journal of Political Economy* 100 (August): 776–800.

Howson, S. (1985). "Hawtrey and the Real World." In: *Keynes and His Contemporaries*, ed. G. C. Harcourt, pp. 142–187. London: Macmillan.

Howson, S., and Winch, D. (1977). *The Economic Advisory Council, 1930–1939: A Study in Economic Advice during Depression and Recovery*. Cambridge University Press.

Humphrey, T. M. (1971). "Role of Non-Chicago Economists in the Evolution of the Quantity Theory in America 1930–1950." *Southern Economic Journal* 38 (July): 12–18. Reprinted 1993 in T. M. Humphrey; *Money, Banking and Inflation: Essays in the History of Monetary Thought*. Aldershot, Hampshire: Edward Elgar.

(1990). "Cumulative Process Models from Thornton to Wicksell." In: *Perspectives in the History of Economic Thought: Keynes, Macroeconomics and Method*, ed. D. Moggridge, pp. 40–52. Aldershot, Hampshire: Edward Elgar. Reprinted 1993 in T. M. Humphrey, *Money, Banking and Inflation: Essays in the History of Monetary Thought*. Aldershot; Hampshire: Edward Elgar.

(1993). *Money, Banking and Inflation: Essays in the History of Monetary Thought.* Aldershot, Hampshire: Edward Elgar.

(1997). "Fisher and Wicksell on the Quantity Theory." *Federal Reserve Bank of Richmond Economic Quarterly* 83 (Fall): 71–90.

Jevons, W. S. (1863). "A Serious Fall in the Value of Gold Ascertained and Its Social Effects Set Forth." Reprinted 1884 in W. S. Jevons, *Investigations in Currency and Finance.* London: Macmillan.

(1871). *The Principles of Economics; A Fragment of a Treatise on the Industrial Mechanism of Society, and Other Papers.* Reprinted 1965 by Augustus M. Kelley, New York.

Johannsen, N. A. J. (1908). *A Neglected Point in Connection with Crises.* New York: Bankers Publishing. Reprinted 1971 by Augustus M. Kelley, New York.

Johnson, H. G. (1961). "The *General Theory* after 25 Years." *American Economic Review, Papers and Proceedings* 51 (May): 1–17.

(1971). "The Keynesian Revolution and the Monetarist Counter-Revolution." *American Economic Review, Papers and Proceedings* 61 (May): 1–14.

(1974). "Cambridge in the 1950s." *Encounter* 42 (January): 28–39. Reprinted 1978 in E. S. Johnson and H. G. Johnson, *The Shadow of Keynes*, pp. 127–150. University of Chicago Press.

(1977). "Cambridge as an Academic Environment in the Early 1930s: A Reconstruction from the Late 1940s." In: *Keynes, Cambridge, and the General Theory: The Process of Criticism and Discussion Connected with the Development of the General Theory*, ed. D. Patinkin and J. C. Leith, pp. 98–114. London: Macmillan.

Jonung, L. (1979). "Knut Wicksell's Norm of Price Stabilization and Swedish Monetary Policy in the 1930s." *Journal of Monetary Economics* 5 (October): 459–496.

Kaergaard, N., Andersen, P., and Topp, N.-H. (1996). "The Danish Economist Jens Warming – Odd and Genius." Mimeograph, University of Copenhagen.

Kahn, R. F. (1931). "The Relation of Home Investment to Unemployment." *Economic Journal* 41 (June): 173–198.

(1932). "The Financing of Public Works: A Note." *Economic Journal* 42 (September): 492–495.

(1933). "Public Works and Inflation." *American Statistical Association Journal (Suppl.)* 28 (March): 168–173.

(1937). "The League of Nations Inquiry into the Trade Cycle." *Economic Journal* 47 (March): 670–679.

(1938). "Some Comments on Mr. Kahn's Review of *Prosperity and Depression*: A Rejoinder." *Economic Journal* 48 (June): 333–336.

(1984). *The Making of Keynes' General Theory.* Cambridge University Press, for the Raffaele Mattioli Foundation.

(1985). "Discussion" (of the Cambridge Circus). In: *Keynes and his Contemporaries*, ed. G. C. Harcourt, pp. 59–60. London: Macmillan.

Kaldor, N. (1937). "Prof. Pigou on Money Wages in Relation to Employment." *Economic Journal* 47 (December): 745–753.

Kalecki, M. (1933). "Outline of a Theory of the Business Cycle." Translated 1966 in

Studies in the Theory of Business Cycles 1933–1939. Warsaw: Polish Scientific Publishers.

    (1935). "The Mechanism of the Business Upswing." Translated 1966 in *Studies in the Theory of Business Cycles 1933–1939*. Warsaw: Polish Scientific Publishers.

Kates, S. (1994). "The Malthusian Origins of the *General Theory*: or, How Keynes Came to Write a Book about Say's Law and Effective Demand." *History of Economics Review* 21 (Winter): 10–20.

Kemmerer, E. W. (1909). *Money and Credit Instruments in Their Relation to General Prices*. New York: Henry Holt.

    (1921). *High Prices and Deflation*. Princeton, NJ: Princeton University Press.

Keynes, J. M. (1911). "Review of I. Fisher: *The Purchasing Power of Money*." *Economic Journal* 21 (September). Reprinted 1971–88 in *The Collected Writings of John Maynard Keynes*, vol. XI, ed. D. Moggridge and E. Johnson, pp. 275–281. London: Macmillan, for the Royal Economic Society.

    (1913). "Review of J. A. Hobson: *Gold, Prices and Wages*." *Economic Journal* 23 (September): 393–398.

    (1914). "Review of L. von Mises, *Theorie des Geldes*." *Economic Journal* 24 (September): 417–419.

    (1919). *The Economic Consequences of the Peace*. London: Macmillan. Reprinted 1971–88 in *The Collected Writings of John Maynard Keynes*, vol. II, ed. D. Moggridge and E. Johnson. London: Macmillan, for the Royal Economic Society.

    (1921). *A Treatise on Probability*. London: Macmillan. Reprinted 1971–88 in *The Collected Writings of John Maynard Keynes*, vol. VIII, ed. D. Moggridge and E. Johnson. London: Macmillan, for the Royal Economic Society.

    (1923). *A Tract on Monetary Reform*. London: Macmillan. Reprinted 1971–88 in *The Collected Writings of John Maynard Keynes*, vol. IV, ed. D. Moggridge and E. Johnson. London: Macmillan, for the Royal Economic Society.

    (1925). "The Economic Consequences of Mr. Churchill." Reprinted in 1931 in *Essays in Persuasion*. London: Macmillan. Reprinted 1971–88 in *The Collected Writings of John Maynard Keynes*, vol. IX, ed. D. Moggridge and E. Johnson, pp. 207–230. London: Macmillan, for the Royal Economic Society.

    (1930a). *A Treatise on Money*, 2 vols. London: Macmillan. Reprinted 1971–88 in *The Collected Writings of John Maynard Keynes*, vol. V–VI, ed. D. Moggridge and E. Johnson. London: Macmillan, for the Royal Economic Society.

    (1930b). Evidence presented to Macmillan Committee. Reprinted 1971–88 in *The Collected Writings of John Maynard Keynes*, vol. XX, ed. D. Moggridge and E. Johnson. London: Macmillan, for the Royal Economic Society.

    (1931a). "An Economic Analysis of Employment." In: *Unemployment as a World Problem: Lectures on the Harris Foundation*, ed. Q. Wright, pp. 1–42. University of Chicago Press. Reprinted 1971–88 in *The Collected Writings of John Maynard Keynes*, vol. XIII, ed. D. Moggridge and E. Johnson, pp. 343–367. London: Macmillan, for the Royal Economic Society.

    (1931b). "A Rejoinder to Mr. D. H. Robertson." *Economic Journal* 41 (September): 412–423, (November): 387–397.

    (1933). *The Means to Prosperity*. New York: Harcourt, Brace & Co. Reprinted

1971–88 in *The Collected Writings of John Maynard Keynes*, vol. IX, ed. D. Moggridge and E. Johnson, pp. 335–367. London: Macmillan, for the Royal Economic Society.

(1936). *The General Theory of Employment, Interest and Money.* London: Macmillan. Reprinted 1967, London: Macmillan. Reprinted 1971–88 in *The Collected Writings of John Maynard Keynes*, vol. VIII, ed. D. Moggridge and E. Johnson. London: Macmillan, for the Royal Economic Society.

(1937a). "The General Theory of Unemployment." *Quarterly Journal of Economics* 51 (February): 209–223. Reprinted 1971–88 in *The Collected Writings of John Maynard Keynes*, vol. XIV, ed. D. Moggridge and E. Johnson, pp. 109–123. London: Macmillan, for the Royal Economic Society.

(1937b). "Alternative Theories of the Rate of Interest." *Economic Journal* 47 (June): 241–252.

(1937c). "Professor Pigou on Money Wages in Relation to Unemployment." *Economic Journal* 47 (December): 743–745.

(1940). *How to Pay for the War: A Radical Plan for the Chancellor of the Exchequer.* London: Macmillan. Reprinted 1971–88 in *The Collected Writings of John Maynard Keynes*, vol. IX, ed. D. Moggridge and E. Johnson, pp. 367–439. London: Macmillan, for the Royal Economic Society.

(1971–88). *The Collected Writings of John Maynard Keynes*, 30 vols., ed. D. Moggridge and E. Johnson. London: Macmillan, for the Royal Economic Society.

Keynes, J. M., and Henderson, H. (1929). *Can Lloyd George Do It? The Pledge Examined.* Reprinted 1971–88 in *The Collected Writings of John Maynard Keynes*, vol. IX, ed. D. Moggridge and E. Johnson, pp. 86–125. London: Macmillan, for the Royal Economic Society.

Kirzner, I. (1990). "Commentary [on Boehm]." In: *Neoclassical Economic Theory, 1870–1930*, ed. K. Hennings and W. Samuels, pp. 242–250. Dordrecht: Kluwer.

Klausinger, H. (1995). "Schumpeter and Hayek: Two Views of the Great Depression Re-examined." *History of Economic Ideas* 3: 93–127.

Klein, L. R. (1949). *The Keynesian Revolution.* New York: Macmillan. Second edition 1966, Macmillan, New York.

Klein, L. R., and Goldberger, A. S. (1955). *An Econometric Model of the United States 1929–1952.* Amsterdam: North Holland.

Knight, F. H. (1921). *Risk, Uncertainty and Profit.* Boston: Houghton Mifflin.

(1937). "Unemployment and Mr. Keynes' Revolution in Economic Theory." *Canadian Journal of Economics and Political Science* 3 (February): 100–123.

Kohn, M. (1987). "Foster and Catchings and the Pollack Prize Essays: A Window on the Monetary Theory of the 1920s." Mimeograph, Dartmouth College, Hanover, NH.

Kompas, T. (1989). "Studies in the History of Long Run Equilibrium Theory." Ph.D. dissertation, University of Toronto.

Koopmans, T. (1947). "Measurement Without Theory." *Review of Economic Statistics* 29: 161–172.

Kydland, F. E., and Prescott, E. C. (1982). "Time to Build and Aggregate Fluctuations." *Econometrica* 50 (November): 1345–1370.

Laidler, D. (1969). *The Demand for Money: Theories and Evidence*. Scranton, PA: International Textbook Co.

    (1987). "Henry Thornton." In: *The New Palgrave: A Dictionary of Economics*, vol. 4, ed. J. Eatwell, M. Milgate, and P. Newman, pp. 633–636. London: Macmillan.

    (1989). "Radcliffe, the Quantity Theory and Monetarism." In: *Money, Trade and Payments: Essays in Honour of D. J. Coppock*, ed. D. Cobham, R. Harrington, and G. Zis, pp. 217–37. Manchester University Press.

    (1991). *The Golden Age of the Quantity Theory*. Princeton, NJ: Princeton University Press.

    (1993). "Hawtrey, Harvard and the Origins of the Chicago Tradition." *Journal of Political Economy* 101 (December): 1068–1103.

    (1998). "More on Hawtrey, Harvard and Chicago." *Journal of Economic Studies* 25: 4–16.

Laidler, D., and Stadler, G. (1998). "Monetary Explanations of the Weimar Republic's Hyper-inflation: Some Neglected Contributors in the Contemporary German Literature." *Journal of Money, Credit, and Banking* 30 (November): 816–831.

Lange, O. (1938). "The Rate of Interest and the Optimum Propensity to Consume." *Economica* 5 (February): 12–32. Reprinted 1983 in *John Maynard Keynes – Critical Assessments*, ed. J. C. Wood, pp. 173–189. London: Croom Helm.

Laughlin, J. L. (1931). *A New Exposition of Money, Credit, and Prices*. University of Chicago Press.

Lavington, F. (1921). *The English Capital Market*. London: Methuen.

    (1922). *The Trade Cycle*. London: P. S. King & Son. Reprinted 1925.

Lawlor, M. S. (1994). "The Own-Rates Framework as an Interpretation of the *General Theory*: A Suggestion for Complicating the Keynesian Theory of Money." In: *The State of Interpretation of Keynes*, ed. J. B. Davis, pp. 39–90. Dordrecht: Kluwer.

Leeson, R. (1996). "Keynes and the 'Klassics': The Macroeconomic Creation Myth." Mimeograph, Murdoch University, Perth, Western Australia.

Leijonhufvud, A. (1968). *On Keynesian Economics and the Economics of Keynes*. Oxford University Press.

    (1973). "Life among the Econ." Reprinted 1981 in A. Leijonhufvud, *Information and Co-ordination*, pp. 347–359. Oxford University Press.

    (1981). "The Wicksell Connection – Variations on a Theme." In: *Information and Co-ordination*, pp. 131–202. Oxford University Press.

Lerner, A. (1936). "Mr. Keynes' 'General Theory of Employment Interest and Money'." *International Labour Review*, 34 (October): 435–454. Reprinted 1983 in *John Maynard Keynes – Critical Assessments*, ed. J. C. Wood, pp. 55–70. London: Croom Helm.

Lindahl, E. (1929a). "Review of *Dynamic Prices* by G. Myrdal." *Economic Journal* 39 (March): 89–91.

    (1929b). "Prisbildningsproblemens uppläggning från kapitalteoretisk synpunkt." *Economisk Tidskrift* 31: 31–81. English translation of revised version (1939): "The Place of Capital in the Theory of Price." In: E. Lindahl, *Studies in the Theory of Money and Capital*. London: Allen & Unwin.

(1930). *Penningspolitikens medel.* Lund: Gleerup. English translation of revised version (1939): "The Rate of Interest and the Price Level." In: E. Lindahl, *Studies in the Theory of Money and Capital.* London: Allen & Unwin.

(1934). "A Note on the Dynamic Pricing Problem." Reprinted 1971 in O. Steiger, *Studien zur Entstehung der neuen Wirtschaftslehre in Schweden: Eine Anti-Kritik,* pp. 204–211. Berlin: Dunkler & Humblot.

(1935). "Arbetslöshet och Finanspolitik." *Economisk Tidskrift* 37: 1–36. English translation of revised version (1939): "The Problem of Balancing the Budget." In: E. Lindahl, *Studies in the Theory of Money and Capital.* London: Allen & Unwin.

(1939). "The Dynamic Approach to Economic Theory." In: E. Lindahl, *Studies in the Theory of Money and Capital.* London: Allen & Unwin.

Lucas, R. E., Jr. (1972). "Expectations and the Neutrality of Money." *Journal of Economic Theory* 4 (2) (April): 103–124.

Lundberg, E. (1930). "On the Concept of Economic Equilibrium." Reprinted 1995 in *Erik Lundberg: Studies in Economic Instability and Change,* ed. R. G. H. Henriksson, pp. 13–47. Stockholm: SNS Foerlag.

(1934). "Report of My Studies as a Rockefeller Fellow of Economics." Reprinted 1995 in *Erik Lundberg: Studies in Economic Instability and Change,* ed. R. G. H. Henriksson, pp. 48–66. Stockholm: SNS Foerlag.

(1937). *Studies in the Theory of Economic Expansion.* London: P. S. King & Son. Reprinted 1964 by Augustus M. Kelley, New York.

(1985). "The Rise and Fall of the Swedish Model." *Journal of Economic Literature* 23 (March): 1–36.

(1996). *The Development of Swedish and Keynesian Macroeconomic Theory and Its Impact on Economic Policy (the 1981 Raffaele Mattioli Lectures).* Cambridge University Press, for the Raffaele Matteoli Foundation.

Maes, I. (1991). "On the Origins of Portfolio Theory." *Kyklos* 44 (1): 3–18.

Marget, A. (1931). "Léon Walras and the 'Cash-Balance Approach' to the Problem of the Value of Money." *Journal of Political Economy* 39 (October): 569–600.

(1938–41). *The Theory of Prices,* 2 vols. New York: Prentice-Hall. Reprinted 1966, New York: Augustus M. Kelley.

Marshall, A. (1871). "Money." Reprinted 1975 in *The Early Economic Writings of Alfred Marshall,* vols., ed. J. Whittaker, pp. 165–177. London: Macmillan.

(1887). "Remedies for Fluctuations of General Prices." *Contemporary Review* (March). Reprinted 1925 in *Memorials of Alfred Marshall,* ed. A. C. Pigou, pp. 188–211. London: Macmillan.

(1890). *Principles of Economics.* London: Macmillan (8th ed., 1920).

(1923). *Money Credit and Commerce.* London: Macmillan.

(1926). *Official Papers of Alfred Marshall,* ed. J. M. Keynes. London: Macmillan.

Marshall, A., and Marshall, M. P. (1879). *The Economics of Industry.* London: Macmillan.

Marx, K. (1867). *Kapital,* vol. 1. Reprinted (1961): *Capital,* vol. 1, trans. from 3rd German edition of 1887 by S. Moore and E. Aveling, ed. F. Engels. Moscow: Foreign Languages Publishing House.

Meade, J. E. (1934). "The Amount of Money and the Banking System." *Economic*

Journal. Reprinted 1952 in *Readings in Monetary Theory*, ed. F. A. Lutz and L. W. Mints, pp. 54–62. London: Allen & Unwin.

(1937). "A Simplified Model of Mr. Keynes' System." *Review of Economic Studies* 4 (February): 98–107. Reprinted 1983 in *John Maynard Keynes – Critical Assessments*, ed. J. C. Wood, pp. 129–140. London: Croom Helm.

Means, G. C. (1935). "Price Inflexibility and the Requirements of a Stabilizing Monetary Policy." *Journal of the American Statistical Association* 30 (June): 401–413.

Mehrling, P. (1995). "The Monetary Thought of Alvin Harvey Hansen." Mimeograph, Barnard College, New York.

(1996). "The Monetary Thought of Allyn Abbott Young." *History of Political Economy* 28 (Winter): 607–632.

Meltzer, A. H. (1981). "Keynes' General Theory – a Different Perspective." *Journal of Economic Literature* 19 (March): 34–64.

(1988). *Keynes' Monetary Theory – A Different Interpretation*. Cambridge University Press.

(1995). "History of the Federal Reserve. Chapter 5: Why Did Monetary Policy Fail in the Thirties?" Mimeograph, GSIA, Carnegie Mellon University, Pittsburgh.

Menger, C. (1871). *Principles of Economics*. Reprinted 1976 by New York University Press.

(1892). "Geld." In: *Handsörterbuch der Staatswissenschaften*, vol. III. Jena.

Metzler, L. (1941). "The Nature and Stability of Inventory Cycles." *Review of Economic Statistics* 23 (August): 113–129.

Mill, J. S. (1871). *The Principles of Political Economy with Some of Their Applications to Social Philosophy*, 7th ed. London. Reprinted 1965, ed. J. M. Robson, by University of Toronto Press.

Minsky, H. P. (1975). *John Maynard Keynes*. New York: Macmillan.

Mints, L. W. (1945). *History of Banking Theory*. University of Chicago Press.

(1946). "Monetary Policy." *Review of Economic Statistics* 28 (May): 60–69.

(1950). *Monetary Policy for a Competitive Society*. New York: McGraw-Hill.

Mises, L. von (1924). *Theorie des Geldes und der Umlaufsmittel*, 2nd ed. Munich. (1st German edition 1912). English translation (1934): *The Theory of Money and Credit*, trans. H. E. Batson. London: Jonathan Cape. Reprinted 1953, Yale University Press, New Haven, CT.

Mitchell, W. C. (1913). *Business Cycles*. Berkeley: University of California Press. Reprinted 1970 by B. Franklin, New York.

(1927). *Business Cycles: The Problem and Its Setting*. New York: National Bureau of Economic Research.

(1935a). "Robbins' *The Great Depression* [review]." *Quarterly Journal of Economics* 49 (March): 503–507.

(1935b). "The Social Sciences and National Planning." *Science* 81 (January): 55–62. Reprinted 1935 in *The Backward Art of Spending Money*, pp. 83–102. New York: McGraw-Hill.

Mitchell, W. C., et al. (1923). *Business Cycles and Unemployment*. New York: McGraw-Hill.

Mizen, P., and Presley, J. R. (1995). "The Evolution of Monetary Theory: Was IS-

LM an Unfortunate Diversion?'' Mimeograph, Department of Economics, University of Nottingham.

Modigliani, F. (1944). "Liquidity and the Theory of Interest and Money." *Econometrica* 12 (January): 45–88.

Moggridge, D. E. (1992). *Maynard Keynes: An Economist's Biography.* London: Routledge.

Morgan, M. (1990). *The History of Econometric Ideas.* Cambridge University Press.

Morgenstern, O. (1929). "A. A. Young." *Zeitschrift für Nationalökonomie* 1 (May): 143–145. Reprinted 1976 in *Selected Economic Writings of Oskar Morgenstern,* ed. A. Schotter, pp. 143–145. New York University Press.

Moulton, H. G. (1916). *Principles of Money and Banking: A Series of Selected Materials with Explanatory Introductions.* University of Chicago Press.

Mummery, A. F., and Hobson, J. A. (1889). *The Physiology of Industry; Being an Exposure of Certain Fallacies in Existing Theories of Economics.* Reprinted 1956 by Kelley & Millman, New York.

Myhrman, J. (1993). "The Monetary Economics of the Stockholm School." In: *The Stockholm School of Economics Revisited,* ed. L. Jonung, pp. 267–289. Cambridge University Press.

Myrdal, G. (1927). *Prisbildningsproblemet och Föränderligheten.* Stockholm: Almquist & Wiksell.

(1931). "Om penningsteoretisk jämvikt." *Economisk Tidskrift* 33 (5–6): 191–302. German translation 1933. English translation, with minor emendations (1939): *Monetary Equilibrium.* London: W. Hodge.

Neisser, H. (1934). "General Overproduction – a Study of Say's Law of Markets." *Journal of Political Economy.* Reprinted 1951, as abridged and revised, in American Economic Association, *Readings in Business Cycle Theory,* pp. 384–404. Homewood, IL: Richard Irwin.

O'Brien, D. (1994). "Friedrich August von Hayek 1899–1992." *Proceedings of the British Academy* 84: 347–366.

Ohlin, B. (1933). "Till frågen om penningsteoriens uppläggning." *Economisk Tidskrift* 35 (2): 45–81. English translation (1978): "On the Formulation of Monetary Theory." *History of Political Economy* 10 (Fall): 353–388.

(1937). "Some Notes on the Stockholm Theory of Savings and Investment." *Economic Journal* 47 (March–June): 53–69, 221–240.

(1977). "Some Comments on Keynesianism and the Swedish Theory of Expansion Before 1935." In: *Keynes, Cambridge, and the General Theory: The Process of Criticism and Discussion Connected with the Development of the General Theory,* ed. D. Patinkin and J. C. Leith, pp. 149–165. London: Macmillan.

Patinkin, D. (1948). "Price Flexibility and Full Employment." *American Economic Review* 38 (September): 534–564. Reprinted 1952 in *Readings in Monetary Theory,* ed. F. A. Lutz and L. W. Mints, pp. 252–283. London: Allen & Unwin.

(1957). *Money, Interest, and Prices; An Integration of Monetary and Value Theory.* New York: Harper & Row.

(1965). "Wicksell's Monetary Theory." In: *Money, Interest, and Prices,* 2nd ed., pp. 581–597. New York: Harper & Row.

(1969). "The Chicago Tradition, the Quantity Theory, and Friedman." *Journal of*

Money, Credit and Banking 1: 46–70. Reprinted 1981 in D. Patinkin, *Essays on and in the Chicago Tradition*, pp. 241–276. Durham, NC: Duke University Press.

(1973). "More on the Chicago Monetary Tradition." *Southern Economic Journal* 39 (January): 454–459. Reprinted 1981 in D. Patinkin, *Essays on and in the Chicago Tradition*, pp. 277–287. Durham, NC: Duke University Press.

(1974). "Keynesian Monetary Theory and the Cambridge School." In: *Issues in Monetary Economics*, ed. H. G. Johnson and A. R. Nobay, pp. 3–30. Oxford University Press.

(1976a). *Keynes' Monetary Thought: A Study of Its Development.* Durham, NC: Duke University Press.

(1976b). "Keynes and Econometrics: On the Interaction Between the Macroeconomic Revolutions of the Interwar Period." *Econometrica* 44 (November): 1091–1123. Reprinted 1982 in D. Patinkin, *Anticipations of the General Theory? and Other Essays on Keynes*, pp. 223–260. University of Chicago Press.

(1977). "The Process of Writing the *General Theory* – a Critical Survey." In: *Keynes, Cambridge, and the General Theory*, ed. D. Patinkin and J. C. Leith, pp. 3–24. London: Macmillan.

(1979). "Keynes and Chicago." *Journal of Law and Economics* 22 (October): 213–232. Reprinted 1981 in D. Patinkin, *Essays on and in the Chicago Tradition*, pp. 289–308. Durham, NC: Duke University Press.

(1981). *Essays on and in the Chicago Tradition.* Durham, NC: Duke University Press.

(1982). *Anticipations of the General Theory? and Other Essays on Keynes.* University of Chicago Press.

(1983). "New Perspectives or Old Pitfalls? Some Comments on Allan Meltzer's Interpretation of the General Theory." *Journal of Economic Literature* 21 (March): 47–51.

(1987). "J. M. Keynes." In: *The New Palgrave: A Dictionary of Economics*, vol. 3, ed. J. Eatwell, M. Milgate, and P. Newman, pp. 19–41. London: Macmillan.

(1990). "In Defence of IS-LM." *Banca Nazionale del Lavoro Quarterly Review* 172 (March): 119–134.

Patinkin, D., and Leith, J. C. (eds.) (1977). *Keynes, Cambridge, and the General Theory: The Process of Criticism and Discussion Connected with the Development of the General Theory.* Proceedings of a conference held at the University of Western Ontario. London: Macmillan.

Pearce, K. A., and Hoover, K. D. (1995). "After the Revolution: Paul Samuelson and the Textbook Keynesian Model." In: *New Perspectives on Keynes* (annual supplement to *History of Political Economy* 27), ed. A. F. Cottrell and M. S. Lawlor, pp. 183–216. Durham, NC: Duke University Press.

Pennington, J. (1829). "Paper Communicated by Mr. Pennington." In: T. Tooke, *Letter to Lord Grenville on the Effects Ascribed to the Resumption of Cash Payments on the Value of the Currency*, pp. 117–127. London: Murray.

Perlman, M. (1996). *The Character of Economic Thought, Economic Characters and Economic Institutions.* Ann Arbor: University of Michigan Press.

Phillips, R. J. (1993). "Marriner Eccles and the Chicago Plan for Banking Reform." Mimeograph, Department of Economics, Colorado State University.

Pigou, A. C. (1912). *Wealth and Welfare*. London: Macmillan.

(1913). *Unemployment*. London: Williams & Norgate.

(1917). "The Value of Money." *Quarterly Journal of Economics* 32: 38–65. Reprinted 1952 in *Readings in Monetary Theory*, ed. F. A. Lutz and L. W. Mints, pp. 241–251. London: Allen & Unwin.

(1924). "Correctives of the Trade Cycle." In: *Is Unemployment Inevitiable?* ed. W. Layton, pp. 91–131. London: Macmillan.

(1926). "A Contribution to the Theory of Credit." *Economic Journal* 36 (June): 215–227.

(1927a). *Industrial Fluctuations*. London: Macmillan.

(1927b). "Wage Policy and Unemployment." *Economic Journal* 37 (September): 355–368.

(1929). *Industrial Fluctuations*, 2nd rev. ed. London: Macmillan.

(1931). "Evidence" (to the Macmillan Committee). In: Committee on Finance and Industry, *Minutes of Evidence Taken before the Committee on Finance and Industry*, vol. II. London: HMSO.

(1933). *The Theory of Unemployment*. London: Macmillan. Reprinted 1968, New York: Augustus M. Kelley.

(1936). "Mr. J. M. Keynes' General Theory of Employment, Interest and Money." *Economica* 3 (May): 115–132.

(1937). "Real and Money Wage Rates in Relation to Unemployment." *Economic Journal* 47 (September): 405–422.

(1938). "Money Wages in Relation to Unemployment." *Economic Journal* 48 (March): 134–138.

(1943). "The Classical Stationary State." *Economic Journal* 53 (June): 343–351.

Presley, J. R. (1978). *Robertsonian Economics*. London: Macmillan.

(1986a). "J. M. Keynes and the Real Balance Effect." *Manchester School* 54: 22–30.

(1986b). "Modern Monetarist Ideas: A British Connection." In: *Ideas in Economics*, ed. R. D. Collison Black, pp. 191–210. London: Macmillan.

(1989). "J. M. Keynes and D. H. Robertson: Three Phases of a Collaboration." *Research in the History of Economic Thought and Methodology* 6: 31–46.

Reddaway, W. B. (1936). "The General Theory of Employment, Interest, and Money." *Economic Record* 12 (June): 28–36. Reprinted 1983 in *John Maynard Keynes – Critical Assessments*, ed. J. C. Wood, pp. 32–38. London: Croom Helm.

Reder, M. W. (1982). "Chicago Economics: Permanence and Change." *Journal of Economic Literature* 20 (March): 1–38.

Reed, H. L. (1930). *Federal Reserve Policy 1921–1930*. New York: McGraw-Hill.

(1935). "The Stabilization Doctrines of Carl Snyder." *Quarterly Journal of Economics* 49 (August): 600–620.

Reeve, J. E. (1943). *Monetary Reform Movements: A Survey of Recent Plans and Panaceas*. Washington, DC: American Council on Public Affairs.

Ricardo, D. (1816). *Proposal for an Economical and Secure Currency*. Reprinted 1951–73 in *Works and Correspondence of David Ricardo*, vol. 4, ed. P. Sraffa, pp. 47–99. Cambridge University Press, for the Royal Economic Society.

Riefler, W. W. (1930). *Money Rates and Money Markets in the United States.* New York: Harper & Row.

Robbins, L. C. (1931). "Introduction." In: F. A. von Hayek, *Prices and Production.* London: Routledge.

(1934). *The Great Depression.* London: Macmillan.

(1935). *The Nature and Significance of Economic Science*, 2nd ed. London: Macmillan.

(1971). *Autobiography of an Economist.* London: Macmillan.

Robertson, D. H. (1915). *A Study of Industrial Fluctuation.* London: P. S. King & Son. Reprinted 1948 by London School of Economics.

(1922). *Money.* London: Nisbett.

(1926). *Banking Policy and the Price Level.* London: Macmillan. Fourth printing 1949. Reprinted 1989 by Augustus M. Kelley, New York.

(1928a). *Money*, 3rd ed. London: Nisbett.

(1928b). "Theories of Banking Policy." *Economica* 8 (June): 131–146. Reprinted 1966 in D. H. Robertson, *Essays in Money and Interest, Selected by Sir John Hicks*, pp. 23–42. London: Collins, Fontana Library.

(1931a). "Mr. Keynes' Theory of Money." *Economic Journal* 41 (September): 395–411.

(1931b). "Evidence" (to the Macmillan Committee). In: Committee on Finance and Industry, *Minutes of Evidence Taken before the Committee on Finance and Industry*, vol. I. London: HMSO.

(1933). "A Note on the Theory of Money." *Economica* 13 (August): 243–247.

(1936a). "Some Notes on Mr. Keynes' General Theory of Employment." *Quarterly Journal of Economics* 51 (November): 168–191.

(1936b). "The Snake and the Worm." Reprinted 1940 in D. H. Robertson, *Essays in Monetary Theory*, pp. 118–127. London: Staples Press. Reprinted 1966 in D. H. Robertson, *Essays in Money and Interest, Selected by Sir John Hicks.* pp. 85–94. London: Collins, Fontana Library.

(1940). "Mr. Keynes and the Rate of Interest." In: *Essays in Monetary Theory*, pp. 11–44. London: Staples Press. Reprinted 1966 in D. H. Robertson, *Essays in Money and Interest, Selected by Sir John Hicks.* pp. 150–187. London: Collins, Fontana Library.

(1949). "Preface to 1949 Edition." In: D. H. Robertson, *Banking Policy and the Price Level.* New York: Augustus M. Kelley.

Robinson, A. (1977). "Keynes and His Cambridge Colleagues." In: *Keynes, Cambridge, and the General Theory: The Process of Criticism and Discussion Connected with the Development of the General Theory*, ed. D. Patinkin and J. C. Leith, pp. 25–38. London: Macmillan.

Robinson, J. (1937). *Introduction to the Theory of Employment.* London: Macmillan (2nd ed., 1969).

(1939). "Review of Myrdal – *Monetary Equilibrium.*" *Economic Journal* 49: 493–495.

Rogers, C. (1989). *Money, Interest, and Capital: A Study in the Foundations of Monetary Theory.* Cambridge University Press.

(1994). "Comment: Michael Lawlor's Own-Rates Interpretation of the General

Theory." In: *The State of Interpretation of Keynes*, ed. J. B. Davis, pp. 91–102. Dordrecht: Kluwer.

Rutherford, M. (1994). *Institutions in Economics: The Old and the New Institutionalism*. Cambridge University Press.

Rymes, T. K. (1989). *Keynes's Lectures, 1932–35, Notes of a Representative Student: A Synthesis of Lecture Notes Taken by Students at Keynes's Lectures in the 1930s Leading up to the Publication of The General Theory*. Houndmills, Basingstoke, Hampshire: Macmillan, in association with the Royal Economic Society.

Samuelson, P. A. (1939a). "Interactions between the Multiplier Analysis and the Principle of Acceleration." *Review of Economics and Statistics* 21 (May): 75–78.

(1939b). "A Synthesis of the Principle of Acceleration and the Multiplier." *Journal of Political Economy* 47 (December): 786–797.

Sandilands, R. (1990a). *The Life and Political Economy of Lauchlin Currie: New Dealer, Presidential Advisor, and Development Economist*. Durham, NC: Duke University Press.

(ed.) (1990b). "Nicholas Kaldor's Notes on Allyn Young's LSE Lectures 1927–29." *Journal of Economic Studies* 17 (3/4): 2–114.

Sargent, T. J., and Wallace, N. (1982). "The Real-Bills Doctrine versus the Quantity Theory: A Reconsideration." *Journal of Political Economy* 90 (December): 1212–1236.

Schumpeter, J. A. (1912). *Theorie der wirtschaftlichen Entwicklung*. Leipzig: Duncker & Humblot. English translation by R. Opie (1934): *The Theory of Economic Development*. Cambridge, MA: Harvard University Press.

(1931). "The Present World Depression: A Tentative Diagnosis." *American Economic Review, Papers and Proceedings (Suppl.)* 21 (March): 179–182.

(1934). "Depressions." In: *The Economics of the Recovery Program*, ed. D. V. Brown et al., pp. 3–21. Cambridge, MA: Harvard University Press.

(1935). "The Analysis of Economic Change." *Review of Economic Statistics* 17 (2) (May): 2–10. Reprinted 1951 in American Economic Association, *Readings in Business Cycle Theory*, pp. 1–19. Homewood, IL: Richard Irwin.

(1936). "The General Theory of Employment, Interest and Money." *Journal of the American Statistical Association* 31 (December): 791–795. Reprinted 1983 in *John Maynard Keynes – Critical Assessments*, ed. J. C. Wood, pp. 124–128. London: Croom Helm.

(1954). *History of Economic Analysis*. Oxford University Press.

Shackle, G. L. S. (1967). *The Years of High Theory*. Cambridge University Press.

Shehadi, N. (1991). "The London School of Economics and the Stockholm School." In: *The Stockholm School of Economics Revisited*, ed. L. Jonung, pp. 377–388. Cambridge University Press.

Simons, H. C. (1934). *A Positive Program for Laissez-Faire: Some Proposals for a Liberal Economic Policy*, ed. H. D. Gideonse. Public policy pamphlet 15. University of Chicago Press.

(1935). "Review of L. Currie's *The Supply and Control of Money in the United States*." *Journal of Political Economy* 43 (April): 555–558.

(1936a). "Rule Versus Authorities in Monetary Policy." *Journal of Political Economy* 44 (February): 1–30. Reprinted 1952 in *Readings in Monetary Theory*, ed. F. A. Lutz and L. W. Mints, pp. 337–368. London: Allen & Unwin.

(1936b). "Keynes's Comments on Money." *The Christian Century* (July 2): 1016–1017.

Simons, H. C., et al. (1933). "Banking and Currency Reform, including Appendix entitled 'Banking and Business Cycles', and Supplementary Memorandum on Long-term Objectives of Monetary Management." Unsigned mimeograph, Department of Economics, University of Chicago.

Skaggs, N. T. (1995). "The Methodological Roots of J. Laurence Laughlin's Anti-Quantity Theory of Money and Prices." *Journal of the History of Economic Thought* 17 (Spring): 1–20.

Skidelsky, R. (1992). *John Maynard Keynes – The Economist as Saviour 1920–1937*. London: Macmillan.

Smith, A. (1776). *An Inquiry into the Nature and Causes of the Wealth of Nations*. London.

Snyder, C. (1924). "New Measures in the Equation of Exchange." *American Economic Review* 14 (December): 699–713.

(1927). *Business Cycles and Business Measurements*. New York: Macmillan.

(1931a). "The World-wide Depression of 1930." *American Economic Review, Papers and Proceedings* 21 (March): 172–178.

(1931b). "Overproduction and Business Cycles." *Proceedings of the Academy of Political Science* 14 (3; *Depression and Revival*): 333–359.

(1935). "The Problem of Monetary and Economic Stability." *Quarterly Journal of Economics* 49 (February): 173–205.

Soddy, F. (1926). *Wealth, Virtual Wealth and Debt*. New York: Dutton.

Spiethoff, A. (1933). "Overproduction." In: *Encyclopaedia of the Social Sciences*. New York: Macmillan. Reprinted 1953 in *Readings in Business Cycles and National Income,* ed. A. H. Hansen and R. V. Clemence, pp. 108–115. New York: Norton.

Sprague, O. W. (1910). *A History of Crises under the National Banking System*. Washington, DC: Government Printing Office.

Sraffa, P. (1932). "Dr. Hayek on Money and Capital." *Economic Journal* 42 (March): 42–53.

Steedman, I. (1994). "*On The Pure Theory of Capital* by F. A. Hayek." In: *Capitalism, Socialism and Knowledge: The Economics of F. A. Hayek*, vol. II, ed. M. Colonna, H. Hagemann, and O. Hamouda, pp. 3–25. Aldershot, Hampshire: Edward Elgar.

Steiger, O. (1971). *Studien zur Entstehung der neuen Wirtschaftslehre in Schweden: Eine Anti-Kritik*. Berlin: Duncker & Humblot.

Steindl, F. G. (1995). *Monetary Interpretation of the Great Depression*. Ann Arbor: University of Michigan Press.

Stigler, G. J. (1988). *Memoirs of an Unregulated Economist*. New York: Basic Books.

Streissler, E. W. (1973). "Menger's Theories of Money and Uncertainty – A Modern

Interpretation." In: *Carl Menger and the Austrian School of Economics*, ed. J. R. Hicks and W. Weber, pp. 164–189. Oxford: Clarendon Press.

(1990). "Menger, Böhm-Bawerk, and Wieser: The Origins of the Austrian School." In: *Neoclassical Economic Theory, 1870–1930*, ed. K. Hennings and W. Samuels, pp. 151–189. Dordrecht: Kluwer.

Tavlas, G. S. (1976). "Some Further Observations on the Monetary Economics of Chicagoans and Non-Chicagoans." *Southern Economic Journal* 42 (April): 685–692.

(1977). "The Chicago Tradition Revisited: Some Neglected Contributions: Senator Paul Douglas (1892–1976)." *Journal of Money, Credit and Banking* 9 (November): 529–538.

(1982). "Note on Garvey, Snyder, and the Doctrinal Foundations of Monetarism." *History of Political Economy* 14 (Spring): 89–100.

(1997). "Chicago, Harvard, and the Doctrinal Foundations of Monetary Economics." *Journal of Political Economy* 105 (February): 153–177.

Tavlas, G. S., and Aschheim, J. (1981). "The Chicago Monetary Growth-Rate Rule: Friedman on Simons Reconsidered." *Banca Nazionale del Lavoro Quarterly Review* 136 (March): 75–89.

(1985). "Alexander Del Mar, Irving Fisher and Monetary Economics." *Canadian Journal of Economics* 18 (May): 294–313.

Thomas, B. (1936). *Monetary Policy and Crises – A Study of Swedish Experience.* London: Routledge & Kegan Paul.

Thornton, H. (1802). *An Enquiry into the Nature and Effects of the Paper Credit of Great Britain.* Reprinted 1939, with an introduction by F. A. von Hayek, by Allen & Unwin, London.

Thorp, W. (1926). *Business Annals.* Publications of the NBER, no. 8. New York: National Bureau of Economic Research.

Timlin, M. (1942). *Keynesian Economics.* University of Toronto Press.

Tinbergen J. (1937). "Review of Harrod, R. F., *The Trade Cycle, An Essay.*" *Weltwirtschaftliches Archiv* 45 (3): 89–91.

Trautwein, H.-M. (1993). "Wicksell and the Stockholm School on Credit and Money." Mimeograph, University of Hohenheim, Stuttgart.

(1996). "Money, Equilibrium and the Business Cycle: Hayek's Wicksellian Dichotomy." *History of Political Economy* 21 (Spring): 27–55.

Tugwell, R. (1933). *The Industrial Discipline and the Governmental Arts.* New York: Columbia University Press.

Tugwell, R., Munro, T., and Stryker, R. E. (1925). *American Economic Life and Its Means of Improvement.* New York: Harcourt Brace.

Uhr, C. (1987). "Davidson, David." In: *The New Palgrave: A Dictionary of Economics*, vol. 1, ed. J. Eatwell, M. Milgate, and P. Newman, pp. 749–750. London: Macmillan.

Veblen, T. (1904). *The Theory of Business Enterprise.* New York: Scribner.

Velupillai, K. (1975). "Irving Fisher on 'Switches of Techniques' – A Historical Note." *Quarterly Journal of Economics* 89 (November): 679–680.

Viner, J. (1932). "International Aspects of the Gold Standard." In: *Gold and Mone-*

tary Stabilization: Lectures on the Harris Foundation, ed. Q. Wright, pp. 3–39. University of Chicago Press.

(1933). *Balanced Deflation, Inflation or More Depression?* Minneapolis: University of Minnesota Press.

(1936). "Mr. Keynes on the Causes of Unemployment." *Quarterly Journal of Economics* 51 (November): 147–167.

(1937). *Studies in the Theory of International Trade.* New York: Harper & Row.

Wadensjö, E. (1993). "The Committee on Unemployment and the Stockholm School." In: *The Stockholm School of Economics Revisited*, ed. L. Jonung, pp. 103–123. Cambridge University Press.

Warburton, C. (1946). "The Misplaced Emphasis in Contemporary Business Fluctuation Theory." *Journal of Business of the University of Chicago* 19 (October): 199–220. Reprinted 1966 in C. Warburton, *Depression, Inflation, and Monetary Policy – Selected Papers 1945–53.* Baltimore: Johns Hopkins University Press.

(1966). *Depression, Inflation, and Monetary Policy – Selected Papers 1945–53.* Baltimore: Johns Hopkins University Press.

Warming, J. (1932). "International Difficulties Arising out of the Financing of Public Works During Depression." *Economic Journal* 42 (June): 211–224.

Wicksell, K. (1893). *Über Wert, Kapital und Rente.* English translation by S. H. Frowein (1965): *Value, Capital and Rent.* London: Allen & Unwin.

(1898). *Geldzins und Güterpreise.* English translation by R. F. Kahn (1936): *Interest and Prices.* London: Macmillan, for the Royal Economic Society. Reprinted 1962, New York: Augustus M. Kelly.

(1907a). "The Influence of the Rate of Interest on Prices." *Economic Journal* 17 (June): 213–220.

(1907b). English translation by C. G. Uhr (1962): "The Enigma of Business Cycles." In: *Interest and Prices*, pp. 223–239. New York: Augustus M. Kelley.

(1915). English translation by E. Claassen from second Swedish edition (1935): *Lectures in Political Economy*, vol. II. London: Routledge & Kegan Paul.

Williams, J. H. (1932). "Monetary Stability and the Gold Standard." In: *Gold and Monetary Stabilization: Lectures on the Harris Foundation*, ed. Q. Wright, pp. 133–158. University of Chicago Press.

Willis, H. P. (1915). *The Federal Reserve: A Study of the Banking System of the United States.* Garden City, NY: Doubleday.

(1932). "Federal Reserve Policy in Depression." In: *Gold and Monetary Stabilization: Lectures on the Harris Foundation*, ed. Q. Wright, pp. 77–108. University of Chicago Press.

Willis, H. P., Chapman, J. M., and Robey, R. W. (1993). *Contemporary Banking.* New York: Harper & Row.

Willis, H. P., and Edwards, G. W. (1926). *Banking and Business.* New York: Harper & Row.

Wright, Q. (ed.) (1932). *Gold and Monetary Stabilization: Lectures on the Harris Foundation.* University of Chicago Press.

Young, A. A. (1920). "Review of *Currency and Credit*, by Ralph G. Hawtrey, and

Stabilizing the Dollar, by Irving Fisher.'' *Quarterly Journal of Economics* 34: 520–532.

(1924). ''Review of R. G. Hawtrey's *Currency and Credit* (2nd ed.) and *Monetary Reconstruction.''* *American Economic Review* 14 (June): 349–351.

(1927). *Economic Problems New and Old.* Cambridge, MA: Riverside Press.

(1928). *An Analysis of Bank Statistics for the United States.* Cambridge, MA: Harvard University Press.

Young, W. (1987). *Interpreting Mr. Keynes: The IS-LM Enigma.* Cambridge, U.K.: Polity Press.

Author Index

367

Subject Index

accelerationism (Hayek and Lindahl), 43–4, 62n12
accelerator: absence from *General Theory*, 291–2, 336; importance of concept, 335; interaction with multiplier concept, 335–6; mechanism in Hansen's cycle theory, 203–5; Mitchell's attention to mechanism, 201–3; Mummery and Hobson's discovery of, 170
allocation, inter-temporal, *see* resource allocation, inter-temporal
animal spirits (Keynes), 256, 329, 336
Austrian economics: capital theory, 33–4; comparison with IS-LM model, 49–50; credit theory, 34–42; criticism of Hayek's ideas, 44–6; cycle theory, 31–2, 34–46; deductivist methodology of, 31–3; forced savings, 13, 38–40; inflation theory, 4–3; influence in United States, 19, 216, 243; intertemporal resource allocation, 32–42; monetary policy, 47–9; saving and consumption theory, 33–4; saving and investment concepts, 253; use of Wicksell's ideas, 13

Banking School (*see also* needs-of-trade doctrine; real-bills doctrine): American economists as heirs to, 214–15; ideas in U.S. monetary economics, 189–95; needs-of-trade doctrine, 18
banking system: adjustment of quantity of money (Myrdal), 65–7; credit granted by (Wicksell), 28–9; in Hawtrey's analysis, 114–16; Hayek's conception of, 37–40; in Marshall's quantity theory, 14; 100 per cent reserve basis, 20, 240–1; pre–central bank in United States, 181; role of credit in (Mises), 35–6; Willis's analysis of pre-1929, 214–15
bank rate (*see also* discount rate): influence

(Hawtrey), 122–3, 138; link to quantity theory of money (Keynes), 138–9; theory (Keynes), 138; used to control cycle (Keynes), 143
Baring Crisis (1890), 182
booms, Keynes's conditions for, 150–2
business cycle, *see* cycle; cycle theory

Cambridge economics (*see also* cash-balance approach): cash-balance version of quantity theory, 113; circus, 133; counter-cyclical monetary policy, 101; cycle theory of Marshall, 81–3; cycle theory of Pigou and Lavington, 83–90; forced-saving mechanism in cycle theory, 96; influence of Marshall's cycle theory on, 83; Keynes's 1930 cycle theory, 144–5; Keynes's 1936 cycle theory, 270–2; market's lack of co-ordination mechanism, 85–6, 96–7; Marshallian tradition, 14–18, 98–9; quantity theory of money, 111–12, 138; Robertson's cycle theory, 90–9; scepticism about market, 85, 97, 99–100, 153–4, 254–5, 339; treatment of monetary factors, 105; variety of viewpoints, 128–9
Cambridge quantity equation (Hicks), 310–11
capital (*see also* investment): formation of fixed (Hawtrey), 119–20; marginal efficiency of (Hawtrey), 292; marginal efficiency theory (Keynes), 253–5, 260–1, 273–4, 299–300; working and fixed (Wicksell), 30; working capital (Robertson), 91
capital market: failure in Austrian economics, 253
capital theory: of Austrian cycle theorists, 33–4; of Böhm-Bawerk, 39, 53–5; of Cassel,

378   **Subject Index**

prices, relative (*cont.*)
  in (Austrian), 32–3; in transmission
    mechanism (Brunner and Meltzer), 339
price theory: of Hayek, 58; of Lindahl, 58–9,
  58–62
producers' expectations (Keynes), 250–6
profits (*see also* losses, in Danaid jar analogy):
  in monetary equilibrium (Keynes), 137;
  profit inflation and deflation (Keynes),
  151–2; in widow's cruse analogy
  (Keynes), 133–4, 151
public-works programs: counter-cyclical
  (Pigou and Robertson), 103–4; Douglas's
  reasoning, 210; expenditures (Keynes),
  148–9; Foster and Catchings view of, 208–
  11; Harris's advocacy of depression-era,
  218; Hawtrey's scepticism of spending
  for, 125–8; perceived effect on
  employment, 173; as remedy for cyclical
  unemployment (Director and Douglas),
  224–5

quantity theory of money: according to
  Fisher, 183; according to Wicksell, 28–9;
  Anderson's critique of, 189–92; cash-
  balance approach (Marshall), 80, 113; in
  Chicago oral tradition, 10–11; in classical
  economics, 9; differences among Fisher,
  Hawtrey, and Wicksell treatments, 330; of
  Fanno, 139n11; Hawtrey's version, 113–
  14, 331–2; of Keynes (*Tract*), 106–7;
  Lerner's approach, 312; Lindahl's
  interpretation, 58; link to bank rate
  (Keynes), 138–9; of the Marshalls, 14–15,
  79, 112, 325, 331; relation of LM curve
  to, 329–32; relation to employment theory
  (Keynes), 267–74

Radcliffe Committee, 112, 337
rate of interest (*see also* discount rate;
  liquidity preference theory; liquidity trap):
  Austrian conception of natural, 34; in
  counter-cyclical policy (Keynes), 272–4;
  criticism of Keynes's interest-rate floor,
  285–7; determinants of (Keynes), 297–8;
  Fisher's theory of, 54–5, 57; in Hawtrey's
  analysis of credit, 114–15; interest rate
  floor (Keynes), 263–5, 285–7; Keynes's
  theory (*General Theory*), 256–9; Knight's

criticism of Keynes's theory, 282; market
  (Keynes), 136–7, 142, 150, 153; market
  or money rate (Wicksell), 28–30, 34, 53,
  55; in Marshall's cycle theory, 79, 82; in
  Marshall's transmission mechanism, 81;
  money rate, 108; natural (Keynes), 135–8,
  142, 150, 153; natural (Wicksell), 28–30,
  34, 53, 55, 138; Pigou's concept of
  proper, 167–8; real and nominal, 57, 82,
  108, 183; relation to demand for money
  (Lavington), 332; relation to level of
  employment (Keynes), 264; Robertson's
  criticism of Keynes's interpretation, 282;
  sensitivity of demand for money to, 313–
  16; Stockholm School conception of
  natural, 53–7; true (Cassel), 544
real-bills doctrine (Mints), 189n8, 194–5 (*see
  also* needs-of-trade doctrine)
resource allocation, inter-temporal (*see also*
  co-ordination, inter-temporal): American
  economists of Banking School, 215–16;
  of Austrian economics, 32–42, 215; of
  Haberler, 216; Hawtrey's analysis, 120; of
  Hayek, 36–7; of Keynes, 106–7, 328–9;
  of Mises, 35–6; Robertson's interpretation, 91–2; role of expectations
  (Stockholm School), 57–62; view of
  Pigou and Lavngton, 85–7; of Wicksell,
  29–30
Rockefeller Foundation, 199n17, 226n16

saving (*see also* Danaid jar analogy; forced
  saving; lacking; thrift): Austrian
  conception, 253; criticism of Keynes's
  idea of, 152–3; Keynes's definition, 132–
  3, 150–1, 252; link to investment
  (Keynes), 252–3; transforming
  involuntary to voluntary (Robertson), 96
Say's law, 169, 210, 301
secular stagnation, 153, 217n7, 267, 292–5
slump, *see* Great Contraction (1929–33)
speculation, Keynes's definition, 255–6
spillover effects, 327–8
stabilization policy (*see also* fiscal policy;
  monetary policy): of American monetary
  authorities (1920s), 195–9; in Hansen's
  cycle theory, 204–6; of Hawtrey, 121–8;
  Pigou's interpretation, 99–101; proposals